ODYSSEY
OF A
BARBARIAN

the biography of
GEORGE SYLVESTER VIERECK

Elmer Gertz, 1906 –

Prometheus Books
1203 Kensington Avenue
Buffalo, New York 14215

Published by Prometheus Books
1203 Kensington Avenue, Buffalo, NY 14215

Copyright 1978 © by Elmer Gertz

Library of Congress Catalog Card Number 78-24801
ISBN 0-87975-108-8

Printed in the United States of America

From the cloistered halls of knowledge where fantastic lights are shed
By a thousand twisted mirrors, and the dead entomb their dead,
Let us walk into the city where men's wounds are raw and red
Three gifts only Life, the strumpet, holds for coward and for brave,
Only three, no more—the belly and the phallus and the grave!

CONTENTS

Necessary First Words   1
1   Why?   3
2   How   7
3   A Hohenzollern Socialist   12
4   Putty   20
5   Wonder Child   31
6   College Boy   39
7   Three Literary Musketeers   43
8   A Game at Love   49
9   A Strange Trinity   55
10   Helping Hands   62
11   Skyrocket!   67
12   The Ghost of Oscar Wilde   77
13   Of Vampires and Such   81
14   Loving Much and Many   84
15   A Barbarian Confesses   88
16   First Efforts as German-American Editor   93
17   The Poet Takes Out His License   98
18   A Very Restless Young Man   104
19   "The International" Breaks Trails   111
20   For the Fatherland   118
21   Marriage: An Interlude   129
22   Struggling Against the Tide   133
23   Making the Most of the War   146
24   The Other Side   159
25   Theodore Roosevelt and the Waging of Peace   163
26   Revenging the War Through Harding and Debs   170

CONTENTS

27   Rebuilding   176
28   The Little Blue Book Way to Fame   181
29   The Progressive Politician   188
30   "Ambassador" of the Kaiser   191
31   Colonel House Forgives His Enemy   197
32   The Chronicler of the Wandering Jew   212
33   The Sexual Relativist   225
34   The Poet Turns Psychoanalyst   232
35   The Brown Pit   242
36   Is It the End?   262
      Postscript   272

NECESSARY
FIRST WORDS

As I write these words, it is almost exactly forty-two years since I began this saga of a damaged soul. I was then a young man, not yet thirty, and almost indifferent to the abuse I was receiving for being interested in a man who was excoriated by much of the rest of the world. I consoled myself with the thought that Bernard Shaw shared my curiosity about George Sylvester Viereck, and I persevered. Shaw and I had shared an interest in another flawed creature—Frank Harris. My book on Harris—subtitled *A Study in Black and White*—had appeared only four years previously and seems to have given me insight into controversial characters. My late wife, Ceretta, phrased it differently. "Do you have any friends who are not bastards?" she once asked me.

My Viereck book was accepted for publication, and I was prepared for the worst. Then the publisher reneged. There were reasons enough for this. Perhaps, I should have been grateful. At any rate, I could do nothing to turn the tide.

It was at this time that Viereck's troubles turned to disasters, including almost five years in prison. I put aside my manuscript, despite my feeling that it was the best literary study I had ever written. After a time, I deposited my manuscript and vast accumulations of Viereck material in the Library of Congress and tried to forget my great expenditure of time and thought. Now and then I dwelt wistfully upon what I had done. Secretly, I was proud of it. Being a person of great faith, I sometimes felt that all would be well in the end.

Just a short time ago, through a series of chance occurrences, an editor of the firm now publishing this book became interested in the fruits of my Viereck labors. Ultimately a decision was made that there was much in my book still worthy of the attention of readers.

For the first time in a generation, I reread what I had written. It seemed fresh and fruitful to me. Perhaps still controversial, it had values which survived the passage of time. I rejoiced that in my seventy-second year I would finally see my Viereck book in print.

I made a decision to which I adhere. The book gains much by appearing in its original form with only slight changes, although Viereck has long since passed away. Thus one captures the flavor of a living man.

Before reading the book, many may still ask, "Who is George Sylvester Viereck?" After they have gone through it, they will learn why Viereck created so much excitement and animosity in his day, and they may agree with me that he should be remembered, not alone for his vices.

Of course, I have added enough to the original book, by way of a postscript, to bring the story, briefly, up to date.

I still feel that Viereck, despite all of his failings—and they were many—has utility for our day. Here, I say, is a man who embodies much that is wrong and some that is yet good. In a very real sense Viereck stood in symbolical relationship to his own age, the previous century, and what is to come tomorrow.

In this book, as when he was alive, I am neither his friend nor his foe, but an objective recorder of a fascinating man and his career.

1 WHY?

This book is presented as a case study for communists and for fascists. Here is a portrait of precisely the sort of individual to be eliminated in a collectivist or a totalitarian state because he is so glaringly an embodiment of the contradictions, confusion and near chaos that characterize our age. The ''gentlemen'' of the right and the ''comrades'' to the left want a measure of unity that is unthinkable to the individual here selected as an uneasy blend of the life of our day. One is tempted to catalog the vices and virtues of the man in all their variety, for their diversity had definite meanings. Poet, propagandist, publicist, politician, editor and journalist, lay psychoanalyst, semiprofessional student of sex, amateur manipulator of scientific ideas, business man and stockbroker, historian and biographer, novelist, adventurer and opportunist—George Sylvester Viereck was a fit megaphone through which to shout the goods on display in our modern Vanity Fair. Rebel in some respects and reactionary in others, nationalist with a double loyalty and internationalist withal, parochial and cosmopolitan at the same time, pantheist and pansexual, Viereck strove to be all things to all men and, therefore, was a synthesis of this age and worth capturing for the sake of the next age.

Ours is the era in which men aspire to reach the truth with bulletlike phrases—''words, words, words,'' Hamlet diagnosed the illness long ago—and so life today is a series of metaphors, missed or mixed. This, more than any other, is the age of dubious action stemming from muddled thought, of good conduct arising from bad motives, of high purpose and low attainment, of understanding and obtuseness. The composite man is like a wanderer in a field of daisies who picks certain flowers and passes others without rhyme or reason. Like an ill-motivated child, he flits aimlessly in a circuitous path, returning ultimately to the unrest of his own soul. No one, perhaps, is more strikingly representative of this vagrancy than Viereck. His career, as here developed, is that of a chameleon who reflected, sometimes directly and at other times inversely, the variable colors of

3

the flora and fauna about him. Through his life story the world of the twentieth century is mirrored as in few other lives—more clearly, indeed, than through a study of his betters. The reflection is twisted and distorted at times, but generally it is of shocking clarity and so, again, worth recording.

Driven by an overwhelming ego, the dominant and irresistible impulse of Viereck's life was to unite himself with those personalities, groups, nations, movements, events, and tendencies which colored and shaped the life of this generation. All of the crowded picture was seized by him. His joy was the conquest, in one fashion or another, of all who have been representative of the basic forces in this age; his method was libidinous, a sort of intellectual seduction; his purpose to take that from others which might lend meaning to his own life. To limn Viereck's character and career is to trace his successive courtships of the ghost of Oscar Wilde and the living selves of Theodore Roosevelt, William II, Bernard Shaw, Freud, Einstein, Colonel House, Nikola Tesla, Eugene V. Debs, and the others who were focal points of world attention. It is to see such causes as artistic and personal freedom, votes for women, the successive progressive plat-forms, and the like, become toys for an eager mind. It is to see such ideas as psychoanalysis and relativity absorbed seemingly with spongelike avidity. Two world wars and the rise of new social orders became to him personal concerns rather than events universal; and so with all tendencies and movements: they became important only insofar as they gave satisfaction to the capricious soul of Narcissus—Viereck.

It was not merely the superficially broad equipment of an important journal-ist, and it was not always a matter of persistent pursuit by Viereck. He acted and reacted on men and events; at times he added colors to the age's palette; he was one of those who helped to distill public opinion. That man who is generally credited with being the person chiefly responsible for America's entry into the first world war on the side of the Allies said that if he had met Viereck early enough, America might not have entered the tragic conflict. True or false, and it is probably unwarranted, the opinion gives some measure of Viereck's sometimes impor-tance. It is cited here as typical of his role in contemporary life. His successful fight against what has been called the War Guilt Lie might also be cited. This book aims to make a definitive statement of his place in the scheme of the twentieth century and thus, by implication at least, to assist in correcting the picture of our times that has been prematurely framed. Its quest is for a useful symbol, the summing up of Viereck in socially significant terms.

It should not be assumed that an attempt is being made here to weave a garland about his once golden head. Many rocks were tossed at that head—and by no means playfully. Brickbats aimed for him have been known to hit others. This was so throughout his life. A book about Viereck, then, must be not an attack, not a defense, but something in the nature of a scientific examination.

To some, Viereck was an unprincipled scoundrel who sold a heritage of dubious talent for a mess of notoriety. They saw him as a man of some ability and more conceit who, drunk with self-love and weakened by the caresses of the Bitch

Goddess Success, played idly with words, with lives, with verities, with principles as if they were only toys in the quest for a self-amusement. To them, he lacked the fundamental virtue of sincerity and was a by no means pretty peacock who flaunted its tattered feathers as if they were the livery of a prince. His poetry they dubbed inconsequential backhouse Swinburne, the rhetoric of a once cute kid. His prose they dismissed as loud and lewd. All they found, finally, was a lackey of whatever ruling group would pay him enough: a man to be had at a price, if a rather high price.

Others, in decreasing number, saw Viereck as a great American poet, a once revolutionary influence on Parnassus, one who had, in his Two Thousand Years saga, created a superior kind of fiction, a blend of urbane philosophy, civilized drollery, sensuous language, and scientific truth. They saw him as a romantic, almost legendary figure of much personal charm, pucklike, capricious, erratic, and playful, but essentially sound. They conceded he had made errors, probably damning ones, and had been guilty of lapses of taste and judgment; but, bathed in the sunshine of tolerance, they forgave his misdeeds as the pecadillos of a man of genius. Compensating for these faults, they saw him as a crusader, in spite of himself, for fine causes, a furious fighter for his conceptions of the right, an apostle of bravery, intelligence and tolerance, with an astonishing arsenal of knowledge and insight. These judgments, it must be admitted, became more rare as the horrible dimensions of World War II, obliterating individuals by millions, came upon us.

The judicious middle-grounders said "yea" and "nay" and "perhaps" to all of the accusations directed against Viereck and "yea" and "nay" and "perhaps" to all that was said in his praise, and they resolved the differences into a formula of paradoxical synthesis, strikingly similar to some inspired doggerel of Viereck's own authorship, written while he was vacationing long ago on the coast of Nova Scotia:

> He longed for love and found lubricity,
> He courted fame and won publicity,
> He had two countries, home in none,
> He wandered between moon and sun,
> Forever with himself at strife,
> He wooed a god and wed a wife.
> Forgot by all, he died A.D.,
> The date is not yet known to me,
> Drowned in the Bay of Fundy,
> Sic transit gloria mundi!

The prevailing feeling was that Viereck was concealing something, perhaps some monstrous secret, that even when he was most candid, he said less than he might and left the true words unuttered. Particularly since World War II, he was, to many, a sinister figure or at least a man of mystery. The hope, not always expressed, was to learn the real truth about him. In this they are not unlike the hero of an early tale by Viereck, a man who pondered desperately as to what is on the other side of the moon and built strong mental pictures of what he hoped was there. Spiteful Fate granted the man's desire, and he saw the other side of the moon. But, alas, that we should attain what we seek! The man returned, a dour, designing wretch, eager to inflict ill upon all. Out of the bitterness of his heart he became a tyrant of unlimited cruelty. He even forced his children to study mathematics! For he learned that the other side of the moon is exactly like the side turned towards us!

Is there a similar disconcerting truth about Viereck? This book tries to give the answer.

2   HOW

To say that it is worth writing of George Sylvester Viereck because he was a mirror of his age is to say, in effect, that a book about him must be pieced together, with painstaking care, out of many fragments. It is not enough to know his every book and his countless contributions to newspapers and magazines and his voluminous correspondence, nor is it enough to have read all that appears in print about him, though it fills many volumes and has a reckless candor. These things afford little more than the superficial coating of a book, not the sinews of a man.

One may know the flesh and blood of the man, Viereck, and derive aid from his family, his friends, his associates. One may search in all of the nooks and corners of his career and traffic with his foes. Still, one may not be equipped to write of him, for a giant shadow is inevitably cast over any book about Viereck. Implicit in the suspicion with which Viereck is regarded is an almost equal suspicion of the one who dares to be his biographer. A sinister cloud of doubt, born out of a fear of propaganda characteristic of the postwar age, seems to envelop the subject. One may say, "Let the book speak for itself." But such a brave show of indifference is too theatrical to serve the purposes of truth. The reader is entitled to know the sources of the information doled out to him so that he may decide for himself whether it is tainted or true. The answer to the preconception of the reader is not the prejudice of the writer, nor easy generalization. To place Viereck in symbolical relation to his age is not to attempt to fit him into the fine groove of a theory, for thesis building is truth wrecking. The biographer should not claim any artistic license; his privilege is to tell only the unadulterated truth.

Necessarily, a chief source of information was Viereck himself, with careful substantiation from other sources. Viereck's aid took various forms. We wrestled with each other, so to speak, and neither of us was the invariable winner or loser. Whenever I sought information, however delicate, I attempted to win it from Viereck, sometimes with success and sometimes without. I engaged in what lawyers call a fishing expedition, that is to say, a cross-examination built upon the hope of unearthing secret things.

Day after day, I was with Viereck, in the privacy of his home and family, at his club, at public gatherings, and on the streets. I was with him when he was serious and when he was playful, when he was silent and when he was communicative. I browsed among his possessions and went through all of his dozens of scrapbooks. Thousands of letters and manuscripts were placed in my lap. Viereck's home was a biographer's paradise to me. His kindness was so overwhelming that it has taken a steadfast determination on my part to tell the full truth, even if I appear to be ungrateful.

Let my meaning not be misunderstood. I do not for a moment think that I know the whole truth, in all of its ramifications, about Viereck. Much less do I think it possible to write all that there is to say about any man. The man may be brazen as a sailor on shore leave, but still there are limits, serious limits, to what one may say of him. Even of dead men one cannot always tell tales; still less of a man who was at the time of which I write in his middle years and facing many days of activity. (Remember: these words were written long ago, when Viereck was alive and unaware of the disasters that were to come upon him.)

I recall saying to Viereck one day, while we sipped beer together, that I thought he was inhibiting or, to be less polite, deliberately concealing things from me. I made the statement in part because I wanted his reactions to a charge often made against him. His answer was in the form of a question: "What have I concealed from you?" Nevertheless, I still say that the whole truth can be told of no man. I believe that Viereck had, consciously and unconsciously, concealed information about himself. The biographer, no less than the reader, must be fortified by the armor of cynicism.

How, for example, can one tell the whole truth about the lovelife of a poet of passion? Candor has more definite limits than one likes to think and the ways of love are so devious that one must be careful not to be trapped in a maze of words.

Pitfalls surround other aspects of Viereck's career. Important records have been lost or destroyed or are witheld; material, for example, relating to financial entanglements. During the period of World War I many of Viereck's records found their way, with curious indirection, into the hands of foreign agents. Other documents dwelt for a while in the archives of the American government and then disappeared, often without explanation. They may yet turn up to confound the biographer. Many people in a position to help refused to do so, for reasons both good and bad. Unfortunately, the missing contributions of some of these people can scarcely be replaced.

Viereck disclaimed any special capacity for conspiracy, but he could not deny that his career had been such that many necessarily suffered from forgetfulness or dismay when they were asked about him. Though there may be no real mystery about Viereck's career and personality, the fact that some believed that there was a mystery made for difficulties. It compelled many to excuse themselves from making a contribution lest they be booted into a controversy. It may be years before some unseal their lips; others will have gone in silence to their heavenly rewards. (And World War II intensified the difficulties.)

This writer has adopted the formula Othello long ago bequeathed to biographers. With his dying breath, the honest Moor asked that his life story be told with nothing extenuated and naught set down in malice. The formula, despite its surface ease, has been beyond most biographers and alien to the public. For many generations Boswell was reviled as often as he was praised because he persisted in limning Dr. Johnson as a fallible human being and himself as an indefatigable student of the intimacies of one man's life. In the age in which Victoria was queen of Britain and Mrs. Grundy was the head of every household, biography reverted to a form of prim panegyric. In our day the prevailing mode is in blatant contrast with the early manner. Today some writers have become ghouls, playing with the bones of the past. One may write nowadays with devastating frankness even of the living. One has to write of George Sylvester Viereck with a full consciousness of the fact that the truth, the whole truth, and nothing but the truth must be approximated. One's mental reservations must be aired; the gaps in one's knowledge must be confessed; speculations, however proper, must not be substituted for the simple facts; interpretation must be given its proper place, and no more.

When dealing with a hybrid like Viereck, it is necessary to utilize all the tools, unknown to the earlier generations of biographers, that modern science has given twentieth-century students of personality. The various schools of psychology have opened new worlds to the Boswells of today. Medicine has made its contribution, largely in the field of endocrinology. A whole new science of sex has arisen. Even physics and mathematics have furnished new and useful concepts; and, of course, the social sciences, particularly Marxian economics, are permanently attached to biography. The insight gained in these fields ought to be utilized whenever a truly ambitious attempt at biographical writing is made. When the subject himself, as here, was in contact with the Columbuses of the new schools of knowledge, it is unforgivable that his biographer ignore such men. This writer must acknowledge with gratitude the aid of psychologists, medical men, and sexologists like Freud (through his books and his correspondence, rather than through firsthand contacts) and Alfred Adler, Havelock Ellis, Wilhelm Stekel, A. A. Brill, Magnus Hirschfeld, Harry Benjamin, and Johann Plesch (these latter men more or less directly). Of the physical scientists, he is chiefly indebted to Nikola Tesla, the patriarch of modern technology; of the social scientists, he is happy to thank Harold D. Lasswell. There are others whose writings have been examined and who have written personal letters touching upon aspects of the career of Viereck.

One device of modern scholarship has been particularly useful. A form of questionnaire, sent to all and sundry, brought back, as in a fisherman's net, a miscellaneous assortment of information. What in Viereck most interests you? Most irritates you? Which of his writings do you prefer? What is his position in literature? What are the reasons for his success or failure?—these and other questions brought conflicting replies, in many cases highly enlightening, from George Bernard Shaw, Thomas Mann, Lord Alfred Douglas, G. K. Chesterton,

Rupert Hughes, Gertrude Atherton, Mitchell Kennerley, Edwin Markham, Don Marquis, Upton Sinclair, H. L. Mencken, Art Young, and many others—the names are a further indication of the immense variety of Viereck's contacts in his quest to catch all of the reflections of the mirror of life. Some of these luminaries replied briefly, even curtly. Others replied with much particularity. But even in their silence they were of unwitting aid.

More valuable than a parade of celebrities was the intimate knowledge of those who had been associated with Viereck for long periods of time. Some of his closest friends were not unknown to fame, but their value was not to be gauged by the barometer of public acclaim. Men and women who knew Viereck as a baby, as a school boy, as a college student, and in other phases of his career tapped their memories and reported their recollections with surprising candor and complete-ness. Even members of his family, his aunt, Frances Schmidt Viereck, and his second cousin, Erna Schmidt Viereck, for examples, wrote with a frankness that served to make an open book of his childhood. William Ellery Leonard, Ludwig Lewisohn, Leonard D. Abbott, Alexander Harvey, Paul Eldridge, Shaemus O'Sheel, Alfred Rau, Ludwig Fulda, Fulton Oursler, Elsa Barker, and Blanche Wagstaff were, indubitably, among the closest friends of Viereck. The first named in particular, were intimates of his daily life, and they were, in each instance, helpful to me. Leonard, Harvey, O'Sheel, Abbott, and Mrs. Wagstaff read portions of the manuscript of this book, in addition to supplying invaluable information and shrewd advice. In fairness to Lewisohn and Eldridge, it must be admitted that their aid was indirect and involuntary, for reasons, stated later, which afford good cause for the writing of this book.

Many survivors of the hectic period of the First World War were generous enough to forget the rancorous hatreds engendered by their conflicting interests and set forth their impressions of the part Viereck played in the struggle. Foremost among these men was, of course, Colonel Edward M. House; but it would be unfair not to thank Frederick Franklin Schrader, Judge Daniel F. Cohalen, Charles Nagel, Dr. Bernhard Dernburg, James Gerard, Hermann Hagedorn, Ferdinand Hansen, Sir William Wiseman, Colonel Norman Thwaites, and others. E. Halde-man-Julius, Isaac Goldberg (with anathemas for both biographer and subject), and Ralph Easley joined many others in helpful impressions of activities in which Viereck engaged.

I should be remiss if I did not mention the aid I received, in various forms, from friends, particularly Allen Crandall, George Herman, Peter J. Pollack, Irving Eisenstein, Leo C. Rosten, Emil Armin, and Alexander J. Isaacs, and from members of my immediate family, particularly my late wife Ceretta and my sister Bernice. This book owes much of whatever value it may have to the kindness of many people. I trust I do not ill reward them by claiming full ultimate responsibil-ity for all that lies between the covers of the book. (For the material in the postscript I am indebted to yet other people and sources to be mentioned there and particularly the Library of Congress, custodian of my Viereck papers.) .

For the rest, in thousands of press clippings, both in English and in German, in magazine articles, books and pamphlets, in the proceedings and reports of official bodies, like the Overman and Dickstein committees, and in the archives and annals of several institutions, material was found dealing, directly and indirectly, with the subject. I attempted to make myself familiar with all of it, not alone because of this book. but because of the fascination of the quest. Informed readers may feel that they detect gaps other than those mentioned, but a reexamination may convince them that what they seek is implicit in the pages of this book. In brief, I have attempted to be a mirror of reconciliation, except where no such synthesis appears possible. I trust that at such times I have not twisted the shape of truth.

The stage, one hopes, is now set.

3   A HOHENZOLLERN SOCIALIST

There are certain morsels of court scandal that must be considered even at this late date, though they be cold and stale. Knowing people in Germany used to speculate, sometimes in a supercilious manner, as to the identity of the father of Edwina Viereck's son. The prevailing belief was that the old Emperor himself, William I, then the heir presumptive, was the anonymous parent; and wise people winked when it was claimed that the dashing young Hohenzollern army officer, Louis von Prillwitz, had fathered the child. The official birth records were, of course, ambiguous. They showed that on March 21, 1851, a son was born to the distinguished actress of the Royal Theatre, Juliane Caroline Edwine Viereck (commonly known as Edwina), and the child was given the formidable name of Franz Georg Edwin Louis Withold Viereck, quite properly shortened to Louis Viereck, or a simple L. Viereck. The records also showed that the godfathers of the child were His Royal Highness, Prince George of Prussia, and His Excellency, the Imperial Austrian General of Cavalry, Baron Franz von Schick. Such well-born godfathers indicated to the knowing that the old Kaiser was the modest father. Did not his absence from the baptism prove it? Lieutenant Louis von Prillwitz was present at the baptism merely as an imperial decoy, it was thought, and, of course, Frau Caroline Viereck, the mother of Edwina, had to be present. Fraulein Ida Hartmann, the other witness, was merely a supernumerary. So it was all settled!

In after-years an old artist, who never forgot that he had painted a portrait of William I, used to tell Louis Viereck, son of Edwina, that the resemblance between Louis and the late Emperor was astonishing. He tried to persuade Louis to dress himself up as the Emperor, with side whiskers and the rest of the royal ornamentation, merely to demonstrate the truth of the theory that William I was his father. But Louis expressed no interest in the experiment. He was quite content to let the late Emperor remain his uncle, rather than his father.

For Louis von Prillwitz, the acknowledged father of Louis Viereck, was himself the morganatic scion of Prince August of Prussia, a kinsman of the Prussian king, and a Hohenzollern of the Hohenzollerns. Apparently this propensity for irregular unions was an old family custom and part of the royal system of old Europe intended, perhaps, as Bernard Shaw has said, to strengthen the weak blood of kings. When such attachments did not exist, they were invented—and cherished—by folklore in each country, old Prussia being no exception.

Thus, through Louis Viereck, his father, the blood of the Hohenzollerns entered the veins of George Sylvester Viereck and helped to determine the course of his career. It was not merely another interesting fact in the life of George Sylvester Viereck; it was perhaps basic. That he could claim descent from the Great Elector and from Frederick the Great and from all the other princes and princelings of Prussia and its satellites was bound to be of great importance to him and to others. It would influence his life, sometimes consciously and more often unconsciously. There was a luxuriant feeling in contemplating one's royal ancestors. It gave an element of romance, of poetry, to one's life even if one tried to stifle silly thoughts of regal grandeur and felt rather ashamed of harboring them. It was pleasant to say that from this royal ancestress a drop of French blood was absorbed and from that one the disposition of a martinet or some vestige of bourgeois conscience. It was still more pleasant to say that such and such regal progenitor wrote poetry of not a little merit. There was an ironic quaintness in the fact that the town palace of one ancestor later became the headquarters of the Nazi Propaganda Ministry. And there was always interest in the game of tracing interrelationships, cross-breedings, court connections. If one carried the process back far enough, one discovered, to one's astonishment, that one was descended from those immortal parents, Adam and Eve! In the line of descent, Viereck found himself connected, however distantly, with Mary Stuart and the British Royal family, as well; to Barbarosa, too, and to Charlemagne.

There has been much nonsense written on the theme of ancestors and the inheritance of their characteristics, and this has been especially true since the time of Mendel. One cannot tell, in truth, through what devious paths the sins and virtues of our progenitors will visit themselves upon us, nor from whom our own pecadillos and major vices and occasional virtues will come. It is possibly enough to say that George Sylvester Viereck's genealogical tablets had written on them many entries likely to count for much in his life. Conceivably the story of his career traced in this book is the result of ancestral characteristics.

Edwina Viereck died many years before George Sylvester was born, but he had read of her beauty and he had found among his father's papers the fragments of diaries in her handwriting, which gave him some understanding of the personality that had charmed his Hohenzollern ancestors. He knew that the really revealing diaries had been committed to the flames after her death, and the fragments themselves told him that Edwina kept the important things in her head, not daring to entrust them to writing. In her head, no doubt, was the real truth about Louis Viereck's parentage. Perhaps it was just as well that the truth was buried with her. Young George Sylvester could look at her picture in his father's home and ponder romantically over her secret. And then later he saw her statue at the Royal Playhouse in Berlin, and for the first time she became more important to him than Helen of Troy or Lilith or the other lovely women of whom he sang in his verse. He confessed that when he stood before Edwina's loveliness hewn in marble, it seemed to him as if he felt the impress of her lips upon his forehead, as a consecration and a blessing. Many years later, when the German consul-general in New York gave him, in behalf of the German government, a replica of the bust of Edwina, the sweet intoxication renewed itself. Often he felt that he was in communion with her ghost. He could see her as she was on the stage, acting in Schiller's *Turandot,* and challenging the beholder to look upon her beauty and not go mad. It must have been in such moments that the Hohenzollerns lost their hearts to her.

King Frederick William IV of Prussia admired Edwina's art and her person. He often intervened to save her from the results of her infringements of the rules in force in the Royal Theatre. She was a privileged character behind the footlights, there could be no doubt, and she doted upon this. She never seemed to feel quite herself unless princes of the blood fluttered about her. William, who later became the first emperor of the united Germany, scarcely concealed his attachment for Edwina, although he maintained a discreet silence about the parentage of her son. He was frequently seen riding with her in the Tiergarten, and at least once he met her child there. His chamberlain, Louis von Prillwitz, was, of course, often seen in her company, and Edwina was, in truth, deeply attracted to him. Von Prillwitz later toyed with the idea of adopting Edwina's son. Nor was it unusual for her to meet, quite casually, to be sure, such gentry as the King of Würtemburg. At one such meeting, her little boy, then three or four years old, asked the king if he was a soldier. The king gravely assured him that he was, much to the satisfaction of the boy. When Edwina traveled about, she was shown every courtesy by the authorities. In one police passport, still extant, she was given the fictitious name of Frau von Lornau and was recommended, with Teutonic flourishes, as well-born and entitled, as such, to respect.

Naturally, such royal favor did not prevent her from being hissed by mobs during the revolutionary uprisings of the memorable year, 1848. She was hissed because she was, perhaps properly, looked upon as part and parcel of the discredited aristocratic scheme of things. The mobs could not have known that there was a revolutionary fringe in Edwina's family circle. Lovely poems, in which *"der Viereck wunderschönes Haupt"* is sung rapturously, could not save her from the revolutionary zeal.

Her brother William courted death because of his loyalty to the insurgent cause. Once he had to hide in the home of his well-favored sister in order to escape the firing squad. She concealed him in the chimney and subsequently helped him to escape to America. Another brother of hers, named Edward, left a written record of the fact that, during the revolutionary uprisings of 1848, some of the revolutionaries got on the roof of Edwina's house and shot at the soldiers, as if to show them that the house of a court favorite was not free from revolutionary disturbances. The soldiers ultimately repulsed the attack and, entering the house, arrested all but three of the insurgents, those three, young students, escaping with the aid of Edwina and another of her brothers. The story was told by George Sylvester's aunt, Erna Schmidt—Viereck, daughter of Edwina's brother Edward and one of the lyric members of the Viereck clan.

Edwina was proud of her baby son, Louis. She displayed him everywhere and took the utmost care of him. In her mind and certainly her conduct, his extramarital birth meant nothing to her. She often took him to the theatre, where he waited for her behind the wings, whiling away his time by memorizing all of her roles.

An actor, too, was his Uncle William, the revolutionary brother of Edwina, who had, with her aid, escaped to America. Among William's roles was the part of Franz Moor in Schiller's play, *Raüber*. He was the founder of the German Theatre in San Francisco, to which city he wandered, after his escape from Prussia. Traveling westward in a covered wagon, he had the nerve-freezing adventure of being captured by the Indians. After winning his freedom, he renewed his trek to San Francisco—certainly far enough away from the vigilant eyes of the Prussian police. William, who was evidently a man of parts, became a big man in the city of his adoption. Besides being a painter of some little talent and an actor and stage manager, he was the Grand Master of the Odd Fellows fraternal order and employed in the United States Customs Service: A career of promise ended when he died from a stroke just after reaching forty years of age and left a widow and children. When one of these children, bearing the lovely name of Laura, was eleven years old, the widow and her children returned to Germany. Laura, in time, married her romantic cousin Louis Viereck and became the mother of George Sylvester.

There were other romantic strains in Edwina's and, therefore, in George Sylvester's largely Nordic ancestry. The Viereck family had probably come to Prussia from Scandinavia during the Thirty Years' war. But some Slavic blood entered through Edwina's mother Caroline Buttney, born in Lusatia, where the remains of the ancient Slav invasion exist, the descendents of the invaders being called Wends. This inspired the once famous and charming Prince Pückler, one of Edwina's numerous admirers, to call her the Princess of the Wends. Edwina's Slavic grandfather Buttney was an alchemist who spent his entire fortune trying to make gold out of base metals. Many years later some said that his descendent, George Sylvester Viereck, succeeded where he failed. Certainly, Buttney may be held guilty for some of the unconventionality of William and Edwina and George Sylvester Viereck.

One of the not necessarily romantic legends is that there was Jewish blood in Viereck's veins. Not long ago a purported genealogy of Viereck was published, showing, with much particularity, that he was descended from one of the tribes of Israel. Strength was given to the theory when George Sylvester's preoccupation with the theme of the Wandering Jew led the immortal scientist, Einstein, to assume Viereck to be a Jew. The episode is reported in *Glimpses of the Great*.

"When I met you," said Einstein to him, "I knew I could talk to you freely, without the inhibitions which make the contact with others so difficult. I looked upon you not as a German nor as an American, but as a Jew.''

"I have written the Autobiography of the Wandering Jew with Paul Eldridge,'' Viereck replied. "Nevertheless it so happens that I am not a Jew. My parents and my progenitors are Nordics from Protestant Germany.''

"It is impossible for any individual to trace every drop of blood in his constitution,'' Einstein retorted. "Ancestors multiply like the famous seed of corn on the chessboard, which embarrassed the Sultan. After we go back a few generations, our ancestors increase so prodigiously that it is practically impossible to determine exactly the various elements which constitute our being.''

Viereck had to content himself with the reply that, so far as he knew, the Vierecks were Northerners, with Ingeborgs and Gretas on the remote branches of the family tree.

"Nevertheless,'' Einstein replied, "you have the psychic adaptability of the Jew. There is something in your psychology which makes it possible for me to talk to you without barrier.''

When Edwina died, her young son was, to all seeming, alone in the world, an orphan child. But he was not really deserted. Von Prillwitz, particularly after his marriage to Countess Moltke, continued to play with the idea of adopting him, but he never took the ultimate step. A little fortune was settled upon the boy; he became a corps student and received a good education and was fitted for a fine career. He attended the universities at Marburg and Berlin and studied medicine, law, and political science. But his position remained equivocal. As a student he loved to be in noble circles, said his cousin Erna, and he was welcome up to a certain point. He enlisted in the War of 1870 against France. But soon enough he was given to understand that his illegitimacy barred him from from the world to which he aspired. His birth thus furnished the conflict of his life.

He served for a while in a minor capacity in the German judiciary. It might have been a stepping stone upward. Tall, handsome, blue-eyed, invincible in bearing and keen mentally, he appeared predestined to a great future. His egotism had a soft charm to it, and few could be offended by it. Had Edwina lived, he might have gone to any height. He might have been a leader in the State, and in spite of her early death, opportunity for preference beckoned to him. But like his Uncle William before him, he became an insurgent, a member of the Socialist Party, devoting his time and substance to the vain effort to establish socialism in Germany. Deeply shocked by the realization that his birth could bar him from the success he craved, he put all his zeal into propagandistic work in the proletarian cause. Thenceforth he was an outcast, the subject of persecution. Because he was falsely accused of being connected with Nobiling, who had attempted to shoot Emperor William I, he was banned from Berlin, and resigned from the Civil Service.

Years later, his father's socialistic career enabled George Sylvester Viereck, as he narrates in *Confessions of a Barbarian*, to break in upon Georg Brandes, then at the height of his fame as the chief ornament of the City of Copenhagen,

Denmark. Viereck, a very young man, had tried every device to gain admittance. He had bandied about the names of those who might have an appeal to Brandes, but the sage of Copenhagen was unimpressed.

"Well," said Viereck, still undaunted. "I am a considerable personage myself."

Brandes looked at him with incredulity and amusement.

"I am the author of several books. My poems mark a new epoch in American literature. I have given a new impulse to the poetry of my age. Besides, for my recreation, I am editing two magazines."

"You're rather precocious," the celebrated man retorted, still amused, to young Viereck's speech of self-praise. Suddenly, he seemed to recall something out of the distant past. "Are you related to Louis Viereck, the former socialist leader?" he asked, his interest beginning to be aroused.

Viereck confessed the relationship, and that broke the ice; the old man was defrosted. He told of a socialist congress many years before in Copenhagen and of how secret police spies dogged the steps of every participant in the Congress, including Louis Viereck, who sought refuge in Brandes's house. The Danish police were in league with the Germans and hardly had Viereck's father been seated when a policeman inquired for him. A white lie by Brandes threw the police off the trail.

Wherever George Sylvester went, he discovered his father's mark. Louis Viereck's picture greeted him from the walls of the Marx-Engels Museum in Moscow when he was there in 1929, and there, too, he saw the correspondence of his mother and father with Marx and Engels carefully preserved. He saw inscribed photographs, which had belonged to his father, bearing the likeness of most of the leaders of the Social Democratic movement in Germany, persons like William Liebknecht, Edward Bernstein, August and Frau Bebel, and others.

In 1881, when Louis Viereck married his cousin Laura, Engels was one of the witnesses at the marriage ceremony in London. Although not herself a radical, Laura Viereck shared her husband's life gladly, a helpmate in every sense. She met and fraternized with all her husband's friends and comforted them when they were hunted and despised. She wrote drama criticism for the newspapers edited by her husband in Munich in the eighties. She did every kind of pedestrian chore for him, and although differing from him in temperament, appearance, and viewpoint, she held him spellbound. He might philander and appear unfaithful, but ever he cherished the vivacious, eager, tolerant cousin who had become his wife. With disarming frankness, he failed to hide the shady side of his life from her—the affairs of the heart and brain that might have hurt her but did not.

As a young man, Louis Viereck seems to have been attracted, like his son after him, by women older than himself, ripe feminine fruit of between thirty and forty summers. One of his infatuations was the now virtually forgotten "Red Countess," the titian-haired heroine of George Meredith's novel, *The Tragic Comedians*. Helene von Doenniges was the fatal lover who had unwittingly doomed the brilliant Ferdinand LaSalle, political leader of German socialism.

LaSalle was neither the first nor the last of the lovely Helene's admirers. Louis Viereck was one in the line of succession, and in time she took a maternal interest in Louis's brilliant young son, whom she fascinated and frightened. Ultimately, she died in a suicide pact with her last lover, who was, incidentally, also her husband. She was one of those who added meaning to the life of the Hohenzollern socialist, Louis Viereck, and his son. Though Louis was faultless in manner and treated the ladies with the utmost courtesy, he had too sober a mind to dally overmuch.

Louis's wife was a devout although unorthodox Christian, while he had renounced all religious affiliations and worshipped all goodly things under the sun with an agnostic's faith. That was just one of their differences, but it mattered little. She cherished all that was his. She thought him the most interesting person who ever lived, superior in mentality even to the child she adored. Above all, she showered love upon the children ultimately born to Louis and herself. When Louis finally found his way to a prison cell because he had transgressed one of the antisocialistic laws of Bismarck—he had participated in a secret session of the Socialist Party—she comforted him from the outside and softened the edge of rancor. Once when the police searched the house and office for socialist literature, Laura, ill at the time, lay on a couch under which the fobidden pamphlets were hidden. Earlier, even before his marriage, when he wandered off to America with Fritzsche to create sympathy for a German revolution, she kept the pots boiling for him at home in the same fashion. Despite her comparatively slight education and the absence of mere cleverness from her makeup, she was, as her cousin Erna said, a lady to her fingertips, even in mean circumstances. She was a very decent person, Erna said, who would rather have bit her tongue than to have passed a mean judgment on anyone.

On his return to Germany, Louis devoted all of his time to socialist journalism, in which his wife assisted him. He established newspapers and published pamphlets on socialist themes that did not find favor in the eyes of the authorities. He was hounded constantly, harrassed wherever he went; but he persevered, although with diminishing faith. He was elected to the Reichstag on the Socialist ticket but constantly came in conflict with the other leaders of the socialist movement. He was looked upon as too moderate and dangerously opportunistic. It could not be forgotten that he had sat at the foot of the blind teacher, Professor Duehring, who had been excommunicated by the patron saints of the socialist movement; both Marx and Engels had written pamphlets and books and articles having as their purpose the disproof of Duehring's notions. There was something in Louis Viereck's bearing that cast doubt upon his allegiance to the proletarian cause. His aristocratic manners and the circumstances of his birth seemed to invite the epithet "parlor socialist."

While Louis Viereck was struggling with his doubts, he was cast into prison at Zwickau, where Bebel, the leader of his party, was a fellow prisoner. The two spent their time debating their conflicting notions. Viereck believed in a form of state socialism, but he could not swallow the idea of the dictatorship of the proletariat. The differences remaining after he was released from prison, he was expelled from the party at the Congress of St. Gallen. Thus the Hohenzollern socialist returned, in a sense, to the fold of respectability, winning meanwhile a black mark in the orthodox histories of Marxism. The chief reproach of the Third International is entered against his name in the histories of the movement: *he was an opportunist!*

Opportunist or not, Louis Viereck had to get on somehow, but the bureaucracy remained unkind. Their harrassment of the former socialist continued so long as he remained within reach. Gradually Germany became less and less desirable to him, although he loved the land with a love that grew more intense with the years. A group of liberals offered him a place once again in the Reichstag, but he refused it. Instead, he sought a position in private life. He made many friends in various fields. He founded the Authors Pension Institute in Munich. He sponsored the first lecture by Magnus Hirschfield, then young and unknown, but subsequently one of the great students of sexual variety. The friendship existed until death, and George Sylvester succeeded his father in the line of friendship. Louis Viereck discovered Father Kneipp, who was responsible for the science of hydrotherapy. When he became much interested in hygiene, he established a permanent hygiene exhibition in Berlin in the old Reichstag building, which he hired from the Prussian government. Ironically, the old socialist had at length achieved complete control over the Reichstag! Few fields of knowledge were alien to him. But the feeling of disenchantment remained. No amount of knowledge, no intellectual attainments, could bring contentment.

Finally, the sole question that remained was the choice between North America and South America—to which continent should he and his tribe migrate? His wife's sister had her new home in Brazil, but his wife preferred America, the land of her birth. That decided him. Leaving his wife and two little children, one of them George Sylvester, under the wings of Edwina's brother, Edward, he departed for America to survey the landscape. His oldest son, Frank, child of another union, was already there and apparently prospering. Louis sought to do likewise. One could not help wondering how well-suited his tribe was for the American soil.

4   PUTTY

With a careful regard for the symbolic connotations of the event, George Sylvester Viereck was born betwixt the dying year 1884 and the year 1885, which was then, like Laura Viereck's baby, struggling to be born. In his apparent eagerness to see light on so noteworthy a date as December 31, 1884, the baby came prematurely, in seven months. Indeed, guests had been invited that stormy New Year's Eve, and, to make the occasion more memorable, a shot rang through the house and came perilously close to snuffing out the life of the tiny new visitant, who as yet knew nothing of such gaiety. It was suspected at first that the shot was directed against the elder Viereck, out of political motives or for revenge. Laura Viereck had reasons sufficient to remember the advent of her first-born, and her husband, the Hohenzollern socialist, thought the circumstances fairly romantic. Both agreed that the baby was extremely small and delicate and in need of warmth, like a Lilliputian character out of *Gulliver's Travels*. He was rolled in thick wadding and was covered with so much ticking that his tininess was accentuated. "My Lilliput!" his mother whispered to him. These were her first words to her baby. Those closest to Viereck thought of him as Putty, the German diminutive of Lilliput. More formally, he was called George, after the poet-prince of Prussia who had been one of the godfathers of Louis Viereck, and Sylvester, because he was born on the Eve of St. Sylvester. The name George Sylvester Viereck had a resonant roll, truly, like a line out of Swinburne, or a passage by the future poet of *Nineveh*.

The baby was born in Munich, Germany, where Louis Viereck was editing Socialist papers and pamphlets and seeking vainly to bring about a form of state socialism. The Vierecks then occupied an apartment in a very large and commercial-appearing building on one of the corners of a street in the Bavarian capital. It was not a Potsdam palace, but simply the modest home of two cultured Germans, who had been married, just three years before, in London, England.

Laura Viereck won an early battle over the child's future. Despite her husband's protests, Putty, unknown to his father, was baptised in a church of the realm by a clergyman Laura was then visiting. He was made a Christian in good standing and given the blessing of an orthodox start in life. The holy water soon enough lost its potency, and in time Putty became, like his handsome father, a freethinker.

Louis Viereck's first reaction to the new-born was that he cried too much. The baby's yells, growing in volume as the days went by, forced Louis to leave in despair. There was business at the Reichstag, and Laura could take care of the squawking Lilliput. With seeming reluctance, Louis began to direct the career of his offspring, and he was not always charming in his methods. The child loved to nestle to his mother. He clung to her as if her love were the one thing he needed to save him from the impatience of his father. The utterly blond child, dazzling in his whiteness, kept a safe distance from his father. He would gaze wistfully at the little rubber donkey that he cherished most of all his toys and seem to wish that papa would be as gentle and as reasonable. Which is not to say that the child was completely estranged from his male parent; far from it, in fact. As if in imitation of Louis Viereck's ways as an editor, the child would play with scissors and daily newspapers, cutting out items in a knowing way, for all the world like a big city journalist, his intelligence obviously precocious.

Louis Viereck believed in self-reliance. He would have his baby face the world unafraid, even if Mama would have him held to her apron strings. When Putty was in his third year, Louis decided to send him to the Kindergarten—by himself. He ordered the child to cross the broad street all alone and instructed the fearful mother to keep her distance. Hidden behind the curtain of the window, she observed her baby cross the street and sighed with relief when no mishaps occurred. Louis Viereck had his own ideas about children's diseases too, no doubt stored in his memory by his experiences as a medical student. When Putty, in common with the other children of the neighborhood, had the measles, Putty recovered soonest, for his father insisted that he be treated with cold water baths and showers! Putty stole the father's thunder by ordering his half-brother Frank around the house, though Frank was his senior. Then, in repentance for his dictatorial conduct, Putty would cling fondly to his brother. He could not be a whole tyrant like his father!

Putty talked early and well. As soon as he could write, he began to make use of written language. He would write letters and notes to his Aunt Frances and to others, making use of all the lore that he absorbed in school, including arithmetic problems. He cherished the memory of his aunt, from whom many of these reminiscences emanate, and when she had left Germany, he constantly wrote to her, asking her to return. When she did return six years after her departure, he greeted her joyously. Mrs. Schmidt found her nephew to be the same nestling child, fairly clinging to his mother. Withal he appeared receptive to everyone and to all things, prematurely ripe in wisdom and filled with the most unbelievable ideas. At that time, she said, he had a passion for recitation, particularly for those things which were beyond his understanding. He wanted to be an actor, a spouter of grand language. One day his aunt went for a ride with him. He stood in the wagon like a matinee idol and declaimed at the top of his voice with gathering strength. He exulted luxuriously, literally intoxicated with beautiful language. Only with difficulty was he quieted. Yet Putty contrived to suggest tragedy, suffering of an intense variety. His aunt felt that he was not altogether happy. One day Putty returned from school, excited to the point of hysteria. He cried with the anguish of a broken heart and would speak only with his mother. In time his mother learned the cause of his tears: a little girl friend at school had just told him of sex and its consequences! He clung to his mother more passionately than ever, while she explained the nature of sex to him, as an antidote to the poison the little girl had poured into his aggrieved ears. Only gradually did his hysteria vanish.

The episode lingered in his memory, just as it had remained in his aged aunt's memory. It was perhaps the most revealing event in the childhood of the poet who was destined to bring passion into the verse of his adopted country. Instead of making a little prude out of him, the episode had a totally opposite effect: the boy developed a heightened curiosity about sex.

Other life-long characteristics could be seen with some clarity in those distant days. As Alfred Adler, the father of individual psychology, brought out, Viereck was always inordinately interested in death and in its counterpart, life. The dread of extinction, the fear of Narcissus to see his own sweet image destroyed, perhaps explained Viereck's interest in a formula for immortality and, lacking that, rejuvenation. As a small child, he recalled, he raced up the stairs, fearing that the nameless terror—later he knew it was death—was pursuing him. When he walked upstairs, he walked sideways, with his back against the wall. Throughout his life he found it insufferable to sit with his back against a door, especially an open door. And only under compulsion would he attend funerals. He swore not to attend his own!

The fear of death may, in his case, have been ancestral. Were not his royal forebears in constant danger of assassination? Or perhaps there had been some infantile shock. As a small child in Munich, Putty used to go to the cellar and set up a sort of throne on top of a huge vat, and with a stick he used to beat against the vat, making reverberations like thunder. At his right would be a bottle filled with blood, the blood of oxen, purchased at the butcher shop. Putty fancied himself a king of the underworld, a king of sudden terror. There perhaps was the future admirer of the Nazis! At any rate, there was the genesis of the worshipper of clamorous heroes.

One of Putty's first recollections was of his father's imprisonment for violating a law aimed at the Social Democrats. It was shortly after the boy was born, but he remembered saying with some frequency, as people inquired after his father, "Papa, Zwickau, far away." Zwickau was the prison Louis Viereck shared with Bebel, and it was at Zwickau that he became disillusioned with socialism. Perhaps, too, the little golden-haired boy that Laura Viereck guarded made her husband's mind run from any subject which might impair the boy's future. For on that future he pondered constantly.

In Munich, Putty attended a public school and absorbed a knowledge of the German language and the subjects then taught in the schools of Germany. None of his teachers made a lasting impression on him; nor did the instructors at the gymnasium, which he later attended in Berlin when his family moved there. He saw little of the land of his birth, taking trips with his parents to the Bavarian mountain resorts and forests. Something of the loveliness of south Germany became a part of his inheritance. He absorbed what he saw with the avidity of a bright child.

When Putty was about ten, he lived in the home of his parents' cousin, Erna, a woman of culture and independence and with literary ambitions. She had written poems, and a play about Edwina Viereck. She was, in short, a woman to inspire the articulate youngster. She recalled Putty as a delicate little boy in appearance, showing clearly the marks of a feminine upbringing. He had spent most of his time with women perhaps twenty years older than himself. Yet he was loud and bold, a little rascal of exigent personality and constant interest. He was three or four years younger than Erna Viereck's children, who were thoroughly normal and average in outlook, but he felt himself too grown up for them, too mature for their play and warfare. Naturally, a feud resulted; for what child will tolerate the superciliousness of one younger than himself? Putty and his distant cousins battled endlessly, but to Erna, who had the poetic vein of the Vierecks, he would bring the verses that he composed. She regarded the poems as nonsensical and would sternly reject them. She would caution him to think of less dangerous subjects than those of his poems. She began to fear that Putty was unfitted for a Philistine world, that he was overripe and sensuous and would find himself soon enough in difficulty. When later he was taken to America and occasionally wrote to her, the early impression was intensified. Yet when she visited him about twenty years later, when he was a man of thirty, she found him "a thoroughly proper and dependable character."

When Putty lived with Erna, he projected a series of impressions of famous personalities. The boy of ten decided that he would set down for the world what George Sylvester Viereck thought of those—as yet—of greater renown than himself. The series was dedicated to Erna's governess, and the first essay was about the last days of Napoleon, the conqueror, then as later an object of worship to Viereck. More than thirty years later Viereck saw his youthful rhapsody on Bonaparte and wrote on its first page, with evident relish, a final benediction: "Seen and read and approved."

"The world creaked in her joints. A second war of nations was begun; thousands lay on the field of battle; the glorious god of war crashed to the ground—yes, crashed physically and morally"—so, with youthful melodrama, the essay began. "Europe was triumphant. The course of steady victory was at an end. The fall of Napoleon had to come, for such is the inevitable law of nature and the earth is round." The victor necessarily must be vanquished. The sun that rose at Austerlitz must set elsewhere.

The boy saw the philosophical consequences when a great spirit decays. "Napoleon," he said, "found it necessary to convince himself of the thanklessness of his people. Here he learned that he was degraded. And here, because a poison failed to harm him, he formed new courage. But that which had motivated him in all his acts—self-control—began to pale. Without self-control he was Napoleon no longer." At Elba, and later at St. Helena, he became a "ghost sovereign," the boy said, and dwelt disconsolately on the incidents of the Emperor's exile. To him, the chief lesson Napoleon learned was the foolhardiness of confiding in the English. He told of the "shop-keeper soul, a son of Albion," who acted as Bonaparte's jailer and who was so niggardly in his kindness. "The said one pulled out his watch as Napoleon drew his last breaths (just like the hypocritical English!) and made light of the phantasies of the dying man and gave himself to his joy in an entirely unconcealed manner as his regal prisoner departed."

It is hardly too much to say that this youthful essay affords additional proof of the juvenile roots of Viereck's excessive admiration of those who have aroused the attention of mankind. The antipathy towards the English is, of course, to be noted also, thought it is probably a boyish echo of the attitude that prevailed on the continent, where England was hated, patronized, and feared. The boy was quick to absorb opinions and manners that might seem mature.

A few years later, in the first month of the new century, Putty set before himself the duty to write some souvenirs of the brief life of his departed little brother, Eddy. He called them, in Heinesque fashion, *Pictures from the Life of the Little Man Eddy*. "Almost two years have sped by," he wrote, "since our little heart-thief wandered to that unknown land from which no traveler returns. Two documents—a birth notice and a death notice—are perhaps all of him that we possess. . . . And to keep this memory fresh, I write these lines, not intended for strange hands." The manner was grand; the mood that of a boy poet conscious of his position in the world.

Eddy was born on the twenty-second day of September, 1895, in Berlin, "in the holy room once occupied by the German Parliament, where Bismarck delivered his famous orations, where so many historically important acts were considered." Putty, shown his little brother, awakened indeed to see him, marvelling at the tininess of the smiling new-born child, scarcely realizing that he himself had been just as inconsequential in size at his birth.

Came more business failures on the part of Papa Viereck and more intrigue against him, and these meant more journeyings forth of Laura and Putty and Eddy. At this time, when Putty was about ten years old, Louis Viereck decided to leave the land of his fathers. He scarcely realized that he could not truly rid himself of his love for the Fatherland. But he fancied that somewhere in the world there was a haven that would enable him to tear Germany from his heart, as he might an unsympathetic and unloving parent. That land, he finally decided, was the land in which his wife had been born. She had left America when she was about the age Putty now was—almost eleven years old. Putty was left at Schoeneberg with Uncle William, and his mother and Eddy stayed in Berlin. Later the two children and their mother were reunited in Berlin, where Laura maintained herself by giving lessons. Eddy, developing rapidly in every way, never bothered his mother while she held classes, but, once classes were finished, the little fellow would stick his head through the door, much to the delight of the doting pupils, and say, with a childish lisp, "May Eddy enter now?" At that time, in the absence of Papa Viereck, Eddy was baptized by a Protestant minister, the child watching with alert blue eyes each motion of the pastor and counting every drop of the baptismal water, as if to say, "Papa does not approve of one little drop on his little boy." Even Mama, despite her religious susceptibilities, could scarcely keep from laughing.

To New York the mother and two children went, by way of Hamburg and a long ocean voyage. Eddy took even more joy in the street cars and elevators in Hamburg than he had in the horse cars of Berlin. Everything seemed to please his bright, inquisitive eyes. The youngster sang like a lark. He was soon to see his Papa! Mrs. Viereck and Putty taught him a bit of responsive recitation with which he could greet Papa. "What will Eddy call when he sees him," they would ask. "Hipp! hipp! hullu!" Eddy would shout with abandon. "Then Papa will take him—" they would suggest; "on his arm," he would answer quickly; "and will Eddy—" they would insinuate, "be happy!" Once again he would shout. It was a merry game. Their happiness was at its crest.

But as the port of New York neared, the little boy, who had been called by the ladies the best behaved child on the boat, became restless and irritable. He cried and cried, and mystified and worried his dear ones. When the boat docked and Eddy saw his father, he said "hipp, hipp, hullu!" in a very quiet voice. It was the beginning of the poor fellow's end. He was shy—even afraid—of the father for whom he had longed. This and other things puzzled the attending physicians. They could not determine what was wrong.

There were moments when Eddy seemed to be restored to health. Then he would pick up a few crumbs of English speech. These he would love to parade, as he rocked himself in the comfortable chair the family had taken with them from Berlin. How he loved that chair! In the dead of the night, he would beg, "Momma, rock me!" The movement to and fro seemed to lull away the pain and unrest of his tiny soul. He would sing to the one on whose lap he found himself:

> Rocking, rocking, here and there,
> Eddy is a shaggy bear!

The Vierecks had moved from a dismal boarding house far out in Brooklyn to a modest apartment in Harlem and the change seemed to brighten up Eddy. "He loved everything that was beautiful and good," remembered Putty; "the flowers, poetry, music—and candy and food." Frequently he would pretend he was writing poems, like Putty's, of the contents of which he could tell little. To the very end, his gift of parody and humor remained, coaxing poor weak smiles from his wan face. He would pretend to read things to himself, though he was too young to know such things, and from time to time he would nod like an oracle and say, "That's so!'' or ''Well, yes!'' A moment later he would be like a carefree child and run around in his drawers or jump upon the lap of Mama or Papa.

So he played and sang and acted until death snatched him with shocking suddenness on the second day of March in 1898. The child almost sensed that his taking-off would be in the very blush of babyhood. Dear God, he had prayed, make me good so that I may enter heaven. Two years later, Putty wrote his pathetic life story.

Laura Viereck renewed her American citizenship, which had been hers by birth but which she had lost by marriage. She regained it when her husband took out his citizen's papers. He was determined to be a faithful adopted nephew of Uncle Sam, for he envisioned a hopeful future under the Stars and Stripes. Before long, he prepared a treatise for the United States government on the teaching of the German language in American schools, and he was on his way to a career of usefulness in his adopted country. He made his living by lecturing and writing. Soon he got to know the leaders of American life. Even the occupant of the White House, the robust Theodore Roosevelt, knew and liked Louis Viereck. Viereck's circle of friends was large. It numbered educators, journalists, and men of culture in general. He became a leader among German-Americans. He took his rightful place among his compatriots, this former member of the Reichstag, this self-created exile about whom strange whisperings were heard. Was he, indeed, the son of the old Kaiser? Why was he here? Such questions, heard with increasing frequency, did not impede him.

In time he became the New York correspondent of the *Berliner Tageblatt,* a journal of world fame. Under an inner compulsion to go abroad in the land and see what it held, Louis Viereck traveled much. Almost constantly he seemed to be called away from home. Thus his growing boy, young Putty, was separated from his father during the formative years of his life. His father became a romantic figure, a man totally unlike the parents of his playfellows. And when Louis Viereck was at home, strange ideas for his boy's future sometimes coursed through his mind.

Shortly after the boy's arrival in the United States, Papa Viereck became convinced that cultured people were impotent in the material struggles of the workaday world. He, therefore, decided that Putty should be apprenticed to a gardener in Baltimore and thus learn to make his way into the world. There the child resided for six months, while his father vicariously returned to nature in the style of Rousseau, as Putty later recorded in *My Flesh and Blood*. The decision was not wholly impractical, for Putty's half-brother Frank was then residing in Baltimore and was a successful florist.

Putty's employer was a Scotsman named MacRoberts. This dreamy soul, who loved poetry more than the tending of flowers, gave the young boy the first experience he was destined to have with manual labor. There was really very little labor to it, for MacRoberts took up the boy's time with long discussions of poetry. Putty was then writing German verse in a humorous vein. He had written the libretto for a musical comedy called, prophetically, *The Rustic Don Juan*. The boy wrote poetry because of an inner compulsion, while MacRoberts discussed poetry because of a similar compulsion. They were two of a kind, the lad and the man. Naturally, the business did not thrive, and the wife of MacRoberts became desperate. She wrote to Putty's papa, imploring him to take back the boy, who really was not earning the bread with which he was fed. MacRoberts, grief-stricken but still murmuring poetry, fell into one of his own water tanks and was drowned. Viereck's pen thus had its first victim!

When Putty was safely returned to New York, a new job was found for him as a florist's errand boy. Neither knowing nor caring for exactitude in directions, he delivered too many bouquets to the wrong addresses, making the wrong people happy and, incidentally, losing his second job. He left a poem with the boss' wife, so that she might remember him, as if she could forget the golden-haired young flatterer! Putty had learned much since he had first cried over the forbidden knowledge a naughty little girl had imparted.

That completed his experiences as a florist's assistant. By this time he had acquired the beginnings of a knowledge of the English language. He spoke with delightful inaccuracy and with an accent upon which one could skate, but it was a beginning. And he was proud of it. He was ready to write poems about it—in German. He was sent to an American school for the first time, Public School 43 at 129th Street and Amsterdam Avenue in New York City. There, alas, his wall of superiority collapsed and could not be rebuilt for some while. Putty was exceedingly shy and fearful. One time, when Putty got up to recite, some of the other boys tormented him, causing him to burst into tears. America was not such a joyous land, after all! One boy, apparently not liking his appearance, threw a stone at Putty, leaving a permanent mark on his forehead. With his insufficient knowledge of English, the boy could scarcely follow the lessons. He never learned the rudiments of grammar and could not do the simplest examples in arithmetic.

But gradually his schoolfellows became accustomed to him and granted him a certain measure of admiration, if not of liking. In time, he was elected to deliver the valedictory of his class, in spite of his pronounced German accent. The Valedictory of the Class, delivered by Master George Viereck, was sandwiched in between the more ambitious speeches. Also sandwiched betwixt and between was the singing of the *Graduate's Farewell,* with words by Master Viereck:

> Farewell! Farewell! Dear 43,
> We now our parting give;
> Where e'er our place in life shall be,
> With thee our thoughts shall live.

> *Chorus*

> O dear old 43,
> Of thee we sing in praise;
> Our future path lies free.
> Farewell! O fond schooldays.

And so on, much to Putty's later chagrin.

It was the same sort of weak triumph as his recitation of *Barbara Frietschie* in a Pennsylvania Dutch version. The New York Superintendent of Schools had congratulated him on his perfect rendering of the strange idiom, not knowing that that was the boy's natural speech.

Back in the days when he was in Baltimore, he had written a much finer poem—on the death of Bismarck. True, that poem was in German, but it had been written on American soil, when the boy was scarcely a year in this country. And the May 12, 1898, issue of Hearst's powerful New York German newspaper, *Das Morgen-Journal*, printed, on its editorial page, a poem by George Sylvester, hailing Columbia in her battle with Spain:

> *Stumm an Deinem Graben stehen,*
> *Die Gefallenen der Maine,*
> *Doch im Hintergrunde Sterne*
> *Und der Freiheit Banner wehn.*
>
> *Heil, Columbia, Dorn-Roschen,*
> *Das aus tiefem Schlaf erwacht,*
> *Durch die Finsterniss zur Wahrheit*
> *Und Zur Tages-Sonne Pracht!*

The tone was sufficiently chauvinistic to delight Hearst himself, and there was obviously some poetic merit in it. The editor printed the poem under the patronizing caption:

> *Noch so jung und schon so—poetisch!*

"Yet so young and already so—poetic!" It was true enough. Putty was on his way to becoming a wonder child.

The boy of thirteen was careful to send with his poem a letter to the editor. He had learned his first lessons from Wilde!

Through her love for the boy, Laura Viereck was able to forgive all of his beliefs and conduct, including the Wildean pose. She might inwardly fret and outwardly express concern over his erratic, willful, wayward conduct, but she was infinitely wise and infinitely understanding and so had the good sense not to impose her will upon the child. She had confidence in his star and that he was following it properly when he was little more than an infant and still, as Dr. Ludwig Fulda later described him in affectionate playfulness, a little monster. Their differences were, in theory, limitless and were never concealed. Yet their devotion was absolute all the days of their lives. They never tired of confiding in each other. Theirs from the start was an almost ideal mother-and-son relationship, each respecting the other's integrity.

And as he adored his mother, he admired and revered his father. From his babyhood, his father was enshrined in his eyes, long absences only intensifying the regard in which he held the author of his mundane being. Once his father playfully called him Oedipus to denote that he had an almost incestuous regard for his mother. Later Freud himself showed him that, just as he had a mother complex, he had, to the same degree, a father complex.

"Year after year you have sought the outstanding figures of your generation, invariably men older than yourself," Freud said to him as he reported in *Glimpses of the Great,* long years after his Munich boyhood. "There was Roosevelt, the Kaiser, Hindenburg, Briand, Foch, Joffre, Georg Brandes, Gerhart Hauptmann and George Bernard Shaw."

"It was part of my work," Viereck protested.

"But it was also your preference," insisted Freud. "The great man is a symbol. Your search is the search of your heart. It is part of your father complex. Your 'Wandering Jew' extends this search into the past. . . . You are always the Seeker of Men."

Viereck said that he constantly wavered between two magnets of affection: mother-love and father-love; pole and antipole. He said that the conflict of loves gave him his ambivalent outlook on life.

And his father, just as his mother, was temperamentally unlike him; almost the antithesis of him, indeed. His father, for one thing, was wholly incapable of understanding the poetry that Putty later wrote. He liked the infantile humorous verse. But the aesthetic mood, the lyric temperament, the artist's contempt for the practical, were beyond him and utterly alien. Intellectually, he could understand his son's attitude towards sex and he had, as a matter of fact, lived a life not wholly confined. But instinctively he revolted at such things. His emotions could not always follow his brain. Yet these things did not lessen the mutual respect and love of father and son.

But dangers flow from too glib generalization about so definite and clear a childhood as Viereck's. There is too much point making indulged in by debaters, logicians, psychologists, and human beings in general. Does a man love his wife? Then a point is made of it; it is given a significance that fails to take into consideration the fact that to love one's wife is not a particularly novel state of affairs. Or is it? A man clings to his mother as if he really cares for her, and, lo, he has a mother-complex. He respects his father, and, behold, a father-complex is the epithet he wins for himself. Given a name and habitation, the obvious becomes something strange and pointed.

Nevertheless several very important results flowed from Putty's relations with his parents. He began to feel that friendships and loves are simply matters of biochemical affinity rather than intellectual agreement and that, indeed, intellectual and philosophical differences are unimportant. He began to tolerate all opinions, so long as they were the opinions of friends. Principles, as such, began to mean little to him, while personal loyalties commenced to mean everything. Increasingly, he felt that he could easily scrap every set rule of life, so long as it meant the preservation of friendships. His life, from childhood, became the story of a temperamental antipathy towards the enthronement of principles. Such things were not apparent during Putty's boyhood in Munich and elsewhere, but the seeds were there, ready to sprout, as they did soon enough.

And as much as Viereck loved his parents, he was never able to express his feelings for them in one adequate poem, though he dedicated two books to them. All of the fundamental esteem, all of the many thoughts crying for expression, had to be inhibited by the compulsion of some "guardian of the nether mind." He was, however, able to express the sense of impotence, of causeless inhibition, in a poem of that name, which he inscribed to his parents:

> O for the blithesomeness of birds
>> Whose soul floods ever to their tongue!
> But to be impotent of words
>> With blinding tears and heart unstrung!
>
> Each breeze that blows from homeward brings
>> To me who am so far away
> The memory of tender things
>> I might have said and did not say.
>
> Like spirit children, wraiths unborn
>> To luckless lovers long ago,
> Shades of emotion, mute, forlorn,
>> Within my brain stalk to and fro.
>
> When to my lips they rush, and call,
>> A nameless something rears its head,
> Forbidding, like the spectral wall
>> Between the living and the dead.
>
> O guardian of the nether mind
>> Where atavistic terrors reel
> In labyrinthine chambers, bind
>> Old nightmares with thy mystic seal!
>
> But bar not from the sonant gate
>> Of being with thy fiery sword
> The sweetest thing we wring from fate:
>> Love's one imperishable word!

That word never came, but Louis Viereck did not ask for it. As he lay on his deathbed, after the fullness of years, his tired fingers formed one word upon a little slip of paper. That word was "Putty." It was "love's one imperishable word" as far as he was concerned. His son framed the little slip of paper together with other memorabilia of his father, and his eyes often glanced at these tokens of love.

5   WONDER CHILD

After being graduated from public school, young Viereck enrolled as a subfreshman for a while at the College of the City of New York, and at the end of that time he matriculated as a regular college student. It was an eventful period in his life. His childhood—that is to say, the infantile phase—was of the past. His foliage, so to speak, had begun to spread. The figure of the man was emerging. One knowing the Viereck of his later life could have no difficulty in discerning in 1902 the roots and branches and even the trunk of the man. Of course, there was something green in what one saw; the fruit was yet unripe; harvest time was hardly at hand.

And it was also written in large, if unkempt letters, in a bookkeeping journal that the boy Viereck turned into a diary late in 1901. On the cover of the book, the boy had written the telltale words, "Precious for George S. Viereck." The words were in the English language; but most of the diary was in German. And all of the entries, whether written in English or in German, were revelatory to a degree. At the end of the year, the diary was discarded, put aside, and, to all seeming, out of the mind of the boy. It was buried with other relics of the past, only to come to life again after a rest of more than thirty years. Read a generation after its composition, it had a compelling power that seemed to brush aside the years, stripping off layer after layer of veneer and showing, at long last, the quintessential Viereck.

The diary began, as it ended, with Oscar Wilde and Swinburne, for it could not otherwise have given a true picture of the boy's mental and emotional life. It began, and ended, too, in a spirit of self-esteem. It displayed contempt for the ordinary usages of life and letters. It reveled in high-spirited ignorance of mere facts. It gloated in triumphs, petty no less than basic. Reflecting the boy in all his assumed rudeness, it gave a Viereckian interpretation of the world as it was during the first year of the twentieth century. One reading Mark Sullivan's account of the *Turn of the Century* or any more or less staid and sober chronicle of those distant days could have no clear understanding of Putty's world view, to dignify his first strivings for expression with so imposing a term. The world was quite different to

31

Putty; it could not possibly resemble the earth upon which his elders stumbled and of which Mark Sullivan and others have written.

Even before the 1900s dawned upon the world and upon young Viereck, the boy had enunciated, as he expressed it, a new cosmogony. He was eleven or twelve years of age when he had made a fantastic attempt to show the evolution of man to godhood. He envisioned a heaven of many gods, a celestial kingdom of sublime men who had become gods, and no doubt he chose a comfortable spot for himself in this haven of sublimity. He may have thought of himself as eventually the best of gods: the king of kings in a land of crowned heads. He certainly preened himself before the mirrors, real and imaginary, which he placed before his young Teutonic face.

And circumstances conspired to heighten his conceit. He could not help feeling himself an exceptional being, a young Apollo in glory, a Solomon in triumphant wisdom. The mysterious whisperings about his father's regal ancestry, when hardly understood by the boy, helped to elevate him in his own eyes and in the sight of others. His first poems, published in German-American newspapers when he was still strutting about in short pants, helped even more, for they were praised as the first offerings of a child of genius—a Wonder Child, a *Wunderkind*. It was asserted by many that German America had at last found its lyrical voice. It is this exultant shout of triumph that the diary, "Precious for George S. Viereck," echoes in strident tones.

It was an extraordinary busy youngster that the diary mirrored. Although there was no tuition fee at City College, the boy had to meet all other obligations, and they were considerable. The Viereck family was then poor, though not poverty-stricken. Still, the boy had to do his share. For one thing, he assisted his father in connection with his work as correspondent of the *Berlin Tageblatt*. Almost weekly, he wrote articles for that great newspaper—sometimes under his own name, but more often in the name of his father. When Louis Viereck was away, and he sometimes wandered for months at a time, his son substituted for him, taking care of the regular articles and of the cable service. He kept none of the compensation received for such contributions; that was his offering for the support of his family. Indeed, it seldom occurred to him that he ought to receive money for partaking in the supreme joy of literary creation. He was then an inspired amateur in the very best sense. He had not yet sunk to the artist's hell of writing solely for money, and it was not yet certain that he would fall to any such level of bondage. He might, like his Hohenzollern forbears, inherit the earth without effort.

He also wrote articles for the Sunday *Staats-Zeitung*, then as later a distinguished German language newspaper. He wrote on Swinburne and other such congenial subjects, as well as many fantastic short stories, and received compensation at the rate of five dollars per column. Since many of his articles and stories filled pages in that paper, he earned perhaps hundreds of dollars annually from that one source alone. These considerable sums helped him to finance his contributions to other publications: a column in Herman Alexander's weekly literary sheet, *The Echo*, innumerable articles for the *Deutsche Korrespondent* in Baltimore and for other Teutonic newspapers, reflections on events in thriving Manhattan, dramatic criticisms, stories, all things upon which the Wonder Child cogitated. It was work sufficient for more than one boy, and it was, by no means, all that he did.

His father, it should be remembered, was acting as a sort of pioneer for German culture in America. He required recruits at all times, for German-Americans seemed to be lacking in racial solidarity, so far as Louis Viereck could judge. His son was his first assistant, almost by compulsion. Putty, like most boys, preferred foreign service to domestic chores, but he assisted his father as well as he could. His father gave him important assignments, but they remained, in a sense, the tasks imposed by filial obligations. Acting as editor of *Der Deutsche Vork-ampfer* when his father was absent could not wholly reconcile the boy to the demands of duty, nor could he face with enthusiasm the many German-language meetings and gatherings that he attended for his father's sake. In his youth, he was by no means a Germanophile.

There was at least one humorous interlude in duty's siege. Some league for liberal immigration, reflecting the views of Louis Viereck, had promised to pay Louis's son and those he could marshall as his assistants some small sum, perhaps five or ten cents, for each signature they could procure to a petition against restrictive legislation, talk of such legislation being very much in the air. Sylvester forthwith put his college mates to work, commencing with those in his own fraternity and extending to a mob of outsiders. Soon the whole school was collecting names at an astonishing rate that outran the funds allowed to Putty. To add to the boy's chagrin, the league authorities had no difficulty in proving to him that many of the signatures had a singular similarity; that they were quite obviously the results of diligent copying from the fast-growing telephone directory and perhaps contained tombstone markings as well! It was a considerable problem to learn what to do to save himself from ungentle treatment at the hands of his schoolmates. Putty assembled all of the name-gatherers in the College Chapel, perhaps because prayer if not fasting was required to solve his difficulties, and dispensing with both prayer and fasting but protected by a bodyguard made up of members of his fraternity, he acquainted the boys with the fact that they would receive not a nickel or a dime for each signature but only a fraction of a cent. It was like pulling down the castles in the air built by many of his schoolmates, for some of them had worked conscientiously, scorning the city directory and the tomb-stones, and had instead won the assistance of their sisters and their cousins and their aunts. It was, indeed, a Gilbert and Sullivan situation, although Putty was not wholly aware of its humor, and at least one German newspaper, Hearst's *Morning Journal,* played it up as a grand farce.

Putty wrote during these Wonder Child years all of the poems that subsequently appeared, as we shall see, in *Gedichte* and *Nineveh und Andere Gedichte*. He translated the *Ballad of Reading Gaol* into German, a notable achievement in every respect. He translated innumerable poems by Wilde, Poe, and Swinburne, some of which were never published in books but most of which graced the columns of the German press and helped to make the boy an important personage.

He began, hesitantly, to write his first verse in the English language and his first prose, the plays later collected in *A Game at Love*. Not exhausting but only augmenting his verbal fertility, he carried on a series of ambitious exchanges of letters with many American and Teutonic poets and writers. Some of these men almost worshipped the golden-haired boy. Ernst Henrici, a strange blend of adventurer and man of culture, a bigoted anti-Semite and a dreamer, dedicated poem after poem to the much younger lyrist. Sylvester gathered the elder poet's harvest with much joy but did not pay similar poetic tribute. He was content to receive, and repayment he left for another season or other hands. Not even Konrad Nies' touching sonnet to Sylvio moved him to an adequate reply. That sonnet, as well as offerings by Martin Drescher, deserve quotation because of their astonishing humility before the child. Men were awed by him; sometimes they were left speechless; often they were like singing birds in the expression of their admiration.

The adoration stemmed not only from masculine sources. Louis Viereck delighted in claiming that a mature lady used to visit his son at college, bringing candy for the boy. This woman with so vast an admiration for the Wonder Child was herself an extraordinary person, an influence wholly for the best. Almost an anarchist in viewpoint, she yet paid homage to the boy. She gave Putty not only candy, but mental sustenance. Later she began to feel that success had perhaps gone to his head. Other women and girls supplied nourishment for his amorous soul. He said he had innumerable casual erotic adventures and four or five "serious" love affairs. The figures need not be totaled. In any event, there apparently were enough to keep the lustiest of young men busy. His escapades, real and imagined, supplied material for a library of passional poems, and those he wrote. He was like a lyrical geyser in his outpourings. The library, also, gave him much material to help satisfy his lustful curiosity, but it never could wholly quench his enormous sexual appetite. Some of his amorous tastes were dubious and troubled a few of his peers and elders. Putty's too rabid admiration for Wilde and his coquetting with the roses and raptures of Swinburnean vice showed the direction counter to the general direction in which his mind and instincts ran. He read, with overmuch zeal, Casanova, Krafft-Ebing, the Marquis de Sade, Zola, and Havelock Ellis. The esoteric in love fascinated him because it afforded new whips with which to scourge the Philistines. Out of his reading grew, inevitably, a monstrous manuscript in the German language, called, with youthful delight, *Elinor, the Autobiography of a Degenerate*. Dedicated to the author of *Nana*, the book is an orgy of lust, but it is too cerebral to be pornographic. The heroine, a slut of unbridled passion, experiences every phase of sex. Only the normal is apparently alien to her. She dotes on her perversions, little and big, and treats them like loving children. She acts like a bitch begotten by the illicit union of a panderer and a harlot. The book is a veritable catalog of lust, more varied in the recital of amorous experience than *Fanny Hill*. Of course, it was not published! Particularly, perhaps, because the boy was careful to blame society for his slut's lapses. How could it be published in America during the lifetime of Anthony Comstock, Herdsman of the Lord? The boy hardly expected it to be published. But it was talked about in the Viereck circle. More than ever, the little monster Putty was looked upon with big eyes. Where would he go, to what heights, or depths? Perhaps the way of Villon to the scarlet Parnassus? Putty joined in the speculations. He was of lively interest to himself at all times.

The lengthiest passages in Putty's diary for the year 1901 concern Lord Alfred Douglas, the Jonathan in Oscar Wilde's life. Lord Alfred was in America at that time in search of an American heiress, as he later confessed in his strange autobiography. Viereck did not know that. He only knew that the friend of his literary god was in New York. Lord Alfred had just been excluded from the Metropolitan Club at Washington where he had been staying as the guest of his cousin, Percy Wyndham. The club objected to him because of his "friendship for objectionable persons," and Putty favored him for the same reason. He wrote to Lord Alfred, sympathizing with him because of the ill-bred action of the club. The boy's letter pleased the romantic and headstrong Scottish lord, and he invited Viereck to visit him.

After a lapse of thirty-five years, Douglas still treasured that first encounter. He wrote that he found Putty in 1901 an unusually brilliant youth with whom, in spite of his youth, he could talk on literature and almost everything else. To Putty, the meeting was epochal, as page after page in the diary evince. He asked and was granted permission to translate into German some of Lord Alfred's poems, notably his first sonnet on the dead poet of Reading Gaol. Douglas wrote it out for him and Viereck treasured the holograph to the end; Lord Douglas, no less than Wilde, remained one of his poetic gods. He, as much or more than any man, with the possible exception of Frank Harris, praised Lord Alfred's poems in season and out and was one of the comparatively few who placed the Douglas poems on a pedestal. But, of course, at that time it was Wilde, rather than Douglas, who interested him. Wilde had just died; to Douglas and to Putty it seemed today, and not yesterday. The two talked familiarly of many things, and the diary sets forth the conversation with uncommon particularity.

There were carefully labeled subdivisions in the book, marking off the various topics that were discussed. The boy felt that he was preserving something for posterity: a detailed account of a contact with a lord of literature.

Especially to be remarked is that one of the carefully labeled subdivisions concerned Wilde's attitude towards the Jews. Douglas told him, and Putty set down, the fact that Oscar disliked the Jews. Nor did Douglas himself express any love for them. But despite Douglas and Wilde and Henrici, the boy Viereck, like his father, fraternized with Jews. He seemed to prefer them to all others. At college, he could hardly escape contacts with Jewish boys, for a Gentile face was indeed rare in the school corridors. City College was predominantly Jewish in student composition. Perhaps 90 percent or more were of that faith, and Putty gave no hint that he did not like it. He was a member of a nonsectarian fraternity (it would have been difficult to support wholly Gentile organizations at City College). And Putty was soon to meet perhaps the greatest of the Jewish influences in his life. That individual, perversely enough, was to seek to run away from his Jewish heritage, only to come back to it long years later and to shout his Jewishness from the house tops. This Jew was to be the most temperamental of Viereck's friends, and in their periods of estrangement Viereck was to wonder if perhaps there was something in the Semitic character which caused tantrums.

One of the elder friends of the boy was the quaint and redoubtable Julius Auspitz, who styled himself *Dr. Kritikus* and published a little magazine of that name. To *Dr. Kritikus,* Putty would often contribute; and how he loved talking with Auspitz. After a long conversation with him Putty would go away with his tags of speech upon his lips. *Meschugge,* this was the Judaeo-German word that most delighted him. Yet the boy's critical sense, with respect to Auspitz, was far from dormant. Writing in his diary, after citing Auspitz's belief that he should write in English, because of the absence of "considerable personages" among the German-American journalists, he says of Auspitz: "His *Dr. Kritikus* seems artificial and mannered. An effort to cover up thoughtlessness with pretty form— and this ironic attitude towards himself, is it genuine or original? But he is nevertheless an inspired and talented man. Like Nietzsche, he is a master of the language and, like Heine, he swings the lance."

It is worthwhile going through the diary for touches such as these. In the very first entry, he gives evidence of realizing the borrowed sources of his own inspiration. He says of his poem, *Das Herz* that it "has some Heinesque echoes," and of his *Tannhauser* that it "was born out of Swinburne's *Laus Veneris;*" of *Lesbian Chants* that they were inspired by Swinburne's *Sapphics* and *Faustina.* Of another poem he says, with refreshing amusement at his own expense, "I do not know to this day from whom I stole it." He says that another poem is "influenced in diction by Poe and Swinburne, in ideas it follows a poem of my own, and the music is after an old folk song"; he would not fool himself, this astute Wonder Child.

Constantly he complains of his lack of poetic fecundity. Under the heading "June—July—August," he says, complainingly, that he "wrote only seven original poems—which makes only two per month." In mid-September he takes stock of himself: "Only eighteen new poems this year, among them two transla- tions. Which makes an average of: every seven days something about me or by me in the newspapers; every eight and a third days a poem from my pen; every fourteen days a new poem about me." Garlands of song were already woven about his golden head. There would be more until he grew too accustomed to them.

After much effort, he completed a letter to his poetic god, Swinburne. Suddenly he wondered if Swinburne was alive. He had not known that the author of *Poems and Ballads* was then under the care of his dry nurse, Watts-Dunton. After much trouble, he learned that Swinburne was among the living. A long delay; but no letter from Swinburne. He wrote a letter to his dear old friend, Mrs. Anna Herberts, the sister of the artist Cronau, who was going abroad, asking her to visit Swinburne. "That fellow should answer!" he wrote, petulantly.

Mrs. Herberts was an old family friend. As an old gentlewoman of eighty some years, she wrote to me her fleeting recollections of Putty. "One could amuse oneself with him, almost like with a grown-up," she recalled, "and his original thoughts and expressions frequently gave us much delight." This was before the turn of the century. She recalled that when Putty was about twelve years, the little fellow brought her a poem that astonished her. Since she was going the next day with her own manuscript to the editor of the New York *German Journal,* she took along the youngster's poem to get the editor's opinion of it. No one could believe that so young a lad had written it, and the editor insisted upon publishing it—perhaps the first verses of Viereck's to appear in print. Mrs. Herberts, like everyone else, began to build assured pictures of his future.

By this time he was building such pictures himself in his diary, uniting seriousness with humor, common sense with quaintness. It was a gala show. "And will this book bring a thousand dollars in fifty years—when I'll be famous!" he asked, while bemoaning an ink spot on one of its pages. "And what will they say about my character? Bad or worse! Moral ladies, like moral books, bore me," he continued, without a pause. "Innocent love always has a ridiculous side to it." And he asked his diary, "Will I ever be a great poet? In a strange land? To the German a Briton, to the Briton a German?"

He told of the books he read, the esoteric rather than the orthodox usually appealing to him. He found Balzac's *Magic Skin* "tedious." He thought that the book had "too much ado and no principal theme." He found the same trouble with Swinburne's essay on Victor Hugo. Halle's *Free Love,* like Balzac's *Magic Skin,* he believed "tedious." Tedious was a favorite epithet of his. He thought Nietzsche's *Beyond Good and Evil* more inspired than *Thus Spake Zarathustra.* Max Nordau's *Degeneration* he called a "grand book, even though, for the sake of maintaining a brilliant theory, he does not always take the truth too seriously." "Isn't necessary," the cynical boy added at once. Was this the birth of the propagandist? At least the streak of worldliness was to the fore. "Wilde is my favorite," he said again, and there can be no doubt that he was, as witness this rhapsody which ended in a note of tomfoolery, written, incidentally, in English:

"Wilde is splendid. I admire, nay I love him. He is so deliciously unhealthy, so beautifully morbid. I love all things evil. I love the splendor of decay, the foul beauty of corruption. What I hate is inquisitive cold, freezing rays of the sun. Day is nausea, day is dullness, day is prose. Night, Beauty, love, splendor, poetry, wine, scarlet, rape, vice and bliss! I love the night—*und Meschugge ist Trumpf!*"

"And hysteria is trump"—that phrase was ever at his pen's end when he was too solemn with himself. Auspitz has taught it to him. *"Herrgott, Donnerwetter, Sakrati!"* he could write, in that same spirit. "Nothing written in eight days. But I have too much to do. Not a poem has appeared lately. I don't give up writing, anyway. Nothing matters. . . . ." The same disillusionment characteristic of the mature man; the seed about to sprout. "Moony of the *Tribune* says that I have imagination and the art to attain form now. What do I buy with that! *Meschugge ist Trumpf!*" The propagandist grew a day older!

One day, Putty wrote in his diary that he has "Nothing to tell." It was a rare day, indeed. Forty-eight hours later he conceived the idea for a tragedy and started to polish *Elinor*. The plot is simple, he said: "A talented author, a disciple of Ibsen and a foe of the 'great lie,' falls in love on his wedding day with the brother of his bride. The struggle within himself awakens him and forces death into his hand. At his funeral his physician speaks: 'Glorious Mother Nature, why didst thou give us this sadness which comes in conflict with thy laws. Why?—oh, why?' The lover of the hero is twenty and blase to a degree. He has gone though much to be up-to-date in vice." In short, he was what Viereck aspired to be during his cynical moments.

A few days later Viereck was busy writing campaign poems against Tammany. "Tammany will lose this fight," he declared. The reason? Apparently because Viereck so willed it. By October 7 he found that "not much news has exploded; a few campaign songs and a little *Weltschmerz*." He contemplated himself once more. The mirror was filled with his image, and he was not quite as much pleased as before. "Why do I really indulge in a comedy with myself?" he inquired. An editor rejected a Lesbian poem of his. The boy commented: "He is no Philistine, no mutton-head, but he has to take the public into consideration, otherwise he'll be hanged and drawn—Damn the Public!" Meanwhile, various poems had been sent off to the press and been published. The diary keeps careful count of these. When a person commented that his poems are good but far too pessimistic, he wrote in his diary, "The beast, man, does not like to hear that he is imperfect and mortal."

A sudden and savage bit of anti-German feeling crept into the book in mid-November: "Swinburne writes in a sonnet: Each lie that falls from German boors and slaves, Falls but as filth dropped in the wandering waves. And he is right. Those lies in German papers can be traced to envy only." This was his way of voicing his resentment over sympathy in the Fatherland for the Spanish cause during the late war. The chauvinistic verses in Hearst's journal a few years before evidently were a sincere expression of his viewpoint.

On the previous day, he mentioned that he had just translated Wilde's "glorious poem, *Bittersweet Love*." Then for several days all of his thoughts seemed to concern Wilde, his admiration reaching a summit in his conversation with Lord Alfred Douglas. A glorious feeling to meet one who had clasped the hand of god and known and loved him in the flesh! To Putty the meeting with Douglas afforded a marvelous close to a memorable year. That year of true grace, 1901, did indeed represent an important juncture in Putty's career. Of this the precious diary was sufficient proof.

6   COLLEGE BOY

From September 1902 to June 1906 Viereck attended the College of the City of New York as a student in the Classical Course. He received the degree of Bachelor of Arts, but he was an indifferent student, or worse. Only in English did he receive, throughout the four years, grades above the average. He studied Latin, Greek, and French and showed an astonishing ability to escape a knowledge of these languages. He was impatient with them because the teachers did not immediately reveal to him the beauties of Catullus and Baudelaire. During his first year Viereck failed in Mathematics, Physics, and Drawing and secured passing grades in the languages and in Natural History. Inasmuch as he succeeded in writing several poems he liked, including an ebullient chronicle of a night of love, he did not waste a moment's thoughts on the various "flunks." He did, however, reform somewhat during the balance of the course and failed only in Greek and Chemistry, but he did come perilously close to disaster in several other courses. When he received a comparatively high grade during the first semester, he invariably was content to take a low one at the end; and when he received a low grade at the beginning, he managed to get a higher grade at the end. He used, in other words, no more effort than was required. For the rest, his course consisted of Logic, Public Speaking, Philosophy, Chemistry, and Pedagogies: a curious assortment, indeed. There was nothing in it relating to the social sciences or to the workaday world. It was a liberal arts course, with little real liberality about it.

The faculty was generous to permit Viereck to graduate with so undistinguished a record. He was, in many respects, a privileged character. His talents as a poet and writer and his irresistible confidence bedazzled the faculty. All of them, with the exception of a prosaic physics instructor, treated him as they customarily treated only athletes. One teacher deliberately left a textbook in the room so that Viereck might pass the examination. On one occasion, a sonnet by Viereck against descriptive geometry was a sufficient reason for the youth's being given a passing

39

grade. A distinguished Catholic scholar, the Latin professor, treated the boy with amused respect, despite his horror of the views held by the young poet. He was in this typical of the faculty. All of them found something in his character to regret. Time has a way with all men's memories, but Prof. Lewis F. Mott's recollections are worth attention. He said that Viereck never strove for high standing and preferred his own reading to the prescribed studies. "He knew all of his teachers and was known by them," wrote Mott of Viereck in March 1935. "In his essays for me, he always took a view contrary to the prevailing one, apparently preferring to take a stand that was different rather than to seek a just opinion. He was one of the editors of the *College Mercury*, then a general college paper, publishing news, opinions and literary articles. To this paper he contributed a good many poems, some excellent, others rather poor. I remember that once, when I criticized a line in one of these, he flushed with anger, but the next day he came to me and said that I was right. A sonnet of his was, through the help of President Finley, published in the *Century Magazine*. A writer whom he greatly admired at that time was James Huneker, whose acquaintance he had made, and, judging from a remark Jim made to me, his attentions must have been a trifle importunate."

Evidently Professor Mott misjudged Huneker's attitude toward Viereck; in truth, Huneker regarded the boy with profound interest and eagerly sought to assist him. An extraordinarily enlightened woman, Amelia von Ende, was another who took a parental interest in the extraordinary lad. To her home came Viereck and the young hopefuls who were his friends. In the group was Leon Dabo, the celebrated artist and man-of-affairs, some years Viereck's senior. He watched Viereck grow from short pants and some conceit to long pants and prodigious self-esteem.

The various college publications—the *Raven, Cap and Bells, Quips and Cranks,* as well as the *Mercury,* and perhaps others—gave a good account of his self-esteem. He was looked upon not merely as another college hopeful, but as a writer of parts, although his conceit was discounted. During his sophomore year one of the publications, echoing the general belief, said that Viereck "has the proud distinction of being the greatest poet in the world—I beg your pardon, I mean the college has ever seen." The same magazine published a parody, in its way typical of the many that were to be written in future years. It was called *The Story of George Viereck, By Himself and for Himself,* and was not the sort of article that would have been written about any other student at the College. It was an amusing picture of a young man whose opinion of himself was by no means modest.

Viereck's contributions to the school magazines were generally of little value, except for their revelation of the boy in the process of growth. His English style was not easy and unforced, and too often Viereck felt inclined to run away from a serious effort. Scarcely concealing his modest opinion of the school audience, he wrote down to their level, mere cuteness taking the place of true wit and humor. Sometimes his writings fell between the two stools of epigram and wisecrack, as when he wrote a series of quips entitled *Short and Sweet.* "The Bill of Fare of Love ought to be changed from time to time," he said in one of the lines;

"One cannot eat caviare every day," he said in another; "To have one's affections bound up in one person all your life, is like eating apple pie every day," he opined in a third quip. These very early statements, by no means profound, were beliefs he always cherished.

It was only occasionally that he felt minded to send a serious effort to the student journals. There is one poem of some beauty—there may be others—which he styled *Paradise*. It appeared in the *Mercury* and narrated that

> In the Golden Garden of Paradise
> The stately Silver Lilies nod,
> And the Seven Virtues sisterwise
> Walk side by side in the face of God.

This approaches the powerful turn of phrase of the boy's best English verse. There was at least one serious essay by him on modern literature which aroused controversy and won a sedate reply by an alumnus. Viereck could not help feeling flattered by the attention. He could appreciate the justice of his critic's complaint that "We read Lawson and Upton Sinclair because we *must*,—Swinburne, Shaw and Viereck, because they stimulate a morbid curiousity; but we are ignorant of the Bible, Dante, Shakespeare, Milton and Wordsworth." Another article on Swinburne, rapt in its admiration for the Poet of *Dolores* and *Faustine,* was quoted in the metropolitan press and had serious consequences. In it Viereck had protested against the absence of Swinburne's works from the college library. As a result, the school authorities gave thought to the desirability of removing Swinburne's defender from the premises. Viereck narrowly escaped being made a martyr for decadent poetry.

Viereck was a frog of size in the City College pond, as his election as class poet evinces. Several of his fellow students wrote charming accounts of him; but only with Ely Simpson and Morris Abel Beer was he really intimate, and with these two he remained on friendly terms. Simpson acted as his attorney occasionally, and Beer's verse was published by Viereck from time to time. With one or two others, Viereck was fairly friendly but not intimate. One student recalled that Viereck's mannerisms set him apart from his classmates. This student recalled that on one occasion Viereck came home with him for lunch, "and before entering the house he stopped in the entrance hall, pulled out a mirror and comb from his pocket, and carefully brushed his hair," with a fastidiousness unlike that of the average college student. On the least provocation, he quoted from Swinburne and Wilde, *Faustine* furnishing him with his most prized quotations. Nor was he bashful about praising and quoting his own poems, the classmate said. On one occasion, according to him, when the instructor in English asked Viereck to name the three outstanding figures in English literature, Viereck selected Shakespeare, Swinburne, and himself! With an amused expression and a polite bow, the instructor congratulated Viereck on his modesty in naming himself last.

Several classmates said that Viereck was much better informed on a great many subjects than were most of the students, especially those subjects which touched on forbidden ground. He was considerably more mature than the other boys and impressed them as knowing much more about women than any of the others. His classmates looked upon him as a sort of Casanova, much attracted by women and undoubtedly attractive to them. Some thought him obsessed by the subject of free love. Others disliked his apparent sympathy for the abnormal. At least one fellow disliked Viereck's black flowing ties, his "rather superior" ways, and his excessive pride in his left-handed relationship with the Kaiser. (Viereck denied he made such claims at that time. He contended that the man confused his later impressions with earlier ones.)

The students could see that there was a curious blend of qualities in Viereck and that he could not be dismissed with categorical finality. One student, a member of the same fraternity as Viereck, met him every day at lunch time and got to know him rather well, he thought. His impressions stressed certain aspects of Viereck's personality that are not always remembered. Viereck, he said, "was rather slight and effeminate in those days and yet he was not lacking in personal courage. This was demonstrated during his initiation into the fraternity. He was shown a large basin filled with broken glass and when later he was blindfolded and told to jump bare-foot from a chair into the broken glass, he did it without hesitation. He really jumped into cracked ice, but he did not know it." Viereck then was, this man said, of the same nervous, dynamic temperament characteristic of him in later life.

When asked years later if any instructor at college had had any profound influence on him, Viereck replied in the negative. He had, strangely enough, forgotten Alexis Irenee du Pont Coleman, his instructor in English literature! Coleman gave him what he most needed: sympathetic understanding. "A tall, stooping figure," Viereck recalled him, "out of touch with reality, he was completely lacking in commercial instincts. A dreamer and a scholar, the academic life was his haven." Coleman defended Viereck when his Swinburne atricle raised such a stir that expulsion stared the young critic in the face. Coleman was profoundly interested in Viereck's German verse and later translated much of it with skill and sympathy.

When asked how much knowledge he had, Viereck, recalling his college days, was quick to reply: "I learned nothing and I know nothing. I managed to graduate by sheer force of individuality and the grace of the teachers. Formal education has done me small good, no harm—possibly some slight mental training. Education as it was then constituted and as it is today is utterly wrong. It is wasting of ideas and time."

His college course was preparation sufficient for a poet of passion, it may be said. But would it do for the other activities in which Viereck was to interest himself?

7 THREE LITERARY MUSKETEERS

A thin, elongated, tense Yankee scholar of twenty-five returned to America in 1902 from extended studies in Germany and travels in England and on the continent, gained in spite of virtual poverty. The knowledge of many books was his and the wisdom that results from burdensome problems, but he was not wholly assured of himself or truly a man of the world. The young man, William Ellery Leonard, was a poet, a dreamer of the quiet beauty of character and the turbulent stuff of experience. He was determined to justify, by his life, the poet as scholar. Leonard had been at Bonn, where he had been a contemporary of the Crown Prince, and at Göttingen, and elsewhere, but these universities did not quench the poet-scholar's desire for knowledge. Like a true devotee of wisdom, he could never give up the quest for enlightenment, and being a poet, he believed that beauty is a lovely veil making the glowing form of wisdom more seductive.

Returned to America, Leonard enrolled without loss of time at Columbia University so that he might write his thesis on Byron and Byronism in America and equip himself for his work in life as poet and scholar. He had already studied at Boston University and at Harvard, the mecca of American scholarship. There he had been on terms of intimacy with the great psychologist and philosopher William James. Leonard was not a socialite; but he was more of an athlete than the average scholar, and he wanted a certain measure of companionship, of physical fellowship in addition to intellectual stimulus without end. He found companionship, also, in a few choice spirits older than himself. But still he longed, almost despairingly, for something he could not define. His life at that time was a series of spiritual aches and pains.

Leonard wanted to retain his newly acquired knowledge of the German language, and he wanted to continue his contacts with Teutonic culture. Languages and folkways lured him (he eventually was to know twenty-six tongues). It occured to him that it would be useful to live with a German-speaking family of some intellectual breadth. He did not know that the course was going to be more than useful, that it was going to be a basic fact in his life. Nor did two young Germans, both, like Leonard, enamored of the sweet true voices of the Muses. One was sixteen years old, the other twenty; but both, like Leonard, followed the star within them.

Old Professor Tombo of Columbia suggested to Leonard that he call upon Louis Viereck, one of the cultural pioneers in German America. Perhaps that debonair fellow in his bright middle years might give the eager young scholar asylum in his home. It would be worth attempting, Tombo told Leonard, who took the advice and called upon Louis Viereck, who then was living in a little home in the upper reaches of Manhattan.

Louis Viereck's son, George Sylvester, at sixteen was a cerebral elf, Leonard said. To the very end of his life, Leonard recalled that on his first visit to the Viereck home, George Sylvester followed his mother down the corridor of the house and, upset that Leonard did not notice him, popped out from behind her skirts to proclaim himself with the cry, "Ich bin ein Dichter; ich bin ein dichter." ("I am a poet; I am a poet.")

And, indeed, he was a poet, Leonard found soon enough. In his heart of hearts, Leonard was in awe of the boy. More than thirty years later he confessed to me that he felt in the presence of the young Viereck as if he were near the youthful Goethe. The boy seemed to have the intensity and the genius of one destined for immortal renown. He posed and primped and play-acted, but to Leonard there seemed to remain an essence that was of breathless interest. It portended accomplishment beyond Leonard's wildest dreams for himself. He began to feel concern for the boy, lest he be deterred in his immortal course. Putty's erratic, capricious qualities worried Leonard, as they did the boy's parents. Leonard took a brother's concern in George Sylvester. The nine year's difference in their ages gave Leonard the right to act as a mentor, and he felt that to act as such was the least homage he could pay to genius. He discussed poetry and love and life with the boy. They took the same restless delight in sheer brains. They felt the same contemptuous dislike for pretense and for the intellectual and spiritual bareness of the Philistines.

The elder Vierecks looked on with mild, hopeful amusement. Neither parent could understand the poetic temperament, but they could understand ambition, intelligence, verve. So they welcomed the stranger to their home and made him one of the family. At no time was he the mere roomer, the tolerated guest, the humored outsider; he was one of the Vierecks. He could share the family's hopes and fears. He could laugh over Louis Viereck's humorous grumblings, his retreats from the house in the face of invasion by young poets who were friends of the two poets of the household, his refusal to wear full dress when "Teddy" Roosevelt invited him to the White House. Leonard could sip coffee within the family circle and talk, in German, of the international reaches of the arms of culture.

To Leonard's corner bedroom at the Viereck's would come another miserable, the future author of *Upstream* and *Israel* who was then trying, with little success, to forget his Jewish origin. The Lewisohn of 1902 was by no means one weeping over the fall of Zion. Leonard, in his autobiography, painted a remarkable picture of Ludwig Lewisohn as he was when he became a member of the Viereck entourage at approximately the time Leonard did. Later Lewisohn occupied Leonard's room. The two were graduate students at Columbia, Lewisohn had just arrived from the South to which his family had moved from Germany a few years before the Vierecks had come to America. Lewisohn was trying to be a Southern gentleman, transplanted to the north, although he was of definite Jewish appearance. This inner conflict was helping to form the character and the career of one who was destined to enrich the literature of America. Lewisohn became part of a strange trinity. He and Viereck and Leonard were three literary musketeers, inseparable and mutually inspiring. The hopes of the one were the hopes of all. They shared each other's fears, and they trembled together and joyed in common.

Leonard left a memorable picture of Lewisohn seated at the typewriter in Leonard's room, ticking off Leonard's verses as they came from Leonard's own lips as he reclined on the bed, like a poet holding court. Unshaven, ever excited, Lewisohn's appearance was enough to startle the dead. In sonorous sentences and phrases, Lewisohn would recite the praises of Leonard's poetry. Mankind, especially the professors, should read his poetry. Leonard could not type his poems? Lewisohn, his friend and discoverer, would type them. And he did, night after night. His devotion was without limits.

The attachment of all three was boundless.

Yet even friends such as these could not supply the every want of passionate young men. Leonard fell madly in love; an unreasonable, utterly foolish infatuation drove him frantic. The entire Viereck household sought to console him. Lewisohn discussed his plight in long, resonant phrases. "You are experiencing the grand passion," he told Leonard with utter seriousness, and Leonard perhaps wished he would not rub it in. Sylvester had a cure for Leonard's heartsickness; he would bring little gifts, such as apples, to his friend. He would attempt in a soft, almost feminine manner to cheer him up. It did no good. One day Leonard sent his lady love a feverish letter, proposing marriage. Her answer began, "Ellery, Ellery, Ellery, Ellery, Ellery," like the blows of fate on the casket of his soul, and it ended in a refusal, good-humored but final.

Leonard could no longer tolerate America. Germany was the one spot for solace. He decided to depart at once, almost without leavetaking. "*Spielen Sie uns eine comodie vor?*" asked Louis Viereck of him, by way of bewildered farewell. Of the Columbia professors, his and Lewisohn's favorite, the ever-inspiring Trent, was the only one to whom Leonard confided his reasons for leaving. Both agreed that Leonard seemed to be falling apart and that Germany was the cure.

Now letters took the place of personal contacts. Viereck and Leonard wrote to each other frequently and warmly and with mutual admiration. They exchanged their poems and offered helpful suggestions. One day Leonard sent Viereck a poem from Germany. Viereck praised it by saying that it would have been worthy of a Byron but not of Leonard. From Ellery he expected much more! Could any friend ask for more? Leonard and Lewisohn had been helping Viereck to acquire a knowledge of the English language, and the separation did not terminate the lessons. To no one was Viereck more indebted that he was to these two for knowledge of the structure of a difficult language, and he was the first to recognize his obligation.

In the absence of Leonard, Lewisohn moved into the Viereck home. He was already virtually a member of the household; but this move intensified his relations with Viereck. Their friendship became lyrical, tense, trying, much too deep for their own comfort and well-being. Lewisohn wrote poems to the light-haired and light-hearted boy. He sung to his graces. In a very real sense, he was enamored of Viereck. He posed as a man of the world and spent all of his spare money to entertain Viereck. He wanted to dazzle him with his gallantry, and Viereck voiced no objections. Meanwhile, both young men gained in poetic power and fervor. Viereck particularly began to do inordinately good work. Soon Lewisohn and he agreed it was time that America learned of the incomparable gifts of Viereck. They decided to share the expenses of issuing a pamphlet of Putty's best German poems.

Just fifty-four pages in length, paperbound and simple in appearance as the book was, the boy of twenty was yet proud, justifiably so, of his first book, his maiden offering before the shrine of the Muses. There were only sixteen poems in the little volume, but they were all his—his to proclaim from the housetops; his despite echoes and unconscious borrowings; his even if he and Lewisohn did pay for their printing! They were written in German, it was true, but they were a springboard, he knew, to triumphs in the American tongue. Already he knew that he was going to make his ultimate reputation in the language of Walt Whitman.

It was fitting that a special note should proclaim as the purpose of the long appreciation, written by Ludwig Lewisohn as a preface to the volume, the making of Viereck's poetry more accessible to the American public. The appreciation had earlier been published as an article in the *Sewanee Review*. There it bore an insinuating title, indicating that it was a general survey of German American poetry. Actually it was the same article that later served as an introduction to *Gedichte*. This was perhaps Lewisohn's super-subtle way of boosting, by indirection, the poetic stock of his young friend, of whose genius he was then certain. Yet the appreciation has the same measured gravity and critical balance which always distinguished Lewisohn's prose. Even a lyrical friendship could not force him to unleash the hounds of praise.

In an extremely quiet tone, Lewisohn told of the exotic literary phenomenon of German poetry written by men residing on American soil and away from the main currents of German life. Konrad Nies and Viereck were coupled by him as the two chief representatives of the genus, Nies the older "and in some respects the more accomplished," Viereck the more modern. Lewisohn then proceeded to sing Viereck's praises as a poet. He honored the young poet's offerings by superbly translating certain snatches of his song. He treated the individual poems in the little volume with respect. Each one was given its measure of praise. With acumen, he discussed their technique and content. It was evident that he wanted to say more, but his dignity as a critic and elder friend forbade. Perhaps, too, he feared that unrestrained praise, however well intentioned, might harm his precious friend, the "dear little boy" of his own lyrical letters and poems.

So he closed with a note of warning and of sad prophecy. "The best poetry cannot be written without a far profounder realization of the beauty and terror, the splendor and solemnity of the external world; without a keener consciousness of those great issues of human life and destiny which transcend even love," he lectured sonorously. "But within his own limits Viereck is a true poet. He has originality, he has power, he has imagination, and his extreme youth gives his talents large possiblities of development."

Lewisohn properly felt that the poems in the little volume were representative of Viereck's talents, in that they limned, with sustained fury, the sinner triumphant and the sinner repentant, the intellectual wanderer and the prober of ageless mysteries. Leonard, by then returned to America and with access to one of the sacred journals of the Brahmins, sang the praises of the cluster of German poems in the columns of the *Boston Transcript*. Though not as restrained in his praise as Lewisohn, Leonard's language possessed a calm that carried conviction. "In maturity of art I know not where to find his parallel in English letters, unless in the Rowley poems of the marvelous boy who perished in his pride," said Leonard. Later, altering a familiar word, he wrote a sonnet in Viereck's honor and there called him the marvelous boy who conquered in his pride. Certainly Leonard felt *Gedichte* to be a conquest. "I am aware," he said, "that any comparison of an obscure New York schoolboy with Goethe and Byron must strike the reader unpleasantly, but the critical conscience should not wince at that. . . . On one reading you pronounce him a decadent. But if you read him again you must admit some noble elements of thought and strength and pathos."

These two men, Leonard and Lewisohn, were, after all, intimate friends of the poet, and their praise of him was to be expected. But they were joined by others in a full blast of honor. That sweetest of academic souls, W. P. Trent of Columbia University, wrote to the boy in the same encouraging strains as he talked to Lewisohn and Leonard: "You seem to me to have the qualities of the true singing lyrist, and I hope that you will continue to sing despite the fact that nowadays poetry is, in the main, its own award. I am sure your genuine poetic qualities will finally win at least fairly adequate recognition." Hugo Munsterberg, ever alert for German American contributions to the cause of international goodwill, was more sanguine than was Trent. He wrote Viereck: "Your book of poems arouses the liveliest hopes. Many things in it are of a deep, pure and melodic beauty." The *Washington Post*, the *New York Sun*, the *New York Herald*, the *New York Times*, the *London Literary World*, the *New York Globe*, the *Review of Reivews*, and dozens of magazines and newspapers published both here and abroad sounded the tocsin of praise.

There was a curiously revealing notice in the *New York Herald*. Viereck had sent that paper, as well as others, a copy of *Gedichte* with a letter suggesting that the poems ought to be reviewed, "not because they are my poems, but because they are good." "One may smile at this youthful impetuosity, but one can truthfully admit Mr. Viereck's estimate of his own productions," the *Herald* commented, in seconding the other laudatory reviews. Real talent, probably genius as well, deep passion and true poetic fire—this was the general verdict.

It could not fail to please the three conspirators, Viereck, Leonard and Lewisohn, and cement their friendship. They gloried in it; the one urged the other to join the ranks of published poets. "We three will become the leaders of American literature," Lewisohn repeated. The prophecy might well have been realized. But life itself was cruel, insistent. It left too little time for high dreams. Viereck could remain in New York to pursue his career while earning his living, but Lewisohn and Leonard were necessarily cast adrift. They were compelled to earn a livelihood and had a harder time than Viereck, though better equipped with knowledge. Dreams of immortal fame had to abide the financial issue, especially with Lewisohn, who took to himself a wife.

By painful steps, Leonard became a teacher at the University of Wisconsin. He rolled logs in Lewisohn's behalf, and the future author of the *Island Within* became an instructor in German at Wisconsin, though he longed to teach the language of the land of his adoption. Naturally, the friendship of the two older members of the trinity was solidified and sealed. Too soon, however, Lewisohn accepted an appointment at Ohio State, and Leonard remained at Wisconsin where he remained a glory of that institution to the time of his death. He was bound to Madison, Wisconsin, by the cruelest ties of fate. The story is given lasting form in Leonard's *Two Lives* and *The Locomotive-God,* his major contributions to literature. Lewisohn was unable to wander more than a few blocks from his home by reason of his phobia. It was as if he were strapped by some demon to a fixed spot. Lewisohn, too, was stirred to great utterance by the experiences of his youth. Implicit in his *Up Stream* is the story of his association with Viereck and Leonard, although he says comparatively little of them. Lewisohn, in the thrall of work, could forget anybody, just as Viereck, when a prisoner to ego, could fail to think of his friends, though a generous measure of personal loyalty always remained in his knapsack. And Leonard, schooled by life to expect anything, went his lonely way, thinking often of the two great friends of his youth. Their friendship was one of the truly notable ones in American literature. The greatest of gods, Caprice, brought them together and estranged them at moments, but their friendship left its lasting impression.

8   A GAME AT LOVE

"Those plays certainly show marked originality and ability of an unusual order," one of the heads of the then important publishing firm of Doubleday Page & Co. wrote to the boy, Viereck, on October 23, 1905. "But I'm sorry to say that after reading them myself and having them go through the regular 'machine' here, we do not feel certain enough of our ability to sell such a book to warrant us in making you an offer. . . ."

It was easy to read between the lines of such a letter. It was obvious to everyone except a boy intoxicated with his first successes that America was intent upon ignoring the entire current of modern literature that was already a commonplace in France and in Germany and, to a lesser degree, in England. Nothing that might offend the prim maiden aunts who guarded the literary nurseries stood a chance in the reading rooms of the respectable publishing houses, as Theodore Dreiser, David Graham Phillips and others had already discovered. It was not until long years later that so sexually alive a book as *Susan Lenox* could be published here. The boy Viereck would not learn the lesson because he was determined not to.

A few days before he had received the letter from Doubleday Page & Co., he had received an even more significant one from the editors of the *Smart Set,* then the publication nearest to a sophisticated journal in America. Belated tribute has been paid to the *Smart Set* by Burton Rascoe and others. An anthology of some of its representative pages has been published, and the attention it has received has been merited. But in the year 1905, there were definite limits as to what the editors, Henry L. Mencken and George Jean Nathan, could publish, and they were sharply aware of those limits. It was obviously with regret that they turned down Viereck's plays.

"We are greatly indebted to you for the privilege of reading these plays," they wrote to him, "but they are really unsuitable for publication in 'The Smart Set.' Indeed, we can not think of a magazine in this country which would dare to publish them. This seems a great pity, since your style is so rarely exquisite. If you should ever do anything with not quite so bold a touch, we hope you will give us the pleasure of seeing the manuscript. Your work interests us exceedingly.''

Huneker, too, was afraid of the plays and told his young friend so in letter after letter. He felt, with the editors of the *Smart Set,* that perhaps no firm in America could risk issuing plays so frankly amoral or, by the American standard of the day, so rankly immoral, but he persevered in his efforts to find a publisher. He thought that those two young, enterprising men, Moffat and Yard, who had lately broken with the responsible old house of Scribner's and had formed a firm of their own, might be stirred. He talked with them and interested them somewhat; at least they were willing to see the young playwright.

"Make concessions in your copy," Huneker felt constrained to advise Viereck. "Life is a series of concessions—adaptations the biologists call them. 'All or nothing' is lovely as a motto—in print; in life it leads to the gaol or madhouse.''

Then perhaps feeling ashamed of the conventional advice, blunt, honest, lovable Jim the Penman added a characteristic anticlimax to his admonishing letter: "Pardon these truisms. It is Monday morning!''

Viereck probably forgave them. Certainly he forgot them, though Huneker remained one of his major gods. Viereck was not interested in discretion. It did not suit his temperament, and Viereck felt in his bones that the old order in America was definitely changing and it would be a joy ride for him to be in the vanguard of the new movement. The feeling may have been unconscious, but that gave it added strength. It more nearly suited his temperament and paid heavy dividends of notoriety and excitement and eventually fame. He subconsciously knew that he was the restless child of a new age that was rushing into print with scarlet letters in spite of its elders.

Before long, he battered down at least one gate and was able to write to his solicitous elder friend, William Ellery Leonard, that Brentano's had accepted the plays. To Ludwig Lewisohn, the other poet of the trinity, he did not at that time communicate, for they were then in the midst of one of their minor quarrels. The letter to Leonard was written with the least bit of malice, for the atavistic New England conscience in Leonard did not permit him to like the plays with any wholehearted admiration and he had told Viereck so.

In due course the book appeared, a slender little volume in a rich red binding, and across the cover ran the rather invidious title, *A Game At Love and Other Plays.* It was his first book in the English language; his formal bow to that part of the American public not interested in things German. It was a public hardly aware that just five years before Oscar Wilde had passed to an alien grave, a public too engrossed in the imperialistic dreams which rose out of the Hispanic-American War to care much for any thing except robust fiction.

"These plays are unplayable," Viereck assured his readers in a brief preface to the volume. "They were not, at least, written with an eye to the stage.''

Yet they have a dramatic intensity that is not altogether outside the theater. It is worth tracing the particular qualities of the playlets which make them significant and stirring, not alone in relation to Viereck but in their obverse reflection of the life of the senses in early twentieth-century America, as mirrored in the impatient mind of a young college boy casting importunate glances at the wider world about him.

"They point out no moral, they teach no lessons," the boy warned the readers of the plays, "and the reader may feel assured that the obvious interpretation is in no case the author's own. Certain truths, as I have seen them, are here set down, but I decline to be held responsible for anything that my characters may say or do:

> I have taken the climacteric moments of imaginary novels and embodied them in dramatic sketches. This method constitutes a rebellion against that species of psychological fiction which, in six hundred pages, succeeds in telling us nothing. For as intellectual intercourse between nations becomes more intimate, and the body of literature of each country is augmented by that of the others, it will inevitably become a requirement that the individual work of art shall be diminished in bulk. Homer could write a poem in twenty-four books with impunity. Not so the modern artist. Nor is there any legitimate reason why we should take up twice twenty-four hours of a reader's time with a story that could be told no less effectively in ten minutes.

Having gained in confidence by the echo of his own voice, the youthful sage continued with more assurance:

> I have laid some stress upon the fact that men and women communicate with each other not by articulate speech alone, but by a quiver of the eyelid or a curl of the lip. And I have left nothing unexpressed that seemed to contribute to a desired effect, even at the risk of offending such as would close the mouth of the Muse with that muzzle which, if applied at all, should be confined to that many-headed monster—the press.

There is nothing particularly original in this pontification by a boy in whom precocity and conceit were almost inextricably blended. But, fortunately, the plays had more than idle vaunting as their framework; the last one in particular is substantial in its philosophy. Curiously enough, it is styled "a morality" by the author. Striking one of the deep and enduring motifs of Viereck's own life, the play, *The Butterfly,* tells of the parallel defeats of The Righteous Man and The Unrighteous Man.

In the first brief scene, The Righteous Man lies in a simple bed, which bestrides a conventional bed chamber. The gaunt bones of the harbinger of Death sulk in the background and gradually assume definite outline as the scene reaches its height. The Righteous Man muses about his impending death. It frightens him not at all; indeed, he luxuriates in it. He does not console himself with any vain dreams of an afterlife. He cares not that he will not feel the grass grow, while he slumbers in his green grave, nor see the flowers open and the passing swallows beat their wings. It is enough that he has "led a life clean and honourable and triumphant over temptation," that he has fought the good fight not as a fearful child but as a man.

Just as he is ready to die with smug joy, the sound of music introduces a chorus of the Things that Might Have Been. They torment The Righteous Man with his unrealized possibilities: the Crown of Life that never pressed his brow; the happiness whose light his temples never felt; the deeper mysteries his glance never pierced; the lily of might he did not dare to pluck; the perished dreams lost when he let duty to others stand in the way of self-loyalty; the crimson blooms of love upon the Tree of Life, which he dared not grasp; the illicit pleasures from which his conventional spirit fled. The Righteous Man protests; he pleads; he whines—to excuse himself. The Chorus lashes him with the whips of passion. "And because thou didst not know us thou must perish life a moth dancing in a sunbeam, . . ." they tell him, in parting.

Gone is his self-satisfaction; he begs a little space of life, a few remnants from its banquet for him, a late and famished guest. But Death steps forward; he will have no gibbering protest. "It is too late," he says to The Righteous Man. The man becomes desperate. He curses his weeping family. He lashes himself with regrets. And then his weary lips are sealed by the finger of Death, and a gaudy butterfly flutters against the windowpane.

Elsewhere The Unrighteous Man is dying. He, too, is sucking the nourishment of content from a contemplation of his life. He looks upon his bed chamber, furnished with subtle elegance, and his thoughts are of the luscious joys he has dined upon. It matters little to him that the grave is the end.

"Dying as I have lived," he says, "I force even death to yield to me a strange and subtle pleasure from its very pain. I can truly say that I have lived my life, have tasted it with every nerve, have burned my heart in the flame of every passion, and struck each chord upon the gamut of human emotion with a master's hand. . . ."

Hideous noises from the hall disturb The Unrighteous Man's self-contemplation. Green, peevish Ennui, ashen Disgust, painted Pose and The Seven Sins break into his room and announce themselves as old acquaintances of the dying man. They taunt him with their share in the life he is leaving, and at first he is untouched, careless, at ease. They give more particularity to their stories of his past; they reveal the baseness behind their and his grace; they strip themselves and him of every claim to splendor, and at length, as his pitiful soul lets its weary little wings hang down, his armor is pierced. He sees himself as he was, a thing of rags and tatters, an unwholesome guest in the house of life. He tries in vain to speak to Death that he now discerns clearly, as it rises out of the shadows. But it is the end. The Unrighteous Man is no more than a little dove, featherless and limp. Out of the room comes the glittering form of a butterfly.

This view of the futility of choice is reflected in the other playlets in the volume and is reflected, as we have seen and shall see, in Viereck's life. Base or good, our decisions in themselves are inconsequential, the boy implies; the Supreme Ironist will confound all of our values; He will cause romance to rise from the ashes of defeat, while he turns honey into gall. We are prisoners of caprice and must be content with perhaps one supreme moment. For the rest, mild amusement is enough.

These and related motifs run through the four remaining playlets in form varied and cunning. The titular one is in mock praise of pose: "Pose! Pose! What higher compliment can I pay you than to appear before you in my fairest raiment," says the gleaming hero when he is told by one of the women he seeks to capture that he has courted others with identical language. "If you are a master of language," she says, "why do you not at least clothe your thought in new forms?" "It is because I *am* a master of language that I refrain from doing so," he replies. "If I have found perfect expression for anything should I not be the merest tyro to change one jot or tittle?" A kiss and an embrace assure him that he is correct. Love, then, is the repetition of well-learned phrases; success in its pursuit is the badge of a good artist in pose.

In *The Mood of a Moment* young Viereck plays variations upon the same theme. He inquires once again if love is a matter of stage setting, the repetition of like sounds and similar surroundings leading to like effects. He finds that that is almost true; the interposition of a mood is the one variable factor which makes all the difference in the world. Hence a moment of love may never be recaptured, although one may be on the very brink. Incidentally, this little play is the only one of the lot which has been performed—in Japan, of all places. Yet the succeeding play, called, with an apology to Swinburne, *From Death's Own Eyes,* is far more dramatic, far more actable than anything in the little volume, and it is hardly below *The Butterfly* in general worth.

It deals with the deep, autumnal love of a woman of forty for a lad of eighteen or nineteen. The lad, with youthful loyalty, swears eternal love, but the woman knows that fealty is impossible, that other arms than hers must tempt him some day. It is better to make an end, she thinks. Then she asks him what he would do if death were to part them. He tells her that he would kiss her dead hair, water her breast with his tears, and lay the rose leaves of song upon her pallid eyelids, for love like his is stronger than death. She decides to tell him that he is being tested, that some deadly poison is in the wine he has just tasted. He imagines he is dying; he play-acts well the part of the lover faithful unto death. He does not reproach the woman; the luxury of such a death is too sweet. But he is interrupted by the realization that the woman, and not he, is dying. He sobs violently as she passes away with his kisses on her face. His screams awaken the young and comely niece of the woman, who runs into the room where her aunt lies dead. The boy tells her of the pure, fair, and wise love of her aunt, who was like a good fairy to the troubled waters of his youth. The niece, deeply affected by his eloquence, strokes his hair and says tenderly, "How you loved her!" "His hand, entwining her neck as if seeking help, slips down, and is arrested upon her half-bared breast. . . . they both spring up and dare not look at each other." For Love has caught strange fire from Death's own eyes!

The sequel is *A Question of Fidelity.* The boy is now a man of forty-five, having all of the autumnal tenderness of his dead love. A girl of twenty woos him.

He tries to dissuade her, telling her that younger arms will reach her, but she tells him that she wants only him. They are married, and in less than a year she has felt the embraces of arms younger than his. Penitent, she confesses her wickedness, but her husband fails to act like the conventional cuckold. He consoles his wife with the broad philosophy of modernism, the all-forgiving tolerance of the New Man. She, however, takes his attitude as an evidence of lack of love, and he muses: "It is passing strange that in the presence of the New Man the New Woman becomes at once and invariably the Old Eve."

In a play which he wisely refrained from publishing in permanent form, and which he styled reminiscently *The Triumph of Life,* Viereck continues the audacious mood of *A Game at Love* in more exaggerated form. The youth favors marriage to free love, "because when you are married you can at least get a divorce. It's only the law that binds you then, not a sense of personal obligation." And so he marries his attractive companion, both united in viewpoint, both incidentally, finding "nothing more loathsome than a woman about to exercise the absurd function of motherhood." The wife breaches their covenant and bears a child; she is radiant with new-found mother-love. He, maddened by the flouting of his sacred views, spits out words of condemnation: "You are desecrated in my eyes. You are no longer a woman, but a breeding-machine."

It could not be expected that plays such as these could win a warm response in the America of 1905, and they did not. But in the lack of enthusiasm with which the plays were greeted, a certain unwilling admiration could be discerned. It was the sort of admiration founded upon the hope that the child had had better upbringing. The feeling seemed to be that as he grew up, he would learn that the fundamental beliefs of America were sound and should not be desecrated by the loud blasphemy of youth. It was a too hopeful attitude, all things considered. But it was there, nevertheless, for Viereck continued to confound it in the immediate future.

The Nation, typical in this respect, insisted upon seeing the plays as filled with "contempt for all the restrictions which prevent human society from relapsing into barbaric animalism." It felt that "what Mr. Viereck may achieve in the future, if ever his rankly luxuriant boyish fancies acquire the ballast of solid learning and common sense, it would be hazardous to predict. At present, he is devoting precious gifts to futile and unworthy ends." Max Beerbohm, the Incomparable Max, writing in the *Saturday Review,* had much to say of the plays. The review itself was important chiefly because it betrayed the seriousness with which the boy was taken.

The fin de siecle poet, Richard LeGallienne, not yet convinced in his own mind of Viereck's talents, endulged in carefully guarded criticism. "These little plays, cynically catching life at some unnatural angle, as they do, and cleverly, even brilliantly done as they are," he said, "scarcely amount to a *raison d'etre.*" The *Bookman,* then highly esteemed, was less guarded. "The volume is remarkable," it said, "not only for its promise but also for its accomplishment." Its words were soon to be echoed elsewhere. As a matter of fact the review was published in the midst of Viereck's skyrocketing fame.

9   A STRANGE TRINITY

Early in 1905, before the publication of *A Game At Love,* the young college boy submitted an article on Oscar Wilde to the *New York World*. The article was rejected by that journal, then successfully competing with Hearst, as too sensational. By some impish mental process, young Viereck thereupon decided that a respectable magazine would publish the article, and he submitted it to the *Critic,* one of the outstanding literary journals of the time, then edited by Jeanette Gilder, sister of Richard Watson Gilder, who had printed Viereck's first English sonnet. The article, which dealt with the possibility of Oscar Wilde's being alive, was accepted and published by the *Critic,* as if to confound the *World,* and it immediately created a minor stir. It was quoted and requoted throughout the world, much to the gratification of the boy. It had at least one very important result, which, at the time, did not seem of much consequence.

Leonard D. Abbott, then an associate editor of an eclectic monthly magazine called *Current Literature,* quoted from Viereck's article in such fashion that he piqued the curiosity of the young poet, with the result that the two men, Abbott and Viereck, met. Abbott was then twenty-seven, Viereck twenty, and no two men could have been more unlike each other. Though Abbott had rebelled against the authority of his conventional Anglo-American parents, he was not, to all seeming, a wild fellow. There was always something measured and reserved in his personality, despite his ideas, writings and activities, which were not tame. For ten years he was identified with the socialist movement and regarded himself as a firebrand, but at the same time he was on the staff of the once popular *Literary Digest,* certainly not a hotbed of radicalism. He, Dr. Edward Jewitt Wheeler, and Alexander Harvey left the *Digest* and joined *Current Literature,* a publication more alive to the nature of things, they thought, than any journal in the land.

Viereck and Abbott took to each other at once. From the start Abbott was fascinated. He felt that there was not a thought that he could not communicate to

Viereck. He was thrilled by the boy's creative power. He seemed to see the poems ferment within young Viereck. Vicariously, he experienced the pleasure of giving life to great literature, for he felt that Viereck's poems were his, a glorious part of him. Yet he realized the immense differences between himself and Viereck. Viereck was Teutonic, sensual, earthy, Byronic, Wildean, while he was Anglo-American, fastidious, Ariel rather than Puck, and anything other than sensual. Viereck used to twit him: "You believe in free love, but you don't practice it. I do not believe in free love, but I practice it." Abbott tried to see what made the younger man's mind work so brilliantly, but he could not accept Viereck's character. To his dismay, he felt that his own character was being distorted by Viereck. Yet the infatuation held him. Only at times could he draw away and assert his own integrity.

Of course, Abbott talked about Viereck to his favorite associate on *Current Literature,* a fantastic creature who bore the name Alexander Harvey. He told Harvey of the poems of passion and of the plays just published by Brentano. He quoted the plays to Harvey, telling him of their unreal, flashing scenes and striking language. Harvey was interested in a mild way. Perhaps his earlier diplomatic training and his knowledge of the world's ways caused him to restrain his interest; he had been secretary to the American consul-general in Egypt for two years, and he had been a newspaper man for more than ten years. He felt that he could not be imposed upon, and his bearing was often imperious.

One day he and Abbott stood in front of an office building in New York, attempting to keep out of the rain.

"Look," said Abbott. "There's Viereck."

Harvey looked. He saw a young boy dressed in a cheaply made suit, on his head a freshman's cap. Harvey looked closer. The boy's cheeks were hollow, yet rosy. His chin was disproportionately large; his mouth insisted upon opening at intervals in a grin and then snapping shut, as if controlled by strings; his hair was cut short; his face totally beardless and altogether boyish. He looked like an imp or a sprite, Puck with a touch of Caliban, Harvey thought.

Abbott presented Viereck to Harvey. They shook hands and exchanged a few polite phrases. Harvey felt constrained at that moment to ride a high horse and act reservedly, for in a flash he took a dislike to the boy, and later, as Abbott talked to him of Viereck, the dislike was intensified.

As if to confound Harvey, Viereck soon became a member of the staff of *Current Literature,* largely through the good offices of Dr. John H. Finley, the president of City College. Viereck got the job immediately upon his graduation from the college and retained it until 1916—the one job of his life. And it was of inestimable importance, not least of all because of his association with Harvey and Abbott, an association that rivaled his friendship with William Ellery Leonard and Ludwig Lewisohn. Harvey's initial feeling of dislike for Viereck died hard, but eventually they were bosom companions.

Viereck said that Harvey was "a deacon with the pen of a satyr." Abbott called Harvey "a fantastic conservative, like G. K. Chesterton." But Harvey himself had penetrated through their minds to their true feelings about him. "They thought me fantastic," he said, "bizarre, possibly a hypocrite but not quite a humbug." Harvey's reverence for the mysticism of Swedenborg and his disparagement of their purely earthly experience, made them feel as they did, and Harvey knew and did not resent it.

Viereck had not been long on the staff of *Current Literature* (later called *Current Opinion*) when Harvey obviously amazed him by professing a vast admiration of the German mind, especially its pioneering qualities and its capacity for exploring the domains of knowledge.

"The Germans," Harvey said to him, "are our intellectual superiors."

Viereck was at a loss for words.

"The difficulty with you," Harvey assured him, to confound him further, "is that you are really anti-German."

Was Harvey confusing a German inferiority complex with bias against things Teutonic? Harvey stopped to listen to Schumann's *Serenade*, played exquisitely by a large orchestra led by a German-American violinist of note. They were at the restaurant of a great department store owned by a German-American. They discussed Goethe, Nietzsche, Lessing, but Viereck persisted in turning the conversation towards the American, Poe.

"You," Harvey interrupted him, insistently, "being German can criticize things German out of the recourses of the consciousness you have inherited. I can't criticize anything German, even if I knew enough."

Viereck passed once more to the subject of Poe: "His poems are few—but everyone is a masterpiece or so nearly a masterpiece that it will live."

Harvey sardonically reminded him that Dr. Wheeler, the editor-in-chief of *Current Literature*, did not think much of Poe, but Viereck was undaunted.

"Poe's position is unassailable," he insisted.

"He will not sink into a minor poet?" the older man queried.

"Never!" the boy said, with finality.

Again and again the two men returned to the subject. It was a refrain running through their curious friendship. Harvey saw the young poet in his lodgings about that time or a little later. In the corner was a painting of a young woman in nude splendor, and under the picture was a lush, invidious sofa. The floor was richly covered with rugs and carpets. A bust of Napoleon adorned a table; a crucifix in the Italian style was on the wall; pictures of Oscar Wilde and Poe stared from other walls. And Viereck wore an Oriental dressing gown that shouted with loud colors. Viereck was an impudent dream come to life.

"I am driven to write original pieces, original criticism," Viereck said to him. Harvey reminded him that their magazine only quoted, that it published nothing original.

"When I can find nothing to quote that is worth quoting," Viereck persisted, "I write something original and send it to a German paper. When it is printed, I quote it in English. It makes some of our pieces piquant."

The Oriental dressing gown flashed new colors, and Harvey smiled approvingly.

Harvey similarly marvelled at the spell Viereck seemed to cast upon Edward

Jewitt Wheeler, the editor-in-chief of the magazine. Wheeler felt at the outset that Viereck's genius was patent and permitted no doubt. He was delighted at the articles that the boy prepared for his magazine.

"There's something!" he said one day, showing Harvey three papers by Viereck, his first editorial contributions. "This is the stuff." The Methodist philosopher, Wheeler, seemed to clap his hands in glee. Harvey read the articles, one a discussion of the philosopher Hartmann's views of a certain practical problem (Hartmann had written a book, *The Philosophy of the Unconscious*, which profoundly influenced Freud), the other two literary, all vivid and piquant and paradoxical. Harvey sensed that Wheeler really did not grasp Viereck's viewpoint, but was under his spell nevertheless.

One day Wheeler asked Viereck to write on Anthony Comstock, who was then riding the witch's broom in an energetic campaign against what he deemed to be obscene literature. Harvey, knowing Viereck's utter contempt for Comstock, was astonished at Wheeler's choice and waited for the fur to fly. About an hour after he had received the article, Wheeler emerged from his private office, his face a study in chagrin and pain. Putting on an innocent expression, Harvey asked his chief about the article. The man's face showed how deeply hurt he was. It was the Puritan soul in revolt against Apollo, Harvey felt, and the article was not used.

Thereafter a reservation or two in regard to Viereck found harbor in Wheeler's troubled mind. He still admired the boy almost beyond words, still took his suggestions and printed his articles, still defended him with touching loyalty. But he could not surrender completely. And this was ever the way of Viereck with Puritan souls of the Wheeler type, Harvey felt. "He was pagan in the nudity of his soul. He feared no revelation of himself on any plane. He shocked. He charmed. He shocked again. The antagonism at times seemed almost violent. But still the charm was there . . . after a first repulsion."

Viereck felt impelled to discuss sexual problems with Harvey and with others. Like a modern Aretino, he dwelt upon sex, constantly finding something novel. Or he would talk of money with a strange passion, for he regarded himself as poor. To William Ellery Leonard he had written at this time of his efforts with *Current Literature:* "Work: pleasant; remuneration: comparatively good." His real meaning was that the compensation did not satisfy him. He would say to Harvey, trying to make himself believe that he was sincere: "You never save. You spend all as you go along. You are wise." For himself, he cultivated friends who showed him how to accumulate, the international banker, Otto H. Kahn, for one. His list of securities became curiously large for a poet who had started at scratch. In time he could say to Harvey with bourgeois vaunting, "In order to ruin me, the government would have to be bankrupt, the steel trust would have to be bankrupt, the big bank downtown would have to be bankrupt—six great concerns would have to be bankrupt."

Harvey found it more pleasant to contemplate the intimacy of Leonard, Abbott and Viereck. His interpretation of it made Abbott loom even larger in Viereck's life than Viereck believed. Abbott was inimitably charming, Harvey felt, because he was not Narcissus, but the pool of Narcissus: a miraculous mirror that reflected a face in a thousand lights and in every conceivable aspect. One got to love oneself not out of conceit, but because Abbott mirrored all that was beautiful, inspired, and angelical in one. So Viereck generally delighted in Abbott without knowing why.

"Abbott is nebulous," Wheeler once complained, hardly realizing what he had in mind. This nebulousness of Abbbott was just his reflective quality, Harvey contended. Just as Abbott had in the past reflected Ibsen and Freud and Jung, he was now reflecting Viereck in glowing, dazzling lights, like a rainbow of thrilling beauty. Viereck became aware of a thousand traits in himself, a thousand facets to his personality, and he grew self-enamored, forgetful that it was Abbott who made him see himself, trailing clouds of glory.

"Without Abbott in his life George Sylvester Viereck would have been a glaring effulgence, shooting rays pitilessly into dazzled eyes," Harvey said. "The verse of George Sylvester Viereck must have penetrated but it could not have charmed. For while Abbott did not write a line of the verse of Viereck, there was in the verse of Viereck the charm it caught from Abbott."

Abbott, truly one of nature's noblemen, exquisitely proportioned in mind and spirit, might well have played the role Harvey says he did play in Viereck's life. And he was troubled because Sylvester Viereck, unlike himself, did not sigh with longing to mold things "nearer to the heart's desire."

"Sylvester is destitute of thé purely altruistic impulse," Abbott explained sorrowfully to Harvey. "He is like the true artist in that he is all for self. Fancy his dismissing the socialist ticket with the statement that he does not mean to vote for a party which will make all of his stocks and bonds worthless!"

While Viereck might discuss Goethe and Nietzsche and Lessing with Harvey, he discussed Wilde, Swinburne, Baudelaire, Verlaine, D'Annunzio with Abbott, and both admired Walt Whitman and had a fascinated intellectual curiosity about the variation of the sex instinct.

Viereck, in his own way, reciprocated, introducing Abbott to Otto Kahn, Rudolf Eucken, Leon Dabo, James Huneker, Childe Hassam, Hans Heinz Ewers, Theodore Roosevelt, visiting German professors and celebrities without number. Viereck, Abbott observed, had something of the climber's instinct and "counted a day lost in which he did not make some new and advantageous contact."

Viereck could write to another of his dearest friends, the ever interested William Ellery Leonard, that all was well, that he and Leonard and Lewisohn were all three on the way to fame. He could write that, for one reason, because he and Lewisohn were then, in October of 1906, once more on speaking terms. For another reason, Leonard, tired in his quest to find a publisher for his poems, had issued them himself, just as Viereck's first book of poems had been published. "I shall use whatever little influence I have to help your book along," Viereck wrote Leonard and did, indeed, conspire to boost Leonard's stock, just as Leonard and Lewisohn had sought to boost *Gedichte*. The letter was written before *A Game at Love* had appeared.

"You probably know that Cotta is bringing out my German poems and Brentano my plays," Viereck continued in the same letter to Leonard. "I am at work upon a novel or rather a novelette." It was the book that appeared later as *The House of the Vampire.* "I am also collecting my English poems which will be brought out in February or about that time. I have done some pretty decent stunts since we met last. My work here is very satisfying all around. This is the most progressive, the most modern, the most literary magazine in the United States, if not in the world. Toward the middle of December I shall go to Chicago for a series of lectures and readings (in German) from my plays and poems. Perhaps I can arrange to see you then. (Is Wisconsin very far from Chicago?) Write soon, and meanwhile, 'Good Luck!' "

Viereck could wish good fortune to his friend, for his own approaching triumph filled him with gladness. The world seemed, indeed, a goodly place. The great, the good Dr. Ludwig Fulda, renowned German poet and dramatist, already a classic in his lifetime, had been in America. Young Viereck had interviewed him for the *New York Times:* it had been his first important paid article—and it paid better than he thought possible. He instantly won the eager admiration of the great poet of the Fatherland. Fulda became, in a sense, Viereck's German discoverer, one of those who built the structure of Viereck's wider fame. He took back with him to Germany the manuscript of some of Viereck's German poems. He would find a publisher, he swore, and he did—the famous house of Cotta, original publishers of Goethe! Could any young aspirant, even a Wunderkind, ask for more?

The book contained many new poems, *Nineveh* and *The Magic City* being especially important. It created some interest in Germany but, alas, not a sensation. Herman Sudermann and other important men expressed admiration for the verse, but the book was not really in conformity with the spirit of the times in the Fatherland. Viereck's German verse stemmed from English sources. The rhyme, the rhythm, the ideation, as Viereck realized, were more English than German. Viereck was estranged from his homeland; he was by now an American; his German verse, born under the Stars and Stripes, belonged to an earlier period. He might become a distinguished German poet, but not if he remained in America, and he wanted to remain here.

In a book which he wrote a few years later, Viereck told, in mock heroics, of his transition from German poetry to English. "There was a time when I wavered between two literatures," he said. "I consulted with friends on both sides of the ocean, and it was finally agreed upon that America, being poorer than Europe, needed me more. I decided to become an American classic. I voluntarily deserted the company of Baudelaire and of Heine, for that of Longfellow and Whittier."

In a way, the Fulda Symposium held by The League of German Writers in America at Hotel Astor in New York City on April 14, 1906, was the farewell to Viereck's career as a German literateur, although he long continued to write and edit in the German language. All of the important German-American poets and writers were present or represented in some way, and the gathering was *echt*

Deutsch in the best prewar sense. Song and speech and verse hailed Fulda, in particular, and German-American writers in general. To the tune of the *Kaiser-marsch*, the gathering sang *Hoch, Fulda!*

And then, with the melody of *Deutschland, Deutschland uber Alles*, they hymned themselves and Fulda, once again, and Kaiser Wilhelm over the seas, and "Teddy" Roosevelt. It was definitely prewar, happily prewar, and pre-Hitler, too. And so it was joyous.

One ballad, by H. F. Urban, celebrated the genius of German-America's wonder child, Sylvester Viereck, and the talents of the older poet of St. Louis, Konrad Nies, through many verses, both apt and inept. The respect with which the younger poet was treated was remarkable. And finally, by way of farewell, a drinking song to the tune of the *Lorelei* was sung by the gathering:

> *Es dunkelt in riesigen Fernen,*
> *Verdachtig der Abendwind weht,*
> *Verstummt sind die Strassendaternen,*
> *Kalender im Mondlichte steht.*
> *Wir sitzen so fest wie gamauert,*
> *Im Antlitz den Heiligenschein;*
> *Gott gebe, dass lang noch es dauert,*
> *Eh' leer mid das Fass in dem Wein!*

Would that the mood had endured!

10   HELPING HANDS

In the American literary desert of the first years of the twentieth century, there were two once famous, now almost forgotten nomads who traveled from oases of beauty to oases of thought, tending the frail flowers of culture that grew in the stray gardens of the continent. Having little to work with, they yet achieved wonders. They almost succeeded by themselves in creating an American civilization where none existed before. These two pioneers, James Gibbons Huneker and William Marion Reedy, were in their prime when Viereck arrived on the scene and helped, in no small measure, to shape his career.

The two men had much in common. Physically and intellectually they were of approximately equal stature. Both were big men, bulky and benign in appearance, loud of voice and affable. They loved the good things of the earth and reached out for such things greedily. Men and women, food and fornication, thought and gaiety, every manifestation of the capricious spirit of humanity dazzled and delighted them. They experimented. They seized upon the novel. They reexamined the old. They toppled standards and ignored shibboleths. They were high priests of such splendid gusto that the superficial were inclined to forget that the two were at all times dedicated to their high calling.

Reedy was the reigning luminary in the literary world of St. Louis. For a generation, Reedy was, in the phrase of Edgar Lee Masters, the "literary boss" of the Middle West, and he ruled through the dominance of his personal journal, the *Mirror*. Its circulation was never more than a few thousand, but its influence was incalculable.

Reedy himself wrote with sparkling clarity on a myriad of subjects. Nothing which man has thought or done in any of his moods was alien to him. He set no limits to the sacred gift of expression and placed no sentinel on guard over any one's morals or modes. An astonishing scholar in many fields, encyclopedic in knowledge, the master of six or seven literatures, yet he was not a pedant. Shrewd, sane, sober, he judged works of art, not by comparison with certain fixed models, but by their own special virtues. He always could be counted upon to exercise the broadest tolerance and he could criticize without spitting venom.

The secret lay perhaps in the curious turn his career took at its outset, before the *Mirror* had become the food of starved young seekers. His father had been a police officer in St. Louis, which meant that Reedy had been nursed on the realization that "bilk and boodle" are the prevailing American motif. Though he was educated in a Jesuit school, young Reedy yet showed an astonishing aptitude for the American game of graft. He extorted money by every means at his command. It was a sorry game for one of his talents, he was the first to admit; but the experience gave him a rich measure of human understanding. He did not throw stones idly for fear of hitting himself. He was thus, in a sense, imprisoned by his own kindness. His condemnation of shoddy literary merchandise took inverted forms. He stepped upon cheap stuff by extolling the better brands. He was at times shrill in his laudatory accents, but that was that he might be heard, and he was heard, just as was his Eastern counterpart, Huneker.

And all that might be said in praise of Reedy could with equal truth be said of Huneker. Benjamin De Casseras called him the American Columbus who discovered Europe. Huneker was responsible for introducing to America most of the supreme artists and thinkers of the Old World. Brandes, Nietzsche, Shaw, Sudermann, Ibsen, Flaubert, Cezanne—to name only a few of an extraordinary number—were among those who largely owed their American fame to him. All of the arts were his domain. His field was richer even than Reedy's. His pen, too, jumped and laughed and galavanted with more ecstasy than did Reedy's. He was the best talker in America and one of the best writers; with Reedy, his influence was incalculable.

Reedy, in spite of his extraordinary gifts and ecstatic love of literature, wrote no books. This narrowed his influence during his lifetime and accounts for the fact that his fame and influence died with him. But roaring Jim wrote books, many of them, big with sprawling ideas. He wrote essays, stories, biographies and a novel, although he preferred reading other men's superior volumes to creating poorer ones himself. How both of them loved to encourage other writers, especially young ones. These two big men were the first to grasp the hands of literary rebels, the first to encourage them with approval and unpatronizing advice.

Both men hailed Viereck with enthusiasm when first he swam into view and were, from the first, determined to lend helping hands. Huneker preceded Reedy, perhaps because he was physically closer to Viereck's home. Viereck was still in college when he became, in a sense, the protegé of the Glad Literary Warrior of Philadelphia. He had read one of Huneker's bizarre cerebral stories, and it had appealed to him strongly. In youthful zeal he wrote to Huneker, and that was the beginning of a long and fruitful friendship. Huneker was all too familiar with the poison of American Puritanism. He himself was so blighted by it that he could not reach his real stature. He was too good humored to fight against many of the prevailing standards. He had too many personal loyalties; he was weighted down with religious inhibitions; he was too close to the nineteenth century to be the wild and unconcerned leader of a literary rebellion. He was eager to salute the younger rebels who began to roam the land, and he sensed at once that Viereck was a born shouter of the good news of freedom, a predestined rammer of closed doors. And so he gloried in Viereck, just as he later gloried in Mencken. Before either man had done memorable work, Huneker hailed them as masters. It was altogether proper, then, that Viereck should dedicate his first book in the English language to Huneker, just as it was fitting that Mencken should later write two of his best essays in praise of Huneker.

Huneker had been the first to sense that Viereck had certain capabilities in the field of the drama. His earliest letters to Viereck were filled with as much practical advice as either he or Viereck could stomach.

"I have read your poetry with unmixed admiration," he told the boy, no doubt conscious of the joy it would give. "You are—to paraphrase a remark of Franz Liszt—too young to write so marvelously well. Your essential peril is the peril of the lyric soul—you may end in a cascade of subjective verbal harmonies like Swinburne. I hope not. Character study, objectivity, the broad, enveloping study of a Goethe—These are your cues. I am glad you think of the theatre. It is often a pit; in your case it may prove a salvation."

And then he read the plays, eagerly sent to him by Viereck, and wrote of them in such fashion that Viereck could not help profiting. "Of course, my dear Mr. Viereck," he began, "a snowball has a better chance of surviving hell-fire than your plays of finding a publisher." He was a better critic than a prophet, as we have seen, for *A Game at Love* was published in spite of its amoral tone. Huneker's views were, nonetheless, the soundest that the young man could have mustered. "You are still too lyrical, that is too subjective for the broader canvas of the drama," Huneker told him. "But there is good metal in the plays."

"Have you ambitions toward the drama?" the older man asked. "If so you must sacrifice—especially in America—all notes of defiance, of rebellion against conventions, and write for the many-headed monster of a public. Before you were born, *Cher poete,* the world had its head filled, indeed, packed with the concepts of duty, of love, of religion, of patriotism. You can't expect to drive out these *Grundideen* in a few years. It will take centuries. Pardon the critical curtain lectures. (I don't practice what I preach!)"

"Don't be in a hurry to print in English," he warned Viereck. "The ravens are circling critically in the sky; your bones would be picked clean, your very soul bleached if you fell short in your first book. Avoid Swinburne for a year. Read the *English* Bible, Shakespeare, Milton, Keats. Leave Shelley, Byron, Coleridge for another season. . . . You have a brilliant future; don't as Heine would say, have it *behind* you! Work, read Goethe—and look out for Eros. He is a treacherous God at best." Indisputably the advice was needed, if scarcely heeded.

His whole heart was in the simple words he wrote to Viereck on June 29, 1909, and the words represent his own appraisal of the respective merits of the old critic and the young poet: "A critic—especially an American—is of no particular importance in the scheme of things. And thus far beyond writing words I've done nothing. The older I grow the more futile all manner of ink seems. When one has the lyric gift as you have in a splendid degree, then you can sing."

Reedy never visited New York without calling upon Viereck, until a world war threw its shadow across their friendship. In the midst of the war, however, he was sane enough to proclaim the self-evident truth that a Hun and a traitor, no less than a Boston elder statesman or an Oyster Bay orator, can write great literature. He never denied Viereck's great gifts, though he hated Viereck's advocacy of the German cause. He let others sling the mud of vituperation. He was eager to keep a balance and to place first things first; neither war nor personal stress could shake his view that art is the supreme good of man.

For years Reedy wrote letters of encouragement to Viereck; for years he reviewed his books with understanding and with discrimination, tossing to the young man sly hints as to how he might better his writings and thus come nearer the goal of perfection. He published Viereck's poems, stories, and essays in the columns of the *Mirror*. He published articles, poems, and skits about Viereck written by others. He threw his correspondence columns open to the friends and to foes of the young man. He beat a steady drum and sounded a loud bell for the man. More than any other man, he spread the name and fame of Viereck in the hinterland. Viereck conquered New York himself, but it was Reedy, more than any other man, who conquered the rest of the country for him.

Never could this poet of passion justifiably claim that hands were not lifted to aid him. From childhood he had been blessed, possibly beyond his deserts, by kindly spirits like Huneker and Reedy. In his early boyhood Alexander, Auspitz, Henrici, Mrs. von Ende, Dr. Baruch, and a host of others had traveled out of their way to assist him. Then had come two of the greatest literary and personal influences of his life, Leonard and Lewisohn, followed by Wheeler, Harvey and Abbott. And there were others; Michael Monahan, for one, a close friend of Reedy's and on terms of intimacy with most of the country's men of note.

Richard Watson Gilder, the respected editor of the *Century*, one of the justly esteemed literary journals, was another of Viereck's guiding lights. He was the first important American editor to publish a poem by Viereck, and it gave him much joy. He followed Viereck's career with a paternal interest, though he sorrowed at the erotic impulse of the young poet's verse. In conversations and in letters, he offered assistance. For Viereck's sake, he examined the manuscript of some of William Ellery Leonard's early verse. Whatever was of moment to Viereck was of interest to him. In his heart he knew that a young rebel like his German-American friend necessarily despised many of his favorite prejudices. But this did not diminish his liking for Viereck and his verse. He introduced him to Stedman, the banker-poet who had known Poe, one of the gods in Viereck's poetic firmament. He introduced him to Mark Twain and other dominant literary men. His aim seemed to be to lead the young man to Sinai that he might overlook the Promised Land. Perhaps he hoped that the quiet pastures, rather than the turbulent seas, might appeal to Viereck in the end.

More important to Viereck, in some ways, than the friendship of Gilder and Monahan and Reedy and Huneker was the parental guidance of Hugo Munsterberg, the world renowned head of Harvard University's philosophy department. Munsterberg was intensely Teutonic. His role in life, he felt, was to interpret Germany to America and America to Germany. To that end, he wrote many volumes in English and in German which achieved a wide fame in their day, among them a once classical work on American traits and institutions. He placed himself on terms of intimacy with the leaders in every field and was universally respected. Perhaps no man in the years before the war had a more solid reputation on two continents than did Munsterberg. While he rejoiced in his fame, he did not abuse it. He was ready at all times to assist any worthy cause or person, especially if that cause or person tended to aid German-American relations.

Because he had been a poet himself in his youth, he doted on the precocious boy and watched him grow in assurance and mastery. He read his every word and observed his every activity and exhibited him to everyone. Even the exclusive Boston literary cliques were invaded in Viereck's behalf. Munsterberg introduced him to all of the Brahmins. He helped father many of the boy's ventures and never denied any request Viereck made of him. He, as much as any other man, helped to make Viereck's path an easy one. Neither Viereck nor Munsterberg could dream of the debacle that was to take place in the America they loved. The world war was to choke the life out of Munsterberg, and it was to affect Viereck profoundly, changing the entire course of his career. But that was far, far in the future. Both men now appeared secure in their mutual loyalty and in the offerings of friendship they received on all sides. Munsterberg apparently had lasting fame, and Viereck was about to achieve it.

These men, the generous souls who were part of the life of Viereck and part of the American background as well, gradually receded. They ceased to mean much to Viereck and, alas, to America, but no study of Viereck's career ought to ignore them. When the star of the young poet flamed in the night, they were the ones who pointed it out.

11   SKYROCKET!

At length, in April 1907, Yard & Company published Viereck's first book of poems in the English language, his true bow to America. *Gedichte,* of course, had been published in German for a limited circle, though it had attracted surprising interest. The volume published in Germany by Cotta attracted still more interest, but like *Gedichte,* it had the barriers of a foreign language and a strange public to overcome. *A Game At Love,* though in the English tongue, was a comparatively little known first offering; unplayable dramas never have a wide appeal. Necessarily the book could not attract the interest Viereck hoped it would, but the new volume, called, resoundingly, *Nineveh and Other Poems,* was something else. It was a full blast of the trumpet of triumph, a fanfare from the orchestra of the Muses, sufficiently loud and long to give the true measure of Viereck. It introduced the young poet of twenty-two to a world that, curiously enough, was waiting for him. The news of his talents had been heard in the land before *Nineveh* had appeared. The earlier volumes had filled many discerning people with a feeling of anticipation, heightened by the random verse by Viereck which appeared here and there. Despite the qualified tone of some of the reviews of *Nineveh,* the enthusiasm was unconcealed. *Nineveh* skyrocketed Viereck into fame and made him a bright star in the firmament of American letters.

It is not difficult to understand the sensation caused by this volume of poetry. Looking back over the period, we can see now that contemporary poets were, as one literary historian has said, "mild, hushed souls, compared to the philosophers, the critics, the social prophets." They were chained by a tradition of gentility that had grown shabby. They had become tame, sometimes dignified rhetoricians whose function it was, as the same literary historian has said, "to adorn the commonplace with a pseudo-literary grace." They were all minor Tennysons, embedded in syrup, and out of them oozed stale thoughts. They affected a grand style, but they lacked substance. To be sure, there were exceptions; William

Vaughn Moody, Edwin Markham, Lizette Woodworth Reese, Elsa Barker, and Ridgely Torrence rose at moments above the merely rhetorical and wrote with simple beauty, and Emily Dickinson, a voice out of the past, was suddenly discovered. But these men and women lacked the youthful rebelliousness of the young Viereck. Their revolt was an implicit one; there was no clarion ring to it. Viereck's verse succeeded, where theirs failed, in arousing the attention of the timid.

In art, as in life, the golden mean often goes unnoticed. It is wise understatement and brilliant overstatement that challenge attention. Viereck excelled in the latter, though he had his quiet note, too. "Today no one is likely seriously to deny that Viereck was the most conspicuous American poet between 1907 and 1914 and that there were few dissenters from the chorus of praise, almost of adulation, that greeted his successive volumes," wrote Ludwig Lewisohn in *Expression in America*. Men "were sure that the spirit of modern poetry had now first reached our shores. Nor was this all. Viereck's volumes of verse sold; they made money. They bore witness, in other words, to the utter weariness of men of the conventional mouthings of the genteel versifiers and to the perennial need of the poet."

In the same book, Lewisohn, in spite of his praise, also pointed to the defects in Viereck's poetry. "Unluckily," he said, "the poetic school and manner which Viereck represented in America, that, namely, of the French and English late Victorian decadents, was even then on the point of extinction and may be said, in fact, to have enjoyed its last flicker of life in America and in him. Nothing seems more old-fashioned today than this loud sonorousness of execution and this public exaggeration of private sin and unnecessary repentance. Nevertheless Mr. Viereck's goings-on both as a man and as an artist had a definitely liberating influence on American life and letters at their particular moment; from their influence an astute prophet might have foretold the imminence of many of the revolutions which did, in fact, take place almost immediately."

Here is the same measured tone with which Lewisohn had years before appraised the little booklet of Viereck's German verse, but now the calm exterior is not a literary device. It is, rather, an expression of Lewisohn's critical conscience at its best. It is difficult after this cold wash of candor to recapture the first flush of enthusiasm that was expressed for young Viereck's poetry. Lewisohn declared that Viereck wrote "better and better as the years went on and it is only his public clamorousness, compensating no doubt some private inadequacy or fear, that still keeps from their just place in the poetry of the period such fine sonnets as 'The Poet' and 'Finale' as well as a few among the subtler and quieter of his earlier poems. The always honorable experience of espousing an unpopular cause, which made poets of Abolitionists, also made a better poet of Viereck." But the judgment lacked the fervor that Lewisohn and others must have felt then. The fire is rekindled by an examination of *Nineveh* itself.

"The splendid heritage of two languages has fallen to me from a German father and an American mother," Viereck wrote in a provocative preface to the volume. Viereck's prefaces always struck an insistent key in their summary of his beliefs of the moment. Brimming with self-confidence, he stated that he had "extended the borderland of poetry into the domain of music on the one side, into that of the intellect on the other." The poetry of tomorrow, he said with no uncertainty, will "become once more the vehicle of great thought."

Changing his tone, he acknowledged his debt to "lyric England." In a sonnet, his first important one in our tongue, he told of the contrasting gifts of Germany and England. He rose to genuine eloquence in repaying his debt to the land of Shakespeare and uttered a prayer that catches one's throat:

> "Lord," sobbed I, "take Thy splendid gift of youth
> For the one boon that I have craved so long;
> Mould Thou my stammering accents and uncouth,
> With awful music raise and make me strong;
> A living martyr of Thy vocal truth,
> A resonant column in the House of Song!"

One begins to feel that he will achieve his purpose—that, indeed, he already had achieved it. The premonition of an early death, expressed in a sonnet, bade him hasten with his harvesting and lent a solemn tone of sincerity to his verse, and this, strangely enough, was missed by the public, possibly because of Viereck's own clamorousness.

He plunged, forgetful of his role of supplicant, into the gloating verses of *Nineveh,* the title poem, in praise of the fever of Manhattan:

> The splendor and the madness and the sin,
> Her dreams in iron and her thoughts of stone.

It is easy to understand that those Americans of 1907 who were young in spirit and were tired of mere gentility thrilled at the words of Viereck; whether as rhetoric or as high poetry—and one cannot be sure which they are—they have the force of a thundering cataract. The final stanzas, summing up what is implicit in the rest of the poem, throb with the irresistible pulse of youth:

> I, too, the fatal harvest gained
>   Of them that sow with seed of fire
> In passion's garden—I have drained
>   The goblet of thy sick desire.
>
> I from thy love had bitter bliss,
>   And ever in my memory stir
> The after-savours of thy kiss—
>   The taste of aloes and of myrrh.
>
> And yet I love thee, love unblessed
>   The poison of thy wanton's art;

Though thou be sister to the Pest
    In thy great hands I lay my heart!

And when thy body Titan-strong
    Writhes on its giant couch of sin,
Yea, though upon the trembling throng
    The very vault of Heaven fall in;

And though the palace of thy feasts
    Sink crumbling in a fiery sea—
I, like the last of Baal's priests,
    Will share thy doom, O Nineveh.

It is not simply the delight in sin, the pretense to an exotic joy in wickedness, that distinguished the poem. Theodore Roosevelt and others who should have known better told the young poet that he was painting New York as too wicked. Nor was the poem simply the catch-penny shocker played up in the Sunday newspaper supplements of 1907. It was a hymn, rather, to all of the life that swarmed in the metropolis, an inverted apotheosis of the excitement that welled in the city and in the young man's heart. Those who missed that point missed the point of all of Viereck's poetry.

There were many moments of brooding seriousness in the volume. And there were unwilling tears beyond the spirit of gaiety. His preoccupation with the Sphinx and related themes was another evidence of his essential concern with the verities, belying the popular picture of a lad enraptured with a fanciful portrait of Dame Sin, with whom he jousted amorously. In the book there were no less than three fairly long poems about the Sphinx, two of them of considerable merit. He himself marveled at it, this preoccupation with age-old symbols:

O strange beyond the strangest fears
    And hopes and ancient questionings,
That I who am so young in years
    Have loved the oldest of all things!

He found a "beast the mansion of the soul," and it was enough to take the spirit of youth from him and to reduce all of life to weariness:

And lo, the spring's breath faded from Love's charm,
    The sunshine from his hair,
And in his arm
    The arrows turned to rods.
        He heeded not the silent years that crawl
        Like uncouth spiders. Weary, cynical,
Self-conscious, disenchanted stood he there,
    The oldest and the saddest of the Gods.

Seriousness is only the other face of the youthful optimist. It may be that the face simulates sorrow, while the heart knows only joy. After all, Viereck was too young to know profound grief; life was necessarily gilded for him; his playing with grief was like knowledge not yet tested by life. When his sorrow was based upon an actual personal incident, as in *When Idols Fall,* it had not the forlorn appearance of maturity but only the petulance of a child deprived of his toys and pouting so that his mother may hear:

> Amidst the gloom I grope for song;
>> The fires die out that passion fed;
> Thou art not what I thought thee long,
>> And oh! I would that I were dead!
> Yet worse than all the pain of loss,
>> The smile that seals a traitor's will,
> Is this: that knowing gold for dross,
>> I cannot choose but love thee still!

It was youth's wonderment, after all, and not the weariness of age. It was poetic vaunting for Viereck to write of "endless pleasure's endless woe"; it gave him the luxury of experience. He had the glorious gift of youth, as Huneker had said, and could have only an academic view of an old fellow's thwarted desires. Viereck, in the summer of his triumph, could not think convincingly of any sad end.

He sounded much more genuine in the chants of *Love Triumphant,* a poem written when he was only sixteen and, fortunately, included in the volume. The effort put into the writing of the poem caused him to flunk a mathematics examination. "Your body's treasures are mine today," he intoned to his lady of love, a woman, incidentally, much older than himself, who satisfied him only in retrospect. "Your body's treasures are mine today," he gloated and made them his; from head to foot his kisses played, and naught was kept from his sovereign will:

> The God in me and the beast in me
>> And all deep things come up to light;
> And I would barter my soul to be
>> The prize of love for a single night.
>
> One long, long night of supreme desire,
>> One long, long night of rest and rage;
> For you are the sea and I the fire,
>> And old as the world is the war we wage.
>
> The old, old strife of woman and man
>> That ever has been, and still shall be
> Until the day when the vaulted span
>> Shall sink a wreck in the whelming sea.

My life is poured in the stream of yours,
    But fire and flood were not meant to mate:
We shall never be one while the world endures—
    And the meaning of love at the last is hate!

He envisioned the whole kaleidoscope of passion. Whatever its form, love's
end is the same, he said: "a thing of horror at the last." His disillusionment, real or
feigned, was unquestionably given its supreme statement in *The Haunted House*,
a poem which is, as Richard La Gallienne had said, as unique in its way as Ernest
Dowson's *Cynara*. The poem demands quotation in full, as the final expression of
a universal mood:

I lay beside you . . . on your lips the while
Hovered, most strange . . . the mirage of a smile,
Such as a minstrel lover might have seen
Upon the visage of some antique queen—
Flickering like flame, half choked by wind and dust,
Weary of all things saving song and lust.

How many days and years and lover's lies
Gave you your knowledge? You are very wise
And tired, yet insatiate to the last.
These things I thought, but said not; and there passed
Before my vision in voluptuous quest,
The pageant of the lovers who possessed
Your soul and body even as I possess,
Who marked your passion in its nakedness
And all your love-sins when your love was new.

They saw as I your quivering breast, and drew
Nearer to the consuming flame that burns
Deep to the marrow of my bone, and turns
My heart to love even as theirs who knew
From head to girdle each sweet curve of you,
Each little way of loving. No caress,
But apes the part of former loves. Ah yes,
Even thus your hand toyed in the locks of him
Who came before me. Was he fair of limb
Or very dark? What matter, with such lures
You snared the heart of all your paramours!

Tonight I feel the presence of the others,
Your lovers were they and are now my brothers
And I have nothing that has not been theirs

No single bloom the tree of passion bears
They have not plucked. Beloved, can it be?
Is there no gift that you reserve for me—
No loving kindness or no subtle sin,
No secret shrine that none has entered in,
Whither no mocking memories pursue
Love's wistful pilgrim? I am weary too,
With weariness of all your lovers, and when
I follow in the ways of other men,
I know each spot of your sweet body is
A cross, the tombstone of some perished kiss.
My arms embrace you, and a silent host
Of shadows rises—at each side a ghost!
With all its beauty and its faultless grace
Your body, dearest, is a haunted place.
When I did yield to passion's swift demand,
One of your lovers touched me with his hand.
And in the pang of amorous delight
I hear strange voices calling through the night.

Here, in incomparable form, was the search after the mystic meanings beyond the flesh, transcending poetic devices. It was the quest that heightened the spirit and purport of Viereck's every passional hymn. A public and a press blinded by Puritanism could not see this; but the more astute critics did discern it and to them it was a token of achievement and of greater promise.

Soon enough, he adopted the less fleshly view of Man's partner, a view that does not forget the wondrous body of Woman, but sees beyond it. In what Viereck called post-coital contemplation, the poet gazed at the creature reclining before him. He could not retain the dark picture his mind has formed of her. It is only her loveliness that now beguiled him:

Eternal Woman! Good or ill
    Has left its stamp on charms like these:
Your body is a wonder still,
    And you creation's masterpiece!

Away with visions that recall
    Your nameless lust, your stranger woes,
For whiter than the first snowfall
    Your immemorial beauty glows.
Lean back in all your loveliness
    Soft-bedded where red roses bleed!
A fool who would your secret guess,
    And who has guessed it—poor indeed!

As was to be expected, the repressed general public completely ignored the high thought of the passional poems, and many of the critics, being true mirrors of their age, were guilty of the same obtuseness. Perhaps it is more accurate to say that the public and the critics felt that the characteristic element—at any rate, the element most out of tune with the prevailing mores—was sexual. As a result, many of the reviews were in reality critiques of the particular attitudes toward love to which Viereck gave voice. The reviews were in toto an important document in the history of American letters, for they showed the reactions to the frankest voice in American poetry since Whitman. The less blunt language Viereck adopted obscured somewhat his candor, but his disregard of the prevailing code was patent enough.

In perhaps his most penetrating essay, that on Puritanism as a literary force in America, Mencken, the one-time terror of the Philistines, showed with devastating completeness and with an absence of too easy generalization that Puritanism has blighted American letters, not only because of the outward forces supporting it, such as the police and the law makers who are dominated by moral entrepreneurs and hard-fisted salvation hunters, but as much or more because of the inward sense of guilt from which the average American writer finds it impossible to free himself. Mencken cited virtually every prominent writer of the American race to prove his thesis.

During the age of Anthony Comstock, who was, as is generally known, the Good Lord's Minister in Charge of American Morals, the ethical test was virtually the only test. A book and its author had to tread the straight and narrow path of virtue, or both author and book were damned to everlasting hell fire. For the average writer, the public inhibition was no great hardship. He had only to utter the beliefs upon which he was raised and in which he had a genuine faith, and he was safe. He was not conscious that the dull weight of conformity pressed down upon him. He paid matter-of-fact homage to household gods and did not feel any sense of oppression. Occasionally, however, a restless spirit arose who felt that he must not yield to outward pressure. Such men were few and too likely to feel conscience-stricken because of their inward rebellion. Generally, they stifled the nascent spirit of revolt within them and counted the beads of propriety in public. Such, occasionally, were the men who gave revolutionaries like Viereck cautious welcome and paved their way to triumph. In private they talked in kindly, unpatronizing tones; they wrote privately to Viereck as proud fathers to a young son of genius. But in public, they guarded their phrases and their praises. There were reviews, of course, which praised the poems and the poet beyond measure, veritable deluges of praise. But it was not in these reviews that one got a critical approach to Viereck's poems, the sort of approach that placed them in relation to the popular standards of the day.

The then well-known critic, Clayton Hamilton, was enthusiastic enough in his praise of the volume, in the columns of both the *North American* and the *Bookman*. There was, however, a careful balance in what he had to say that succeeded admirably in its purpose of lauding the verse and yet placing Viereck and the poems in their proper perspective. Hamilton opined that Viereck owed something to the world in return for his poetic gifts. "His recent volumes prove him to be indisputably a poet," said Hamilton. "It also indicates the lines along which he must develop in order to fulfill his promise. As yet his genius is greater than his talent. His verse has spontaneity, but not perfected art; and it behooves him to study carefully the master poets and grow to greater sureness of technical effect." This was an oblique method of hinting at other sins.

Akin to Hamilton's review were dozens of others—by William Aspenwall Bradley, Richard La Gallienne, Richard Watson Gilder, James Gibbons Huneker, Charles Hanson Towne, and others of great repute. There was more than a page about the book in the *New York Times,* and for weeks its columns contained discussions of Viereck. In the *Saturday Evening Post* of August 31, 1907, then as later respectable in the conventional sense, there was eloquent proof of the tremendous sensation caused by *Nineveh.* Under the headline, *Believes He Is a Genius,* Lorimer's journal recorded the incidents of young Viereck's triumph in surprisingly spirited language.

"The most widely-discussed young literary man in the United States today is George Sylvester Viereck, the poet," it said with assurance. "Not in a decade, perhaps, has any young person been so unanimously accused of being a genius. And Viereck agrees very heartily with his accusers. At twenty-two years of age he has produced a volume of verse that has kicked up more controversy and inspired more 'letters to the editor' than any similar book in years. In a way, it is the Keats episode all over again but with the characteristic twentieth-century exception, aptly expressed by Viereck . . .: 'I want to be heard while I am living, and I don't want to starve. I believe in activity, even if it is about myself.' "

Viereck, the article went on to say, differed from the traditional poet in that he did not mind acting as his own press agent. "In fact, this excessive overflow of himself has made him a literary exhibit without precedent. . . . Some one asked Viereck the other day if he minded the criticism that was being heaped upon his young head," the article reported, "whereupon he pointed to his face, which was freshly sunburned. 'That is the only roast I ever got that hurt,' he said." The article concluded with an admission that was sanctioned by many of the young poet's detractors: "Despite the flood of conflicting opinion about his work and the incessant play of his own personality, the fact remains that he has the promise of real power."

Elsa Barker, herself a poet of consummate skill, was one of those who recalled this first season of Viereck's fame. She had met him less than a year before the appearance of *Nineveh.* He bubbled with joy at being a poet and was eager to proclaim himself, eager for recognition. Unhesitantly, he would recite his poetry, so that one could not help noticing him. He was vital, terse, fresh, startlingly original, essentially different, like his poetry. He had a deep and serious artistic purpose, Mrs. Barker felt, but he glossed over it all with a touch of wit and whimsicality. In less than a year, fame came to him, real fame that not even his worst enemies could deny. He would often run in to see Mrs. Barker, carrying a fresh sheaf of reviews of *Nineveh* under his arm; sometimes, too, he would recite a new poem, while intoxicated with the success of *Nineveh*. Of course, Mrs. Barker and many others helped Viereck to celebrate his new fame. They gave parties for him; it was enough to turn anyone's head, this miracle that had been wrought in one year.

Viereck neither smoked, drank, nor swore, and, as of that time, had never been in jail. And he did not hesitate to say so in print. But he was actually intoxicated with success, reeling in ecstasy, though he tried to carry himself with easy grace. He made many friends and more enemies. He was quoted widely; he was hailed as the leader of the rebel choir and was dubbed the poetic hope of America. He rammed in doors for the new movement in verse and prose and life. The sensational press, Hearst's yellow sheets, no less than the more august publications, featured him. He received flattering letters; he carried on important correspondence with distinguished men; love, in all of its forms, was thrown in his lap. No wonder he staggered; no wonder he was fascinated with himself; no wonder he made serious strategic errors. His conceit, his audacity, his unworldliness, and the heady wine of success left him bereft of the power of leadership. He did not form cliques; he did not capitalize properly his heavy earnings of notoriety; a *bon mot* meant more to him than a lasting contact or a manifestation of sober leadership. These things concerned him little in 1907; but very soon they were to matter much.

Elsa Barker, much interested in the fates foretold by the stars, cast his horoscope shortly before *Nineveh* had appeared. The stars were plausible in the fate they forecast, and Mrs. Barker accepted their story with full faith. They said he was destined to be a poet of vigorous and resonant verse; that his House of Friends was dangerously afflicted; that his reputation would sometimes be seriously attacked, but that he would respond fearlessly; that brilliant though he was, he was under a nervous tension which forebode some catastrophic conjunction with Uranus, that he had a unique but eccentric character which would make him take strange and unaccountable attitudes; that the immediate prospect was fame—full, glorious fame—within a year. And fame did come, as we have seen. Mrs. Barker had more confidence than ever in the horoscope. She looked forward to the rest of the story—sometimes with uneasiness. But Sylvester Viereck worried not at all. He even forgot the dire prophesy, the Lord forgive him! For what can a comet, a rocket of the skies, think of the stars?

12   THE GHOST OF OSCAR WILDE

In one of the odd volumes exposing German activities in the United States before our entry into the First World War on the side of the Allies, there is adduced as proof of Viereck's utter viciousness the fact that he treasured a violet from the grave of Oscar Wilde! The great minds responsible for the book in question might just as well have carried the charge further. They might have said that Viereck was the chief disciple of Wilde in prewar America: the high priest of the Wilde cult in America. The ghost of Oscar Wilde walked arm-in-arm with him, whispering inspiration in his ears, until Viereck was in his thirtieth year. Then suddenly the spirit vanished. Viereck had by then imbibed all that Wilde had to offer: too much indeed. There had been, perhaps, no greater influence in his life. Not even Lewisohn or Leonard seemed to count so much then, except for a few lyrical moments. They had never had any appreciable influence on Viereck's style of writing or habits of thought nor his mode of living.

In the first flush of the sensation aroused by the publication of *Nineveh,* Viereck had told the reporter sent by the *New York Times* to interview him, the new celebrity, that Christ, Napoleon, and Oscar Wilde were the only three gods in his heaven—and he lingered particularly over the name of Wilde. He might have substituted other names for Jesus and Bonaparte, but no name could have taken the place of Wilde's. Because many in the America of the year 1907 considered Wilde taboo, unmentionable, Viereck, intent upon violating the canons of conventionality, found it necessary that the poet of *Reading Gaol* be elevated to godhood. He afforded leadership to the Wildean "art for art's sake" school, American branch.

Viereck might have told the *Times* reporter, sent to pry into his soul, that he could remember vaguely the trial and conviction of Wilde, though he was a mere child at the time. The savage treatment of a great man had angered his parents. He might have mentioned that while other boys were gorging themselves on adventure stories, he was studying the writings and life style of Wilde. He might have mentioned his boyish tribute to Wilde, a superb German translation of *The Ballad of Reading Gaol*. He might have mentioned his vicarious contacts with Wilde through Lord Alfred Douglas, who had played so tragic a role in the poet's life. In an impish mood, he might have mentioned the tour de force, involving Wilde, which had appeared under his signature in the *Critic* magazine of July 1905. In that article, Viereck had posed the question, *Is Oscar Wilde Living or Dead?* With halting breath, he had recounted rumors that the author of *De Profundis* was not dead at all, but a recluse in the bosom of the Church, perhaps in New York! The wish giving credence to his argument, Viereck had confessed some belief in the bizarre story and had told of whisperings by unnamed men. It was a hoax, a harmless one; but it would later plague him, and be used as proof of his unreliability.

He might have told the tales repeated later by William Ellery Leonard, little episodes which had lingered fondly in Leonard's memory for more than thirty years—tales of Wildean poses, these, harmless in themselves, but giving point to many rumors. One day young George Sylvester had run to Leonard and had, in the very accents of the immortal Oscar, shouted: "Ellery, teach me some new vice!"

Instead of telling the reporter these things, he had told her of the literary and intellectual qualities of Wilde, of the barbarity with which the outcast poet had been treated, and of his influence on his own writings.

Viereck has paid rather inadequate tribute to Wilde in a poem called *The Ghost of Oscar Wilde:*

> Within the graveyard of Montemarte
> Where wreath on wreath is piled,
> Where Paris huddles to her breast
> Her genius like a child,
> The ghost of Heinrich Heine met
> The ghost of Oscar Wilde.

And more in that vein.

In the receptive columns of *Reedy's Mirror,* Francis Medhurst had replied to the poem in verse aping Viereck's own. It was difficult to see where malice ended and good humor began; but much of the parody shows insight, lopsided, it is true, into Viereck's personality:

> "No piffling plagiarist am I
> To hunt your garbage through,
> I have my own pre-empted sty,
> And it's a gold mine, too!
>
> I pander to the torrid taste
> Of many a hectic hen.
> My patrons all are matrons chaste
> And maids—but never men."

For many years, there was hardly a review of Viereck's poems that did not lug in some comparison with Wilde. Sometimes he was praised in Wilde's name, though more often damned. His lifelong detractor, the chronic anthologist, Louis Untermeyer, found some subtle distinction between Wilde's merits and Viereck's demerits; he and others thought of Viereck as a pinchbeck Wilde. It is possible to write a sketch of Viereck as some sort of Teutonic-American reincarnation of Wilde. Wilde, through Viereck, gave German American verse new forms and content. He added to Viereck's personality certain graces, chiefly of effrontery and courage, that Viereck might otherwise have lacked. Perhaps it was through the histrionic background supplied by Edwina Viereck and her brother William that Viereck was predisposed to the essentially theatrical Wilde. "I had my experience as an actor before birth," Viereck once said with Wildean flippancy.

Viereck was content to let the vulgar view of the matter stand, for he thought it gave him a certain distinction in some quarters, not always the best. As a result, other doors were barred to him or at least not opened with enthusiasm. He should have known that here one must sneer, in masculine fashion, at the mere thought of sexual eccentricity. The wonder is that Viereck did not meet with total disaster. He got off comparatively easy, for all his vaunting of strange sins. Many people did not feel as did the discoverers of great German conspiracies that taking pride in possessing a violet from the grave of Wilde was a sign of moral turpitude.

In the spring of 1911, Viereck was in Paris for a few days and called upon Elsa Barker at her picturesque old studio court. Would she go with him to the tombs of Oscar Wilde and Baudelaire and Heine? She would. Laden with flowers of the season, they started, in an open victoria, on their lyric pilgrimage. They began, of course, with Père-Lachaise and Oscar. Viereck saw to it that Oscar got most of the flowers, and this meant replenishing the supply. He was determined to lend solemnity to the occasion; he posed himself on the alien grave and recited poems, appropriate and inappropriate, to the ghost of his dearly beloved mentor. He persuaded Elsa Barker to recite her sonnet on Wilde. She was not sure the dead poet would be pleased; but she obliged his disciple by reciting her sonnet that begins, "Laureate of corruption on whose brow the bay-leaves are all slimy with the worm," and ends, "For when the angels fall they fall so far."

Mrs. Barker took more pleasure in showing Viereck the tomb of Abelard and Heloise and in telling him of her good friend Mildred Aldrich, later the author of *A Hilltop on the Marne*, who was the mysterious woman mentioned by the Paris newspapers as having attended the burial of Wilde. This gave them the feeling of being closer to him.

Then the two went to the grave of Heine at Montmartre, and Viereck recited a poem in Heine's honor and some of Heine's own incomparable lyrics in the original German. Mrs. Barker, not understanding German, busied herself with the arrangement of the flowers and occasionally listened with respectful attention. And on the way home, they visited the eternal home of Baudelaire at the Cemetery of Montparnasse. Appetites aroused by the strenuous posturing, they had dinner at the Restaurant L'Avenue and drank toasts to three dead poets—and two live ones.

It was a memorable gesture, and it brought the author of *De Profundis* nearer to his American disciple. It marked, indeed, the high point in his adoration of Wilde. Thenceforth Wilde's influence was to be increasingly on the wane. A few years earlier, in the days when everyone was composing limericks, Elsa Barker had written her little tribute in limerick to the young poet Viereck:

> There is a young man named Sylvester
> Who revels in lilies that fester—
> Or so he pretends
> To incredulous friends.
> He's a poet, a child and a jester!

He remained a child and a jester, and a poet, for some years. But it was not until he could see Wilde objectively that Viereck really put aside childish things. This is to be found in the things he has written since Freud usurped Wilde's place in his life.

Justifying his original choice of Christ, Napoleon, and Wilde as his sacred Trinity, Viereck said they are "each the supreme embodiment of a type, the ethical, the dynamic and the aesthetic, and each a martyr to his ideal." Wilde, he said, is the youngest of the classics, not the oldest of the moderns, for he belongs to the past by temperament and by tradition. He was not, after all, an aesthete completely freed from bourgeois misgivings. In his heart, he believed in the old moralities; his paradoxes and glitter only hid his devotion to the old order. Because by nature he was addicted to certain forbidden things, he writhed in an inner conflict and felt constrained to justify himself through experimentations in various fields of art: the essay, poetry, romance, comedy, tragedy, his other poses and banter aside. Viereck, in this respect like Wilde, felt the same need for self-justification and attempted to satisfy it in the same way.

Wilde's conceit, Viereck concluded, was only a mask to conceal his weakness, his paradoxes only an oblique compliment to the things that are; in brief, that he was a slave to the law. Once Wilde learned his true nature, his pose of scarlet sin failed to deceive or to console him. "Unable to glory in the flesh without a stab of conscience, Wilde was neither a pagan nor a Greek. He was an Irishman moulded by the atmosphere of Nineteenth Century England."

Thus do the gods of our childhood perish!

13   OF VAMPIRES AND SUCH

Heralded by much fanfare, the book, *The House of the Vampire*, appeared in English and in German in September 1907 in England and in America. Viereck could not complain of neglect; the impetus of *Nineveh* assured the book a measure of success.

Viereck dedicated *The House of the Vampire* simply "To my mother"; but it is not the sort of book his mother would ordinarily have liked, nor many other mothers. It is a perfervid, if mannered, account of the vampirelike habits of one Reginald Clarke, a light-hearted thief of the ideas and the language of others, whom he leaves drained and exhausted. With the air of a conqueror—affable, self-possessed—Clarke takes what he wills from the brains of men and women and leaves them like stricken deer. It is a story which, if written by Viereck after he had attained maturity, might have had some lasting value, for the idea is original and daring and of some philosophical and psychological wealth. Years later, after Viereck had become associated with Paul Eldridge, he hoped to rewrite the story in collaboration with Eldridge; unfortunately, that has never been done. Yet even in its published form, the story has considerable interest and value. The story deserves attention as a literary curiosity, belonging on the same shelf as *Dracula, Frankenstein, Dr. Jekyll and Mr. Hyde,* but in a humbler position. Incidentally, it struck a chord of approval in the strange minds of some Theosophist leaders.

The plot has an obvious bizarre appeal.

Ernest, the stricken hero, struggles against Clarke, the Vampire, as he gets visible proof of Clarke's strange powers. He becomes determined to rid himself and the world of the monstrous creature who makes each man's talent his own; he knows that he must be careful. Fortunately, he has Ethel to aid and comfort him. They plot and plan—all to no avail. The Vampire conquers in the end with horrible completeness. "Without a present and without a past . . . blindly . . . a gibbering idiot . . ." Ernest stumbles down the stairs of the House of the Vampire—to be replaced by the boy who had been his best friend and comforter.

This is the gist of the less than two hundred pages of Viereck's first published novel. It might have been momentous, but it was merely strained. It did not live up to its own possibilities; Viereck, like the tragic figure of his protagonist, Ernest, was apparently bereft of the power to create the splendid things suggested by his basic idea.

There is, as Viereck himself soon realized, too much self-consciousness in the book; too much overwrought language; too much shrillness and no compensating calm, no quiet mastery. The book, in short, is the open grave of what might have been.

One more reason for the book's failure is evident. Viereck showed sympathy in the book for the vampire's victims. Seldom was Viereck in his later writings to err on the side of charity. Viereck's sympathies for the defeated Ernest were purely verbal, called for, he mistakenly thought, by the exigencies of the story. The great man, good, bad or indifferent in human qualities, especially in defeat, appealed more to Viereck than did an assemblage of saints. His heart did not bleed for the downtrodden; unlike Shelley, he was not the nerve o'er which did creep the else unfelt sorrows of mankind. He liked to believe himself a lute for the fingers of wickedness to play upon. In his case, at least, compassion was an artistic mistake that ruined his book.

The reviews of the book were deservedly unfavorable. But the success of *Nineveh* was too fresh in Viereck's mind and in the public's for him to pay much attention to unflattering views. There were, besides, enough adulatory reviews, and admirers still swarmed about him, and ideas for new books filled his head, leaving little room for uncomfortable thoughts. And surely the praise of one great critic, in this case Arthur Symons, meant more than all of the abuse of dwarfs. Symons, he thought, had written the true words: "The idea is original and the form is well wrought and brought to an end which justifies and expresses the whole course of action. . . . Mr. Viereck has made a really impressing story out of a symbol. It rather suggests Wilde, but Wilde would have spoilt it by decoration and left it vague in the end. There is certainly force in it and it insists on being read straight through." To be compared, this time not unfavorably to Wilde, was praise indeed.

A further boost to his pride came in the form of a dramatization of the novel by his college friend, Edgar Allan Woolf. The dramatization was made with the nominal collaboration of Viereck. The library playwright of *A Game At Love* thus became overnight a practicing dramatist with a play on Broadway. The play had a run, Viereck could say, though it was not a marathon, as he good-naturedly realized. The professional critics found much to criticize; but the public attended. Pictures of the stars and of some of the scenes appeared in the feature sections of the papers. It was talked about, given front page space because of the mutual recriminations of Viereck and another person, each claiming the other had plagiarized his incomparable idea. With pleasing abandon, Viereck threatened to sue for hundreds of thousands of dollars; so did the other man. But the suits were buried with the play. "Poet's Nights," honored by the presence of Edwin Markham and others, did not help. The run was certainly not a marathon.

New York was not the only stage for the Viereck play. Two road companies went to the hinterland. Providence, Rhode Island, seat of Brown University, was given a performance of *The Vampire*. "The ways of Providence are unaccountable," said Viereck to Alexander Harvey, when he asked Viereck for the details. "As we entered the door, four people were streaming in." Those four people were Viereck, Leonard Abbott, and the Heins, who accompanied him to the Providence Opera House. Viereck felt constrained to compliment the actors, as did Abbott.

After the performance, Abbott and Viereck went on to Cambridge to see Viereck's paternal friend, the distinguished Hugo Munsterberg. The professor and the poet at once began to discuss German affairs, until Abbott got exhausted and went out for air. The conversation then turned very naturally to the state of Viereck's soul. Munsterberg said Viereck suffered from intellectual katzenjammer. He did not prescribe Wilde-and-water as a cure. Nor can we be sure that he joined Huneker in prescribing Goethe.

The poet and Abbott took a temporary leave of the professor and tramped to the Harvard Stadium. There Viereck, taking advantage of the empty seats, declaimed his poem, *A Little Maid of Sapphc*. Abbott listened with awe.

Of such quaint stuff did Viereck build his life. In addition to such activities and his journalistic work, he also found time in that magical year 1907, during which he rose to the height of his fame, to edit and publish for the New Immigrants Protective League a little volume of verse, a poetic tribute to the various races commingling in the United States. His own contributions to the pamphlet were an indifferent introduction of two pages and two mediocre poems. But by the promise of much publicity and with a little cash, he beguiled his friends, William Ellery Leonard, Ludwig Lewisohn, Elsa Barker, and Alexis Coleman to contribute poems. The verse, if not of the highest quality, yet suited its purpose and served a worthy cause: the defense of liberal immigration legislation. It was significant that Viereck, then in the height of his Wildean period, could yet interest himself in such a cause. Without fully realizing it, he was demonstrating that an artist could be frivolous in his art and earnest in his life. The phase was apparently a passing one. He could not then see himself as a crusader for anything of mortal consequence, except the untrammeled freedom of art. The traditional artist's splash against censorship could interest him, not because a social principle was involved, but because a Comstock cramped his style.

14   LOVING MUCH AND MANY

"Sex allures me at all times," Viereck had said. "I seek not merely passion, but the meaning beyond it. I do not know if I am essentially passionate or essentially intellectual, whether I employ the images of passion to cloak the coldness of an analytical mind or whether passion colors all my cerebral processes." His constant quest was an answer to the inquiry he himself propounded in glittering language:

> Whence springs that hunger beyond the flesh
> That only the flesh can appease in me?

He sought the answer in poetry and in prose and, to the surprise of the cynics, in life. The best expression of his quest can be found in a saga of passion.

A chapter or two in *Confessions of a Barbarian,* the book to be discussed presently, afford examples of Viereck's passional rhetoric; but he was then a very young man and so to be forgiven. "There are born three types of the female," he there declared, "—the Eternal Harlot, the Eternal Woman, and the Woman in Scarlet. The Eternal Harlot bears the fragile vial of transitory delight. She is all of the earth, earthy. Less robust, still of the earth, but spiritualized and transfigured, mistress and mother, the Eternal Woman brings loving kindness and peace into the world. Unlike the Woman in Scarlet, she has no aspiration beyond the Race. Unlike the *demi-mondaine's,* her eyes are set toward the future. Through her, evolution works its indomitable will." And so through the various categories of the female. Viereck, in his book, told of the various amorous girls he met in Germany. He hid them under such names as Ermengarde, Madeleine, Aholibah, Thusnelda. Worse, he made them unreal under a flood of storybook language. And since his amours had nothing to do with Europe, he asked the good folks to accept his apologies.

Yet at least two facts of consequence stand forth. "I have never loitered with prurient interest in the love-marts of the world," Viereck said. "I have been intoxicated with the glitter and glare of Broadway, but even as a boy I never glanced twice, except in pity, at the vendors of passion." In short, love purchased by money did not appeal to him; love had to be acquired by other charms before it won his approval. And there had to be something strange in the object of his love: "the virgin and the strumpet blent in one" or some other such impossible combination. Just as the infinitely wise Francis Bacon felt that there had to be something strange in all excelling beauty, the infinitely passionate Viereck feels that the heart of love is the anomalous.

We must turn to his poetry and, above all, to his lyrical autobiography and the novels written many years later to find Viereck's account of himself as a masculine George Sand, loving much and many. The immortal Heine forgave Sand because of such love, but, in Viereck's case, it is a matter of understanding certain unusual qualities in his love life rather than a matter of forgiveness or damnation.

Even as a child, Viereck had two simultaneous loves, he says, one with a dreamy, epicene girl whose brown locks and faunlike face charmed him, the other with a somewhat older girl, who was buxom and tempestuous. No specific sex acts entered into these early affairs, nor in his mild interest in a dark schoolfellow of feminine gracefulness; but they showed, in a vague way, the duality of Viereck's love instincts before puberty. He seldom dreamed, he said, in youth, indicating perhaps that he rid himself of repressions, by expressing, in one form or another, all of the urges that tempted him. It is the old story of conquering temptation by yielding to it.

When still a student, Viereck once visited a brothel, but the prostitute aroused in him only slight physical pleasure and much pity and disgust. His friends, not having his sensitive and complex makeup, extracted infinitely more physical pleasure. Nor did he derive any keen delight from the embraces of a married woman who gave herself to him when he was sixteen or seventeen. The episode somehow fell short of his expectations and stirred him only in retrospect. When he pondered over the woman's caresses, he gave birth to his most feverish love poem, *Liebesnacht,* poetry acting as a compensation for the deficiencies of his paramour. Often in the future, poetry served the same compensatory purpose.

Until he was thirty, most of his love affairs were with women older than himself, and in this he was not unlike his father before him. There was unquestionably something of the search for the Mother in this predisposition to older women. There was something, also, of the feeling that, being older, his loves had mastered and could teach him the amatory refinements.

In his sophomore year at college, Viereck knew an elderly physician who sought to renew, vicariously, his own love life by creating amorous opportunities for younger people. Viereck was one of his beneficiaries and became an observer of many blends and varieties of love, carnivals and comminglings and perversions of all kinds. He could observe such things with an interest that was intellectual rather than morbid, but he could not respond emotionally or physically when desire became pathological. His amusement ceased when perversion was a matter of compulsion or pain. When a certain lyric female told him that she had burned the arm of her lover with a cigarette to show her power over him, she lost her charm for him, the scent of burning flesh acting as a barrier.

Neither the frigid nor the too passionate female appealed to him. He once told of a married woman who intellectually accepted all of the ways of love and who asked him one day to name what would give him most pleasure. But he could not arouse himself amorously, for he felt that an armor of frigidity guarded the lady's bizarre beauty. He felt the same chill when with a young woman of melting disposition, who had no understanding of his personality. His ardor died when he felt that his partner loved the ways of love, rather than his particular self.

He said that he liked the stir of adventure in his love affairs. The possible presence of husbands or fathers, latent dangers of all kinds, excited him and sometimes compensated for the deficiencies of his companions. He was an amorous freebooter, in a sense, and carefully cultivated that reputation, but he had certain bourgeois restraints as well that kept him out of the law courts. Perhaps it would be more accurate to say that his dissatisfaction with conventional love kept him within certain limits. Not finding the realization of his impossible dream, he did not linger. He was ever on his pilgrim's way to discover what he styled the double blossom of passion, the union of all of the varieties of sex, the creation of a partner who was all things to all persons and in no sense gross or monstrous, a creature, in short, who transcended the limitations of sex. It was the theme of his best poetry; it was to be the theme of the saga of passion he was to write many years later.

In his poetry he adopted certain symbols to denote his quest for the impossible synthesis of the sexes. In a way, it was the quest of Faust all over again, and his language is decidedly Faustian:

> I am the Pilgrim of Passion who ever must choose and grieve
> Between the earth-born daughters of Lilith and Eve.
> For I have lost my way twixt Heaven and Hell and Earth . . .
> Let Lilith and her sister both back into night be thrust.
> Fashion woman anew out of their astral dust!
> Dreams of impossible joy and impossible loveliness meet
> When beautiful Helen of Troy shall be one with the Blonde Marguerite.

There was no one Lilith and no one Eve. Neither was there a single Helen of Troy. Several women in his life represented each of the types. And his preference depended upon his regal mood or, as seemed seldom to occur to him, the mood of his love mate. But gradually the Blonde Marguerite became the type of types for him. And there was in time only one Blonde Marguerite for him, and she remained the only one, sung in poem after poem and hymned in prose until a second world war destroyed this.

The triumph of the Blonde Marguerite is another story and a later one. In the

Nineveh period, the poet of passion was much too busy sampling all of love's viands to limit himself to any one person or type or diet. He was content to receive the love offerings of many women, be the offerings in verse or in the poetry of reality. Many sonnets were delivered to him by those lyrical women who desired possession of his heart; but he wrote few in reply. An Encyclopedia of Passion was gradually forming itself in his mind. We shall return to it at length, just as we shall turn the cold light of objectivity on this largely subjective account of his sexual life.

But the insistent person will ask again and again what truth there is in the account. Were there so many lights of love shining for Viereck? Years ago the editor of the magazine *Current Literature* asked Viereck and others to select the most beautiful line in the English language. Viereck replied that it is not possible to name a single line, for a total rhythmical effect is needed. He gave as his first choice a stanza by Wilde:

> For surely it is something to have been
>   The best beloved for a little while,
> To have walked hand in hand with love and seen
>   His scarlet wings flit once across thy smile.

15   A BARBARIAN CONFESSES

One of the important results of young Viereck's pilgrimage to Europe was a little book embodying his experiences and the ideas that coursed through his head. The book was modest in size—just the least bit longer than *The House of the Vampire*—but it boiled over with Viereck's temperamental immodesty. *Confessions of a Barbarian* shows Viereck, still in the summer of his triumphs, morally certain that what has been will continue. The book is the assured chronicle of a series of triumphs and the matter-of-fact prelude to greater triumphs.

The book appeared serially in Reedy's *Mirror*, where it aroused much interest and precipitated a controversy. The reviews, in general, were highly favorable. Some of the journals which had disliked Viereck's earlier books found much to praise in this one. *The Nation*, which had been highly critical of his earlier efforts, wrote that when Viereck gets away from the subject of sex, "he is often better than brilliant." *The Review of Reviews*, which had also been critical, thought the book would do much "to interpret German ideals for America, and conversely something toward making the Germans understand the realities of things in the United States." Hutchins Hapgood, writing in the pages of the *Bookman*, thought the book was needed in America—"not that it is a great book . . . but it is a small book in the right direction." Hapgood apparently was not aware of the direction.

Such giants as Huneker and Reedy were delighted by the jaunty air of wisdom with which the young poet carried himself. Publicly they expressed the thought that the boy still had much to learn, that he was immature, despite all of his cockiness. Privately, especially in the case of Huneker, they said that the boy had reached a man's estate, that he was no longer a baby but a man of the world, splendid in his wisdom. They looked forward, with Viereck's own confidence, to what the years would bring forth. Huneker did feel that a little ballast was needed and perhaps some jetsum should be thrown overboard. He thought Viereck should bathe himself in cool classical springs so that modernism would not wholly corrupt him. He was ready, as ever, to act as tutor to the headstrong boy, but, as always, he knew that his good offices would be refused.

Viereck loses no time in telling the reader that his book "reveals America to herself by interpreting Europe." And he immediately gives the reason for his prescience: "I stand in symbolic relation, so to speak, to both hemispheres. My twofold racial consciousness serving as platform, I am enabled to pry two worlds—Archimedes aspired to lift but one—out of the furrow of their mutual misconceptions."

He says that he has seen "the soul of the subtle siren Europe" and has chronicled facts from her unwritten history. "From her I also learned verities greater than facts," he says in the same spirit. "I may speak *ex cathedra:* infallibility I claim not. . . . Having navigated unknown seas of Germanic psychology, I chart them. I trace the tangled lines of an elder civilization. I record spiritual data that elude Baedeker."

Having dived through troubled waters, Viereck feels, he has found many pearls of wisdom. As a result, he urges Europe's gospel of tolerance. He wants to lead an exodus from "the Babylonian captivity of Puritan prejudice," but the most important sections of the book do not deal with prudes and Puritans. Instead he contrasts the political, social, and economic institutions of Germany (which Viereck persists in calling Europe) and America. Near the middle of the book is a group of four chapters which are indispensable to an understanding of the later career of Viereck. These chapters deal with "The State Idea," with "S.M." (the vernacular for the Kaiser), "The Philosophy of Militarism" and "Inspired Bureaucracy." These chapters show infallibly the trend of Viereck's mind, his instinctive defense and rationalization of things German, notwithstanding their conflict with his own professed beliefs and practices. Incidentally, these chapters were the basis of the charge that was made in the years preceding the outbreak of the World War that Viereck was underwritten by the so-called reptile fund of the German government, the fund used by the Kaiser's government to win adherents abroad. That suspicion was to gain in strength as the years passed.

Americans remember our country only when they are in trouble, Viereck says: we have no conception of the state idea; indeed, we actually fear it, when we don't ridicule it or shame it. In Germany, however, the state enters into relations with every individual. The state there is an all-powerful, all-caring father. It may be paternalistic to a degree, but it does not run away from responsibility. It feels a concern for everyone, and in turn it wins the regard of all. No one there would think of robbing the state; here no one thinks of anything else! Indeed, graft and thievery are public duties here. Viereck leaves no doubt as to his preference for the state idea, as contrasted with our catch-as-catch-can system.

The state idea in Germany has led to a military system and to a bureaucracy, Viereck says. "Germany is an inspired bureaucracy," he insists. "The men at the helm of German affairs today have maintained the Prussian tradition of strict adherence to duty. But their horizon has widened. Sustained, not ossified by routing, they follow the star of the new." Viereck credits William II with the success of the German bureaucracy, and he has much to say in favor of the German bestowal of titles upon all and sundry who serve the state. "We may regard inherited titles as absurd," he says, "but titles earned by service are certainly sensible, one may even say, democratic. It's the one chance of the burgher to get even with the nobility. While the system establishes a differential social tariff, it creates no obstacles that cannot be overcome by merit."

Very astutely Viereck builds his defense of the German military system. He mentions that, through some error, "a uniform, spick and span, and with brass buttons" is waiting for him in Germany; but he does not want it—he'd rather wear his blue serge suit. "Yet there are moments when it is sweet to grow out of the shell of self. There is, perhaps, dangerous intoxication in crowds; to be swayed by the common impulse when the mysterious force psychologists call 'mass suggestion' sweeps through the channels of the brain, breaking the floodgates of mental reserve. Such must be the soldier's experience in war or some great maneuver. Think of a million young souls swearing fealty to one flag, made one by the ties of comradeship and obedience, and a new sense of brotherhood born of common experience." And so on in that vein, adding reason to reason and yet remaining what it necessarily mu be—unreasonable. The fact that Viereck feels called upon to defend the system is one of the sad commentaries on such pseudo-glamorous order as the German military system of 1910. Such blindness to realities was bound to have disastrous results.

Again and again Viereck feels called upon to defend the nobility as a necessary prop to the German scheme of things. "We live in a curiously transitional period," he says apropos his defense of the aristocracy. "Probably authentic democracy lies at the end of the road. I should prefer some transfigured aristocracy. The greatest individual development is perhaps possible under a cultured tyrant. He is the man of destiny. His brain is the scroll of the *Zeitgeist*." It is only one step from this to the acceptance of fascism.

This necessarily leads him to say:

> The giant Modernity everywhere shakes his fist against the lavendered glory of mediaeval tradition, impotent to obliterate its immemorial traces. William II is the living incarnation of this great contradiction. He is logical, because he is illogical. He is the only logical monarch in Europe. He is an ideal Kaiser. He is in tune with the *Zeitgeist*. If Germany were to be declared a republic today, and a president had to be chosen, the unanimous choice of the people would be William II.

"I wonder if the blood of kings is really like other men's?" he asks, his answer indicated in the very question. "A brain where the divine right of monarchs has been rooting for generations must be different from the brains of other men"; it must be specially endowed for the business of kingship, he answers. And the best one in the business is the kaiser—Viereck's kinsman whom he had not as yet met, through no fault of his own. Circumstance had prevented the meeting.

The Kaiser, he says without benefit of firsthand knowledge, is two distinct personalities: "the sole legitimate offspring of Romanticism and Modernity." His charm is more potent than that of Circe, for he turns his admirers, not into swine, but into patriots. All Germany vies to please him because all know that he has Germany's interests always at heart. Even the Socialists must secretly revere him.

This chapter dealing with *Seine Majestat* is impassioned, hot with reverence for the monarch who had unconsciously played so important a role in Viereck's life and who was destined to play a greater one in the very near future. Whether he realized it or not, his excessive admiration for the Kaiser was to make him a marked man. It was to give a certain color to his defense of things German, to make it unconsciously too personal to be palatable. Years later Emil Ludwig, in anger, referred to the illegitimate defenders of legitimacy and the monarchist principle, having Viereck in mind. Others, less overt, had still more to say—and it was said with increasing frequency.

In discussing "the morals of Europe," Viereck makes some observations in regard to himself that are of peculiar interest in the light of his subsequent career.

"Ladies and gentlemen, who have followed me so far, are you not astounded at my conservatism?" he asks. And he immediately answers:

I described myself once as a conservative Anarchist. I am afraid there is little of the Anarchist in my composition today. Europe has transformed and converted me. I have set my face toward order. I fear that a suspicion of respectability always lurked in my heart. Of course, people will never believe me. They imagine that I live the life of an aesthetic tramp, break up homes, and am continually in debt, merely because my name is attached to certain passional studies. A bank account, it seems, is irreconcilable with a poet of passion.

"Dear souls," he is quick and eager to assure the ladies and gentlemen,

I am really a Philistine. I am scrupulously honest, and as for wild oats, I have never sown them. Poets, like the comets, those celestial Bohemians, are privileged to deviate from their orbits. My actions may at times contradict my words. Do not, therefore, question my sincerity. I certainly must refuse to live up to all the things I am preaching. At the present, however, I believe in them. I have forsaken my radical affiliations. I have returned to the fold. But, alas, no fatted calf is in sight. I made more money when I was supposed to be wicked.

And at the very end of the chapter, he returns to the engrossing subject of money, which interests him in spite of himself. "I turn an honest penny wherever I can," he admits. "While my attitude toward the Golden Calf is not one of worship, I approach it with considerable respect. Every dollar is so much potential energy imprisoned. But I refuse to water my literary stock for any amount of money. That is the only way an artist can be immoral."

For the rest, the chapter is a Viereckian preachment on the theme that "sex has nothing to do with morals" and belongs to the sphere of passion, "being natural, it is unmoral." Europe has a realization of this, Viereck says; America has not. Hence in this country, we forgive the most astonishing lapses in our masters of wealth and power. They may rob us and shamelessly deceive us, but as long as they succeed in their piracy, they are heroes. Europe, on the contrary, expects personal integrity from its leaders. It will forgive their sexual lapses and pecadillos, but it will not countenance theft of the public treasury. The European concept of morals is, in other words, a higher one than ours.

Chapters on "Adam and Eve" and "Some Women" of his life, the "Intellectual Drama," "Things Literary," "The Sage of Copenhagen," being his celebrated interview with George Brandes that led to a curious exchange of letters with Brandes, and chapters on "Gambrinus and Bachus," "We and Europe," and, finally, "I and America" complete the book. A close study of the volume is the prelude to a definitive study of the Viereck who was then all of twenty-four years old. Much of the content of the book is implicit in what we have narrated of his youth. The book merely gives an autobiographical version of what we have, more or less objectively, set forth. Viereck necessarily writes of himself, when his subject is ostensibly some dead emperor. There is a passage which must be taken as a final quotation from the book because of its particular aptness.

"Already an aura of myths surrounds my head with a nebulous halo," Viereck says with evident satisfaction. "I shall be a legendary figure before I die. That is the reason why I have deliberately courted a bad reputation. It is a valuable asset for a poet of passion. When Swinburne lost it by moving to Putney Hill with Mr. Watts Dunton, the savor went out of his song. I am convinced I shall never lose my evil glamor. I have builded too well for that. And an hundred hands were stretched out to help me. Even if I weary, my friends, I feel sure, will persist in supporting the tottering structure."

Withal, he had very little knowledge of the future he was building for himself and the parts his friends would play in it. Greater prescience might have daunted him, might have caused the cream of his wit to sour. Some friends may have suspected it, but certainly they did not advise him. The author of his existence—his father—to whom, in full parade, he dedicated the book—did not suspect it, nor did he advise him. It might be more accurate to say that they made no particular point of their advice, for inevitably they felt confident that their ever-assured offspring would flout all that they might say! Curiously enough, the American ambassador to Germany, David Jayne Hill, took great pains to give Viereck some fatherly advice. He knew and admired the talents of Viereck, but he was afraid of them and, like a worried parent, attempted to steer the young man's course. Viereck enjoyed the attentions of the genial ambassador, but he preferred to be his own pilot.

16   FIRST EFFORTS AS GERMAN-AMERICAN EDITOR

Viereck confessed that his early associations with German-American affairs bored him. He rebelled against his father's preoccupation with German *kultur* and politics. He was a literary man in the Anglo-Saxon lyric tradition, while his father was of heavier paste. His friendships, as if to spite his father, were more frequently Anglo-Saxon, Irish, or Jewish than German, and he was trying to be American. But a change came over him when his father returned to Germany around 1911. He suddenly discovered that he had a father complex, and, as if in atonement for his not always concealed impatience with things German, he became more strongly pro-German. Alexander Harvey could no longer call him anti-German! In truth, Viereck disliked only the bourgeois element of his people. The Hohenzollern blood reasserted itself, at first gently and then with more insistence. *Confessions of a Barbarian* was one of the first important results.

At the celebration of "German Day," August 3, 1908, in Columbus, Ohio, young Viereck delivered a speech in the German language, under the auspices of the National German-American Alliance. "Twenty-five thousand Americans of German descent listened to the speaker and by their cheers and applause expressed enthusiastic approval of the views" of Viereck, claimed the publication which reprinted Viereck's speech in full. "Germans of Ohio," the speech began, at once capturing a Teutonic spirit, "The fathers of the republic, with the help of German blood and brain, have freed our country from *external* shackles, but it is the Teutonic spirit that preserves its freedom *within*." Then Viereck launched into an attack on the prohibition forces which were gathering strength. Viereck took his stand as a liberty-loving Teuton. "Above all," he said,

> the friends of personal freedom must beware of concessions, however
> justifiable or small they may seem. There is a German proverb to the

effect that if you give the devil the little finger he takes the whole hand.
Local option is the little finger of prohibition. Alcohol is food, just as
coffee and bread. But who would dream of leaving it to the jurisdiction
of any locality to decide whether the use of coffee or bread should be
legal within its limits? The principle of compromise is English; it is
un-German. We should persevere in that unyielding faith to a principle
once avowed, which is the distinguishing mark of the German.

The fight against prohibition in the prewar years was essentially a Teutonic
fight, for the very good reason that the breweries of the country were largely in the
hands of wealthy German-Americans. Viereck joined in this fight for a combination of reasons. Naturally he was for personal liberty, his professional interest was
to support German-American causes, and (not least of all) he was on terms of
intimacy with many of the leading brewers, Adolphus Busch, for one. Busch and
other German-American interests advertised in the pages of Viereck's publications; indeed, their advertisements gave Viereck's magazines the bulk of paid
matter that the magazines carried. When Busch died, Viereck wrote a poem in his
praise. He was closely associated, too, with members of the Busch family, the
most important in the brewing industry. There was a curious little article by
Viereck in one of the issues of the *International* concerning a temperance drink put
out by Busch to compete with other soft drinks and to confound the prohibitionists.
It is no worse to praise a drink than a work of art, said Viereck, as if to free himself
from the suspicion that he was writing an unlabeled advertisement.

Similarly, in the course of his speech at Columbus, Ohio, the adroit young
man was careful to get in words of praise for the magazine he and his father were
then editing: "The great German movement, of which even the National German
Alliance is only a part, has found its own magazine in *Der Deutsche Vorkaempfer*."
Viereck acted as a sort of literary editor of the magazine, furnishing whatever
lightness distinguished its more or less heavy pages, and when Papa Viereck and
his Frau returned to Germany to regain their lost youth, young Viereck assumed
complete control of the magazine. His interest in German American *kultur* increasing, Viereck sought to augment his own usefulness and importance. He was then a
member of the staff of *Current Literature* and beloved of Edward Jewitt Wheeler,
his editor-in-chief. That gave him large ideas for his future as an editor. He felt that
there was room in abundance for a magazine or scope which would cater to the
intellectual needs, not only of Germans in America, but of Germans in the
fatherland and throughout the world. It was to be a magazine that would interpret
America to Germany and Germany to America. Built upon the same general plan
as *Current Literature* it would appeal to the same sort of public, a public united by
racial ties.

But such things cost money, much more, indeed, than poets generally have at
their disposal. Viereck suggested to Wheeler that it might be a good policy on the
part of *Current Literature* to adopt his idea—to sponsor his new magazine as the
German edition of *Current Literature*. Wheeler was willing to do so, provided that

substantial financial guarantees were forthcoming. Such a proviso is likely to mean first a dash of cold water, then a chill, and finally sudden death and burial. But to the young enthusiast it was a challenge. He remembered that the international banker, Otto H. Kahn, had promised to spread "the protecting wings of finance over poetry." He remembered other contacts, his wealthy brewery friends, the ever-faithful Max Hein who, with his wife, was as a foster parent to him, Professor Hugo Munsterberg, and Hugo Reisinger, the art patron.

One day in October 1910, he was able to write his parents a letter brimful of joy. *"Liebste Maus und vielgeliebte Pentarch,"* ("Dearest mouse and well-beloved Pentarch), he began with the quaint greeting he had adopted for his parents, "Preserve this letter, because it is historical." The letter was indeed epochal, if a bit overwrought. "The Hundred Million Dollar Lunch has taken place and was socially a bombshell." True enough! It was something in the nature of a social bombshell, this luncheon to raise funds for a new German magazine.

At ten minutes to one—the time, like all the other details, made a permanent impression on Viereck's mind—on the momentous day of the Hundred Million Dollar Lunch, Viereck called at the office of Theodore Roosevelt, at the headquarters of the *Outlook* magazine, in order to escort him to the luncheon. The reception room had been filled with those many persons who wanted to see the great man, but "Teddy," putting on his favorite smile and displaying his best teeth, had the young poet ushered into his most private office.

"If you were the right sort of Dutchman I'd say this to you," the former president said in a tone of familiarity, making a complimentary remark in Dutch, which Viereck could not wholly understand.

The two were in the elevator, and Viereck felt he had to say something to express his intense satisfaction. "Mr. Roosevelt," he said, "this is a historic moment for me." Again the teeth of Teddy flashed with pleasure.

"Es soll der Dichter mit dem König gehen," Viereck said to Roosevelt. "Let the bard walk with the king."

"Yes," Roosevelt laughed, "—but in this case a retired king."

The young man felt that it was quite enough for his purposes. Presently the two were at the National Arts Club, where Viereck had assembled those who were to be his guests with Roosevelt: Munsterberg, the poet Brachvogel, Wheeler, Alfred Rau, Otto H. Kahn, and a few others. Viereck seated himself to the left of Roosevelt and gazed across the long table. While the turtle soup was served, he thought of Kahn and observed with satisfaction that Kahn ate with an appetite, knowing well that each bite was to be paid for dearly. With the bluefish a la Meuniere, Viereck's thoughts dwelt upon Reisinger, the kinsman by marriage of Busch. The last luncheon to which Viereck had invited him had cost Reisinger one thousand dollars and Busch an equal amount by way of contributions. Through the food and liquor and cigars and cigarettes, Viereck added up the costs of his guests, and with a little less satisfaction it occurred to him that he himself was spending all of one hundred dollars.

The luncheon featured a monologue by Roosevelt; only the author of *Nineveh* got in a few words edgewise. Teddy felt completely at home, as if he were among his old cronies. He professed an extravagant admiration for things German; for Wilhelm of Potsdam, he expressed liking and respect. "With the exception of the Kaiser," he said, speaking of the crowned heads of Europe, "there was not one of them whom I would treat as an intellectual equal if they were here at this table." There was a pause of only a moment's duration: "I told the Kaiser, that of all the Kings I have seen you are the only one who could carry his own ward, if you were an American politician"—the supreme tribute in a political mind! "The other kings are good fellows, but not men of culture."

After the dessert, Viereck rose and delivered a flaming oration. "You loomed large in that speech," Wheeler whispered to him. The peroration fit the occasion: "and if the most representative American in the world today, a former president of the United States, lends us his enthusiastic support, shall we German-Americans shirk our share in the work?" "No," was the answer, to the tune of ten thousand dollars. Roosevelt sought to stir up more enthusiasm. "As patriotic Americans we must welcome the interpretation of German ideals," he said in the course of another long monologue which followed Viereck's talk. Again Teddy told of his dislike of the English: "I have always treated them in a patronizing way," he said, feeling no doubt that Germans necessarily relished anti-British speech. As a matter of fact, the non-German, Wheeler, was impressed to an extreme. He later said to Viereck, "I have the same feeling in Roosevelt's presence as I have in reading Shakespeare, because of the universality of the man. I always knew he was great, but he is even greater than I thought."

In leaving, Roosevelt thanked his young host for a "delightful time." "It was most instructive," he said. Later he thanked Viereck, once again wishing him success in his magazine project. Still later, in a letter dated December 23, 1910, Roosevelt reemphasized his good wishes. "I feel that in America there is especial need of keeping alive a thorough knowledge of German," he wrote to his young admirer, "and I believe that your magazine will not only help in this direction, but will help in the converse way, by interpreting American events to your readers beyond the ocean." And, like a good politician, he permitted a photograph of himself to be taken, showing a copy of Viereck's new magazine upon his desk.

Thus, blessed by a former president of the United States, the magazine, *Rundschau Zweier Welten,* was launched auspiciously. The renowned Jacob H. Schiff had a good word to say for it, as did the German consul-general and the well-known congressman Richard Bartholdt, Paul Warburg, Munsterberg, of course, and many others. A broadside issued by the Current Literature Publishing Co. hailed the launching of the magazine as an international event. "It will be one of the essential periodicals," said the broadside, "to all who read the German language, whether resident in Germany, in the United States, in South America, or in other parts of the globe." The sixty-eight pages of each monthly issue of the magazine were, indeed, sightly and sprightly. Each issue had a review and commentary on world events and departments relating to "Men and Women of the Hour," (the first one dealt with "the future German Kaiser"—whose "future" has not yet arrived!), "Science and Technique," "Ethics and Religion," "Music and Drama," "Literature and Art," "New Poetry," "German Affairs," "Trade, Finance and Industry," and "Wit and Humor." It was a well-rounded publication and it should have succeeded, but, alas, it died after a year's ambitious effort, becoming part of the *International*. Did the failure stem from weakness in the German-American ranks? Viereck's German interests remained and gathered strength. They were to require strength in the years that followed.

17   THE POET TAKES OUT
          HIS LICENSE

There are at least three reasons for designating the years 1910 and 1911 important ones in the career of the playboy of Parnassus who bore the name George Sylvester Viereck. The three reasons or events are interconnected and should not, perhaps, be treated separately, though at the time they seemed fairly distinct from each other.

The first event was the publication of a volume of poetry called *The Younger Choir*. The volume was not ambitious in size—there were hardly more than one hundred pages in it—and it did not bear the imprint of any established publisher. The editors of an insurgent magazine, called *Moods*, forerunner of *The International*, had issued the volume. The editors had been fortunate enough to persuade the generous-hearted old poet, Edwin Markham, to write an introduction to the volume, but that good fortune carried with it a certain sobering influence on Viereck. Markham had exercised the prerogative of watering down the contents of the volume, not enough, to be sure, to destroy the rebel note, but enough to make it less audible. In his introduction to the volume, Markham drew certain interesting parallels. Wordsworth and Coleridge, he said, had sent forth their *Lyrical Ballads* at the end of the eighteenth century; out of that joint venture came two immortal poems, *Tintern Abbey* and *The Rime of the Ancient Mariner*. A half-century later the Pre-Raphaelites, under Rossetti, issued *The Germ,* an artistic publication from which sprung one immortal poem, *The Blessed Damozel.* From these two instances, Markham concluded that the world belongs to the young; to them God lends inspiration. And now, said Markham, there is a group of young people in America who are carrying on the apostolate of poesy. These men, he said, are represented in the volume, *The Younger Choir*. Markham was glad to observe the moral health of the poems in the volume, the absence of the hectic fevers of the decadents, the freedom from the eroticism of sodden satiety. He found a wholesome spiritual atmosphere in the book, a sweetness and warmth that pleased him.

Included in the volume were poems by thirty-six poets including, besides Viereck, Elsa Barker, Zona Gale, Joyce Kilmer, William Ellery Leonard, Ludwig Lewisohn, James Oppenheim, Seumas O'Sheel, George Sterling, Ridgely Torrence, Charles Hanson Towne, and Louis Untermeyer. Not all of the poems had the tone of sweetness and light that had been blessed by Markham. Viereck, for example, had hymned "iron passion" in a poem of that name. He had asked love to come to him with cruel, loveless eyes. The significance of the volume, then, was not that the younger choir had turned saintly—that would have been an unforgivable reversion to the outmoded tradition of gentility. The true significance of the volume almost escaped Markham: it was simply that there was so large a number of genuine poets practicing the lyrical art in America. More than ever before in the literary history of this country, poetry was an art independent of churchly precepts and popular for its own sake. The reason for the happy change was evident; it could be summed up in George Sylvester Viereck. The publication of *Nineveh* three years before had unlocked the floodgates of song. *The Younger Choir* was a visible token of this.

It has more than once been said that in 1910 few would have denied Viereck's leadership of the insurgents. Many, like Louis Untermeyer, regretted it, but they could not deny the fact. In the nature of things, it was fitting that Viereck was selected as the first American Exchange Poet, sent to lecture on "America as a Land of Poets" during the summer of 1911 at the University of Berlin. In Berlin the event was treated as a great one; it was thought proper to have the young American poet introduced by three distinguished Germans. Privy Councilor Dr. Alois Brandl, professor of English literature at the University and an eminent Shakespearean scholar, joined Dr. Ludwig Fulda and Hugo Munsterberg in presenting Viereck to the large audience. Fulda and Munsterberg took particular pride in the occasion, for they could truthfully call themselves leaders in the discovery of the gifts of the young poet. "George Sylvester Viereck is Germany's first contributor to American literature," said Munsterberg.

Viereck spoke of an "undiscovered, esoteric America, where religion and poetry dwell." In America, he said, poetry stood in strange contrast to our feverish industrial development. In seeming protest against the prevailing materialism, our poets address themselves chiefly to the spirit; they concern themselves with the ethical and the speculative. But missionaries are needed for this esoteric America of song, so that poetry might raise its voice above the turmoil of American life. One difficulty, continued Viereck, was that our poets employ erudite language and substitute philosophical problems for elementary emotions; our poets isolate themselves in the chilly regions of ethics. The erotic element is lacking in the younger poets; they betrayed beauty for ethics. The hopeful fact that emerged, however, was that there are at least fifty poets in America who sound their own notes, not borrowed tunes. Viereck called the attention of the audience to the volume, *The Younger Choir,* as evidence of the promising situation here.

The poets of America, he said, can be divided into four groups: *first,* the ones like Whitman, who were of the soil and who sang of comradeship and pantheistic democracy; *second,* the poets like Poe who were apart from time and space, real aristocrats and aesthetic egotists who were infallible in rhythmic beauty; *third,* followers of Longfellow, Whittier, and other traditionalists, who were the middle class of the spirit; and *fourth,* the lyric insurgents, disciples of Poe and Whitman who heard the passional strains of Swinburne and Baudelaire.

Of course, there were variations and blends. Whitman, said Viereck, was not as spontaneous and naive as he pretended; he had some of the tricks of Barnum, as well as genuine greatness and a tremendous individuality. His poems were studies in the psychology of sex rather than authentic poems of passion, and his empire fell apart in the hands of his disciples: Horace Traubel, Richard Hovey, Bliss Carman, Edwin Markham, and others. Among the poets without habitations, so to speak, who were followers of Poe, Viereck placed George Santayana, Louise Imogen Guiney, Lizette Woodworth Reese, and William Vaughn Moody.

He named, with varying degrees of praise, as representative of the lyric insurgents the poets included in *The Younger Choir.*

"These poets," he said, "are the true heirs of Whitman and of Poe. They have inherited Poe's technique and added thereto the element of passion. From Whitman they have received the Americanism which makes itself strongly felt, especially in their fantastically impressionistic pictures of American cities. They dare to attack the great problems which fascinated Whitman and they possess at the same time the plastic sense which is absent from him."

America is not one country culturally but many, he went on. There are literary cliques in various localities, but between them no intimate connection exists. One of the purposes of the newly organized Poetry Society of America is to create a belletristic center for America, Viereck said. The society bids fair to become a "lyric academy" and it may, in the best sense, popularize poetry. Viereck expressed the hope that there would be an exchange of poets between America and Europe, so that Puritanism might be dispelled. "After me others will come," he said, "worthier than I to proclaim the poetic gospel of the New World in the heart of the Old." It was an unexpectedly humble attitude in one who had thought himself the greatest of American poets. The first result was that the *Amerika-Institut* in Berlin, founded by Munsterberg, requested a complete library of American poetry for the benefit of German students.

In his German lecture Viereck had mentioned the newly formed Poetry Society of America with *The Younger Choir* as a sign that American poetry was coming of age. Viereck had been instrumental in organizing the society. Despite his extreme individualism, he felt that the poets were in need of some craft solidarity, some greater degree of fellowship, so as to combat the Philistines. He interested his friends in the project, notably Isaac Rice and his talented daughters, whose luxurious New York apartment was thrown open to the poets as a sort of salon. Greystone, the home of Mrs. Samuel Untermeyer, was dedicated to a similar purpose. Invitations were sent out to prospective members in the winter of 1909–10, not only to practicing poets but also to lovers of letters, artists, actors, writers, all who might have some interest in high endeavor. The movement gained momentum under Viereck's leadership in part because the staff of *Current Literature* took to the idea with enthusiasm. Viereck acted as a provisional secretary and Wheeler as chairman. At length the first meeting was held in the Rice home. Leon Dabo, the brilliant artist and *causeur,* spoke of the beauties of the salon, and others joined in the song of praise. But suddenly it became apparent that what was required was not a salon, which was construed to be more or less private, but a more formal society free of dilettantism. Viereck, despite his feelings of friendship for the Rices, accepted the more inclusive idea. At once ambitious plans were formulated. A larger group of poets was invited to join and a greater air of seriousness developed. More satisfactory results were obtained, largely through Jessie Rittenhouse's acceptance of the permanent secretaryship and not a little because of the continued efforts of Viereck.

The newspapers seized the idea as a humorous one. It appeared to them as a matter for laughter, not always good-natured, that the poets of America had formed a union, just like the plumbers and carpenters and steam-fitters. Column after column appeared in the press, dealing particularly with Viereck as the ringleader. Cartoonists were kept busy. If attention meant anything, the society was assured of a great success, and it did, indeed, win such a success, though some poets agreed with the newspapers that poetry was an individualistic art that should know nothing of trade solidarity. Ridgely Torrence, for one, had serious misgivings; but he and most of the best poets joined the Poetry Society of America. Membership in it was taken as a matter of course by all who aspired to serious lyric poetry.

Among those who Viereck proposed for membership in the society was Mrs. Corinne Roosevelt Robinson, sister of the former president of the United States. Years later she joined the movement for Viereck's expulsion from the society, but at the time no one thought of expulsions. No one could think of any reason for expelling a poet from the society of his fellows. It was to be a poetry society, not a political party. The group devotion was to be to the Muses, not to the demogogues. Unlike the Supreme Court, the society was not to follow, in the words of Mr. Dooley, the election returns. So it was thought, at any rate, in 1910 and the first season thereafter.

Viereck maintained his interest in the society for a while; then other matters began to engross him. He began to be impatient and discomfited; his anarchistic mind began to revolt. He did not need a union card to practice his art. He did not need a license. The society ceased to amuse him, though he did not regret his part in its formation. It was a toy that he would fondle at times, but not with any overwhelming interest. There were other playthings, and he turned to them with more pleasure.

But these three events—the publication of *The Younger Choir,* Viereck's lecture in Berlin, and the founding of the Poetry Society of America—were clear proofs of Viereck's dominance of American poetry and, at the same time, tokens that there were other poets in the land. A fourth event began in the nature of a triumph for Viereck, but its ultimate meaning was that American poetry was about to take a different course from that charted by Viereck. Ludwig Lewisohn is authority for the statement that Viereck anonymously planned and inspired the anthology, *The Lyric Year,* which ushered in modern American literature in 1912. Lewisohn, seconded by others, has selected the year 1912 as a crucial one of American letters because it saw the first issue of *Poetry: A Magazine of Verse* and the first volumes of William Ellery Leonard (other than private and semiprivate ones), Vachel Lindsay, and Amy Lowell, and the publication of *The Lyric Year,* which contained, among other things, *Renascence* by Edna St. Vincent Millay. The net meaning was that Viereck's struggle against Puritanism had become obsolete, almost as old-fashioned, in a way, as the moral sermons of Channing and Beecher and Everett. American poetry began to concern itself with the experimentation with technical forms and patterns of thought alien to Viereck. Believing that free verse is mostly "degraded prose" and looking with suspicion on the bizarre contents of the poetry that began to be written, Viereck found himself once more out of step with the crowd. He began to feel that if American poetry has been diverted from the course he proposed, so much the worse for the American Muse. But the poets did not think so, and Viereck's poetic dominance was at an end. For two more years, he was the most conspicuous American lyrical poet, and then he was sent to coventry, seldom to be mentioned as a poet.

One of those who knew him best during this critical period in his career was Blanche Shoemaker Wagstaff, who drew an unusually valuable full-length verbal portrait of Viereck. In many respects, they were akin. They were both in their early twenties at this time and planning to conquer the world. She had begun to write ardent love poetry at seven and of "satiety" at sixteen. They both had a natural interest in biochemistry and in the more daring thinkers and poets, a devastating group that shook their foundations but led them to stabler, profounder truths. Their intellectual explorations were, as Mrs. Wagstaff said, a sort of vagabondage, almost orgiastic in nature, though their personal relations were platonic. They first met in the days of poetic fervor at the meetings of the newly formed Poetry Society of America:

> There, with flaming tie, gold-glinted hair, seductive hands and voice of bell-like beauty, he would discant to groups of neophytes on the 'New' poetry—or rather, exclusively, his poetry. . . . His magnetism was something electrical. During the gathering of poets in the old grim corridors, he would rise to his feet in flamboyant argument, gesturing with fine grace, and invoking intellectual fusillades. Not everyone liked Viereck. Many feared him. In this fear of his caustic brilliant tongue and exotic personality, there was jealousy, as well as dislike of his aggressiveness, his glorious assurance, his abundant talents. May there not have been in all this dominating brilliance and egoism, a lack of some essential equilibrium which mitigated against his broader success with more substantial people?

Viereck and Mrs. Wagstaff were constantly together, engaged in thrilling literary labors: writing for *The International;* "discovering" Amy Lowell; launching Robert Frost; repudiating Gertrude Stein. They carried on a correspondence on a very intense scale—Mrs. Wagstaff was "Lilith," he "Lucifer"—the temptress and the arch-corruptor. Lilith felt that Lucifer's letters were extraordinary; she never read more brilliant outpourings. But the execrable calligraphy caused her to lose much. They exchanged many poems. Viereck was seldom happier than sitting in the ornate Louis XV room in the Wagstaff home and reciting one of his latest poems. He left his listeners breathless. "The words would die away on his lips, a cadence soft as a lily." Mrs. Wagstaff wrote her best prose and poetry under his influence. She said that he was tremendously generous to other writers, if he liked them, and because he liked her, he did all he could to assist her. She felt that she possibly would have been a better writer if she had not become estranged from Viereck.

Looking back on those years, she contended that Viereck's streak of exhibitionism was the source of both his success and failure. We can reveal only so much of ourselves, she said, without causing complications. "Taking the scalpel to one's emotions is justified to a certain extent." Viereck overstepped these limits and as a result suffered. When he was disrobing as a young man, he was fascinating, but soon he became too bold, too eroticized. Even in her later years she considered him an influence in American and perhaps world poetry. His egotism, a defense left over from a mother complex, crucified him, she felt. "But he is a unique American—now of an almost remote age, but nevertheless a vital force in the currents that in the early years of this century were to forge what is present-day American poetry. His passion, his exuberance, his classic flavor, his romance, his fervid sincerity, his wealth of erudition, his splendid respect for form, make him one of the last of the *ancien regime*. His influence has been so well assimilated that only those who were associated with him realize its proportions. None have come to replace his high tradition, for modern poetry has a different character today. Then it expressed the experience of soul and sense. Now it is hard and machine-made and passionless as the age it represents."

In her mind the period when he wrote *The Candle and the Flame*—the book appeared in that miraculous year 1912—was his best. Then he was super-sensitive to beauty, to love, to the things of the intellect. It was his time of exploration, his best because he was most free from everything, save the purest aesthetic ambition. But in this she was mistaken. She failed to see the schism in Viereck's personality that came to a head in that same year, 1912.

18   A VERY RESTLESS YOUNG MAN

In 1912, five years after *Nineveh* had appeared, the publishers issued a second volume of Viereck's poetry. Though it was approximately the same size and, superficially, of the same general nature, it actually was vastly different in meaning. Five years is a long while for a poet to refrain from publishing a second book of verse if his first is as sensationally successful as *Nineveh* was. Stray verses by Viereck had, of course, appeared in many magazines, and he was still at the head of the Younger Choir. His displacement was not as obvious as it appears now in retrospect. But it was, nevertheless, something to be remarked upon, this absence from the poetic book marts, and it called for explanation. The explanation is, in a very real sense, the elucidation of Viereck's entire career and is found, not very well hidden, in an examination of the new volume and those which had preceded it.

The Candle and the Flame, the new book of verse, was mysteriously dedicated ''to Poppy.'' There was no word as to her identity, though there was some special significance to all the other dedications in the book. Individual poems in the book were addressed to the several persons, who at that time were influences in Viereck's life. In at least one respect the subsidiary dedication was of more importance than the principal one. A modest, tender poem, Viereck's chief contribution to Woolf's dramatic version of *The Vampire,* was inscribed to a slip of a girl, a yellow-haired, silk-white child named Margaret Edith Hein, generally called Gretchen. The poem, tucked away in the middle of the book, was the first printed acknowledgment of an infatuation that was to grow into the great love of Viereck's life. Other poems were dedicated to Viereck's associates on *Current Literature,* Dr. Edward Wheeler, Leonard Abbott and Alexander Harvey, with whom his relations were still of the friendliest; and the *Plaint of Eve* was addressed with good reason, to one of the many Liliths of his life and letters, Blanche Shoemaker Wagstaff.

But it was not in the dedications scattered throughout the volume that its significance lay. The poems, seemingly passional studies like those in *Nineveh,* were much different in tone. By then the full force of the sexual views of Dr. Magnus Hirschfeld, an old friend of the Viereck family, had dawned upon Viereck; and Freud was no longer a name to him but a fascinating reality and a force of incalculable importance. Viereck's earlier readings in Havelock Ellis and Krafft-Ebing were still fresh in his memory, and Wedekind's dramatic presentation of the problems of puberty weighed upon him. These things were reflected in the poems included in *The Candle and the Flame* and, particularly, in the marginalia appended to the book, offered gratuitously to assist his readers in "finding" him. I have found myself, he told his readers; now, with the help of these notes, you may find me.

The book began with a preface far longer than that which had opened Viereck's previous volumes, a preface not only longer but of greater import. It was provocative to a degree, for that was the identifying badge of the young Viereck. And not only in manner was it provocative. It was Viereck's valedictory to a certain phase of his career. Sensing the importance of the book in his own life and suspecting that it might be of general value, Viereck talked in shrill notes that he might be heard; his singing, fortunately, was less loud.

"This, in all likelihood, will be my last book of verse," said Viereck, feeling that he was making a momentous announcement. Without pausing to learn the effect, he went on to give the reason for his strange prophecy: "I no longer worship Beauty. Art for art's sake seems a jest, literature only a sickly mirage of life. My temperament is more dynamic than aesthetic. Activity, as such, allures me. Brooklyn Bridge seems to me a far more marvelous accomplishment than the most precious of sonnets. If I were not Viereck, I would gladly be Edison." "The spirit of America has eaten into my heart. Wall Street is more interesting to me than Parnassus."

Half hopeful that he is not expressing his innermost convictions, Viereck states the reason for his curious repugnance for poetry, and the reason suggested the cure. It was simply that "poetry, being the child of tradition, must necessarily lag behind the times"; poets "must write of the new in terms of the old," for "the new terms have not yet acquired the connotative poetic values which . . . take decades for their growth." Since poetry cannot catch up with life, he will live life and cease creating poor transcripts of it!

Viereck was careful to distinguish *The Candle and the Flame* from the *Nineveh* volume, and the distinction is certainly a real one. "In this book," he says, "I pass from the physics to the metaphysics of passion." But he feels that, living in America, he cannot go far enough, thanks to Mrs. Grundy and the keepers of the nurseries. "I am too far ahead of the pageant of American life to go one step further. . . . Seated by the roadside, I shall wait for America to catch up, dividing my time, perchance, between love and the ticker. America forces its poets to deny poetry or leave the country! . . . But the touch of our lyric fire still burns and will continue to burn when it has passed from my hands into those of a younger poet."

Pose or natural to the man, it was an exhibit worthy of preservation. It was the same note that he had sounded, in a milder way, when lecturing at the University of Berlin a year before. "I have no reason to be ungrateful to America," said Viereck, in spite of his distaste for the prevailing mores. "Few poets have met with more instant recognition than I." He went on to rehearse the long list of his triumphs, an impressive list indeed. He could, with confidence, call himself one of the leaders of the lyric insurgents. He had, in truth, given a new impetus to poetry in America. He had added a novel note of passion. He had made sin a "part of the quest of the human soul for the ultimate good," as is abundantly demonstrated in "The Pilgrim," the most strikingly original poem in *The Candle* and possibly the most audacious Viereck had ever written:

> There knocked One nightly at the harlot's house,
> Wan was His mouth as kisses without love.
> His groping fingers followed tremulous
> The winding of her delicate thin veins;
> He traced the waxen contour of her breast,
> And then, as baffled in some strange pursuit,
> Drew her to Him in weariest embrace;
> And, as she shuddered in His grasp, He watched,
> Still passionless, the working of her throat,
> The woman's cheek grew crimson as He gazed,
> But He, a scowling and disgruntled guest,
> Rose white and famished from her body's feast.
> Yet one night, pausing half-way, He turned back,
> Lured by the wraith of long-departed hope;
> And then He asked of her a monstrous thing.
> The strumpet blanched and, rising from the couch,
> Spat in His Face.
>
> Straight way the Stranger's eye
> Blazoned exultant with the pilgrim's joy
> When ends the quest. He lifted up His hands
> In quiet benediction, and a light
> Miraculous upon His forehead shone.
> But she, being blind, still cursed Him, and reviled:
> "Albeit I sell by body for very shame
> I am a woman, not a beast; but thou . . ."
> "And I" quoth He, "a Seeker after God."

Is this not, indeed, the very metaphysics of passion, he could ask, while pointing out that "the monstrous thing" causing the strumpet to blanch is nameless, a hint sufficient that sin and shame are purely subjective and a hint which is the motif running through the whole volume, from the haunting title poem to the last one, a quieter one, called *The Plaint of Eve*.

The title poem tells of the thing in the eye of Love that makes the poet half afraid. As he muses on it and the utter horror of the Infinite enters into his soul, he sees, vaguely, that the passions of mankind, like mystical torches, illumine the darkness of the universe! ''We are the Candle, Love the Flame,'' he expresses it. the consequence appears inevitable to him:

> No bar to passion's fury set,
>> With monstrous poppies spice the wine:
>> For only drunk are we divine,
> And only mad shall we forget!

That is the mystical justification for sexual variety. He carries the thought further in *The Parrot* and extends it beyond the ordinary realms of passion into regions that are as broad as the universe:

> The Life-Force with itself at war
>> Moulds and remoulds us, blood and brain,
>> Yet cannot quench us out again,
> And after every change we *are*.
>> The soul-spark in all sentient things
>> Illumes the night of death and brings,
> Remembered, immortality. . . .

Here, then, is religion in its best sense, linked somehow, if only vaguely, to passion. *Gerisund,* the poem that tells of the child filled with monstrous corruption who was beloved of Charlemagne, is metaphysical and not at all blasphemous. As the grave spits forth the foulness of the harlot-child, the poet is there with her in the night, holding her shrunken hand and praying, with the fine charity of understanding, until dawn. In *Nero in Capri,* passion's embers become a flame that sings and leaps,

> In the concupiscence of heaven,
> And in the incest of the stars!

Passion thus follows the whole course of life. Several poems, including the *Ballad of Montmartre,* the *Ballad of King David* and the incomparable *Children of Lilith* tell of those unfortunates, who live in the forbidden byways of love:

> Made for what end?—by God's great hand,
>> Frail enigmatic shapes, they dwell
> In some phantastic borderland,
>> But on the hitherside of hell!
> Children of Lilith, each a sprite,
>> Yet wrought like us of Adam's clay,
> And when they haunt us in the night
>> What, brother Villon, shall we say?

For all the ways of passion Viereck's Muse expresses lyric sympathy; the way that is tender and the way that is cruel are both trod by him. He can sing of the old, old ways of lass and lad and at the same time call for the iron whips of refusal:

> Wearing the crown of unassuaged desire,
> Break me or bless me—only love me not!

Most of the poems in the volume might be summed up as the successive, distinctive hues of the rainbow of sex. The soul of good in things hideous and the tangent of virtue in the course of evil are the general themes of the poems and of the marginalia appended to the book. But in the end, life becomes to Viereck, in the resigned mood of *The Cynic's Credo,* something purely physical, the metaphysical resolving itself into the highly dubious:

> From the cloistered walls of knowledge where
>   phantastic lights are shed
> By a thousand twisted mirrors, and the
>   dead entomb their dead,
> Let us walk into the city where men's
>   wounds are raw and red.
> Three gifts only Life, the strumpet, holds
>   for coward and for brave,
> Only three, no more—the belly and the
>   phallus and the grave!

The critics, including the more sympathetic ones, did not like the volume as much as *Nineveh* in spite of the fact that the 1912 volume gave not only more of Viereck but more of value. The comparative lack of praise was proof that Viereck the poet was at the end of the road, so far as America was concerned, and as he realized. Of course, he continued to receive some praise and attention; but he himself began to feel that the well was running dry.

In 1912, heralded by a brochure of ebullient praise, his publisher issued the *Works of George Sylvester Viereck* in five volumes. This might superficially be taken as evidence that, far from nearing the end of his popularity, Viereck was approaching the high tide of his career. *The Complete Works of George Sylvester Viereck* told a tale that made it easier for Viereck to be supplanted in the kingdom of poesy.

This was sensed, first of all, in the extreme variety of his works and then in their surprising brevity. The first volume, *A Game At Love,* was less than a hundred pages in length and consisted of rapid-fire playlets of passion. The second volume was the memorable *Nineveh,* one hundred pages of poems, most of them very short and none exceptionally long. Then came the novel, *The House of the Vampire,* less than two hundred pages in length, and the critical study of America and Europe, which Viereck styled *Confessions of a Barbarian* and which he could not stretch past two hundred pages. Finally, there was *The Candle and the Flame*, the later volume of poems, only slightly over one hundred pages, which differed basically from the earlier volume of poems. *The Complete Works* consisted, in other words, of seven or eight hundred large-type pages of poems, plays, essays, and a story, nothing, it appears, of a really sustained nature. Viereck's talents were thus tossed to the winds like bits of confetti. The two little volumes of German verse only reemphasized the fact. Size, it is true, has no bearing on quality, and variety may indicate great ability, but in Viereck's case the notable fact that arose from the brevity and variety of his writings was the extreme restlessness of his nature. He experimented, not out of the largeness of his genius, but because he wanted to find himself.

Between times, to be sure, Viereck wrote for various magazines both in English and in German, edited other magazines in two languages, traveled, engaged in business activities and in politics, and played at love and at living. All of this is implicit in his life until 1912 and is given the sanction of Viereck's own approval in the challenging preface to *The Candle and the Flame*. That preface also made evident that basic changes were about to take place in Viereck's life. Would the stars scanned by Elsa Barker, the stars which had foretold a transvaluation of all Viereck's values, begin to remold his fate? She continued to wonder about and he to forget the prophecy made in 1906.

The political campaign of 1912 presented something in the nature of an answer to the question. Motivated, he thought, by his new-found admiration for the man Theodore Roosevelt and by the welling within him of pools of social consciousness, Viereck found himself taking an active part in the historic Progressive campaign of that year. He attended the Republican and then the Progressive conventions. He wrote Roosevelt's campaign hymn, which he declaimed from a dozen or more platforms. Day and night he campaigned for Teddy until his efforts were known to the leaders and won their warm approbation. In recognition of his services, he was given a place on the Progressive ticket as a Roosevelt elector in the State of New York. Blinded by his partisanship, he thought the election of Roosevelt a strong possibility. It thrilled him, and it compensated for some of the deficiencies of his poetry. It also created some of his dissatisfaction with the Muses. Having tasted the sweets of action and played a part in a dynamic political campaign, Viereck began to see Parnassus as a barren hill. Necessarily, he cast his eyes about for new steeps to climb and new victories to win over literature. Viereck was seeking some cause to which to fasten himself with deep loyalty. Whether he knew it or not, he was prepared to make fatal decisions and perhaps illogical plunges into mad seas. When *The Candle and the Flame* appeared in 1912, Viereck was less than two years away from the most dynamic phase of his career, and he was reaching for it, longingly, gropingly, perhaps ignorantly. As Elsa Barker might have said, the stars took their predestined course, and his life was being touched.

To enter into the details of Viereck's efforts in behalf of Roosevelt would add nothing new to the story and would hardly indicate the goal Viereck had in mind.

One could have sensed an essential falseness in the tone of the campaign hymn he had composed. Politics was not to be the promised way of redemption for Viereck. There was no conscious hypocrisy in the language of the poem; Viereck felt he was sincere. He did try to capture a mood of social sympathy and, in a fashion, succeeded. His success was in versifying the Progressive platform of 1912; his failure was in not giving ultimate expression to ageless longings for meliorization. It is no answer to say that Roosevelt himself was essentially tinsel and that, therefore, a deep and abiding poem could not be written about him. Masterpieces have been written of lesser men. The simple fact is that no social program could strike a deep chord within Viereck and still his emotional aches and pains.

Social principles meant little to Viereck; they could not cause him to invite the hemlock with a glad heart, and so he could not win a philosophical peace. He used to tell his friend, Leonard Abbott, that the magazine, *Current Literature,* for which both worked, was ruining Abbott's career, for the magazine's eclectic policy made it impossible for Abbott to adopt a positive course of action and of thought. No matter what one said to Abbott, he could comment indecisively, "There is some truth in what you say." Though Viereck thus realized what Abbott's difficulty was, he failed to see that he himself suffered from a similar ailment of uncertainty. Writing each month in explanation of the most contradictory ideas current in the world of thought and depicting many strange animals, Viereck lost his native sense of direction. He began to be troubled as fears arose within him that he was lost. These fears led him to experiment impatiently, but he could pursue no experiment to its end. He flitted about the world of ideas and of action like a butterfly blinded by the light. Suddenly he saw what he thought was a star, and he was guided by it while it shown in the skies in the midst of other suns.

19 "THE INTERNATIONAL" BREAKS TRAILS

The cover of a magazine bearing the date January 1914 and the fate which befell it tell, in brief, the story of a generation from one viewpoint. The cover advertised an article by Havelock Ellis called "The New Freedom," and it suggested an article on Richard Strauss' "Rosenkavalier" music, but it was not because of such things that it was of importance. After all, Havelock Ellis had already established his fame, and the prosecution of the publisher of his opus on the psychology of sex was distinctly in the past; Ellis was almost a respectable man now; so, too, the long controversies over Richard Strauss had abated.

It was a drawing of a "nyked lydy" that caused all the difficulty. There she was on the cover of *The International* of January 1914, almost like a Beardsley drawing, except that there was something human and invidious about her. Her nose and face strained upward, as if better to reveal her subtle throat, her breasts pointed outward, one hand placed symmetrically above one breast, subtly accentuating it, the other hand clenched feelingly at the side of her body, her whole being tapering to the strong, upraised toes. There was, in fact, little to distinguish the drawing from the many that now grace magazines found on every newspaper stand in every hamlet of the land. It was neither good nor bad art, just indifferent illustration. Yet in January of 1914 the cover was described with snickering, that is, really salacious, detail in all the metropolitan newspapers; it occasioned men's room whispers; it was a sensation in its day and invited attack and defense. And it sent the post office on the trail of the editor, one George Sylvester Viereck. Viereck offered to cover the lady's unmentionables with a notation that it was done by order of the postmaster, but his offer was not accepted. The cover had to go.

The International was edited by Viereck during the same period that he was conducting more than one German journal and assisting in the editing of *Current Literature*. It was the joy of his heart then and later, for it was evidence that he was

111

blazing trails, destroying rank weeds in the Philistine fields. His tiff with the post office over the comely maiden was only one of the battles.

William C. Lengel, one contemporary literateur, described firsthand the extent of the influence of Viereck's magazine:

> From the time I first came to New York, I heard editors, writers, Greenwich villagers, the intellectuals of the period and radicals talk about Viereck, . . . Most of them talked about him in a sort of awesome way and to me he seemed to be a sort of literary knight in armour who was blasting conventions, setting a new path for freedom of expression in America, and generally being a dominant and dynamic individual. He battered down prejudices and opened the way for others.

And it was in large measure through *The International* that this was done. Many a rebel found the magazine a medium for his shouts of freedom.

Viereck was not the founder of the magazine. It had been started by a group of Columbia University undergraduates, essentially the same group involved in the formation of the organization that ultimately became the League for Industrial Democracy. Walter Lippmann was one of that group, perhaps the leader. B. Russell Herts, Phil Moeller, Ralph Roeder, George Cronyn, Edward Goodman, and Shaemas O'Sheel were others. Associated with them were various forward-looking young men, largely socialistic in viewpoint and rebels by nature. This group had definite views, definite feelings, definite impulses, and the magazine they started reflected these views, feelings, and impulses. It was called *Moods*, and the title was meant to imply that the magazine was a forum of many views, not a narrow organ of one cult. As it was later expressed, the magazine believed in freedom of speech—even for its editors! B. Russell Herts was its first formal editor.

Gradually the magazine absorbed a host of other publications, including the *Rundschau Zweier Welten,* the German language publication which Viereck had founded and edited; Leonard Abbott's *Free Comrade; Progress,* a political, social, and economic review; Michael Monahan's *Phoenix;* and other less important journals. As an editorial in the issue of April 1913 pointed out, with each edition the magazine increased not only the number of its readers, which was never large, but also the number of its contributing editors. It expanded not only in size, but in variety. At the outset it was a journal for literary rebels; then it aspired to be "the great liberal organ of America, liberal not only in its outlook on art, but also in its outlook on life." In the beginning, Viereck was only one of the contributing editors, but gradually he acquired control of the magazine and became its editor-in-chief.

Current Literature, with which Viereck remained connected, aspired to reflect a cosmopolitan viewpoint, but it was limited because it was essentially a mirror or compendium of other publications. *The International* had no such limitations. It could print what it willed—provided the police let it. The cover of

January 1914 could not help but serve as a warning. *The International* was almost alone in its field. Its only consequential rivals were the *Smart Set* and *Reedy's Mirror,* but Viereck's magazine differed from its rebel competitors as Viereck's personality differed from the personalities of Reedy, Wright, Mencken, and Nathan. Even the personalities of Viereck's associates had only minor influences. Whatever the talents—and they were considerable—of B. Russell Herts, Richard Le Gallienne, Blanche Shoemaker Wagstaff, Leonard D. Abbott, Herman A. Metz, and the others in *The International* menagerie, they did not give the magazine its tone. It was essentially Viereck's forum, although it contained comparatively little of his own writings. He determined its strong pro-German leanings, its pro-Roosevelt stand, and its attitude on moral questions.

While Viereck was only its contributing editor, a brochure was issued vaunting the merits of *The International.* "Have you never experienced an extreme and perfect distaste for all the periodical literature of the day?" the readers were asked. "Have you never felt disgusted with the superficiality of the magazine to which you subscribe? Have you never felt that the press of the country was appealing, in large measure, to the lowest instincts of the public?" A pause to permit affirmative responses, and then the moral:

> If you have experienced this sensation, you are one of those who will delight in the discovery of the really vital, interesting interpretation of life; the clear, well-balanced and illuminating views that are presented in every issue of *The International.* . . . The aim of *The International* is the creation in America of a maturer critical standpoint toward life and conduct. By the fearless discussion of all questions in fiction, articles and verse, it endeavors to awaken a greater self-consciousness in American thought. *The International* is a magazine of personality: the organ of the literary insurgents.

This same brochure offered proof of the contentions of superiority. Its symposia were made up of contributions from men and women who had things to say: Charles W. Eliot, John Dewey, Anna H. Shaw, Michael Monahan, Leonard D. Abbott, Hugo Munsterberg, W. J. Ghent, Champ Clark, and others. Its political notes, prepared by Walter Lippmann, were already beginning to receive wide acclaim by European and American experts alike. Its fiction, by Eden Phillpotts, Floyd Dell, Richard Le Gallienne, and Alexander Harvey, together with translations of the stories of Strindberg, Tchekhov, Knut Hansum, and others, represented the finest literature of its day. Dramas, whether in the original or in translation, were works of equal merit, and critical articles were by leading writers. Its literary criticism included discussions of the work of Upton Sinclair, Jack London, and Theodore Dreiser. Its articles on music and art were by Henry T. Finck, Phillip Moeller, Felix Grendon and others, prominence being given "to the noteworthy experiments of able, unrecognized men no less than to the works of established" artists. Then there was original verse by Sara Teasdale, George

Sylvester Viereck, Louis Untermeyer, James Oppenheim, Blanche Shoemaker Wagstaff, Mrs. Wagstaff also contributing reviews of new verse. It is difficult to name a poet of the period who did not contribute. And there were editorials on political, social, or ethical topics by Viereck and on literary and general matters by Le Gallienne and Herts.

In truth, it was an interesting magazine over which Viereck gradually assumed control. It had already won the praise of such varied voices as Mitchell Kennerley, the book publisher who was doing with books what Viereck and his cohorts hoped to do with periodical literature; Charles Renn Kennedy, the author of *The Servant in the House*; William Reedy; Edwin Markham; Henry Frank; Havelock Ellis; and Charles Ferguson, editorial writer of the Hearst papers.

Because Viereck had a wider fame than the editors who had preceded him, the magazine immediately won a wider fame than it had enjoyed in the past, yet the policy and contents of the magazine did not differ markedly at first. It was still the same eclectic rebel journal, and it remained such for a long time. The editorials following the heated election of 1912 were typical of the split personality of the magazine. Viereck had, of course, been the poetic ally of the indomitable "Teddy" Roosevelt and had, in fact, played an active part in the campaign of the Progressives. To him it was truly Armageddon and the editorial, "Of Woodrow Wilson," reflected his chagrin at the defeat suffered by his strenuous hero:

> Wilson is President; long live Roosevelt. For, although Mr. Roosevelt was not elected, he is responsible for the moral renaiscence of American politics which demolished the old guardsmen of the special interests and swept Mr. Wilson into the White House. But for the nomination of Mr. Roosevelt, the Baltimore Convention would have chosen a man far less capable and progressive than the Governor of New Jersey. . . . The Progressive Party supplied the yeast of the campaign, even if the Democrats have the dough.

> Roosevelt was the first, Wilson the second choice of the present writer. The people have decided for Mr. Wilson. Whether we agree with him or not, we must place the country above the party and support the new President where he deserves support, even if partisan interest dictate a different course. For Mr. Wilson will have no child's play if he regards his party's promises as a program. . . .

Not a word was said by Viereck of the one million votes cast for Eugene Debs, an unprecedented total. It remained for Leonard Abbott to comment in the magazine upon the phenomenon. "An agitator with the heart of a poet, magnetic to the finger tips, sincerity incarnate, keen, incisive, eloquent, warm-hearted— this is Eugene Debs," said Abbott.

Abbott saw what Viereck in his spiritual blindness could not see: that one Gene Debs was worth a menagerie of Roosevelts. But Viereck was gradually approaching political wisdom. More and more the pages of *The International* were filled with discussions of economics, political, and social problems. At times such articles seemed to crowd out the purely literary ones. And more and more articles on Teutonic themes found their way into the magazine. It was easy to see the direction in which Viereck's mind was traveling. He may not have been wholly aware of it himself, but he had some rudiments of understanding which found expression at the time.

In the issue of April 1913 there was an editorial by him called, with unusual prescience, "Germany at Armageddon." The article had apocalyptic overtones which carried conviction in spite of their rhetorical manner. "The thunders of war which have been rumbling for decades," said Viereck,

> are growing louder and louder. The nations of Europe are preparing for the battle of battles, Armageddon. France, Russia, Austria, Germany, England, each groans under the heavy burden of preparing, on land and sea, for the inevitable. . . . The world, startled, asks itself: "Is Europe mad?" Germany, above all, must bear the brunt of accusations hurled against this renaiscence of militarism by weak-kneed and weak-brained lovers of peace. The enlightened opinion of the world regards expenses for army and navy as a premium paid for the insurance of national prosperity and national existence. . . . The editorials of the New York *World*, well written though they be, are powerless to change the physical, financial, and commercial necessities out of which, like the beast of the Apocalypse, rises the spectre of war. The German Emperor, once heralded as the War Lord, has proved himself, in his long reign, a very Prince of Peace. . . . It must be with bleeding heart that Germany's statesmen consent to uproot, for a season, the peaceful crops of commerce to plant, instead, the iron teeth of war. . . . To be or not to be, the old Hamlet question, is confronting the German people. War, when it is forced upon them, will be a struggle of life and death, with legitimate expansion as the prize of victory. It is therefore easy to understand that the German nation intends to fight that battle with the same determination with which a century ago it fought its battle for independence.

Running through the files of the magazine, one finds the pro-German, anti-British viewpoint voiced with increasing frequency and greater forcefulness.

In November of 1913 an editorial by Viereck bitterly denounced President Wilson and Walter H. Page, his ambassador to the Court of St. James, because Page had said "that America is still English-led and English-ruled." The editorial demanded the recall of Page. In the same issue Munsterberg dealt roundly with those who accused Germany of starting a certain newspaper in the Fatherland as an organ of sinister attacks on America. In February 1914, *The International* published an article by Frederick F. Schrader, former secretary of the Republican Party, on the subject of Germany and the American press. "Today the American press is ready to find an extenuating excuse for any policy of Great Britain and to commit itself unqualifiedly to an alarmist attitude toward Germany at the first unsupported rumor of some German international move, however improbable, flimsy and unsubstantial that report may seem," complained Schrader, who went on to blame the influence of Great Britain for the prevailing distrust of Germany. The reason, he explained, was the fact that all European news fed to America was predigested in the editorial offices of London. A few months later Schrader published a second article on the same subject.

Viereck undoubtedly shared Schrader's views and was perhaps more biting in his resentment of the greater success of Britain in winning public sympathy here. When Wilson capitulated to England on the Panama Canal tolls, Viereck editorialized with mounting anger, only slightly toned down by irony. "There is no truth in the rumor that the files of the State Department have been removed to London," he said. "The administrative offices of the Government will remain in Washington, D.C.; it is merely the foreign policy of the United States that is dictated in Downing Street." Over and over again Viereck insisted that Germany beyond doubt prized cordial relations with the United States. There was all of the intensity of a preconceived campaign. Was there such a campaign?

These pieces give the heart of the situation. They show that Viereck had thought out the whole problem and that his mind was thoroughly made up. There could be no doubt as to where he would stand in the event hostilities broke out. He was a son of the Fatherland. He had had his rendezvous with the spirit of his ancestors, and he was with them. His Americanism was really only epidermal. He in fact was now more Germanic than when he had edited German language papers, so much so that it was rumored, as when *Confessions of a Barbarian* appeared, that German money supported his magazine. Certainly the advertisements stemmed largely from German-American businesses.

The magazine was, however, much comfort to Viereck's old temperamental friend, Ludwig Lewisohn. Lewisohn felt that *The International,* under Viereck's editorship, restored his faith in culture. He felt that his friend was making the magazine a rallying ground not merely for lovers of German civilization but for lovers of all culture. It was during this period that Lewisohn composed *A New England Fable,* generally regarded as one of his best poems. And that third member of the triangle, poor, distressed, distraught William Ellery Leonard, published in *The International* the first portions of his immortal work *Two Lives.* It was the summit of Viereck's editorship.

Despite the brilliance of the magazine, its existence was precarious. Viereck constantly found it necessary to apply the pulmotor. Various wealthy friends contributed to the support of the magazine, but Viereck rightly felt that its salvation lay in a union with a more robust publication. Naturally, his ambition was to achieve some alignment with William Marion Reedy, whose magazine, the *Mirror,* had achieved a much-merited fame. As early as July 1911 Viereck made overtures to Reedy but met with no success. Reedy wrote to Viereck good-naturedly, reasonably, and with astonishing prescience. He said that he felt certain that his ''general attitude toward economic conditions would not be satisfactory to anybody with money enough to put into'' Viereck's magazine. ''I go considerably further than you do in principles,'' he said. ''I am pretty close to being an anarchist, and my view upon political subjects I am sure would be strongly objectionable to any of your stockholders.'' For that reason, he had refused all overtures to capitalize the *Mirror,* although he knew that he was thereby turning away money that he could use. Reedy was intent upon reasserting his intellectual integrity, and he was careful not to fall into any intellectual traps, even if the bait was appealing.

''I take it for granted,'' he told Viereck, with his habitual candor, ''that back of all this there is the suggestion of the propagation in this country of a sentiment friendly to Germany as against England in the event of a clash. All this thing is confidential between you and me, and, therefore, I tell you right here as between Germany and England in a clash I would be with England.''

In March 1914 Viereck wrote a curious little letter to Blanche Wagstaff. ''I do not know who the anonymous person is who sends you those awful letters about me and *The International,*'' he told her. ''The District Attorney is not investigating our affairs. As a matter of fact, I am on good terms with his office and there is no danger from Anthony Comstock.'' Such rumblings showed that Viereck's enemies, whom he took so lightly, were active, indeed. He would presently give them real cause for whisperings and even shoutings. All the ado about *The International* and other activities of the restless young man was to lend a perhaps tragic significance to the career of the poet of passion.

20   FOR THE FATHERLAND

In accordance with his habit of making trips to Europe every year or two, particularly after his parents had returned to Germany, Viereck embarked for the Old Country late in May 1914. He was there less than two months, spending virtually all of his time with Mama and Papa Viereck in Berlin and Wildungen. The Vierecks had much to discuss: the state of American politics and culture, German-American affairs, the return of Teddy Roosevelt, Putty's petty disappointments with *The International*, his plans for the future, the restless yearnings of his soul. But all three Vierecks were more interested in the waters restoring Papa's youth than in the waters separating the Old Country from the New. Naturally, Sylvester had little time for travel. He did see several personal friends, but no government officials. He had made the acquaintance of the genial American ambassador to the Reich, James Gerard, and had given him a copy of *Nineveh;* and he had once again interviewed Bernard Shaw in England; there, too, he had been entertained by Elsa Barker and her friends. In a general way, he realized that war was going to break out some day very soon, but to him it did not then have any personal urgency. He did not consider what he would do in the event hostilities came; he hardly gave it a thought. Curiously enough, he heard no talk of war. Armageddon seemed a place mentioned in the Bible, not some intimate catastrophe that was soon to overtake him and the world.

But one day in June he found himself with his father in Wildungen, reading a newspaper. The date on the paper was June 29. His father's face paled as he read a dispatch telling of the assassination of the Austrian heir and his wife in the town of Sarajevo. The elder Viereck regarded it as a matter of grave importance, and he tried to impress that fact upon his son, who could not see why the killing of two people should have anything except a local importance: it was interesting, as all sensational murders are interesting, but why should Papa give such ominous meaning to it?

It had been Sylvester Viereck's intention to return on the *Imperator,* but his financial embarassment dictated the choice of another vessel. Next time, he decided, he would travel in style.

The next time was some years later. For Viereck arrived in Boston a day or two before July 28, 1914, and on the twenty-eighth of July the headlines of all the papers of the world announced that Austria-Hungary had declared war against Serbia. On the first of August, the papers exclaimed that Germany had declared war on Russia; on the third France countered against Germany and Germany against France. On the fourth Great Britain joined the fray.

It was Armageddon at last! Every detail became of the utmost importance to Viereck.

At once the war became a struggle of land power against sea power, between England and Germany. The respective allies of the two nations immediately took subordinate positions and became important only insofar as they reflected the fortunes of the two great opposing powers. Few troubled to weigh the sins and virtues of any of the combatants other than England and Germany. France was merely the battlefield, Russia the footrest of Germany. Little Belgium was in the nature of an orphan over whom to shed tears, rather than a belligerent. Men took their places in grocery store arguments as advocates of the British or the Teutonic point of view, not the French or Russian or Austro-Hungarian viewpoints. Thus simplified, it was easy for everyone to have his say, and much was said. The troubled president of the American nation pleaded for strict neutrality—of thought no less than of deed. But he was a supernumerary on a crowded stage. True, some offered pious "Amens" to his prayer for neutrality, but the boys at the corner and the girls at their sewing circles were too busy prejudging England and Germany and too busy with their own vicarious roles in the battle to pay much attention to the preacher in the White House.

England or Germany? Armageddon, indeed. The giants were in battle. Who would be the victor? And would there be a victor and a vanquished? Might not both lie prostrate in time? No—England or Germany! It had to be one. And the American people, like the rest of the world, made their choice—too willingly, too glibly, on insufficient knowledge, and heedless of consequences.

Germany started out with certain disadvantages, so far as America was concerned. They were apparent at the outset and became more apparent as the war continued. Looked at with the superior wisdom of hindsight, it now seems that everything was stacked against the Kaiser's empire. The cards were all marked against Germany, and its advocates were playing a losing game from the start.

To begin with, Austria-Hungary and Germany had been the first to declare war. The American public refused to accept the excuse that Germany's formal declaration of war might have been only a defensive act, that Germany, perhaps, could not wait until Russian mobilization was completed. Then there were the invasions of Belgium and Luxemburg and the rumors that the Germans had contemplated marching through the Swiss cantons, in spite of Germany's solemn pledge to respect the neutrality of all three states. The average man could not understand Germany's dilemma: it was fighting on two fronts, not to mention the northern seas. A free passage through Belgium might give it a much-needed strategic advantage. America saw only the rape of a smaller nation by a larger one. It was easy to imagine the bully committing unspeakable atrocities, and these were supplied for American consumption; the very tales of Belgian atrocities in the Congo now did yeoman's service in Belgium's favor.

And was not the Kaiser always rattling the saber? America agreed with Elbert Hubbard, the flamboyant publisher, that "Bill Hohenzollern" had blown the lid off hell. All Germany, led by the War Lord of Potsdam, was running stark mad. It was rampant militarism, America believed, and Germany's first triumphs confirmed the belief.

Even Germany's advantages became liabilities. The admitted superiorities of Germany only fortified the prejudices against it. Its unbelievable rise to a position of leadership in the arts, in commerce and industry, and in political and social sciences and public affairs created the rancor and envy that too often dog success. Germany seemed too strong for American comfort. There seemed to be black magic in its triumphs, something fearful and foreboding. German *kultur* was only another name for ruthless efficiency, conscienceless triumphs, God-affronting cruelty. To many Americans, it was pitiful to think that not an inch of German territory felt the touch of the invader. While America wept crocodile tears over the bleeding soil of France and Belgium, it forgot that Britain's soil, no less than Germany's, was untouched. And the German submarines, the German poison gas, the German Big Berthas, all of the astonishing instruments of war that Germany had developed, made for fear and trembling in America. There could be no denying here that Germany was a soulless monster, a Frankenstein creature built by the twin demons, junkerism and *kultur*.

Of course, England's greatest ally was the language it shared with America. The British viewpoint could come to this country without the byplay of translation. As Frederick Schrader had pointed out in the columns of *The International*, the sources of America's news were almost entirely British. Serbian news, Russian news, even French and German news generally bore a London date line. Were the lanes of communication direct, it would yet have taken the Central Powers many precious months to capture the eyes and ears of America. But the lanes were not direct; all of them led to London; in the very first week of the war, England snapped Germany's one cable to America. Thenceforth Germany had to depend upon the wireless and the mails to put across its viewpoint, and these sources, too, were crippled. Could emissaries in America bridge the many gaps? This could hardly be expected.

Meanwhile, the grip of economic compulsion held America to the Allied cause. The highways of the sea were soon cleared of German ships. America could not hope to trade with the Central Powers. Its only important European trade had to be with England and the Allies, for Brittania ruled the waves. American trade was dependent more and more upon the success of England. America could be neutral only if it would be content to suffer financially. But the House of Morgan decided otherwise. It became the fiscal agent of the Allies, supplying more and more of the money and credits the Allies needed to carry on the war. The Allies had to win!

Germany could not hope to win the active support of the United States. The most it could hope for was American neutrality, some cutting of the edge of partisanship.

There were three principal catastrophes that marked America's road to war against Germany, and they were intimately a part of Viereck's life. The sinking of the *Lusitania,* the loss of Dr. Albert's portfolio, and the leak of the Zimmerman note: these were tragedies in Viereck's life as much as in the history of the Fatherland. Various actors took part in the drama, some villains and some heroes to Viereck and his cause. In the White House there was the troubled president, Woodrow Wilson, heartsick over the loss of the wife of his youth. Somewhere in Europe was Wilson's friend and confidential agent, the mysterious Colonel Edward M. House, whose comings and goings set men wondering. Close at hand was a man who swayed millions and yet was held in none too secret contempt by Wilson and House: the Great Commoner, William Jennings Bryan. And roaring through the land was Theodore Roosevelt, unable to forget that Wilson occupied his seat in the executive mansion. There were others, serious and comical, but these were the principal actors, just as were the three unforgettable catastrophes.

Viereck immediately took his place in the interplay of men and events. His role was soon enough to become a unique one, in every sense satisfying his restless nature and answering the inner call that began troubling him as soon as the success of *Nineveh* wore off. The unfolding of Viereck the political activist is an extraordinary chapter, for Viereck became not a footnote in history, as he said, but an important personage during a stirring period of American history. Viereck's first utterance was almost as lyrical as it was polemical. Hard upon the declaration of war, he hymned the German Emperor in a poem called, perhaps impiously and certainly impishly, *William II, Prince of Peace.* The words were quoted throughout the world, sometimes with derision and occasionally with approval, but they immediately passed into currency:

> O Prince of Peace, O Lord of War,
>> Unsheath thy blade without a stain,
> Thy holy wrath shall scatter far
>> The bloodhounds from thy country's fane.

> Into thy hand the sword is forced
>> By traitor friend and traitor foe,
> On foot, on sea, and winged and horsed,
>> The Prince of Darkness strikes his blow.

> Crush thou the Cossack arms that reach
>> To plunge the world into the night!
> Save Goethe's vision, Luther's speech,
>> Thou art the Keeper of the Light.

When darkness was on all the lands,
    Who kept God's faith with courage grim?
Shall He uphold His country's hands,
    Or tear her members, limb from limb?

God called the Teuton to be free,
    Free from Great Britain's golden thrall,
From guillotine and anarchy,
    From pogroms red and whips that fall.

May thy victorious armies rout
    The yellow hordes against thee hurled,
The Czar whose sceptre is the knout,
    And France, the harlot of the world!

But thy great task will not be done
    Until thou vanquish utterly
The Norman sister of the Hun,
    England, the Serpent of the Sea.

The flame of war her tradesmen fanned
    Shall yet consume her, fleet and field:
The star of Frederick guide thy hand,
    The God of Bismarck be thy shield!

Against the fell Barbarian horde
    Thy people stand, a living wall;
Now fight for God's peace with thy sword,
    For if thou fail, a world shall fall!

To Viereck it was the day foretold in the apocalyptic vision of John. The Roosevelt campaign was nothing. Here was the cause of causes. By inner compulsion and outward pressure, he had to help the land of his birth. The sole question was the nature of the services that he would render.

Viereck and three of his friends, Hans Hayo Hinrichs, Alfred Rau, and Fritz Borgemeister, sat at dinner in the New York Athletic Club on the night of August 3, 1914. The poet, the broker, the banker, and the chemist, all four young men—Viereck was only thirty—discussed the topic of topics, the great war, which had just commenced. They were amazed that the entire New York press—all seventeen newspapers—had espoused the cause of the Allies and seemed to regard Germany as the common enemy of humanity. The headlines uniformly told a story of German aggression and barbarism, while the Allies were painted lily white. The animus against Germany was common to all of the New York newspapers, even at this time—before the invasion of Belgium, before England's entry into the war, before there were any atrocities to report. The four young men were shocked, grieved, indignant. They felt that something ought to be done immediately by way of self-protection and to assure fair play to the Central Powers.

"Why not publish a magazine that will print the truth?" Viereck suggested, at once envisioning himself as its editor. It seemed an answer to his yearnings.

"It must be a weekly because events move quickly," someone countered. It was agreed.

"And what shall we call it?" The interest mounted. Names were mentioned and discussed. As a gesture of defiance, Viereck says, they decided to call it *The Fatherland*. Had they not the same right as Englishmen to cherish the land of their fathers? Other details were considered. Viereck announced that they could print ten thousand copies for a bare two hundred dollars. Each of them thereupon pledged fifty dollars toward the first number of *The Fatherland*.

But it was never necessary to invest cash, for the magazine was printed on the credit of *The International,* which had somehow managed to survive. It was an immediate and unqualified success, a sensational success, this new baby of the poet of passion. The first number passed into more than one edition. Thousands of extra copies were printed. An office was hastily equipped, and *The Fatherland,* with Viereck at the helm, was in full blast.

Viereck and his young friends were not alone in sponsoring *The Fatherland*. For very few issues, Louis Sherwin, a writer on the staff of the New York *Globe,* was one of the co-editors, but the editor of the *Globe* forced Sherwin to resign. It was casualty number one; there were to be many others.

Frederick Franklin Schrader, who had written articles earlier that year on the pro-British, anti-German bias of the American press, was another co-editor of *The Fatherland*. Viereck directed the magazine editorially, determined its policies, and wrote most of the leading editorials. Schrader attended to the details and wrote many articles and editorials. Politics, drama, and personal invectives were his specialities. He controlled the *Dramatic Mirror* and continued to edit it throughout his connection with *The Fatherland,* until war hatreds crowded him out.

At first it was agreed that those working on the magazine would not draw pay. It would be a free offering in a great cause. But soon such altruism became impossible. The paper required much time at the sacrifice of other means of livelihood, so modest salaries were soon drawn. Ultimately the magazine became Viereck's chief source of income.

The first issue of the magazine was an impressive sight. In bold letters across the cover were the words: "*The Fatherland*/ A Weekly/ Price: 5 cents/ August 10th/1914/ Fair Play/ for/ Germany/ and/ Austria-Hungary." And in red and black challenge were the seals and scepters of Germany and the Dual Monarchy. No less provocative were the contents, which included a preamble, and Viereck's poem on Kaiser Wilhelm, and five articles: by Herman Schoenfeld ("The True Motives of the European Conflagration"), Shrader ("The Germanophobe Press"), Professor Kuno Francke ("Germany's Defensive Aggression"), Sherwin ("The Other Side"), and Hugo Munsterberg on "Fair Play." By and large it was impressive and dignified. The preamble struck the keynote with becoming solemnity as it stated the threefold purpose of the publication:

First: To place the German side of this unhappy quarrel fairly and squarely before the American people.

Second: To review, week by week, the actual events of the war so far as they can be authoritatively ascertained.

Third: To review, week by week, the attitude of the American press, to combat, as far as lies in our power, the misstatements and prejudices of the Slavophile and the German-hater, to point out discrepancies and to protest against injustice towards a race that has rightfully earned the sympathy and admiration instead of the jealousy of the so-called civilized world for its industry, its art, its philosophy and its humanity.

There was nothing unduly flamboyant in this, and large sections of the American press applauded the new paper. "Marse Henry" Watterson's *Louisville Courier-Journal* had kind words of welcome for *The Fatherland* and greetings to its editors. *The Outlook,* the magazine which had voiced the views of Roosevelt, looked upon *The Fatherland* with hopefulness, as did the Springfield *Republican* and other leading journals. Was it possible that American public opinion would be conquered, despite the British inspiration of the news cables?

But this initial kindliness was just a lull in the storm. Viereck became, so far as Watterson was concerned, "a venom-bloated toad of treason." Other American journalists became no kinder, if less pungent. Viereck was to be in hot water constantly, and scaldings were to be his daily experience.

Viereck had scarcely embarked upon his new editorial venture when new duties devolved upon him—the particular duties with which he would be associated in the public mind and which would cause his greatest problems. The odium of the paid propagandist immediately was attached to his name, and the reputation persisted. Tales of various kinds were told of him, some true, some apocryphal, but all bizarre and mysterious. These tales will persist as long as the name of Viereck is known to anyone. They account for the suspicion with which he was regarded by some of his friends and for the feeling that he was morally irresponsible and basically unstable. One cannot understand Viereck's character, his personality, and his career, until the mystery, if such it is, of his world war activities is solved.

There is no dearth of material on the subject. There are Viereck's own writings, found in *The Fatherland* and *The International* and in the books he subsequently wrote. There are the volumes of evidence taken before the once notorious Overman Committee and during the libel actions of Mayor William Hale Thompson against the *Chicago Tribune.* There are the many books and articles and newspaper dispatches dealing with the subject of war propaganda, most of them spurious and vitiated by hysteria, sensationalism, and mendacity. There is much of a serious nature—books and articles by Harold D. Lasswell, Edward L. Bernays, and others. The mass of evidence—good, bad, and indifferent—is mountainous, many winters' reading for any serious student. And the minions of the law were vigilant. The United States Secret Service, the Attorney General's office, the various local law-enforcement agencies, and volunteers without number, kept a constant vigil, and their records have been available from time to time. The ever solicitous British operatives aided ours. All of the world seemed to be in a mood for espionage.

One might therefore say that all of the evidence is in and that one may faithfully record and appraise the wartime activities of so public a figure as George Sylvester Viereck. That is the easy way out of a difficult situation, perhaps the sensible way as well. But we are confronted with the fact that subjective motives are as important as objective activities. How does one arrive at them? We are confronted with the admission that many records were destroyed. Were they incriminating records? It must not be forgotten that others, besides lovers, have learned not to put anything in writing.

Shall a case be built by circumstances? Then what circumstances are to be considered? And is it not conceivable that circumstances can be created with malice aforethought? The culprit may arrange his alibi in advance; he often does, as every law-enforcement officer knows. He may have good fortune and loaded dice. He may be the brains rather than the executant, the planner rather than the mechanic.

Fortified by a determined skepticism and a critical intelligence and in the light of the prior career of George Sylvester Viereck, it is clear that *The Fatherland* arose spontaneously and the rest grew out of it. Events crowd upon events in times of stress.

The Fatherland was no more than a few weeks old and already was an established institution, outgrowing its office and staff. Inquiries and contributions and subscriptions poured in. The volunteers had to become professionals. Inevitably they would become intoxicated with the excitement, the responsibilities, and potentialities. And so too would the master of the show, a young man of less than thirty years who did not dislike attention and in whose nostrils was the scent of fame. Nor did he place a low valuation upon his own abilities. He was eager to second those who had hailed him as a Wonder Child; he could add chapter and verse to the citations of his worth. And he did not despise Mammon, for he saw much that could be purchased not with fame but with cash. He was quite familiar with the system of subsidies and saw nothing wrong in freewill offerings, provided only he was being paid for what he already believed. And he was a German of the Germans, a Hohenzollern as closely related to Frederick the Great as was the Emperor himself. His parents were at that very time on German soil, intending to remain there. He had just left them and he hoped to see them once more—in Germany. He was restless, too, ever so restless, it cannot be repeated too often; literature in itself began to pall; it hardly seemed related to the life about him; it smacked too much of the library and too little of the arena. Now all would be changed. The whirlwind had gathered strength and he was in its grasp, to be carried to a different world. He hardly resisted.

Scarcely had the declaration of war come than did the propaganda machines begin to work full blast in America. Someone once said that when the Liberty Bell first rang in Philadelphia, it was to extend a welcome to all the propagandists of Europe. Dr. Heinrich Albert, then, was simply one in the line of succession; Dr. Bernhard Dernburg was another; so were Dr. Karl A. Fuehr and Dr. Mechlenburg. All learned doctors of propaganda. And there were others. Viereck was already here. They all met at 1123 Broadway in New York City. They and their assistants were the German propaganda cabinet here.

It happened apparently in this fashion.

German shipping in the United States was paralyzed. The British cut off virtually all direct highways between America and Germany, and the ships of the great German lines lay in dock, none so foolhardy as to venture forth. The steamship companies had large forces of idle men and women eager to be placed at the disposal of the Fatherland in all legitimate ways. The chief German steamship men and Viereck and other influential German-Americans readily welcomed Dr. Dernburg and his cohorts when they arrived in New York after the commencement of hostilities. Embassy officials were there, too. It was a gathering of the elite of the German cause. Out of the talk of that first meeting grew the German propaganda cabinet, and Viereck was a member.

A more select meeting was held. The aura of cooperation which had graced the larger meeting vanished almost at once. Instead, fur flew. Dr. Hanns Heinz Ewers, a literary bird of strange plumage, and Prince Hatzfeld, of the Embassy, were the principal combatants. Ewers, strongly seconded by Hugo Munsterberg, urged an alliance between Dernburg's cohorts and Viereck's magazine. Prince Hatzfeld objected strenuously, but Dernburg sided with Ewers and Munsterberg.

Munsterberg's motives were totally selfless, without even a hint of avarice. The truth of this was universally recognized. But Viereck was much more suspect. He held, as he subsequently admitted, the German-American portfolio in the propaganda cabinet and shared with William Bayard Hale the portfolio of publicity. Hale, a former friend of President Wilson, had been retained at Viereck's suggestion at a salary of approximately $15,000, an enormous sum in those days. What did Viereck receive, directly or indirectly? Opinions differ, and the exact figure is difficult to ascertain. How much of it was in cash? How much of it came through third parties? How much did he retain? How much did he pass on to others? These are questions which must be answered and are answered only partially here. More important are certain other questions: What was done with the money? What was its ultimate destination? To what extent did it color and even determine Viereck's views? Again there is no conclusive answer, only surmise. But certain activities are known.

"Sooner or later a German U-boat will sink a large passenger steamer carrying many Americans," remarked Viereck one day to his fellow propagandists.

"Something must be done," Viereck insisted, as his associates listened glumly.

"Done about what?" inquired one of the steamship company officials.

"Sooner or later some big passenger boat with Americans on board will be sunk by a submarine. Then there will be hell to pay. Public opinion is veering around once more to neutrality," Viereck replied, his gloom dissolving into semi-optimism. "The American people are equally disgusted with the transgressions of both belligerents against the freedom of the seas, but dramatize the resentment against submarine warfare by sinking one of the large passenger ships and it will be difficult to prevent a rupture of diplomatic relations."

A German naval expert, then present, insisted that war is war and that "the British blockade, starving thousands of German children, is more inhuman than our submarine warfare."

"I agree, but," Viereck countered quite properly, "it is easier to visualize the pitiful face of a little child drowning amid the wreckage caused by the torpedo of a German submarine than to visualize one hundred thousand or a million children starving by slow degrees as a result of the British food blockade."

Dernburg listened to the argument intently. Albert grasped the point at once. Dr. Hale was asked if the American secretary of state might be persuaded to issue a warning to Americans against entrusting their lives to ships of the belligerents. He thought the administration, rather than Bryan, was dead set against any such warning and that a bill to the same effect could never pass Congress.

"What do you propose, Mr. Viereck?" asked Dr. Dernburg. Viereck was pacing up and down the room restlessly.

Viereck thought it the duty of the German government to issue a dramatic warning that would reach every American passenger—the Guardian Angels of the Allies, as they were called, because of the unwitting protection they afforded the munition shipments of the Allies. He thought that an indirect warning would not do. Nothing short of an official and widely publicized warning would satisfy him.

"What is the date of the departure of the next passenger ship?" Dr. Fuehr asked.

"The next large passenger ship is the *Lusitania*," he was told.

"Then publish a warning before the *Lusitania* sails," Viereck responded.

It was put to a vote and unanimously carried. Viereck and Hale were delegated to prepare such a warning, which they did without delay, but it was decided that the German ambassador had to be consulted. Bernstorff considered the matter so vital that Berlin had to be consulted. Delays. Delays again. One week before the *Lusitania*, pride of the Cunard line, cleared port, the German Embassy inserted paid advertisements in newspapers throughout the land, reminding passengers that a state of war existed between Germany and its allies and Great Britain and its allies and that passengers sailing in the war zone on ships of Great Britain or its allies did so at their own risk. The announcement created a profound stir—but it was ignored.

Meanwhile, Viereck rushed from the propaganda cabinet meeting to his desk in *The Fatherland* office and wrote a strong editorial for the forthcoming issue of his magazine. "Before long," his editorial warned, "a large passenger ship like the *Lusitania*, will met a similar fate as the *Gulflight*," a smaller vessel which had just been torpedoed.

The issue of *The Fatherland* containing Viereck's editorial of warning was hardly on the newsstands when newsboys shouted the sensational news of the sinking of the *Lusitania*. As Viereck had predicted, all hell broke loose. The British ambassador filed an official complaint with the American State Department accusing Viereck of "guilty foreknowledge" of the sinking of the ship. Colonel House, President Wilson's emissary in London at the time, felt that America had to go to war against Germany. So did almost everyone else. If one could wager on such things, it was a virtual certainty that disaster was about to overtake the German cause in America, even if President Wilson implied that we were "too proud to fight"; May 7, 1915 was a fatal day in the history of German-American relations and a fatal day in Viereck's life.

21   MARRIAGE: AN INTERLUDE

One Sunday evening in 1908 at the elder Viereck's home, Elsa Barker saw a shy little girl of less than ten whom she scarcely noticed until Sylvester Viereck whispered to her: "I think I shall marry Gretchen when she grows up." Mrs. Barker thought that this little interlude was delightfully Germanic.

Alexander Harvey, miraculously observant in spite of his seeming other worldliness, often asked himself in later years why he never divined the destiny of little Gretchen, who was to become the wife of Sylvester Viereck. He wrote a little masterpiece, unpublished as yet, in praise of the girl. Late one afternoon he called at the Hein home, a small wooden house in the upper reaches of Manhattan, where Viereck was then living. Viereck was ill and lonely, so lonely that he had written to Abbott with terse command: "Rat: Have you deserted the sinking ship?" Naturally, Harvey, too, felt constrained to call upon his young friend. But when he arrived, the ship was anything but sinking. Viereck was in a zestful mood and quite evidently in the throes of work. After a bout of talk the two joined Mr. and Mrs. Hein and their daughter, little Gretchen, at an informal dinner.

Gretchen flashed forth in a white dress, with a long braid of yellow hair tied, school-girl like, with a ribbon, and falling far below her waist. She had entered the room suddenly, silently, like a beam of white from the sky. She captivated Harvey immediately, even if "Oh, how do you do?" was all that she said at their introduction. Of her voice Harvey sang for many a season. It remained, he said, what it was when he first heard it—"a subdued flute, suggesting in eager moments a trumpet and then dying into its first softness. It conveys through many intonations rapture, grief, ecstacy, amazement, entreaty. . . . It is a voice that floats. Seldom loud, it is now melodramatic, again caressing, or perhaps a whisper to be heard from one end of a room clear across the floor. She seems to deprecate herself. . . . I have heard her tell all sorts of things strange and bizarre . . . but the quality of her accents renders all her talk appropriate and natural."

During that first dinner, Harvey noticed how different Gretchen's voice was from her father's, and her eyes, too, held him. To the very end of his life he was convinced that her eyes changed from a light gray to a deep blue even while she spoke. They were eyes, he said, which conveyed every emotion, every impulse in the depths of Gretchen's being.

"What a white, white girl," Harvey thought. He studied her every nuance with the care of one who is bewitched. She became afraid of him, not physically but intellectually. She suspected perhaps that Harvey might find her simple, smelling of bread and butter and the nursery. Harvey began to suspect that Viereck had told the girl things about him that filled her with a kind of dread, and he swelled with an unaccountable pride.

Harvey experienced a thrill when he saw Gretchen again at a sort of musicale at the home of Isaac L. Rice. Swarms of people were present; but through the throng appeared the floating form of the girl-woman, Gretchen. She seemed to swim up the stream of humanity like a seraph, all in white and with a long golden braid. The impression, to Harvey, was ethereal. He watched the white apparition like a man in a dream; but she did not see him. Her eyes searched the field of vision, and found what they sought: George Sylvester Viereck!

Harvey expected to see her rush forward and throw her white arms around Viereck's neck in the self surrender of a first requited love; but a friend interrupted the longing of her eyes. She chatted with him for a moment and once more she resumed her progress through the human stream. Her eyes saw only George Sylvester Viereck. But again a friend interrupted her worship. She was not resentful. She chatted affably. She looked at the man with an expression totally unlike the one she had bestowed on others. Harvey began to feel that her facial expression had an infinite richness, out of which she gave each person something that was uniquely his. He began to be thankful that he was not alone in watching Gretchen.

Thus Harvey watched her that night as she flitted by him in the throng until she was close to George Sylvester Viereck. Then, says Harvey, she seated herself and gloated over him; worshipped him in a thousand ways with her eyes, in ten thousand ways with her smiles. From that hour George Sylvester Viereck was authenticated to Harvey as a great poet, not only writing great poetry, but living it.

Harvey recalled the Viereck wedding with vividness. Viereck wore a black cutaway coat in which the tails extended to his knees. The trousers were striped. Viereck's shoes were not patent leather. His collar had a somewhat old-fashioned choker effect and his tie was fastened in a style that made it puff. Harvey was amazed at the paradoxical tallness Viereck achieved, or rather which his tailor achieved. Viereck, rather short in actuality, on his wedding day seemed tall. A spectator got an impression of some change in the man.

The bride appeared. She came forward like a worshipper, adoring her beloved. Her rapt face seemed to intoxicate Viereck; he seemed to tremble. Gretchen seemed to be transmuted into a figure of snow, the sculptural effect heightened by her motionless attitude. The voice of the clergyman pronouncing them husband and wife seemed unreal. "Viereck was intoxicated with Gretchen. He absorbed her as if she were a rare essence, a cup of nectar from Olympys. If woman yearns to be understood, man longs to be worshipped. She worshipped him on her wedding day. She worshipped him long before that perfect afternoon. She has worshipped him ever since"—until unexpected events in the distant future, which transformed her and Viereck as well.

The warm glow of Harvey's delicious impressions requires a cooler, contrasting view—perhaps Viereck's own. We were in the same great room that held so many thrills for Harvey. The poet and his wife and the biographer and his wife chatted in a sabattical mood. The conversation veered to Harvey's romantic portrait of Gretchen. "Was Harvey in love with you?" the biographer's wife asked, while the poet smiled. Viereck began to speak:

"My marriage, as you see, has turned out fairly happily," he began, his eyes laughing. Remember: this was many years ago. "This does not change my fundamental view that marriage is a monstrosity. Personally, I—or at least most of my selves—are not and were never intended for marriage. But I presume there is also a bourgeois ego in me which adapts itself to marriage, or I would not be married. My marriage has not been wrecked because my wife is an extraordinary woman. I am fond of her in spite of, not because of the fact that she is my wife."

His voice became more insistent: "The theory and practice of mortgaging one's affections, one's soul and one's body to another human being is barbarous and irreconcilable with the integrity of the individual."

"And your children?" the biographer queried, enjoying the sensation of a man thus discussing his wife to her face.

Viereck replied in the same spirit of detachment and his wife listened with humorous indulgence.

"The children amuse me," said Viereck. "They flatter my ego. They are bright and I see myself, or phases of myself in them. I have always told them that they are probably superior to me. In the first place, there would be no sense in the theory of evolution unless there was some improvement in our issue. To sum it up: I like my children because they are likeable, not because of the biological accident which we call paternity."

In the same mood, the biographer ventured to suggest that since Viereck had been so successful in his marriage as of that time, he ought to take to himself a few more wives, as a sort of amatory experiment in the spirit of modern science.

"One wife is enough," Viereck laughed, in spite of himself glancing fondly at Gretchen. "Monogamy is absurd, but it is better than polygamy." Then, as an afterword: "But all of these are matters of individual taste. Perhaps you need several wives. Like my quaint friend, Kotikokura, you may be able to take care of a harem."

Our conversation, in which Mrs. Viereck played the part of an active, if largely silent, participant, was typical of many similar exchanges between the Vierecks and their friends, for whom they never ceased to hold charm. The poet Shaemas O'Sheel told of a similar exchange that has a curious attraction. He had met the two before they had been married. Gretchen had turned to O'Sheel and had said, delightful girl that she was, "Our first child will be named Peter." And Viereck, remembering that they were not yet married, had countered in mock rebuke of such indelicacy. Inwardly, however, he enjoyed the conversation of the girl, and to O'Sheel it was to remain as a symbol of the relations of Puck and Gretchen.

So on September 30, 1915 Gretchen and Viereck were married at the Plaza Hotel in New York. When reporters interviewed the thirty-one year old groom, he announced that he had a surprise in store for his bride—a honeymoon in the Fatherland. In a matter-of-fact tone, indicating his profound conviction, he told the reporters, "We are going to Germany this year. The war will be over before this year goes to its close. I am so sure of this that I have made all of the necessary plans already."

Of course, he did not go to Germany that year. He was just whistling in the dark! He needed the adoring and adorable Gretchen to lend simple courage to him at home. She was predestined to be his mate and was fitted in every way for the position. Intellectually she had a certain amount of maturity that gave balance to his quicker mind. She found herself able to assist him in his work, his literary efforts no less than his other enterprises. Often she gave human character to the unreal figments of his imagination. And her mind could adventure, just as his could, and she had spunk to match his. Once in the early days, Amy Lowell was talked down at a meeting of the Poetry Society, and it was little Gretchen who came vigorously to her defense in a spirited rejoinder to the attacks made on Miss Lowell. Long afterwards, Amy Lowell spoke with feelings of gratitude for the girl who had thus defended her. Others, too, found good reason to cherish her, not least of all Viereck himself, particularly in the days which followed the disasters of the German cause.

22　STRUGGLING AGAINST THE TIDE

A letter Viereck wrote to his mother immediately after Hugo Munsterberg's funeral in December 1916 gave a memorable picture of the curious life that Viereck led at the time, a life hardly reflected in *The Fatherland* or in *The International* or in Viereck's public utterances. "I am glad the wonder ship has reached its destination," he said, commenting on the safe return of the submarine, *Deutschland,* to its home port. The "wonder ship" had attracted sensational interest because it successfully penetrated the British blockade. It had succeeded in winning a rare burst of sympathy for the Germans, for the public liked the gallantry of Captain Koenig and transferred its liking in some measure to the German cause. It was a bright interlude which the propaganda cabinet appreciated greatly. To Viereck the safe return of the *Deutschland* also meant that his father had received a large number of letters from him, copies of *The Fatherland*, and a picture of his firstborn. Viereck had adopted the wise course of choosing more than one route for his letters to his parents; it was rather expensive, but it comforted him to know that his communications with his parents were kept up even if Germany was blockaded. His Christmas gifts (cash) to his parents, he entrusted to telegrams, but since that service was constantly being interrupted, he could never be sure that they had received his gifts.

"My invitation to you to come here is always open," he reminded his mother in the same letter. "We can very easily accommodate you and make things pleasant for you and Papa. In fact, if peace is declared you should certainly come, and if the war continues there is all the more reason why you should seek the comforts and the fleshpots of 230 Riverside Drive. You simply must not expose yourself to the strain of living in the midst of excitement, and to the difficulties of keeping house under the conditions now prevailing in Europe. I regret that you will not be with your grandchild on his first Christmas.'' A first child—a real war baby—had been born to Gretchen and Sylvester Viereck and he was called Peter as Gretchen had prophecied. ''But you should certainly come here as soon as you can conveniently arrange matters. Papa is an American citizen and will be in no danger whatsoever. Moreover, I have friends connected with the British Embassy, as well as friends in the State Department who can safeguard him.'' An anomaly to find the outcast having hands lifted to aid him in the very stronghold of the enemy! Viereck was instrumental in saving the life of a British officer who had been captured in a U-boat.

Viereck, between verbal shots at his foes, looked with a parent's proud glance upon his first-born, the heir apparent of the Hohenzollern commoner. ''The baby is developing beautifully,'' he wrote to Mama Viereck. ''He has lovely blue eyes out of which he looks rather critically at the world. He has inherited this look from you; the blueness of his eyes from Papa. We are still perfectly happy. Things are going well.''

Only a war clouded the landscape! And war was not as bad as it might have been. After long years of absence, Viereck saw William Ellery Leonard again, and the moody Ludwig Lewisohn, and he printed their pro-German verse. Leonard had taken to Gretchen immediately; all through his stay in New York, during his temporary release from his phobic prison, he called Gretchen daily—to find out the progress of the yet unborn child. He advised her, cautioned her, consoled her, like the dear friend that he was. The common ills of the world could be forgotten at moments when one had such a friend.

''If they have not reviewed my book,'' Viereck had said in his letter to Mama, ''they have not hurt me very much.'' It was, however, a strange sensation to find his newest book scarcely noticed, though he knew it to be a good one, containing not only topical verses but paeans of passion and of thought. It was some considerable recompense to know that a Britisher of tolerance, Mitchell Kennerley, who did not permit war hysteria to cloud his literary judgment, had issued *Songs of Armageddon* in 1916. It was good to know that Blanche Wagstaff remained his friend, if only for the moment, and praised his verse, even his war verse, publicly. She had said of his battle poems that they ''are lusty outcries, full of irony and scorn and an almost blasphemous power.'' He was pleased that the New York *Times* had forgotten its animosity against him long enough to admit that his war poems were ''the most spirited expressions of the German point of view that have been made in English verse.''

Viereck, quite uncharacteristically, because he was too busy, had issued the volume without the blessing of an introduction, and it could well stand on its own feet. Each of the three sections of the book was worthy in its own distinct way. ''The Book of Armageddon'' was Viereck's lyrical reaction to the world aflame. The section began, of course, with his panegyric of the Kaiser—''O Prince of Peace, O Lord of War''—the poem that had traveled the world as soon as it came hot from his enraged Teutonic pen. In *The Iron Chancellor* Viereck returned to his boyhood love for Bismarck, forgiving the great man for having caused the imprisonment of his father. In truth, Viereck had scarcely harbored any resentment against the man and, strangely enough, his father had admired Bismarck, despite personal grievances. Viereck envisioned Bismarck stirring in his grave as the ravens screeched war alarms.

He was infinitely finer both as a humanitarian and as a poet in a sonnet addressed to Woodrow Wilson, *The Neutral:*

> Thou who canst stop this slaughter if thou wilt,
>   Lo, how with death we freight the unwilling sea!
> Lift up thy voice to end this infamy:
> Hands may be blood-stained that no blood have spilt.
> Into a people's heart, yeah to the hilt
>   Is plunged the sword of thy Neutrality.
>   Though each wave brings some golden argosy,
>   Each on our souls heaps a new load of guilt.
>
> Curses for us commingle with the tears
> Of anguished mothers, Man, hast thou no ears?
>   Upon thy white Honor falls a streak of red
> From Europe's carnage. In the long night-tide
> Canst thou not see them marching side by side,
>   The mute accusing army of the dead.

The full blast of his inspired rhetoric Viereck let go at Italy after her desertion of her former allies, Germany and the Dual Monarchy. In accents that sometimes resembled Kipling and sometimes William Watson, he became devout in his self-righteous wrath:

> Tear from thy brow the olive wreath!
>   Thy laughter sickens to a leer:
> Behold thy honor fall beneath
>   The hammer of the auctioneer.
> Now Cain shall claim thee for his own
>   And Judas keep thee company.
> Hell, when the blackest deeds are known,
>   Shall hail the name of Italy.

And to conclude the section of the book dealing with the world carnage, Viereck published his superb translation of *Deutschland, Deutschland, Land of All Lands*. He made it in English one of the finest of the national anthems, with something both heroic and gemutlich in its inspiring verses:

> When thy children face united
>   Every foe against thee hurled,

From the Meuse into the Memel,
  To the sea, with flags unfurled. . . .

German troth and German women,
  German wine and German song,
Shall retain their ancient glamour
  Though the years be dark and long.

Of course, Viereck's first *Hymn of Armageddon,* the one honoring Roosevelt,
was reprinted in the new book of verse, though his admiration for the Rough Rider
had suffered a sea-change and the two were exchanging unkind, knife-like remarks
about each other. Teddy had suggested that George Sylvester Viereck would
prefer the Kaiserly atmosphere of Potsdam to that of New York and Viereck had
told him to go to a region hotter than Oyster Bay. Before the animosity of the two
men was sealed, Viereck had gone to Oyster Bay with Dr. Dernburg to call upon
Roosevelt. It was their last friendly meeting.

One of the curiosities of the book was a *Song Against Nippon,* dedicated to
Senator Hiram Johnson of California. As poetry it was poor and its humanity was
worse. In sober truth, it was mere posture and insincerity, inspired by Viereck's
zeal for the Fatherland. The pro-Germans believed it good strategy to concentrate
on hatred of Japan and of Mexico, thinking that America's resentment being
turned towards those two countries and away from Germany, the danger of
American intervention on the side of Britian and her allies would be lessened. In
this purpose, William Randolph Hearst abetted them, with screaming headlines
about Japanese bases in Mexico.

As if to confound his readers, "The Book of the Dead" had a short poem in
praise of Huerta, the ruthless Mexican leader who had refused to salute the
American flag, and contained a magnificent tribute to the elder John Pierpont
Morgan, whose banking house Viereck was fighting, tooth and nail, in the
columns of *The Fatherland* and in pamphlet after pamphlet! The explanation of the
seeming contradiction is as simple and as complex as the truth very often is.
Although Viereck was apparently a crusader for what he deemed a righteous
cause, that of the Fatherland, his love of strong men could never leave him; in the
midst of strife, Viereck honored the giants in the enemy camp. He was an
inveterate hero-worshiper.

As the German cause became more hopeless, the propagandists fought more
desperately. There was a battle of books, of paper bullets, of ideas, most of them
bad and the good ones contaminated. Viereck's volume of verse, *Armageddon,*
was one of the casualties of this war of words. At best, it received only grudging
praise. America had more casualties, in a way, than blood-drenched Europe, for
everyone took aim at poor Uncle Sam's nephews. Some of the most advertised
men in America were among the casualties. William Jennings Bryan felt constrained to resign as Secretary of State because he felt that the stiff notes to

Germany made war inevitable, and his Christian soul revolted at the thought. The pro-Germans and the pacifists took heart from Bryan's resignation. Even Viereck, who had always denounced Bryan and laughed at his grape-juice diplomacy, suddenly was forced to turn him into a hero; Bryan's portly frame, smirk and all, graced one of the covers of *The Fatherland*, the same covers which had honored the Kaiser and Franz Josef and Hindenburg and other Germanic heroes.

The propaganda cabinet seized such straws as if they were tall timber. They discussed everything with a desperate care, and Viereck gave an account of the meetings that united humor with drama. He told of the fantastic disguises of the names of the participants, the search for dictaphones, the whisperings, the solemnity and humorous interludes, the whole tragi-comic show. Much to the glee of the British and the disgust of the Irish, the German propagandists considered it their duty to make written records of all transactions. With Teutonic heaviness and utter lack of humor, some attempted to secure privacy for their papers by marking them "confidential" and "very secret"; this practice, coupled with the penny-pinching of the imperial government, was to lead to a catastrophe that rivaled the sinking of the *Lusitania*. It was the sinking, indeed, of the German cause.

This second catastrophe followed close upon the first. Its details are tragi-comic and have inspired every kind of fantastic story. The following version differs markedly from others. Dr. Albert and Viereck were on the Sixth Avenue elevated in New York City. Viereck left before Albert, who thereupon dozed for a moment. With a start, Albert realized that he was about to miss his station. He dashed to the rear door of the car and then suddenly recalled that he had left a portfolio—*the* portfolio!—on the seat. He rushed back, only to find the portfolio gone. Someone had purloined it! Another dash by Albert. He saw the portfolio hugging the body of a stranger. He plunged forward to recover it, but the stranger ran with more agility than Albert and jumped on a moving streetcar. Albert pursued the car, but the stranger warned the gullible conductor that the pursuing figure was a madman. The car passed the next corner, and the stranger escaped—with Albert's portfolio.

The stranger was a United States Secret Service operative, and he turned over his prize to his superior, who in turn showed it to McAdoo and to Colonel House. They gasped at the contents: "A veritable box of Pandora," Viereck said truthfully. "Albert's portfolio unloosed every half-hatched plan of the Germans. The loss of the Albert portfolio was like the loss of the Marne." The purloined briefcase was loaded with dynamite to blast the German cause right out of the water; it had the details of many of the activities sponsored by the propaganda cabinet and by the members of the German staff in America. "If the German Government had provided Albert with an automobile, a bodyguard, this disaster would have been averted," Viereck complained. "Governments, reckless in some matters, are at times prodigiously stingy."

With surprising shrewdness, the American officials turned over photostats of all of the documents to Frank I. Cobb, editor of the *New York World*, perhaps the chief journalistic antagonist of the German cause, with the result that the *World* began, as Mark Sullivan has said, "one of the most sensational serials that any newspaper ever published." Such headlines filled columns of August 15, 1915 and subsequent issues:

HOW GERMANY HAS WORKED IN U.S.
TO SHAPE OPINION, BLOCK THE ALLIES
AND GET MUNITIONS FOR HERSELF,
TOLD IN SECRET AGENTS' LETTERS.

And there were many lines of subsidiary heading, eighteen in the first article alone, including one that read; "Fatherland Financed." And staring from the page was a somehow sinister portrait of George Sylvester Viereck, with the heading: "Letters Mr. Viereck and Dr. Albert Wrote to Each Other." What letters, what letters! The Allies could, indeed, congratulate themselves; it was more killing than bullets! "As I have already received $250 this month I enclose a statement for $1500 for June," concludes one of Viereck's letters to Dr. Albert. "Will you please O.K. this and I shall then send my secretary for the cash. I am sending this letter by boy as for obvious reasons I do not wish it to go through the mails."

How does one explain such letters? It was evident that Viereck had his hands full; he never gave a really satisfactory explanation. Inevitably America's entry into the war was accelerated by the mishap which befell Dr. Albert on the fatal, hot Saturday afternoon late in July 1915.

The carefully wrought reply of Viereck appeared in a leading editorial in the August 25, 1915 issue of *The Fatherland* and was reprinted in every newspaper in the country. "The story in the *New York World* about *The Fatherland* refutes itself," said Viereck:

> The context . . . conclusively proves that no German official had any
> control over the policy of my paper. . . .With every means of cable
> communication the world over under the control of the Allies, with the
> American press literally fed day by day upon false and garbled reports of
> the progress of the war, and manufactured tales of atrocities and faked
> peace-offerings by Germany, all intended to impair her credit and
> prestige and alienate sympathy, it was not only proper but it was her
> highest duty that she should seek the means of neutralizing these influ-
> ences so that the American people—always just when they know the
> facts—might be able to judge between the contending interests.
>
> I have carefully looked over the 'revelations' in the *World,* and I
> have ransacked my memory, I can find in neither anything incompatible
> with my integrity as a publicist or my loyalty as an American citizen.
> The business and the editorial policy of *The Fatherland* rest entirely in
> my hands; there is no arrangement with anyone yielding even an iota of
> its independence.

In the purloined letter of July 1, 1915, Mr. Albert makes clear that neither he nor anyone—even remotely connected with the German government—had any interest in or exercised any influence whatsoever over *The Fatherland*. As a *condition* of financial aid he says: 'We must have an understanding regarding the policy which you will pursue, *which we have not asked heretofore!' I absolutely rejected the conditions suggested by Mr. Albert.*

Albert's desire to influence the policy of *The Fatherland*, Viereck said, was prompted by his hope to tone down the attacks by Viereck on the Wilson administration. These attacks embarrassed the embassy, but Viereck felt that he was fighting Wilson, not as an emissary of Germany, but as an American citizen.

The harm was done. Nothing Viereck or Albert or anyone else said could repair it. And to think that the anniversary number of *The Fatherland* had just appeared, its every page voicing great optimism. A leading editorial by Viereck announced, with finality, "Gentlemen, You Can't Get Away With It!" The "gentlemen" in this case being an ironic reference to those attempting to force the nation into war with Germany. Viereck depended on Vice-President Marshall, Bryan, Hearst, and Senators Stone, La Follette, Borah, Hoke Smith, and Bankhead to protect the country from the "gentlemen" conspiring to bring us into the war. Plans were laid for the future of the magazine; it was hoped that by 1916 peace would be restored. Announcement was made of articles to appear in ensuing issues culminating in a series on "America after the World's War." Birthday greetings for the magazine came from Jeremiah A. O'Leary, head of the American Truth Society, Congressman Richard Bartholdt, E.C. Richardson of Princeton, William R. Shepherd of Columbia, Kuno Francke of Harvard, Frank Harris, and others. The list mounted, but it contained very few non-German names and, perhaps, no one who commanded the support of large sections of the American public. By the test of circulation, the magazine was a success, with thousands of subscribers, perhaps 100,000 in all. There could be no doubt that it was taken seriously. The attempts to curb it showed that. It was cited in the House of Commons in Britain, and the British embassy here felt constrained to take notice of it. Had it not been for the ultimate defeat, Viereck and his cohorts might have taken the notoriety as proof of success.

Some of Viereck's pro-German friends scarcely helped his credibility. There was (in Cecil Chesterton's biting words) the "saintly Mr. Frank Harris"; it is still unknown whether Harris's pro-Germanism was subsidized by Dr. Albert or if it was simply due to his resentment against England for having clapped him in jail for contempt of court. It is difficult to read Harris's motives, but his association with Viereck led Scotland Yard to infer that Harris was in the camp of the pro-Germans. If there was no other payment, Harris was amply repaid when Viereck introduced him to the immensely wealthy Otto Kahn: an expensive pleasure for Kahn!

Then there was Aleister Crowley, poet, pornographer, diabolist, adventurer; in some respects, the most curious animal in the pro-German menagerie. For a price, it was claimed, he could praise anybody with plausible enthusiasm. (The deep sincerity of Crowley's beliefs can be gauged from the fact that he later tried to sell out Viereck to the English, at the same time claiming, much to the surprise of the British, that he [Crowley] was really a British spy!)

Perhaps the worst result of Viereck's association with German propaganda was the certain facile quality that became part of his character and vocabulary. For example, in answering the *World* exposure, he wrote: "The only support my paper has ever received has been *in the form* of subscriptions to a very limited extent. The $250, the receipt of which is acknowledged in my letter, falls under this head *and is so entered on the books* of The Fatherland. In view of a total circulation of 75,000, this can hardly be regarded as very startling." Every word of this quotation should be studied, particularly the underscored words. Strictly speaking, Viereck did not lie in his claim, but it was the sort of truthfulness that gives little comfort to the Recording Angel. Viereck wanted people to believe that the form in which contributions and payments were entered actually was indicative of the substance. These could be pay-offs despite any verbal cover-ups.

A better example stems from a period a few years later and is one of the gems of Viereck's testimony in Chicago mayor William Hale Thompson's later libel action against the Chicago *Tribune*. Curiously enough, Viereck called attention to the passage himself.

"What do you know about propaganda?" the attorney for the "world's greatest newspaper" asked him in honeyed accents.

Viereck remained silent for a moment.

"Do you know whether or not, after the Great War started in 1914, the German Government organized any propaganda system in this country?" the attorney asked, with less honey in his voice.

"I cannot answer your question unless you first define what you mean by propaganda," Viereck replied, with a self-confident smile.

"Don't you understand what it means?" the attorney demanded.

"According to the dictionary, the term is derived from the activities of the College of Cardinals for the dissemination of the Catholic Faith," Viereck continued.

"Is that the propaganda you have in mind?"

The lawyer snarled: "Is that what you think about that question?"

Viereck proceeded calmly: "There was also an attempt in the time of Milton to systemize and propagate Protestantism. Subsequently the term 'propaganda' received different meanings."

"What other meanings?" the lawyer demanded. "I will get the one I want before you get through, I think, if that is the way you want to go at it."

"Sir Gilbert Parker—" began Viereck.

The attorney interrupted impatiently: "You started to give a lot of definitions to the effect that propaganda means a lot of things. What other things does it mean?"

Viereck persisted in telling of Sir Gilbert, and the examiner roared at him;

"Now, will you please answer my question?" he insisted. "What other meanings did 'propaganda' have?"

Viereck had his revenge. "The term is used colloquially to designate an attempt on the part of any group representing some special interest," he said, "to put over its point of view, *irrespective of facts*."

After considerable wrangling, the attorney bit, and Viereck was able to say, triumphantly, that there had been no German propaganda in the United States: "All we tried to do was to put over the facts."

Throughout Viereck's testimony, the attorney for the defense made no effort to conceal his belief that he regarded Viereck neither as a patriot nor as a gentleman. And Viereck's disingenuous definition certainly was not reassuring.

The resentment against Viereck was not altogether justified. Not because of any superior virtue in the Germans but because of the fortunes of war, the program of the pro-Germans should have commended itself to Americans, for it was the way to keep out of the war. The German-Americans knew that they could not prevail upon America to enter the war on the side of Germany; their hope was simply to keep the United States entirely out of the struggle.

The first plank in the pro-German platform was the withdrawal of the protection of the American government from American citizens traveling upon armed vessels of the belligerents. It was the so-called McLemore Resolution, suggested by Sheamas O'Sheel, the brilliant young Irish-American poet and politician, and it almost won, after arousing a storm throughout the country. The near-triumph may be said to be the summit of achievement for the pro-German cause. O'Sheel described his and Viereck's hand in the matter:

> Just before the vote on the McLemore Resolution, someone tipped off the *World* that I wrote the McLemore Resolution. Louis Seibold and a man named Albert, the *World's* Washington representatives, German-Americans both doing the dirtiest of work against Germany, sent for me. They had planted some mare's nests in my lap previously. I had laughed them out of this idea though it was for once true. I was astonished and not a little indignant when, not long afterwards, Viereck admitted to me that others had been, with his connivance, given credit, in the eyes of Bernstorff and the German representatives and the German government, for writing and introducing the McLemore Resolution. It was intimated that these others got not only credit, but money.

Another presidential campaign was upon the country in 1916. The Democrats inevitably renominated Wilson, while the Republicans enthusiastically nominated Charles Evans Hughes. The Socialists also nominated, but unfortunately it did not matter. The campaign would be a race of the two parties. There had been some who had hoped that Theodore Roosevelt would be a candidate, but that was totally out of the question. Although Roosevelt was as vociferous as ever, he and the Progressive Party were dead, not to be revived. Viereck wrote of his old hero:

"Roosevelt is not the man he used to be. He never was." It was high time! Leonard Abbott knew it in 1912, while Viereck was yet a cheerleader for Teddy. Even in 1916, hopeful Hugo Munsterberg, before his death, favored Roosevelt as the candidate of the pro-Germans on the theory that Roosevelt would not stand for nonsense, either from the Allies or Germany. Only out of respect for Munsterberg, Viereck printed Munsterberg's article in the columns of *The Fatherland*.

Both parties sought to win the support of the German-American community, the superstition being that they would control the election. Viereck had a liason officer in the ranks of the Democrats, a trusted henchman of Bryan, with valuable contacts everywhere in Washington. The man was on the payroll of the Germans for the niggardly stipend of forty dollars a week, and for that paltry sum, he performed services of inestimable value to Viereck and the Germans. When the 1916 campaign was under way, the man suggested to Viereck a visit to the summer residence of President Wilson and claimed that he had persuaded the President to use Viereck perhaps in the peace negotiations which Wilson hoped to institute! But Viereck would have nothing to do with Wilson; his hatred of the President was too intense. He did see Postmaster General A.S. Burleson, however, and heard Burleson's tearful remarks about the sinking of his heart whenever he heard the news of a German defeat. Viereck's Washington representative also dickered with the Democratic campaign managers about the sale of a million copies of *The Fatherland*. Quite obviously, Viereck was considered a man of consequence in the Democratic camp. Many years later, Colonel House said that the administration looked upon Viereck as the ablest of the proponents of the German cause, though the Wilson camp considered him misinformed and prejudiced.

The Republicans, too, courted the favor of Viereck and his group, but there was no one to act as a liaison officer. The pro-Germans, including Viereck, flirted with Hughes and got a sort of mild comfort from some of his statements. It was looked upon as a marvelous victory when Hughes said that he would assert American rights against both groups of belligerants. Some newspaper cartoonists, seeking to discredit Hughes, published drawings of a proposed cabinet for Hughes, with Viereck as secretary of state.

The election, in all, centered around the shrill shouts of patriotism. The cry was against hyphenated Americans and for 100 percent Americanism. The candidates and their supporters outdid themselves in their loud protests that they hearkened only to the voices of the founders of this nation, but Viereck was unkind enough to ask what would have happened if a Mr. Schultz were President and acted as Wilson did. The moral was obvious; in spite of the campaign talk about the desire for peace, the country was pro-British. Wilson won English support because he had an inner fervor for the British, despite his determination to keep the country out of war.

One often wonders how the German officials regarded their agents in America. Surely much light would be thrown on the whole situation if even one spoke with the reckless candor of which Bernard Shaw was capable in some moods, or General Smedley Butler in all moods. Ferdinand Hansen, who was one of those present at the gathering of pro-Germans which greeted Dr. Dernburg upon his arrival in New York in 1914, said that at the time he did not like Viereck's hints that more money was needed to carry on with *The Fatherland* on a larger scale. He was one of those who had given funds for the support of the paper; in his case, it was $500 for 10,000 copies which he sent to friends and customers throughout the country. Hansen thought that the German officials who were present took a rather satiric view of Viereck's plea. He said that while Viereck, Geheimrat Meyer-Gerhardt and he were awaiting the elevator, Geheimrat Meyer-Gerhardt (sent from the Embassy) addressed them in a changed manner; his seriousness gone, his Exellency said, with a sarcastic smirk: *"Ubrigens meine Herren wird dies auch ein gutes Geschaft fur Sie sein."* ("By the way, gentlemen, this should also become a good business undertaking for you.") Revealing to a degree, if true! Viereck did not remember if the remark was ever made; but he thought it "quite possible;" also significant, in its way.

Naturally, the Germans were very polite in their published accounts of activities by their adherents in the United States. How could they be otherwise? When von Papen was asked his opinion, he informed the interrogator, through his secretary, that he had to maintain silence. Dr. Dernburg was kind enough to reply, his letter a model of official politeness. "I mistake not," he said, "that from a publicity viewpoint such a work (as this book) may have a certain sensational interest." But—the word is not the distinguished German's—"I have stayed away from the United States these last twenty years and cannot imagine that conditions are still similar in kind as in those days. Mr. Viereck was a friend of mine and a friendly helper in my difficult task in New York in 1914–15. With understanding, initiative and courage, he helped to defend a difficult position. I know how to thank him warmly to this day." To their last days Bernstorff and Fuehr were friendly with Viereck. Only Dr. Dumba, who held the trying position of Ambassador for the Dual Monarchy during the early months of the War, wrote with a certain degree of candor. "As to Sylvester Viereck," he wrote, "I remember him as a very gifted journalist who defended the German and Austrian cause with passion, fire and great go in the weekly *Fatherland* as long as the States were *officially* neutral, although in reality they were far from impartial and reserved mentality and attitude which President Wilson had asked from all American citizens. Viereck wrote also very pretty poetry of a somewhat 'decadent' nature, but during my stay in Washington I had other and more serious work and preoccupations and hardly the necessary leisure to appreciate at their full value verses a la Baudelaire."

"I must add," Dumba continued in his letter, "that Viereck is much more journalist than historian. He writes in a brilliant way, but looks for sensation. He wishes to dazzle and to amuse. As to accurate information, use of authentic sources, I believe he is not very anxious to secure them. He sent me some few years ago proofsheets of his publication on Bryan, especially on my meeting with him and conversation about the Lusitania case. He made his account picturesque and amusing, but it was far from accurate. I corrected some details and told him openly in my letter he ought to remain a journalist and not to try to write history."

There can be no doubt that some in the pro-German ranks harbored resentments and reservations. Some, like Shaemas O'Sheel, openly admitted a certain dissatisfaction with Viereck's methods during the war years. Though there can be no doubt that O'Sheel held Viereck in deep affection, he felt that Viereck was not always fair to him or to others. "Sylvester is not a normal man," O'Sheel wrote with deep sincerity, "and is not to be judged by the judgments we apply to run-of-the-mill homo sapiens. He is a genius—whether or not he leaves evidence that will convince posterity of the fact—a spirit, a spirit of perversity perhaps—and I do not expect a genius to conform to the conduct of the ordinary mortal. I do not expect a poet to have sense or morals. I do not, alas, expect a German to have political sense. Recognizing him as a genius, and loving him personally, I tolerate of necessity all his misdeeds, but I have never hesitated to tell him when I thought his deeds were misdeeds. He is brilliant, I am drab; he is successful, I am a poverty-stricken failure; but I envy him only mildly. I am sure of my own greater wisdom, if that matters; but I rejoice in his dazzling successes."

Differences with so decent a fellow as O'Sheel could do no harm; they were natural and passing. But not everyone had the understanding soul of an Irish poet. Many put up their quills in resentment against slights, real and imagined. Some felt that Viereck was intent upon hogging whatever glory, position and cash there was. Each of the various Germanic groups had its own leaders, its own policies, its own procedures. Each journalist had his favorite ideas and his own slant. There were personal differences, sectional differences, social differences. One erred if he thought that German-America was any more united than the rest of America. Viereck could scarcely be blamed for not relishing the situation. Particularly obnoxious to him were the Germans who, self-conscious over their birth, went about licking all the boots in sight, being careful, however, that none of the footgear belonged to Teutonic kinsmen. Of course, while America remained officially at peace, there were comparatively few Teutons expressing shame for the Fatherland. But when war came to America, the stampede to the flag was in a stride more energetic than the goosestep.

The rattle-brained notion of some minor official in the Foreign Office in Berlin put an end to all uncertainty as to Wilson's—and America's—ultimate decision in connection with the world struggle. It grew out of the German intrigue in regard to Mexico, which had been encouraged in the hope of diverting America from the world war. Zimmerman, acting upon the idea of his subaltern, proposed to Mexico that, in the event America went to war against Germany, Mexico make an effort to recover her "lost provinces"—New Mexico, Texas, and Arizona. It was a stupid proposal, serving no good purpose, and must have been accepted by the Foreign Office only as the result of incredible brain fatigue. And, of course, the ubiquitous British intercepted the Zimmerman note and passed it on to the American State Department. The Thames River must have swelled with pride. To Viereck and other German-Americans, it was too tragic to be believed. Viereck sent wires to newspapers throughout the land announcing that the Zimmerman note was a hoax. It had to be! How could a German statesman be so incomparably stupid as to make so impossible a proposal? How could they, indeed! But soon enough the monumental stupidity was confirmed. The death throes of Germany had begun.

"We cannot," said Viereck, beginning to mend his bridges, "remain the friends of a country that is plotting to destroy our own."

Yet the cause of peace died hard. Bryan addressed the American people in a plea for peace, even after the President broke off diplomatic relations with Germany; huge mass meetings were held; pacifists obstructed traffic in Washington and elsewhere in protest. Many members of both houses of Congress secretly opposed our entry into the war, and a few led by the heroic Senators, La Follette and Norris, openly opposed it. Viereck sent a broadside "To the Friends of Peace Everywhere":

> This is the most important communication that I have ever addressed to you. I urge every reader of this message, every sympathizer with the cause of humanity, every sympathizer with the cause of peace, every citizen who refuses to participate in the desperate conspiracy hatched in London to make our country again a vassal of Great Britian, at once to dispatch his protest to the President, to his Congressman, to the two Senators from his State . . . . War may come in spite of our efforts, but upon us will lie the burden of guilt if we fail to speak out.

The plea was unheeded; America led, so it thought, by a pacifist president went to war. What would Viereck do to make the most of the war? What could he do? Only a few months before, in the midst of the presidential campaign that had been enlivened by the slogan, "He kept us out of war," Senator Stone, chairman of the Committee on Foreign Relations of the United States Senate, had asked Viereck and a group of German-Americans: "What would you do if we were to declare war against Germany?" Viereck had replied, "We would do our duty as American citizens. We would shoulder a gun and fight." "You wouldn't, and you shouldn't," Senator Stone had retorted. "No one would expect you to fight against your kinsmen." But Viereck had persisted. "Senator," he said, "we Americans of German descent are true to our oath of allegiance. We would do our duty. But, after it was all over, we would punish the rascals who got us into this mess."

Now it was no academic question. The test had come.

23   MAKING THE MOST OF THE WAR

America was at war, but the enemy was across the sea and far away. How would we fight Germany, without an adequate sea force, no air force, and scarcely an army? Germany, too, may have wondered, but the answer came with such terrific force as to stun not only Germany, not only our associates in the war, but also ourselves. The war atmosphere in America became thicker than the clouds over France. In our eagerness to atone for not having entered the holocaust sooner, we went at the task of war preparations feverishly.

Because German U-boats destroyed Allied vessels with abandon, the U.S. worked at a mad pace to outdistance their work. Every privately owned ship above a certain tonnage was commandeered by the government; interned German ships were taken over—neutral ones, too; anything that would not sink was taken over. Shipyards grew up overnight, turning out every kind of ship: prefabricated ships, concrete ships, freaks of all kinds, the only requisite being that they keep afloat for a little while. America planned to build 20,000 airplanes, even more, if needed to win the war. America would give without stint, for it was in a holy war against autocracy, a fight for democracy, a war to end war. Americans were the paladins of God. "Onward Christian soldiers into battle!"

Onward—prompted by conscription. American leaders knew at once that the system of voluntary enlistments would be inadequate. An army of millions was raised. All young male Americans seemed to be at camp, drilling for the offensive against the Kaiser. Those who were not at camp were active at home or in the shipyards or on the farms and in factories and workshops. Bureau after bureau was set up, so that all Americans might do their bit.

There was a continuous campaign for the preservation of food, of fuel, of resources in general. Day and night America was told by Herbert Hoover, late of the Belgian relief program, that "Food will win the war," and to confirm that belief, there were wheatless Mondays and Wednesdays, meatless Tuesdays, porkless Thursdays and Saturdays, and economy all the time. America, which had been digging its grave with its teeth, went on a national diet. The war had to be won; the Huns had to be obliterated; the Beast of Berlin had to be skinned alive.

America dug deep into its pockets to finance the war. Everyone, voluntarily or involuntarily, bought Liberty Bonds, Thrift Stamps, War Savings Stamps. There was not a human being in the land who was not placed under terrific pressure to "give until it hurts."

Nobody can catalog all of the many devices employed to make America war conscious. The brains of men were racked so that they might rack other brains. Human ingenuity was at its height, thanks largely to George Creel and his Committee on Public Information. To the unbelievable verve and capacity of that one time Socialist, then a close associate of Wilson, America and ultimately the world were indebted for the information and the misinformation, the ideas and the inspiration, that helped win the war. His committee entered into the daily life of every human being in America. Carl Byoir, who was later, during the Nazi period, to contribute to the ruination of Viereck, was associate chairman of the committee.

National madness set in. It is not too much to say that the Reverend Doctor Billy Sunday was for once in tune with the times when he began a prayer in the House of Representatives at Washington: "Thou knowest, O Lord, that no nation so infamous [as Germany], vile, greedy, sensuous, bloodthirsty ever disgraced the pages of history." In this atmosphere George Sylvester Viereck had to live and work. The son of Louis Viereck, the scion of the Hohenzollerns, the son of the Fatherland, the vociferous defender of the Teutonic cause, the marked man of German America, had to carry on, somehow. It was no simple task by any test—an impossible task by most. How could one keep one's principles and yet remain alive and out of prison? There could be no German gold now, nor would gold be of use when a nation was mad. The young man of thirty-three, now the father of two sons, had a problem or two on his hands!

Shortly after America entered the war, a mob threatened to lynch Viereck, and only his own burst of courage, his wife's quick thinking, and her brother's coolness saved him. They were staying then at Mount Vernon, a suburb of New York City. Viereck's youngest son, his namesake, had just been born. When Gretchen saw the mob in uniform, she innocently asked them if they were Boy Scouts! This restored the mob to some semblance of sanity. Viereck safely passed through the crowd because nobody could imagine so young and mild a person to be the most prominent of the late defenders of the German cause. Why, he did not look at all like Bill of Potsdam! Perhaps he was the infant son or nephew of Viereck! He walked into the house with seeming nonchalance and escaped through the rear.

Then followed a "strategic retreat" to a hotel in New York. He could not visit his wife except when darkness covered the city. Like a thief in the night, he stole into his own home. It was dangerous; it was thrilling; it was romantic. He began to enjoy his existence, even if no life insurance company would insure his life, even if he was attacked daily in the press, even if the authorities hounded him.

Not a day without a threatening letter, not a night of certainty, yet humor was blended with the stern happenings of each day and hour. Some inspired oaf in Texas used to send Viereck daily—for two years—a check for one million dollars, signed by Wilhelm Hohenzollern. A Boston publisher told Viereck's frightened secretary that if he could not get Viereck indicted for treason, he would hire thugs to kill him. (This gentleman ultimately ended his career in jail for some common swindle.) Bookstores and newstands no longer dared to display Viereck's books or magazines. His publishers returned the plates of his early book. "Like so many chickens," Viereck later said, "my songs came home to roost." Viereck's employees and agents were threatened and tempted, in turn. The cry seemed to be, "Get Viereck!" They did not get him. It is a tribute to his adroitness and to his luck.

Once Viereck thought his ill-wishers were on the road to success. One day he received a little box, sealed with suspicious care. He took the little package into his library and cut the string with which it was fastened. Suddenly there was a crackle and a flash. An explosion, he felt certain! Part of his scissors was burned away by the flames. Why had he not heeded the warnings? He ran out to telephone the police. The bomb squad came. Alas, for the hundred percenters, it was only a book! The crackle and the flame arose because Viereck had carelessly cut some electric wires while cutting the cord of the package.

Art Young, the radical cartoonist, gave a vivid verbal sketch of the Viereck he knew during the feverish days that preceded and followed America's entry into the War. He had met Viereck at one of the luncheons of the Vagabonds at the National Arts Club in New York. One day Tom Masson, then a well known writer, said to Young as the two were leaving together, "I don't like Viereck." Young asked, "Why?" And Masson replied, "I don't like his teeth." There was really nothing wrong with Viereck's teeth, but one excuse was as good as any for denouncing the man. Viereck was damned for less by others.

Of the many members of the Vagabonds, Young said that Viereck was one of the very few who defended Germany after 1914; most of the others were belligerently against the Central Powers. They would answer Viereck with considerable heat, and the group ultimately fell apart because of such arguments. It was said that Viereck's bringing Dr. Dernburg to one of the meetings was the final straw. What repulsed the others naturally attracted Young, with his inborn compassion for outcasts. He admired the spunk of "this young man who would speak out like an injured school boy—with the teacher and the class against him." Young tried to make up his mind where Viereck belonged in this world. He recalled reading and wondering about a poem of the young pro-German who "was a glorification of ruffles, lace, jewels, perfumed elegance, and all that goes with luxury and wealth." What did it denote? He would often see Viereck, and always the man was filled with enthusiasm for something: "his Aryan eyes would dance a fox trot as if the future belonged solely to Viereck." Once, during a discussion of plans for a new magazine, Viereck disagreed with some of the proposed plans. "I'm an anarchist," he announced, stimulating the discussion until it took in everything, including the world trend toward collectivism. Young began to suspect that "Viereck [believed] in individual rights and freedom for the nice so-called cultured people, and especially for himself; but [was] not too much concerned with the rights of the uncultured members of the human family. I suspect that he is for ruffles, jewels, lace and elegance, and the rule of those who have the money to buy them for pomp and display." One wonders how evident Viereck's hedonism was during the war years; it could not have been as blatant as it was earlier. Henry W. Nevinson, a good observer, who happened to be in New York at the time and who noticed Viereck's unpopularity as a pro-German, said that "he seemed a thoughtful man—almost overwhelmingly thoughtful, and eloquent too."

When America got into the war, restraint vanished; those who should have known better joined the hysterical mob. Charles Hanson Towne, for one, made a public confession:

> With the arrival of the World War, and particularly after the United States entered it, there was no one we disliked more than Mr. Viereck . . . . We ourselves in the hysteria of vanished time remember (to our shame, now) cutting him dead in a street-car one afternoon. We even glared at him, not content with coldly snubbing him. And yet, deep down in our hearts, we admired him as a poet, though, in 1918, we recall tearing an inscribed fly-leaf from a copy of *Nineveh* which he had presented to us long before.

When Towne edited an anthology of verse about Roosevelt, he carefully refrained from including the *Hymn of Armageddon,* though he must have known that it was perhaps the best of the poems about the Progressive standard bearer.

There were few with Elsa Barker's tolerance. She, too, favored the Allies, yet she did not hold Viereck's Teutonic sympathies against him. Meeting him one day on the bus, quite by accident, she said to him that he could not help being pro-German just as she could not help being pro-Allies, and that was all there was to it; they did not have to quarrel about it. Of course, Leonard and Lewisohn did not desert him, for they shared his Teutonic sympathies and were in the same boat he was. They, too, were in precarious positions because they still cherished the land of Goethe. Leonard constantly found himself twitted by colleagues because of his friendship for Viereck, and the twitting was not good-humored. For the most part, he bit his lip and remained silent, but he let it be understood that he did not desert friends easily. Richard Le Gallienne told Viereck that not even a World War could destroy their frienship, and yet they did drift apart.

Some friends departed in silence; perhaps they were in the majority, but most left only after heaping coals of fire upon his head. Some who had cared for Viereck most were now most bitter in their hatred for him. One young poet, Blanche Wagstaff, who had been united to him by every spiritual tie, shouted against his "nefarious deeds" in her letters to him. Viereck reminded her:

If the military Intelligence Bureau had any record or any proof of disloyalty against me, how do you think I escaped? As a matter of fact, one of its chiefs was incontinently kicked out largely because of his slanderous statements against me. Has it ever occurred to you that even the devil might not be quite as black as he is painted? And has it never occurred to you how imbecile it is for poets to quarrel over politics, or to permit their politics to poison their personal reactions?

With a verbal wink, he asked her to keep controversy on a higher intellectual level. "In spite of all, I bear you no ill will. . . . I have always said that I practiced all Christian virtues without believing in any." His foes exercised no such Christian restraint. When they exhausted prose, they turned to poetry in attacking Viereck. One of the most vociferous, Hermann Hagedorn, published "A Portrait of a Rat," Viereck being the rodent in question:

> A little greasy, not quite clean,
> Conceited, snobbish, vain, obscene,
> Like flying poison are his smiles,
> And what he touches, he defiles,
> A Poet, knowing Love and Art,
> He makes a brothal of his heart;
> A builder, gifted to build high,
> He dreams in filth and builds a sty
> To haggle in with foolish kings
> Over the price of wit and wings
> And when his country calls her men
> With gun and sword, with brush and pen,
> He smirks and quotes the Crucified,
> And jabs his pen-knife in her side.

Viereck felt that Hagedorn knew little of animal lore, particularly that rats desert sinking ships. Viereck felt that, whatever his failings, disloyalty was not one; that he stood by friends and causes, even in the face of war. He replied to Hagedorn with another animal poem, "A Portrait of a Jackal":

> For love of ease he plays the knave:
> He spits upon his father's grave.
> Yea, for his masters' sport his tongue
> Befouls the race from which he sprung—
> While eager, oily, smooth and kempt,
> He eats the crumbs of their contempt.
> A beggar, lacking love and art,
> He sells his malice on the mart.
> He cases a eunich's jaundiced eye

Upon the Prophet's Paradise,
And when his country calls for men,
Gives, all he can, a—fountainpen.
His brave words hide a slacker's heart,
Informer, sneak, he chose his part,
A jackal, ever on the run,
Save where the odds are ten to one!

A group of the leading writers of the country pledged themselves never to mention Viereck in any of their writings. They would regard him, they said, as if he had never existed. They would keep his name out of the anthologies, out of the magazines, out of the books. He would never be mentioned, even abusively. It was a solemn pact, perhaps the first of its kind in literary history, and to a very great extent it was observed. *Who's Who in America* had only a formal reference to Viereck for perhaps twelve years following the war, and his name disappeared from anthologies, from magazines, from books.

The Author's League, stirred on by Viereck's old friends, Roosevelt and Gertrude Atherton, expelled Viereck, in an atmosphere suggesting the performance of a holy act. Various writers, including Hagedorn, Ellis Parker Butler, and Owen Wister, joined in a group called the Vigilantes, having as one of its chief purposes the obliteration of Viereck. Butler issued a pompous broadside against Viereck, and the others said "Amen" in various ways. Many members of the social and athletic club to which Viereck belonged would have been glad to throw him out bodily. The club did expel him, and the welkin rang with self-righteous shouts.

The episode which hurt Viereck inwardly more than anything else was his expulsion from the Poetry Society of America. He had been the one principally responsible for the founding of the society; its honorary president, Edwin Markham, was his great friend; its active president, Edward Wheeler, was his friend and one-time chief on *Current Opinion;* its original membership consisted largely of those with whom Viereck had been most intimate in the past, the men and women who had followed his leadership in the struggle of American poetry against Philistine domination. Viereck had always taken an active role in the meetings and activities of the society. He had stirred the old ladies, male and female, on more than one occasion; he was somebody then, and he exercised the prerogatives of his rank. True, during the early years of the war, his interest cooled and he was critical of the society, but he still wanted to belong to it. When the National Arts Club, on whose premises the society met, demanded that Viereck stay away, Viereck was requested by fearful friends to resign. He refused to do so.

At length loud rumblings were heard on the floor of the meetings. Angry demands were made that Viereck be thrown out. Up rose the patriarch of the gathering, brave, liberal, level-headed Edwin Markham, who had shown his contempt for the hysterical unfairness of the warmongers by visiting Viereck, at a great personal risk. He said: "My friends, this resolution against Mr. Viereck is entirely out of order. There is no ground in our constitution for such a proceeding. Why? Because this is a poetry society and is concerned only with poetry—not in the slightest degree with politics, not in the slightest degree with war among nations. If Mr. Viereck had written a bad poem, then we would have jurisdiction, then we would have authority, then we would have inquisitorial power, to seize this young poet and show him to the door. If he gave us an imperfect rhyme or an unspeakable cliché, then we would have unquestionable authority." It did not help. Neither Markham nor anyone else could conquer the hysteria of the moment. The sentiment against him was by no means unanimous. Edgar Lee Masters and Conrad Aiken and others protested vigorously, but it was not enough to carry the day. Viereck was expelled; he lost his license as a poet.

Bernard Shaw expressed the only intelligent viewpoint when he wrote to Viereck: "If the Authors' League or the Poetry Society or any other organization expels a member because of his political opinions, it thereby constitutes itself a political body and violates whatever literary charter it may have. Literature, art and science are free of frontiers; and those who exploit them politically are traitors to the greatest republic in the world: the Republic of Art and Science." Shaw had also said that the 100 percent American is 99 percent village idiot: perhaps a mathematical inexactitude, for, during the war years, most were 100 percent idiotic.

Viereck said farewell to the grim comedy in a characteristic poem "To Diverse Literary Societies":

> Go, play your Lilliputian game,
>   Ye lisping scribes and ladies lyric,
> While brave men die and oceans flame—
>   Your victory at best is Pyrrhic:
> The future knows your Scroll of Fame
>   But for the expurgated name
> Of George Sylvester Viereck.

Men strove desperately to put Viereck behind bars. They did not relax in their efforts from the moment war was declared until long after the Armistice. Viereck never knew when he might be picked up for examination, and these examinations were seldom gentle, particularly when the district attorney was seeking election to a high post. One night Viereck's child-wife became excessively alarmed. Long past the expected hour, he had not returned to their home. In sheer desperation, she called the police and prevailed upon them to make a search for him. The police found him in the office of the deputy district attorney for the state of New York, being cross-examined with relentless vigor.

One example is typical of several. One morning, late in June 1918, Viereck received a call from a Mr. Blatchford of the Department of Justice. He was asked to come down to see Mr. De Woody, chief of the Bureau of Investigation. Viereck expressed pleasure but inquired as to what it was about. He was told it was nothing of much consequence. When he arrived at the government office, he shook hands affably with Mr. De Woody and was introduced to the big chief, none other than Mr. Bielaski. Again Viereck expressed pleasure. There was scarcely a tinge of irony in his politeness. Men had been stepped upon for less!

"We know each other by reputation," Viereck ventured to say.

A few more polite words by both men, while Mr. De Woody fingered several voluminous documents, apparently bearing on the heinous individual before them. The interrogation then began, De Woody becoming increasingly hostile, as if to spur on the big chief, and whispering mysteriously to another inquisitor of the department, much to Viereck's annoyance. They desired enlightenment, they impressed upon Viereck, chiefly about the alleged purchase of the *New York Evening Mail* by Germans, the amounts of money received by Viereck and others, and Viereck's connection, if any, with a man who was implicated in a strike of stevedores. Whenever Viereck hesitated in his answers, whenever he said that he did not remember, whenever De Woody felt that there was something amiss, he whispered to or nudged his fellow inquisitors or nodded his head doubtfully or smirked or sneered. He was the actor as patriot, and he did not amuse Viereck in the least.

Viereck confessed that he had destroyed many of his records. The inquisitor was upon him at once. "Did you not think that these letters might be of value to the government?"

"No, they were not connected with any illegal act," Viereck replied. "I destroyed them in order to break entirely with the past. I did so, in the majority of cases, long before we entered the war. I wanted no further connection, direct or indirect, with the German propaganda, and I tried to forget as much as I could."

"You have admirably succeeded!" retorted Mr. Bielaski, with heat. De Woody beamed and made notes. They would hang the man yet!

"Moreover," Viereck added calmly, "it is not necessary to keep my correspondence on file, because I understand that a complete file exists in the Department of Justice."

Not a smile this time from the inquisitors.

"You have my letters, my memoranda. I have nothing," Viereck hammered home. "The last four years were full of excitement for me. I edited two magazines, I got married, had two children, participated in a thousand schemes and conferences—how could I remember the details of all of these plans?"

This seemed incredible to the big chief, Bielaski, and he said so. He sought further to trip up the German-American before him.

"I presume some one on the committee would say, 'Let us give five hundred dollars to the *Gaelic American*'," he insinuated.

Viereck refused to fall into the trap: "The *Gaelic American* was never mentioned in our conferences," he was quick to reply. Bielaski informed him, with mock sweetness, that he had given the *Gaelic American* only as an example.

Viereck suggested to Bielaski that before America entered the war, he had the right to carry on "literary propaganda" for the German government and to be paid for doing so. He was in the position of a lawyer or a minister.

Another assistant district attorney came into the room at this point. De Woody showed him some memoranda and made some uncomplimentary remark about Viereck's pro-Germanism, intentionally loud enough for Viereck to hear. When Viereck took exception to the uncomplimentary remark, De Woody grunted contemptuously. He would not bother to be civil to a Hun.

Viereck was questioned about the ladies whose initials he had used in a letter to Dr. Albert. He said the names were used without their consent, and he felt ashamed of his thoughtlessness. Would he reveal the names? The government had them in the official files, he replied, but he would not confirm their information.

"Are you holding back anything else from a similar sense of propriety?" demanded Bielaski.

And so the cat and the canary played for long, and strange to say, the canary won. "You had better return to poetry," said Bielaski, affably. "I shall," Viereck replied. There were other examinations from time to time, but the adroit singing bird who did not "sing" about friends managed to keep his freedom!

In those hectic war days, what the left arm of the government did was not known to the other limbs of the government, or was, at best, unheeded. While a few men in the Department of Justice and certain petty local tyrants harrassed Viereck, he was being commended with surprising fervor by men high in office.

Just before America entered the war, the name *Fatherland* was removed from the masthead of Viereck's magazine and *Viereck's—the American Weekly* substituted for it, together with a phrase or two of rampant Americanism of the variety since associated with the *Chicago Tribune*. Just as the original title of the magazine was provocative to a degree, the editor determined that the new title would be a forthright assertion of his right to speak for America. Others might question that right; he would not; he could not afford to! He could no longer oppose the war, but like others before him, he could belong to the party of indignation. He could become excited about the conduct of the war, insofar as he was permitted to do so. He had no illusions as to the difficulties of the task, but he could not escape it.

He had written to the president offering his services. He said, in effect, that, whatever the differences of opinion in the past, now all good Americans had to unite to win the war. He was, he said, a good American, and he wanted to do his share. Some correspondence with Secretary Tumulty followed, both men no doubt suppressing their innermost thoughts. Viereck was careful to note a reservation in his pledge of loyalty. There was, he said, room for constructive suggestions. He would offer them from time to time.

His first suggestion was that German-Americans be exempt from actual combat against their own kin. He felt that they could do their bit in other ways, and he enumerated some of these ways. It should be "America first and America only," he said, but human nature revolts against combat with one's own flesh and blood. Many powerful members of both Houses of Congress supported Viereck, but he saw at once that his position was an ambigious one, too easily misunderstood, and he abandoned it.

Throughout the war, he insisted that we were fighting not England's war but our own. With President Wilson, he insisted that Britian was our "associate," not our ally. Throughout the war he emphasized his Americanism with painful insistence. Just as Frank Harris did with *Pearson's*, Viereck took his cue from the *Metropolitan Magazine* and the Kansas City *Star*, to which periodicals Roosevelt contributed. They gave him his line of safety, he thought. But copying one of their articles, almost got him in difficulty. As a result, he had to withdraw an issue of his magazine. It is important to remember, however, that, in spite of the to-do in the papers and among the law-enforcement agencies, Viereck was never "indicted" or "arrested"; his office never "raided"; his papers never "seized" or denied the privilege of the mails. It was miracle number one of the world war.

Thus, in one of several letters praising his work, Mr. William Churchill, an important member of the Committee on Public Information, wrote to Viereck: "No one would wish that you should sink your individuality to a dull level of journalistic stupidity. There are too many such papers and they are without influence. Just because you maintain your individuality you make your paper worthy of consideration. I spoke to you of the troublesome times which it is not difficult to forsee as approaching. Despite our best efforts we are not by any means sure that we can control the situation when it is upon us. It will then have to run its course."

How well Churchill knew! Churchill, incidentally, had been born in England.

"You have individuality at the tip of your pen," Churchill continued, in a eulogy that would have made the superpatriotic gentry shriek. "You are experienced enough to know what we must do to win this war. You are as anxious to bring the war to the end which lies on the laps of the gods. You have no desire other than the true triumph of our country. No one will suggest to you how best to voice your conviction, you are an editor and the tripod is yours."

Viereck scarcely knew when it would blow hot and when it would blow cold. He kept his emotional barometer and intellectual thermometer in good shape at all hours. He had to! Once when the Post Office department objected to the form of one of his pleas for pro-Germans to buy Liberty Bonds, Viereck wrote to Mr. Rieg that it was almost impossible for him "to come out with a strong statement in support of the Liberty Loan and kindred matters because my action is apt to be interpreted at once as a specimen of the Greeks bearing gifts!"

Many other words of praise for the war activities of Viereck might be cited, words uttered or written by men high in official circles, even by the President's own son-in-law and Pooh Bah, Mr. McAdoo. "It is certainly gratifying to see a tendency toward patriotic action on the part of those who have been at least suspected of a divided loyalty," he said, with the sententiousness of a would-be diplomat. "In the long run the patriotic policy will be the profitable one." The fellow for once did not lack humor. He needed it to survive the rebuke once given him by Mrs. Samuel Untermeyer when he objected to being in the same house as

Viereck. "Mr. McAdoo, if you don't like my friends, you don't have to come to my house," brave Minnie Untermeyer had said. Her courage probably cost her famous husband dearly. When she died, Untermeyer asked Viereck to write her epitaph.

After America entered the war, Viereck was able to communicate, in a limited degree, with his parents in Germany. The letter he wrote to his father on February 9, 1918, helps recreate, if only by implication, the life he led at the time. "My dear Papa," the letter begins: "On October 27th the Department of State was kind enough to forward $1000 to you through neutral channels. The Department limited the amount and it also added the condition that the money should be used by you in order to return to this country if possible." But the elder Viereck remained in the Fatherland throughout the war. "The reason why the Department limited me to so small an amount is because it is contrary to American interests to permit any money to go into Germany.

"Under our new Trading With the Enemy Act, every person living in the territory of the Central Powers is regarded as an enemy alien. Under this act you and Mama are, technically at least, enemy aliens. The same law makes it impossible for me to write you unless I am able to obtain a license from the War Trade Board." Viereck had license 8999. "Such a license is not easy to obtain and only when it is justified by special circumstances. This letter is written to you under a license specially issued for the purpose."

"We shall shortly take a house in the country, probably in the neighborhood of New Rochelle where the Heins will live with us," he went on. This was the home from which Viereck had to flee when the villagers wanted to lynch him. "There will also be room for you and Mama should conditions permit you to come to this country. However, if we knew that you were coming definitely, we could of course make some different plans. We do not expect to go to the country until June."

At one point seven or eight lines are clipped from the bottom of a sheet (the censor's handiwork?). The son of Louis Viereck was genuinely grateful that he could write at all to his father in blockaded Germany. His letter continued: "I would like to hear from you directly and I would like to have you here, if your health and the vicissitudes of ocean travel permit." "Vicissitudes of ocean travel"—battleships and submarines and mines and every kind of instrument for sudden havoc. It seemed as if only American soldiers could cross the seas in safety so that they might be fed to the cannons. "Peter certainly ought to meet his grandfather and his grandmother. But who knows how long the war may continue?" Why was this not censored? Perhaps the words which followed softened the censor: "Peter looks very much like the picture of you as a little boy with the hobby horse, which we have in the drawing room. He also looks like me and like Gretchen." The boy was many-faced! "He is very blond and very pretty; he walks and talks and even plays the harmonica like the little Pan in the picture by Stuck. He sends his love both to you and Mama; so does Gretchen.

"I am very glad to hear that you are working upon our family history and I hope that you will also construct a family tree for Peter."

And then, recalling the excitement of the world outside his window, he concluded his letter: "I hope that Mama is keeping a little diary of her feelings and thoughts which we can read after the war, since intercourse is practically impossible."

So wrote George Sylvester Viereck to his parents in Germany in the tenth month of America's entry into the war.

The International afforded another pleasant interlude to the harrassed German-American. The magazine survived for a considerable period, although it did appear to be in its death throes early in 1914. A careful report, dated as of July 23, 1915, showed that in less than a year and with practically no promotional effort, the circulation increased from less than three thousand copies to approximately seven thousand. The one who audited the report felt certain that with an increase in the capital stock of the corporation and the right sort of effort, better results could be achieved, for the *International* could appeal to a broader and more intellectual public than that reached by *The Fatherland*. Mr. George W. Bowesman sang a siren's song in Viereck's ears as to what could be done, but Viereck was too busy with *The Fatherland*, the German Propaganda Cabinet, *Current Opinion*, and other activities to give heed to a magazine that no longer interested him as passionately as it had just a year before. Increasingly, he had to delegate the work to less busy hands than his own.

Thus the weary months dragged by. Could Viereck survive all of the wear and tear? Might not a prolongation of hostilities lead to a worsening of the national disease? The fever might go to such a height that no one could survive unless he were as mad as the rest of the country. In Viereck's case even complete surrender might not have helped, for he was too deeply stamped with German dye.

Events in Europe soon put an end to Viereck's uncertainty. Turkey, Bulgaria, Austria, then Germany herself asked for peace, begged for peace. Wilson's fourteen points were the battering rams that broke down all defenses of the Central Powers and toppled the thrones of the Hohenzollerns and the Hapsburgs. Wilhelm II abdicated the imperial scepter and went to Holland in exile. The Hindenburg line crumbled. It was all over. The most savage war in history was at an end. Men might breathe easier—perhaps. On Armistice Day 1918, America and the whole world was delirious with joy. Kingdom Come was at hand, and all of God's children vociferated in the very delirium of happiness.

Viereck walked home from his office as in a daze. He knew then that although he had wanted America to emerge from the war unscathed, he did not want Germany to be crushed. The Fatherland's abject surrender shocked him and induced a psychic trauma healed only by a deep sleep of several hours. When he awoke, he wrote his poem, *The Winners*, dedicated to his wife, who had shared the terror and trials and tribulations of the war years with him:

> Never on the winning side,
> Always on the right—
> Vanquished, this shall be our pride
> In the world's despite.

Let the oily Pharisees
    Purse their lips and rant,
Calm we face the Destinies:
    Better "can't" than Cant!

Bravely drain, then fling away,
    Break the cup of sorrow!
Courage! He who lost the day
    May have won the morrow.

The utterance restored him somewhat to himself. He could now face the morrow
with courage.

24   THE OTHER SIDE

There is a telepathy of the mind that bridges gaps and crosses oceans with the speed of lightning. The lines of mental communication are seldom broken. Physicists, I am sure, will some day learn that love has an electrical quality, called mental telepathy. To be sure, there are limits to such communication; the lanes of the mind too often are hazy and give precarious passage to ideas. But some vague suggestions of otherwhere come to many of us with compelling force, conditioning our conduct in ways that rebuke practical judgment. We think, we pray, we act in response to the messages sent abroad by the mind and heart with which we commune.

Such messages came to George Sylvester Viereck during the months following the fatal day of April 6, 1917, after physical contact with Germany became too dangerous to be attempted. His parents were in the Fatherland, away from him; by legal definition, they were his enemies; by the compulsion of his heart, they became doubly dear to him, more close to him, in very fact, than if they had been at his side—his mother, in particular. A few letters had been exchanged by special permit, but such contacts ceased and a great darkness necessarily descended upon their world. Viereck had suggested to his parents that they keep a diary of what befell them during the years of separation. Perhaps some day he would read the record; it was not impossible that they would be reunited, crippled possibly by their experiences, but having the crutch of love to lean upon; the diary would assist them in after days. So Laura Viereck began the book on November 4, 1917, while her husband worked at his memoirs, intended to be a message out of the once golden and now sere past. It was not until long afterwards that Viereck read the diary and the memoirs, but necessarily some of their substance passed to him by the magic of mental communication.

All of which may be only another way of saying that his rich, imaginative mind dwelt upon those who were so far away and that he built images of their lives. When later he read the actual transcripts, they bore, at times, the impress of something remembered from the past. It seemed to him that he had sensed all that his parents had lived through. The diary only confirmed what he knew and what he felt. Laura Viereck's diary necessarily made her son's pro-German fervor more definitely a part of his being and accounted, in part, for his postwar activities.

The diary told of the depressing atmosphere of the Fatherland, of the tightening of the national belt, of the fear of impending defeat, and of speculations for the future. Laura Viereck, forced to return to housework despite the growing ills of her body, found it a sore experience to tramp through the streets in the pursuit of vanishing food. It was something to mark down if she succeeded in getting a fresh vegetable or a goose leg. The irritations of housework were only aggravated by difficulties with the *Dienstfrau*. Nor was Louis Viereck's disposition improved by the disintegration of the times. He grew old and a little grumpy, and Laura Viereck kept apace in the downward path.

The diary began with a letter addressed to Gretchen and Sylvester Viereck, a letter filled with the little things that add up to so much. Laura ached to see her grandson, Peter. She prayed for peace and love to rule the world, so that she could see baby number two, not then born. "It takes a long while to fill up the dozen!" she told her daughter-in-law. She wanted the next child to be "a little Wendy, a sweet companion for little Peter." She told of friends and kinsmen, of their eager curiosity about Putty's activities. In this first section of the diary, she was cheerful, hopeful even for herself, for that week they had received two letters from Putty! Then came the long and bitter silence and a corresponding drop in the optimistic tone.

Late in April the record became a daily chronicle of little happenings and big worries. Was the second child born yet? That was the question of questions. For a while it loomed bigger than the war itself. It was an escape from the ills of the times. For many weeks Laura refrained from making any entries in the diary. In September the reason appeared evident; she was suffering intensely, physically as well as mentally. The household and the world had become too much for her. Two o'clock one morning she awoke and saw before her, with the sharpness of reality, a vision of Putty being taken in a wagon to prison. Toward morning, she heard him calling, "Mama, mama!" "My heart is so heavy, so heavy," she wrote in her diary. That evening Laura succeeded in getting some news clippings about Putty. They served to confirm her fears. "My poor boy will probably have to suffer much," she wrote, "and poor Gretchen—how sorry I feel for her." She began to reread Putty's letters and look among his papers, not daring to express all that haunted her.

A few days later news clippings about Putty arrived, dealing with his examination by the American authorities. Laura studied these for rays of hope and found none. "Somebody had made a betrayal," she wrote. She felt that Putty would be placed on trial: "Otherwise they would not go so much into the details of his undertakings." Louis Viereck did not seem to believe it, Laura reports, "or doesn't want to believe it as yet." She fearfully agreed with a friend who had told her that after Putty's intense activity, he was bound to be persecuted, even if he did assert his Americanism. She began to wonder where Putty would turn after the war. In sad contrast to her husband, she placed her faith in her God; she felt that He would make it right. But a terrifying news item came her way: an attempt had been made to lynch Putty! (This was probably when Gretchen had made her innocent remark about Boy Scouts.) "And so far away," her pen sobbed. She communicated with the International Red Cross on September 19 and learned that Putty was unharmed as of July 10, 1918: "a sign of life before the catastrophe," she commented.

"I am very disheartened today, on the anniversary of the children's wedding," she wrote on September 30th. "I am tired; would like to lie down and not get up again. . . . I wish that the morrow were over. . . . Today I think much of my boy. What is happening to him? Nothing is left me."

The bitter, personal mood passed for a moment as the general ills became more pressing. Obviously Germany was disintegrating in the fall of 1918. The Chancellor, Prince Max of Baden, asked for the acceptance of President Wilson's terms and a cessation of hostilities. "What humiliation!" Laura Viereck wrote in her book, "even if presumably necessary!" The general excitement mounted; the individual worries of Laura Viereck were heightened. Germany and Putty—what would become of them? The newspapers continued to indicate that her boy would be punished severely, and Laura needed no press confirmation to know that the Fatherland was entering the valley of desolation. On October 15, Wilson's second note arrived, "horrible in tone." "The leaves are getting yellow and fall intensely," Laura wrote in her diary. Meetings for the national defense were called. "But the shock is rather too frightful," wrote Laura. "One should defend himself—but it seems that the means are lacking. If the Kaiser falls? It would seem that he is the very stone of attack. Poor Louis suffers much about it and doesn't even get enough to eat."

On the twenty-fourth Wilson's reply to Germany's note arrived: "sharp, clear and firm." Distraught, Laura sounded the accents of her fear: "Germany must now show if it is great, even though conquered. If the Kaiser abdicates, he will bring peace to his country and to the world. Out of the spirit of Germany, the world shall recover. It is a heavy sacrifice for the poor man. But much as I am sorry for him, the world should not go smash because of the will of one man and one country. . . . Germany has shown that it is not able to lead politically," mourned Laura. "It lacks the national consciousness and political schooling . . . We live in great, great times. The world revolution is being effected, in the circumstances, quietly and quickly. My heart beats for America, despite the misery which is coming over us," wrote Laura Viereck. "I hope with my whole heart that Putty shares my feelings." But, "poor Germany, after all of its great deeds which will remain forever a part of history, abandoned by its allies, will yet better itself. It will overcome all of the different changes."

A friend called upon Louis Viereck. The two restless women talked of Putty, the friend taking the view that Putty would have to live in Germany after the war. "Too good to be true," commented Laura. At last, on November 5, the long silence was broken. Word from Putty was received through the Red Cross, word merely that he was alive, but that was enough to cause rejoicing in the midst of the general sorrow. On the sixth the German delegation left to negotiate for a truce. "Thank God," said Laura and millions of mothers throughout the world, "a ray of light. There is hope for the salvation of mankind." The petty thrones of the little kingdoms within Germany tumbled. Increasingly the demand for the Kaiser's abdication was heard. The Socialists began to take over the reigns of government. To Laura it was a wilderness of confusion, made more terrible by a strange quietness. The stillness vanished. There were street battles, turmoil, mutiny. On the eleventh Laura recorded that the Kaiser has crossed to Holland. She went about her housework; she slept; she fretted. The world outside grew no calmer. Laura recorded that Germany wanted an easement of the frightful peace terms which condemned it to starvation. Laura put her belongings in order; when she dies, a certain red casket is to go to Putty and Gretchen. She learned that the conditions for peace would not be made milder. She cried much, "without cause," she said; she claimed she was not brooding. There is "great danger in the near future for this Spartan people," she wrote.

Before the end of the month she heard once again from Putty, and again the national ills were forgotten. Putty was safe! What else mattered? Perhaps she will yet see him. "Or will we be lost?" she asked with a sudden shudder of apprehension. News came of the investigation in the United States Senate of German propaganda. There were worries anew for Laura; "there is so much to bear now," she wrote. "I am dead tired." Louis Viereck became carping, impatient with everything. The gentle Laura quarreled with the maid. "Everything is so drab," she felt. If only Louis would resolve to leave Germany! "I am so nervous and cranky that it is becoming fearful. . . . I am sorry for Louis; but I simply cannot control myself any longer, because I lack outer and inner peace. How could a quiet nature like mine change so? I cannot manage the household in the present style any longer—and Louis is sick besides and home the whole day. He neither wants to go to bed nor to a physician—and in that way his illness drags on."

So the fatal season drew to its close. Putty's thirty-fourth birthday ended the year with feverish fear on the part of Laura that, despite the close of the war, she would not see him again. A picture of Gretchen and the new baby reassured her momentarily. "Gretchen looks very earnest," she commented; "the poor child has to learn very early the difficult ways of life."

Louis stormed around the house, Laura too ill to answer him. The gloomy street, the frightful cold, the many soldiers made her so nervous that she could almost scream. "All the conditions of life grow harder from day to day. . . . I have to live in a country which brought me very little happiness. Even in my youth I preferred America and England to Germany. I like the English language and the English way of life more than the German. I cannot help myself that I do. If I were there, I would at least have the children and the grandchildren, who would bring me joy and zest for life. But this way! The evening of life seems to get even more difficult."

Suddenly Louis Viereck discovered that Putty was not coming to them, that they would have to go to him. To Laura it was a day of fate, too beautiful for belief. Perhaps happy days were yet ahead.

25   THEODORE ROOSEVELT AND THE WAGING OF PEACE

Leo C. Rosten has said that "men like war" and has written brilliantly to prove his thesis. The theme is an old one and yet essentially fresh. Rosten listed some of the reasons for mankind's perverse fondness for warfare, all of them summed up in the fact that war compensates for some of the deficiencies of peace. Peace lacks romance to unromantic minds; peace lacks thrills for the jaded; peace makes one too conscious of one's inferiorities; peace stifles sadistic instincts. It may be said in half-genuine praise of war that it unifies hatred and thus in some measure destroys the diversified hatreds which might otherwise rage. Once peace arrives, all of these little hatreds which war lulled to sleep in the bed of one great hatred come to life with renewed vigor. The inhabitants of the land begin to cultivate their personal enmities. Every form of rancor is placed on display; there is not one battlefield, but thousands.

Thus it was after the so-called Armistice of 1918. The cessation of hostilities unloosed greater battles on American soil than had been waged in Europe. Each of the racial groups decided to combat the others or some particular segment of society. Each social group waged war against the other. Each geographical section combatted the other. Political differences were emphasized. Individual differences were exaggerated. The national motto became, not "one out of many," but "many out of one." Great apostles of strife arose; princes of peace were clubbed down; many of those who cried out for justice were trampled upon. Personal liberty became a meaningless shibboleth, for it was the era of Prohibition and sumptuary legislation in general. It was the era of the Klu Klux Klan. It was the era of red-baiting and witch hunting. No need to chronicle all of the sins committed upon the return of "peace," but they concerned Viereck deeply and they were of moment to the rest of the civilized population of the then benighted states. He waged war against the Ku Klux Klan—at first a losing fight, and attempted in general to maintain some sane balance, but his was little more than a voice in the wilderness, a voice of particular offensiveness because of the disfavor with which he was regarded.

Viereck's forum was the *American Monthly*. It became his sole organ of expression after he severed his connection with *Current Opinion* in 1916 and sold *The International* a few years later. The magazine became his chief means of support. He earned perhaps $10,000 per year through it, sometimes more, and it provided a sufficiency. He was out of the arena of literature, but he was in the battlefield of life with a dozen fights in which to engage.

After months of uncertainty, the terms of the Treaty of Versailles were announced. Alien armies occupied the precious fields and firesides of his Fatherland. The imperial family was in exile. Their Reich felt the heel of the oppressor, and famine walked in the land. It was necessary to feed his German people, it was necessary to fight for justice for Germany, and it was necessary to destroy the "myth" of war guilt. The *American Monthly* under Viereck unleashed a thundering assault on the sins of the world. It was a period of horrors, and all of them were reported in Viereck's magazine. More than ever, the one-time poet became an almost blind devotee of the land of his birth.

Alfred Rau, a dear friend of Viereck's who had assisted him in founding *The Fatherland*, expressed the matter with much aptness:

> I retained a great affection for the magazine, until later on I could not agree with Viereck's policies any longer. I think *The Fatherland* defeated itself when Viereck became more German than the Kaiser, more Austrian than the Emperor and more Turkish than the Sultan. There was ·nothing that the German side did that Viereck did not applaud. Even when the Central Powers apologized for some action, Viereck vigorously applauded. There was no sense to it anymore, and with the outbreak of the war and the necessary change of name (as usual Viereck did the spectacular thing and switched from *The Fatherland* to the *American Weekly*, the good old *Fatherland* died. What was left of it was not enough even to be called a memory.

There was a strong measure of truth in Rau's analysis. Viereck expressed his intentions in the many letters he wrote at the time, particularly to those who had won his confidence. On October 30, 1919, he told his friend Gottlieb von Jagow, the German diplomat, his special admiration for his "sane statesmanship, . . .a quality of which Germany is in greater need now than ever." Even when his faith in Wilson began to weaken, he still thought it possible "to shame him into an honest and consistent policy." But the hope was in vain. "The fate of Woodrow Wilson," he said "savors of a Greek tragedy. He is the hero who betrayed the gods and who thenceforth can find neither peace nor rest. The furies haunt him from place to place until he finally breaks down prostrate." He called von Jagow's attention to the desire of many sincere men for "a real understanding between the three great Germanic nations," America, Britain, and Germany, but he insisted that though he was opposed to racial strife, he was equally opposed to the dominance of one racial group, that is to say, the Anglo-Saxons.

To his father, who was yet in Europe, he wrote with indubitable sincerity. Louis Viereck had sent him a number of articles for publication in the *American Monthly*, among them one on the anti-Semitic movement in Germany. Early in May 1920, Viereck wrote to his father that although the articles were very interesting to him, he could not use them. He cited in particular the article on German anti-Semitism. "We are the only publication in the United States which fights for fair play for Germany," he explained. "It would not be good policy on our part to print anything that is derogatory to Germany, anything that can justify her enemies of which she has all too many. Our mission is to point out her achievements, her efficiency, to deliver a message of hope." He told his father that his articles "admit too many imperfections in Germany. . . . I do not deny that these imperfections exist, but they are not the things which our readers want us to point out. Practically every other publication in the United States takes care of that." And the articles were "too theoretic"; he preferred writings that were "somewhat more sensational." "We should give our readers food for reflection and indignation. . . . We should under no circumstances, give them anything that will make them indignant with the Germans. It has always been the fault of the Germans to see the mote in their own eye and to ignore the beam in the eyes of the enemy." Viereck then prescribed more clearly the sort of article he wanted by commenting on the ones submitted by his father:

> The article on the Kaiser was excellent, except that I would have preferred a more friendly interpretation of him. Our readers would restore the Kaiser tomorrow, if it was a question of their vote. Our readers regret the fall of the German Empire. They would like to see Barbarossa rise again. I know that this is entirely different from the feelings existing in Germany, but we must not shock our readers by any transition that is too sudden.

Viereck, speaking from the depths of his heart, confided to his father: "As far as I am concerned, I am willing to cooperate with any German government so long as it expresses the will of the German people. However, I too, have my visions of Barbarossa." The words must be borne in mind constantly if one is to understand the shifting views of Viereck during the years which ensued.

United in his hatred of the enemies of Germany was his love for those who served her directly or indirectly. Eugene V. Debs may not have been aware that he was a friend of Germany, but he had protested against the war, not as a pro-German, not as a partisan of any of the belligerents, not as an obstructionist of the American government, but as a lover of peace and brotherhood. He held the whole world in his tender heart and hands, loving mankind as few men have loved it, in the large and in the individual. And George Sylvester Viereck was one of those he most loved. Viereck's admiration for him may have arisen from an unconscious bias in favor of one who refused to go along with the mob when America fought Germany, but Debs' love had loftier motives. He thought that Viereck was

America's greatest poet and greatest genius, a wonderful man withal, who had fought bravely when cowards everywhere opposed him. While Debs was in Atlanta prison, a victim of the national hysteria, he sent messages of love to Viereck. One of them he wrote on an envelope of a letter he sent to someone close to him: "My dear Mr. Viereck, we have never met but I feel that we are close of kin and your personal kindness has brought you very near to me. You are a richly gifted soul. You are a poet, a humanitarian, and a warrior, and if you will permit me to say it, you ought to be a Socialist. You have the courage of your convictions and you are true to your ideals. I shall hold you in grateful rememberance. I respect, admire and love you."

Debs was the noblest American of them all. His words to Viereck are the grandest tribute ever paid to Viereck, whether or not deserved. Viereck may have dreamed splendid dreams and followed at moments the star of social vision; but no man can merit the reverence of Debs, particularly not Viereck, for the reasons implicit in this book. Debs' words are memorable because Debs uttered them. So far as Viereck is concerned, they show that one man at least saw beneath Viereck's veneer a solid base of kindliness. The words, it should be remembered, were written of Viereck during the years he was a German, rather than a humanitarian, an enemy of the victors, rather than a lover of mankind.

Viereck told a friend of Debs that if Debs, out of jail, were to run against the Progressives, he would vote for the Progressives; "but, if Debs is in jail, I should feel inclined to vote for him no matter who his opponent may be in order to voice my protest against the infamous treatment meted out to him." Viereck later wrote to Leon Trotsky, the Bolshevik leader, commenting that in the same mail he received messages from the Kaiser and from Debs. "I am advocate neither of the new nor of the old order," Viereck told Trotsky. "I am interested in all things." His interest was seldom emotional and generally cerebral. His interst, too, was often a peg on which to hang the particular garments with which he clothed himself at the moment.

In 1919, for example, Viereck's first book in three years appeared. It was the slender volume entitled *Roosevelt: A Study in Ambivalence*. A copy of the book was sent to Mr. Henry A. Wise, Viereck's one time attorney, with the request that he give his opinion. Wise did so forthrightly. His conclusion was that "the whole purpose of the author seems to have been the gratification of a personal vanity in linking himself with a great man." Viereck replied to Mr. Wise with equal frankness, giving the real purpose of his book:

> Of course, you did not get my point at all. The important thing for me to do was to get back at my critics and to compel them to pay attention to me in spite of their threatened boycott. *Roosevelt was largely a peg on which to hang my literary artifices.* At the same time, there is a great deal of psychological knowledge in the little book. At least, I am so assured by psycho-analysts. You also entirely ignore its literary quality. That, in a work of letters, is not entirely negligible. [Emphasis added]

The war was over, which meant that many wars were raging, with intensified bitterness. The organized literary lights of the country had proclaimed, "Never again Viereck." And in some measure they succeeded almost at once. Viereck's hope was to break the blockade. At that time Theodore Roosevelt, who had, virtually from his deathbed, applauded the expulsion of Viereck from the Authors' League, died. Viereck saw Roosevelt as the personification of the national hatred, a fallen angel. He saw that Roosevelt was a good subject for anyone interested in the caprices of mankind. So following Roosevelt's death, he began a series of articles, published first in the *American Monthly* and then in the book, *Roosevelt: A Study in Ambivalence*.

The book, including spare sheets and advertisements, is only 160 pages in length. Of this number, 50 constitute an introduction, *Apologia Pro Vita Sua*, and 16 constitute a scrapbook of praise of Viereck's earlier writings. The balance of the book deals with Viereck as much as with Roosevelt, for it is a study, except in a few passages, of the relations of the two men, in which Roosevelt leaves the fray second best. Still it is a shrewd portrait of Roosevelt and surprisingly fair.

"This book, dear reader," says Viereck at the outset, "will be a delightful secret between us. It will not be reviewed in the American press. It will not even be mentioned."

"How account for this phenomenon?" Viereck asks. It is not, he says, because the Poetry Society has revoked his license or because the Authors' League has excommunicated him. Nor does the government warrant any blame. "It is the Invisible Government that interdicts this book," he declares. It is not his egotism nor self-assertion or impudence, he says, or his straying from Philistine paths, or the audacity of his verse and prose. Neither are his political activities responsible, nor his acceptance or money to speak for a cause near his heart. He says his pro-Germanism is not the reason for his being ostracized, and his Gaelic affiliations do not account for the boycott of his Muse.

"My real offense, surprising as this may seem," he declares finally, "is nothing less than my Americanism!" He then tries to justify this amazing thesis, not always convincingly.

"But I have wandered far from the subject of my discussion," Viereck says, after a melodramatic interlude. "Enter Theodore Roosevelt, to whom I yield his accustomed place, the center of the stage."

Viereck builds his portrait of Roosevelt on psychoanalysis, particularly the concept of ambivalence or bipolarity: "the sway of coexisting contrary tendencies," hatred and love as alternative reactions in the one individual and in the mob. Roosevelt, he says, in himself and in the crowd's reaction to him was a good example of ambivalent tendencies. He and the crowd somersaulted so often that it became difficult at times to account for their actions:

> Roosevelt himself is a typical example of bipolarity. He was at once the Progressive and the Reactionary. He was Sophist and Rough Rider, Simple Simon and Machiavelli, rolled into one. He was more English

than George V, more imperialistic than the London Times; yet he hated the English from the depths of his heart, he despised them, and, to use his own phrase, he patronized them. He was at once the faithful Patroclus and the treacherous Apache. He loved the Germans and bitterly denounced them. His attitude toward Wilhelm II was equally ambivalent. He admired the Hohenzollern, yet had no kind word for him. The two men were strangely alike in some respects. For the Kaiser is a similar bundle of contradictions. Wilhelm, as I explained in my *Confessions of a Barbarian* (written ten years ago), is both rationalist and mystic, Anglophile and Anglophobe. The Middle Ages and the Twentieth Century join in the unstable composition of his character. Yet, as I pointed out, the Kaiser is no hypocrite. We must simply accept him as two personalities. Roosevelt, contradictory as this may seem in the light of his inconsistencies, was equally incapable of hypocrisy. We cannot explain him without the theory of ambivalence.

Viereck's own relations with Roosevelt were equally ambivalent—hatred and love alternating within the bosoms of both men. "He was both my generous friend and my relentless foe," Viereck says. "If I attacked him bitterly, the arrow intended for him entered my own heart. Praising him, I spoke in strident accents, in order to drown the secret misgivings, the latent hostility, the hidden distrust in my bosom."

When *The Fatherland* was about to appear, Viereck, who could hardly be conscious that Roosevelt would make a violent about-turn, wrote to Roosevelt for a contribution to the first number. Roosevelt's reply scarcely indicated his ultimate viewpoint. He wrote Viereck, under date of August 8, 1914, that he was glad to hear from him and to know his plans. "But, of course, as you say, my desire is at present to avoid in any way saying anything that would tend to exaggerate and inflame the war spirit on either side and to be impartial; I simply do not know the facts. It is a melancholy thing to see such a war."

He felt confident that Dernburg, the German diplomat, would be able to influence Roosevelt's viewpoint. Roosevelt was willing to receive Viereck and his German mentor and the two journeyed out to Sagamore Hill one day. For hours Dernburg and Roosevelt argued, with Viereck only occasionally chirping in. Neither man pierced the armour of the other. They parted utterly convinced that there was no reconciliation possible. They exchanged voluminous letters, with the same poor results; for, as Viereck has said, "it is impossible to argue with the unconscious."

Only once afterwards did Viereck see Roosevelt. He had been invited by Roosevelt in response to an impetuous letter. Roosevelt told Viereck that he wanted Viereck to understand him and for that reason would confide some of the reasons for his anti-German attitudes. He spoke eloquently, but, of course, did not convince Viereck. Viereck ceased looking upon Roosevelt as a friend. He began to hate his old hero, as they crossed swords. Early in 1915 the poet-propagandist wrote the Rough Rider a hot-tempered, injudicious letter. "I think you have lost every German-American friend you had, with the exception of myself," Viereck said. "Now Germany no longer needs apologists nor sympathizers. Her sword has won the war. But I do not think that the Germans will forgive the attitude of their fair-weather friends on either side of the ocean." Through his secretary, Roosevelt replied that the tone of Viereck's letter was such that he did not desire to answer it.

Within his heart Viereck cherished Roosevelt and possibly Roosevelt inwardly cherished him, for Teddy expressed his surprise to a mutual friend in 1916 that Viereck was so bitterly opposed to him. Viereck had sent him a copy of *Songs of Armageddon*, together with a long and sorrowful letter but received no reply. Instead, Roosevelt inspired the campaign of the Vigilantes to boycott him. But he said in the preface to one of his books that "Germany counts upon such men as Mr. Hearst and Mr. Viereck after the war." During his last illness, Roosevelt declared that the only supporters of Wilson's Fourteen Points were Wilson, Hearst and Viereck, a strange combination if ever there was one, yet he cordially endorsed the expulsion of Viereck from the Authors' League. Nevertheless, as Viereck admits in his book, he could not hate Roosevelt. His heart went out to the tortured, disappointed, and grief-stricken man who was sacrificing himself on the altar of prejudice. "Roosevelt, under the strain of peculiar psychic conditions, was willing to die for his hates," Viereck says. "The Colonel himself never doubted the virtue of his motives. No selfish thought, I am absolutely convinced, entered his consciousness. His unconscious, however, seethed with unlovely forces seeking an outlet in the guise of patriotic devotion. The passing away of Theodore Roosevelt, so silent, so alone, moved me deeply. Divested of his faults, which were many, a man no more but a symbol, Theodore Roosevelt, dead is greater than Theodore Roosevelt living."

So the book ends, with Viereck reconciling himself with the dead Roosevelt. But, alas, there were other hatreds that Viereck nursed. He had rid himself of the Roosevelt hatred. But what of Wilson? What of House? What of all the bitterness of the war?

26 REVENGING THE WAR THROUGH HARDING AND DEBS

Throughout the early months of 1920 Viereck was attempting to pull strings so that his parents might be permitted to return to America. He won cooperation from unexpectedly high sources. Bainbridge Colby, the last of President Wilson's Secretaries of State, aided him as much as he could in the circumstances; so did Senator Phelan, Congressman Siegal, and Samuel Untermyer. Viereck wrote his parents at frequent intervals to tell them what progress he had achieved in this matter and in others with which he concerned himself, matters like the purchase of a new home and the intimate details of his daily life. He speculated as to the reasons for the cooperative spirit shown by men high in party circles. "The fact that I am organizing (with Cohalan) the German and the Irish for the Presidential campaign may not be unconnected with the workings of the State Department," he told his mother. "It may also be due to the fact that Colby is a different calibre man from Lansing." He thought no more of Lansing than Lansing thought of him.

All through April the political activities of Viereck were highly publicized. He helped to organize the then celebrated Committee of 96, and he let it be known that he was cancelling his contemplated trip abroad until after the election. "I think that politicians will think twice before offending me in view of the two million votes which I carry in my vest pocket," he wrote his father. "As a matter of fact, I think that our influence will be considerable in the forthcoming election, although I am certain that no matter who is elected, we will be 'done' as heretofore." He was becoming increasingly cynical, and he was working hard, if in the wrong direction. Curious bodies swam in his eyes. "When I look at a bright surface often in reading," he commented, "I see something like the ghost of a mosquito passing before my eyes." These ghosts did not drive him to relaxation but goaded him to more effort. He made plans to go into the brokerage business, to sell stocks and bonds, particularly of the Central Powers. "Poor Gretchen!" he said, to his mother in mock dismay. "She thought she was marrying a poet and found that she only married a stockbroker. And you too, who thought that you had given birth to a literary genius, find that you have brought forth merely a politician and a business man.'' Such activities were fun to him and less strenuous than literature.

A little later in the year, he went to Chicago, Milwaukee, and Madison. He thought people in Chicago had much vision and he worked with them. In Milwaukee he saw Victor Berger, who was then under sentence for a wartime offense. In Madison he saw Senator Robert M. La Follette (the elder) and William Ellery Leonard. His hope was to consolidate the German forces of the country so that they would be united in the forthcoming election. He preached such unity in issue after issue of his magazine and in the council rooms of the various German societies. He promised woe and damnation to the Wilsonian forces and the wholehearted support of the German element to that party and those candidates who would come out for his program. In the large, he attempted a straddle between the Republicans and the Socialists. The New York State Branch of the Citizens Alliance for Good Government and the Committee of 96 (Viereck was executive secretary of both) endorsed the candidacy of Warren G. Harding for President ''as the sole instrument for rooting out the malignant growth of Wilsonism from the body politic,'' while, at the same time, it favored the Farmer Labor and Socialist candidates in the state: Dudley Field Malone for governor and Rose Schneiderman for United States senator. They were particularly desirous of defeating Judge Giegerich, a candidate on the tickets of both major parties, because of his preposterous injunction against German opera long after the war was ended.

They sent out a questionnaire to all congressional candidates to make sure of their stand on the League of Nations, with or without reservations, on an Anglo-American Alliance, peace with the Central Powers, resuming immediate commercial relations with Russia, the revision of the Treaty of Versailles, the recall of American soldiers from Europe, cutting loose from all European entanglements, recognition of the ''Irish Republic,'' the taking from the postmaster general the power to decide the mailability of printed matter, the repeal of all war legislation, the liberalizing of the Volstead Act, the use of foreign languages in newspapers, churches or schools, the need for a referendum before a declaration of war, and proportional representation. The questionnaire is a guide to the matters and things which troubled the German element and many liberals in 1920. The German viewpoint, at that time, as voiced by Viereck, was largely the liberal viewpoint, and it bordered on the Socialist viewpoint. There was, however, no real united front of the forces of the left. Split by factional differences, the insurgents were bound to be defeated.

When in the midst of the campaign one of the Democratic candidates attacked Viereck for his brand of Americanism, Viereck reminded him of what he had said to Senator Stone when the senaor asked him what German-Americans would do if the United States declared war on Germany. ''We would fulfill our duty as American citizens, but when it was all over we would come back and punish the rascals who got us into this mess,'' Viereck had said. This was now the time for punishment.

The Democrats had nominated for president the governor of Ohio, James M. Cox, and the Republicans had, also, gone to Ohio and the boys in the back room had chosen Senator Warren G. Harding. As the candidate for vice-president the Democrats had named young Franklin Delano Roosevelt, Assistant Secretary of the Navy. Cox and Roosevelt attacked Viereck vigorously in their speeches. The Republicans chose Calvin Coolidge for vice-president. His claim to fame was that he had suppressed a police strike in Boston. In other words, the political parties, fulfilling their functions, nominated politicians, and the country was asked by Viereck and others to choose between two sets of insincere promise makers. Great issues were at stake and men had to choose.

The Socialists, on the other hand, chose as their candidate "the bald, lone, tall man of the plebs," Eugene Victor Debs, who had dared to speak out against the carnage, when war hysteria was at its height. Millions of Americans felt in their hearts that Debs was a symbol of flaming protest, a scorching rebuke to the forces that had sent young Americans to the European shambles and had corrupted the basic morality of the land. In his heart of hearts, Viereck shared that belief, but it was more politic to play with the Republicans. He, therefore, promised Harding six million German votes, and during the rest of the campaign the opposition press twitted Harding about the promised support. Cox and Roosevelt made public mention in their campaign speeches of Viereck's promise, which they regarded as tainted. There were Republicans, too, who were uncomfortable about Viereck's support, but they dared not offend him. Perhaps he did carry votes in his vest pocket!

Viereck corresponded with Harding and his campaign managers in the attempt to win concessions for German-Americans. He urged that no one of German blood be discriminated against in the distribution of high offices. After the election of Harding by landslide proportions, he pursued the successful candidate with more determination, for he felt that he had contributed to Harding's success. Important newspapers like the New York *World*, the Cleveland *Plain Dealer*, the Springfield *Republican*, the Louisville *Courier-Journal* and others gave him some credit—or blame—and he was inclined to agree. On election day, when the results were in, Viereck sent Harding a telegram of congratulations. "I rejoice that six million Americans of German descent have cast their votes for you as I foretold in my messages to you and to Governor Cox. . . . I also rejoice in the fact that you enter the White House a free man under obligations to no group, ethnic or economic. We Americans of German descent hold no promises from you and expect from you nothing but a square deal. Looking forward to your administration as a new era of good feeling both here and abroad I am, etc." It was a politician's message, for Viereck had learned the lingo well. To it, Harding personally replied some few days later, his reply mellowed with hokum. He paraphrased Viereck's telegram, so that German-Americans might find their own words and attitudes mirrored, but he was careful to make no definite promises. Viereck waited a few days and then drafted a lengthy letter, velvety in texture, humble in outward form, but explicit in language and compelling in its innuendo. After thanking the president-elect for his kind message, he ventured to say that since he had made occasional suggestions during the campaign, his suggestions now might not be resented, for he had offered them not to procure favors "but for our common country." He called Harding's attention to the brave bearing of the Germans during the war and their services in defeating Wilsonism. It seemed to him that they ought to get some recognition in the appointments to the cabinet. "I do not mean to intimate," he was careful to say, "that if you have an abler man in mind for the place, you should name an American of German descent for the position. However, other things being equal, I think that this element should find the recognition it deserves. He offered, inoffensively, to prepare a list of men of German descent who were of Cabinet calibre and said that others, like the Ridders, prominent publishers of German language papers, ought to be consulted. He advised that the important thing was to choose a man who was truly representative of the best German element in the country and not to make the mistake of choosing one who, although German-born, was not representative. He cited Roosevelt's mistake in naming Oscar Strauss "in the hope of killing two birds with one stone, of pleasing both the Germans and the Jews." He said that Strauss was not representative of the Germans, nor would Otto H. Kahn be representative. "In fact, the German element would regard his nomination as an insult. I say this in spite of the warm personal admiration which I have for Mr. Kahn in order to call your attention to some pitfalls."

He called the president-elect's attention to the alarm felt because of French and British propaganda. He feared that Britain was seeking to create dissension between the U.S. and Japan, so that under our noses they might capture the trade of Germany, while we were losing Germany's friendship. He expressed the thought that we ought to win German trade, not merely by kind words but by definite action such as terminating the control of alien property. Finally, he asked for the release of Debs. He had made a similar request of Harding while the campaign was in progress, and now he was more persuasive in his language. He urged that this would win world approval, particularly in Russia "with whom we must renew trade relations shortly. . . . You cannot be unaware of the fact that at home too, many liberals fear that your administration may lean too much towards extreme conservatism. . . . What more splendid refutation than to free Debs?"

The two men continued to exchange letters. The president-elect appeared to be friendly. He invited Viereck to call upon him in Florida, where he was resting before assuming office. Viereck, naturally, was delighted and, just as naturally, his foes were enraged. Some of them were high in the counsels of the Republican party and they sought at once to explain away the invitation. When Viereck, at the head of a delegation, called upon Harding and was received by him, certain men at Harding's headquarters stated that Viereck was not there by invitation but only through persistence. Viereck sent forth an indignant denial and wrote to the president-elect. Viereck returned the next day with his wife, and they were received graciously by Harding.

"You look very young for one who has received so many knocks," Harding's secretary had said to Viereck and had gone out of his way to be pleasant. Harding, too, talked informally and in the friendliest spirit.

"There is no hatred, no prejudice, no discrimination in my heart," Harding said. "I believe in reconstruction and my one desire is to restore complete harmony among all groups of our citizens without distinction of race. In fact, to tell the truth, I hope that at the end of my administration, there may no longer be the necessity for a political organization such as yours. [The German-American Citizens' League]."

"Paradoxical as this may seem," said Viereck, "this is also our object."

Yet his new political allignment did not make Viereck particularly happy. In the April 1921 issue of his magazine he published a warm tribute to the president, but before Teapot Dome and the revelations of the activities of the Ohio gang of political buccaneers, he had lost his faith, if he ever possessed any, in Harding. True the human qualities of the man appealed to him, the Nan Brittan tale only making him a warmer human being in Viereck's eyes. But one could expect only disappointment when one trafficked with the Old Guard.

While in Florida, the Vierecks had seen William Jennings Bryan, on the verge of his career as inspired priest of the real estate boom. The two men alternated between friendly conversation and heated retorts. Bryan thought Harding's intentions good but his associations bad. He spoke reasonably of Wilson when Viereck asked him if he could forgive himself for having procured the nomination of Wilson in 1912. Then the subject of Prohibition came up. Viereck told him that Prohibition defeated its own purpose. In his own case, for example, Viereck said that he often in the past refused cocktails when they were offered, but now he made certain that he had one.

"All of my friends drink now more than before," Viereck said.

"*Your* friends may be. Mine don't," Bryan replied in a huff.

Viereck teased him with the thought that Prohibition was a good thing "because it added a new zest in life, by giving us a new and forbidden pleasure." The utterly humorles reformer replied heatedly that if such were the case, the Ten Commandments ought to be repealed. He added that Prohibition was the best thing that could have happened to German-Americans because it took the brewers out of their political life. He expressed resentment over the fact that German-Americans had voted against him, preferring, evidently, their beer to their Fatherland.

The talk veered to more dangerous subjects. Viereck asked Bryan if he favored the pardon of Debs. Bryan tried to evade the question by mouthing generalities about his opposition to violence. Viereck assured him that Debs did not favor violence. "To call a man a revolutionist is not in itself an impeachment," Viereck added. "You forget, Mr. Bryan, that there was such a thing as an American Revolution." Bryan grew red in the face and replied angrily that he had not invited Viereck to his house to preach revolution. Gretchen Viereck saved the day in her way and prevented a break at that time. The conversation continued in fairly friendly fashion. Bryan promised to read a copy of the book *Debs and the Poets*. He expressed admiration for Viereck's poetry, although he said that, as a moralist, he had not identified himself with the sentiment. He remarked that those who do not like our Constitution should go elsewhere. As Viereck was leaving, Bryan said, with simple truth, "It is evident that you and I serve the people along different lines."

Politics and politicans were not Viereck's game, even if he did persist in lingering with them. Friends and strangers urged him to abandon politics, and sometimes he promised that he would, but when one person, unknown to fame, wrote an eloquent letter to him on the subject of quitting politics, Viereck confessed that the trouble seemed to be that he was not in the mood for writing.

At last he was able to take the long deferred trip abroad. He had met a gentleman who had taken a leading part in British propaganda activities in the United States during the war. The man had asked him, very politely, "What are you doing at present, Mr. Viereck?" And Viereck had replied, "I am fighting you fellows," The man thereupon inquired, "What for? We have stopped fighting you." This suggested to Viereck that world salvation could be achieved only by cooperation between the United States, England, and Germany or so at least he wrote to H.G. Wells at that time. Wells had told Viereck quite frankly that he was not sure whether or not he liked him, but Viereck urged that mutual likes or dislikes mattered not at all. The important thing, he said, was to work together for worldwide reconciliation and reconstruction.

Earlier, in the midst of the Harding campaign, he had carried on a heated exchange of letters with the director of the French government's war museum. The museum had requested a complimentary copy of Viereck's *American Monthly*, and Viereck had refused on the ground that France had extorted so much loot from the German people that it could afford to pay for a subscription. That started the controversy and, according to news dispatches, it amused all Paris. The museum director decided to display the correspondence as a public object lesson in the methods of Germans. "I never met you; I never expect to meet you, in this world or in another," Viereck replied to the director. "I assure you that I am not writing to you, a stranger, to air personal differences of opinion, but in the hope that letters such as mine may rouse the conscience of France. Bloodshed is abhorrent to me, war an anachronism. Nevertheless, I am convinced that the conduct of your country, both before and after Versailles, renders retribution inevitable. . . . When the day of judgment arrives for France, there will be no Czar to swing the knout for you. There will be no British Empire. Or if there should be, John Bull, quoting scripture as usual, may side with your foe. These things may be conjectures. But of one thing I can assure you: the American people will never again permit themselves to be betrayed into a war that is not of their choosing."

Which, then would it be, reconciliation or retribution? After Roosevelt's death, he had become reconciled to him, in his heart. He had parted company with his wartime friend, Bryan. He had fought for Debs and for Harding, largely to revenge the war, and his vengeance was not yet complete. But still he talked of peace. Was he only mouthing such sentiments?

27   REBUILDING

In 1922 a Leipzig publishing house issued an edition of Viereck's verse in German. It was the fifth book of his that had appeared in that language and the first one since 1911. The book contained selections from Viereck's poems originally written in German, as well as translations from his three English books of verse by renowned German literary men. Professor Edward Eduard Engel also contributed a lengthy appreciation of Viereck to the volume—no little distinction, for Engel was well known in Germany as the author of a history of German literature, a history of English literature, a life of Goethe, a life of Shakespeare, and other works. "My first and most resounding word of acclaim," Engel said, "must be a tribute of Viereck the man, the bold and fearless warrior, unsheathing his blazing sword for the priceless honor of his land and of ours, for the eternal sanctities of mankind." It was conceivable, Engel said, that Viereck's poetic fame would vanish, "but whatever may be his literary fate, every German history recounting the age of terror now drawing to a close, will cite, with deathless admiration and gratitude, the name of the most valiant champion in foreign lands of justice for Germany." It was gratitude, no doubt, that led to the publication of Viereck's poems in Germany; for his verse was not of the prevailing mood in Germany. The poems were reviewed frequently and favorably, but not eagerly.

This high praise was for the man who was then trafficking with politicians and stockbrokers and keeping clear of literary pursuits. The nearest Viereck came to the writing of literature in the days following the war was in his virile editorials, some of them of surprising force and all of them clear in language and thought. Viereck may have been perverse in his beliefs, but he was seldom muddled in his expression of them. At that time his journalistic contacts were widened, and he entered into a phase of sensational newsgathering. The once-famous editor, S. S. McClure, whom he had befriended in a small way (by attacking him!), introduced him to Bradford Merrill, a power in the organization of William Randolph Hearst, then at the height of his power. Merrill immediately realized Viereck's special aptitude for big stories in the field of yellow journalism, and while he wasn't sure that Viereck's name could be used, he was sure that his material was eminently usable. Issue after issue of the Hearst Sunday papers contained articles written by Viereck, articles which appealed to the chief himself, that sinister figure in American journalism and life, Hearst.

Curiously enough (or perhaps it is not so strange), the two men had considerable admiration for each other, much to the disgust of William Ellery Leonard and others who had learned to loathe all that Hearst stood for. Yet Viereck admired Hearst, and there was reason for Viereck's attitude, some of it of early origin, for Hearst had been the publisher of a German-language newspaper, and as far back as the Spanish-American War, that paper had published some of Viereck's youthful verse, and Hearst himself had applauded Viereck's early activities in behalf of the German theatre. When Hearst ran for mayor of New York as the candidate, self-annointed, of the common people, early in the twentieth century, Viereck accepted the man at his own inflated valuation. In this he was no worse than Art Young and others who ought to have known better. When Hearst was defeated, Viereck wrote a sonnet in tribute to him.

Hearst's stand prior to America's entrance into the war necessarily delighted Viereck. Had not Hearst been the one important editor who had supported the German cause? True, he called it Americanism, just as Viereck designated his own activities, and now he was giving Viereck large sums of money, perhaps, $100,000 in all, for frequent contributions to the March of Events section of his Sunday newspapers. It was not unwelcome, either, to know that Hearst had publicly shouted his approval of Viereck's talents and had written praise of his poetry. The two men had traits in common, summed up in lust for influence, an insatiable opportunism, a curiosity about the secrets of individual lives that in Hearst's case verged on the vulgar, a delight in rhetorical devices, and a capacity for self-deception or at least self-pardon. Viereck's final condemnation may be that he followed Hearst in the path of fascism and reaction.

Viereck also established contact with that spiritual brother of Hearst, Bernarr Macfadden, the physical culture man, and this contact survived many years. To complete Viereck's marriage with the commercial journalism of the time, he was associated with George Horace Lorimer of the *Saturday Evening Post,* ''the great dog Lorimer,'' as Upton Sinclair called him. Viereck seemed to fit only too well into the company of Hearst, Macfadden and Lorimer. For Lorimer, Viereck wrote *Prisoners of Utopia;* for Macfadden he wrote *The Web of the Red Spider;* for Hearst he wrote similar articles, all in opposition to the collectivist ideal. Viereck dismissed the communist state as the kingdom of insects. Once I accused him of blatant insincerity in his attacks on communism. He fought back lamely, preferring, he retorted, to be an eagle than an ant. ''I know and care little about economics,'' he added.

Interviews with the Kaiser, the Crown Prince, the Allied and German generals, with men of action and with men of thought, articles on world conditions, particularly on the state of Germany, features by him with scare headlines, filling columns and pages, appeared in the Hearst, Macfadden, and Lorimer publications. More than once these editors felt constrained to suppress, shorten, or edit what Viereck wrote. To satisfy his intellectual conscience, Viereck made it a point to publish his articles in full in his own magazine, the *American Monthly*. Viereck once felt constrained to tell his readers in a form letter that no newspaper account of the week he spent with the Kaiser was complete. ''The newspapers are not now disposed to give in Viereck's own words and in Viereck's own manner just what passed in the course of this visit,'' the letter said, urging readers to circulate copies of the magazine among members of Congress, publicists, editors, and influential people in general. There was one memorable article that passed unnoticed. Since Viereck could not sell it to the commercial press, it appeared only in his own magazine. It was perhaps the first long article in the English language on one Adolf Hitler, then virtually unknown outside of Germany. This article appeared in 1923. For the moment, only one sentence, the very last, needs to be quoted from it: ''If he lives, Hitler, for better or for worse, is sure to make history.'' There was another article, a very early one, on Mussolini, which he could sell only to an Austrian newspaper for about three dollars in American money. After the article had appeared in Vienna, it was quoted extensively all over the world.

If journalism did not soothe his immortal soul, it certainly did line his mortal pockets, except in such rare cases as the Hitler and Mussolini articles. In 1921, to select a representative year, he earned some $12,000 from the *Saturday Evening Post*, $10,000 from the Hearst papers, $8,000 from Macfadden, $8,000 from his own magazine, and about $12,000 from other publications, dividends and stock market profits. These are pre-inflation sums, yet he was always more or less hard up, as he said, because his expenses, somehow, always outran his income. He had heavy liabilities on many fronts, and they weighed upon him.

In spite of such financially profitable journalism and stock market activities, Viereck's name was largely unknown to the public at large. An investigation like that of the Overman Committee spread his name over the headlines for a few days, as did his testimony in the libel action of Mayor Thompson, ''Big Bill the Builder,'' against the Chicago *Tribune*. The ghost of his wartime activities stalked across the stage, forcing Hearst and others to suppress his name from articles for a brief period. He was styled ''A Special Correspondent of the Hearst Papers,'' and that had to suffice—that and the money he received. Owen Wister, who was still fighting the war and hating the Germans with the intensity of a decade earlier, through his secretary advised Viereck ''that since a German employed the phrase 'A scrap of paper' to describe solemn engagements he treats all communications from Germans as beyond consideration.'' Viereck, through his secretary, opined that hereafter Wister will treat all ''pronunciations'' from the Supreme Court as beyond consideration as the highest court of this land had declared that, in certain circumstances, it is justifiable and necessary to disregard the most solemn treaties. But such semihumorous interludes did not help in any real sense. They only prolonged the agonies of hatred engendered by the war and, from Viereck's viewpoint, postponed his reentry into the literary arena. As long as some men could think of Germans as Huns, there could be no real peace for Viereck.

The year of 1924 came and with it another presidential campaign to distract Viereck. That campaign cleared up the atmosphere and the clouds of hatred. Gradually men began to return to sanity. Some were as manly as Charles Hanson Towne in admitting that they had been hysterical during the war years. Rupert Hughes, Don Marquis, and Ralph Easley, who had thought Viereck should be hanged, began to admit error and to praise Viereck. So did Gertrude Atherton once again. And Blanche Shoemaker Wagstaff. There were many others, too.

It was refreshing to discuss again purely literary matters with such people as his admirer and friend, Frank Harris, and when Harris announced that he was going to include Viereck in the next series of his famous *Contemporary Portraits,* it gave Viereck a thrill. Harris asked for some material about him, and Viereck hastened to send him a sizable package and a long letter of confession, one of the most honest letters he had ever written. Telling of the Wandering Jew novel that preyed on his mind and yet could not be written, he said,

> Perhaps if I ever get out of the trap called America, the trap of business, I may complete this work. It should be my Faust. It appealed to me because it gave me an opportunity to traverse the ages and to have a love affair wherever I chose with every great personality in history who interested me. It is also possible that I have talked too much about the idea to be able to write about it. It is only rarely and with great difficulty that I succeed in squeezing a sonnet out of my soul.
>
> I feel that I have never used more than one-fifth of whatever vital powers the gods have given me in literature. That I have never used more than one-tenth of my powers in anything else. As you yourself know, it is comparatively easy for a man of letters, if he is so minded, to make a success of business, politics or anything else. Literature is the hardest task-mistress.
>
> I must still wait at the cross roads not till 'America catches up' with me, but till my own soul comes back.

When Viereck wrote those words, he was ready for a change, overready. The political work in which he was destined to engage in the presidential campaign of 1924 was unlike any that had preceded it. Robert M. La Follette was assuredly not Harding. One could deal with him and maintain one's self-respect. He was almost of the stature of Debs. Poets could sing of him. Viereck had not, but his friend William Ellery Leonard had in some stirring lines:

> In the Valley of Decision,
> Down the Road of Things-that-are,
> You gave to us a vision,
> You appointed us a star,

> And through Cities of Derision
> We followed you from far.
>
> On the Hills beyond To-morrow,
> On the Road of Things-to-do,
> With that strength of hand we borrow
> As we borrow soul from you,
> We know not sloth nor sorrow
> And we will build your vision true.

If one had to be in politics, then one could ally oneself with no finer personality than glorious, fighting Bob La Follette, the one who had stood before the assembled houses of Congress one fatal day in April 1917 and had dared declare his unconquerable opposition to war. There had been only a handful of senators who had had the courage to defy the warmongers. Viereck had been thrilled at that time by their courage. Now he could repay his debt. It was a poem, an epic, a fit prelude to his return to literature.

28   THE LITTLE BLUE BOOK
WAY TO FAME

Among the sourcebooks that social historians will use in the future none is more curious and few more valuable than an almost forgotten volume called *The First Hundred Million*. The book deals with the reading tastes of the American public in the first quarter of the twentieth century. It is the unmasking of the American mind, not by glib generalities, not by any brilliant strokes of insight, but by statistical tables and by the recital of practical experiences. The author asks, Are Americans afraid of sex? And he gives the answer in sales figures. He tells of the quest for self-improvement, of the desire on the part of the American public for fun and laughter, of religion versus free thought—all through cash register records! He prescribes a hospital treatment for classics, just like the typical American pragmatist. He tells how masterpieces can be rejuvenated, his magic treatment consisting often enough in tacking on to a book a title to arouse in the reader prurient interest. The book, in short, discusses the field of literature from the viewpoint of the entrepeneur, and so it becomes a document for the social historian.

It is the story of E. Haldeman-Julius, the Henry Ford of the American publishing world, and his series of nickel books, the little blue volumes that used to be seen all over the land throughout the 1920s. Those who were young then had reason to be grateful to the Kansas exploiter of the classics and the neoclassical. His presses turned out by the thousands exactly the sort of books for which aspiring adolescents craved, volumes that were not readily obtainable elsewhere. And they were sold, as Haldeman-Julius vaunted, at the ridiculously low price of a package of gum. The man was loud in his manners and methods; he resorted to commercial tricks that aroused misgivings in sober minds, but he was one of the great educative forces of the decade that witnessed the complete collapse of Wilsonian rhetoric. If Calvin Coolidge was in Washington as the symbol of a false prosperity, Haldeman-Julius was in Girard, Kansas, the symbol of genuine enlightenment that might one day topple false gods.

181

And George Sylvester Viereck, with his irrepressible itch to be in the center of things, was one of the henchmen of the Kansan in his business of distributing esoteric goods at low prices. His association with Haldeman-Julius was important in itself, but it was far more important in the lift it gave to his literary fortunes. The two men had met in New York in 1923, when Viereck was at the low ebb of his fame as a writer. The literary vigilantes had apparently succeeded in their aim of wiping out his very name. He was virtually forgotten, and to worsen matters, he seemed to have become sterile. In his own phrase, he had joined the conspiracy of silence against himself and let others pursue the Muses, while he chased after anonymous journalistic triumphs and successes over the stockmarket ticker. At the time he met Haldeman-Julius, however, the will to return to the literary field took eager possession of him, and he seized the straws offered by the Kansan. He became the guardian of German literature, the spokesman for the Decadents, and a general adviser for the Little Blue Book series. Haldeman-Julius's chief bait was the publication and exploitation of Viereck's own verse in Little Blue Book form. Viereck was eager to pay tribute to the poets he most admired and to voice his literary opinions with the devices that he had learned too well from Freud. So he worked hard, employing, indeed, a special stenographer for the one purpose. Haldeman-Julius, himself a man of the utmost resourcefulness and with a restless urge to activity, constantly marveled at the spirit that Viereck put into the work, the results that he accomplished, and the speed with which a task was done.

"Really, you write letters and books faster than I can read them," Haldeman-Julius wrote to him very early in their association. "I can't keep up with you. I am positive that you are not a person but a syndicate."

Viereck replied, with uncharacteristic pomposity, that he was not a syndicate: "I am merely efficient. If I undertake a job I get it done." But, on afterthought, the term appealed to him, and he announced to Haldeman-Julius that "the Syndicate is at work again." Indeed, he had never stopped working. He seemed to be fascinated, as were many others, by the possibilities of the Little Blue Books. The nickels of the masses might yet bring culture to America. He became impatient with everything that interfered with the speedy success of his plans. He constantly complained to the publisher in Kansas about the irksome incidents of their collaboration, and often Haldeman-Julius felt constrained to tell him that his demonlike speed was too much for any one man: "I have always considered myself a fast worker, but when I was put against George Sylvester Viereck my efficiency engine broke down. I believe that there is no editor in the world who can keep up with him."

The two men seemed to have an understanding of each other. Once Haldeman-Julius wrote Viereck a short letter concerning Debs which had appeared in Viereck's *American Monthly:* "You are like myself in one respect—ever ready to turn the limelight on a deserving soul, provided you can find a way to get into the picture. I thought that was exclusively my own characteristic, but I must confess that you do it with a facility that equals my own." Viereck explained, "Defying single-handed the lords of letters and of news, we are compelled to create our own backgrounds. We must keep up our faith and that of our followers. In addition to that, we are both amazingly interested in ourselves. However, I, at least, am tremendously interested in you as well, and I regret that we really know each other so little.''

Haldeman-Julius advised Viereck to talk less about the politicians and to get back to literature. The two men were of mutual aid, even if their association did not long endure—little more than a year, in fact. However, that year was a noteworthy one.

Viereck made valuable contacts for Haldeman-Julius. In his desire to increase the number of Teutonic classics in the Little Blue Book series, he wrote to the German scholars he knew. These people gave him the benefits of their long and intimate knowledge of German literature and philosophy. They told him which authors and titles ought to be used, recommended translations and editors, and otherwise gave him every kind of advice and, in several instances, offered to edit little volumes at the wretchedly bad prices that were paid for such work. Among others, he persuaded Margaret Munsterberg, the daughter of his dear old friend, to edit *Faust* and a volume of old Teutonic poems. He persuaded Ludwig Lewisohn to do some work for the series. He communicated with William Ellery Leonard, H. L. Mencken, Richard Le Gallienne, Michael Monahan, and many others—and Otto Kahn, his banker friend. To Kahn he wrote ostensibly because he wanted his advice on Wagnerian literature. He got that advice—and tips on the stock market as well.

Viereck ransacked his mind and his library for subjects for Little Blue Books. He gave Haldeman-Julius plausible arguments for including volume after volume of Swinburne and Wilde. He suggested Rossetti, Douglas, Davidson, Marlowe, Catullus, Byron, Markham, and Le Gallienne. He said that he would like to do Chatterton, Hood, William Watson, Henley, and Eugene Field. And over and over again he repeated the name of Swinburne; there seemed to be a lilting magic in it. The various names were key words, helping to discover his inmost likes, the influences on his own writings, the ghosts that peopled his brain. More than once, when Haldeman-Julius demurred at paying money for some of the things suggested by Viereck, Viereck offered to donate his services.

The correspondence of the two men reads at times like a series of variations on the theme of money, Viereck alternating between insistence upon every penny owing to him and then throwing away his claims to remuneration for the sake of creating a wider public interest in some of his literary gods. The harmony gradually vanished after several minor flare-ups and one or two major ones. Once Viereck gave Haldeman-Julius a particularly ringing lecture on the conduct of business, telling him that their differences were only partly due to mutual misunderstanding, but more because of the publisher's unbusinesslike failure to reply to businesslike queries.:

I am neither a beginner nor an amateur, and I don't undertake work of this nature without definite compensation. Since you met me in such a

frank and generous spirit and since the amounts involved in any case
were comparatively trivial, I deviated from my rule in this instance.
When the augurs meet they do not pontificate, they smile.

That terminated the relationship. Viereck helped to enrich the series of Little
Blue Books, and the series helped to restore his past prestige. Besides the
contributions he procured from other men, Viereck edited ten little books on
Rossetti, Wilde, Douglas, Villon, Swinburne, and Davidson, and he also edited
two little volumes of his own poetry and his own translation of Schiller's *The Maid
of Orleans*. To each of the volumes Viereck contributed an introduction of striking
originality, inspired by the Freudian ideas dominant at that time. Articles by him,
including memorable ones on Frank Harris and on the Loeb-Leopold trial, appeared in other Haldeman-Julius publications. Reviews of his work and articles
about him, including a vivid one by Alexander Harvey, filled columns. The
relationship, while it lasted was profitable, not financially, although the Little Blue
Books sold by the thousands, but in the renewal it afforded of Viereck's fame.

The introduction by Viereck to the edition of Dante Gabriel Rossetti's *The
Blessed Damozel and Other Poems* is typical of the treatment he gave to the other
poets about whom he wrote. "He writes of the heavenly in terms of the carnal,"
Viereck said of Rossetti, at once distilling the essence of the man's poetry. He saw
the clash of the Latin and Anglo-Saxon heritages of Rossetti as "the source of the
psychic conflict from which his poetry springs." Rossetti's sexuality, he said, is
diffused; present everywhere in his poems, it scarcely ever is climactic, and in that
respect is distinctly feminine.

As is to be expected, he had penetrating observations to make on Oscar
Wilde. He concluded that Wilde was neither a pagan nor a Greek, but a secret
moralist: "The duality of his sexual constitution, wedded to a consciousness of
sin, for better or for worse, made Wilde a poet. His genius was a compensation for
his sense of inferiority."

Viereck's two little volumes of Lord Alfred Douglas's poetry represent the
only form in which Douglas' poetry was available in America. The Wilde blight
had affected Douglas' reputation, with the result that few lovers of literature knew
that he was one of the great poets of the day, much above the one whose name had
cast a dark shadow over his own. Viereck deserved credit for having done more
than anyone else in America, unless it was Frank Harris, in the effort to place
Douglas in his rightful position. Of this the Scottish lord was himself cognizant, to
the extent of forgiving Viereck and Haldeman-Julius for having pirated his poems!

"Unlike Swinburne, Douglas never wearies," said Viereck. "Unlike Rossetti, he is never concerned merely with verbal felicities. Unlike Browning, he
never lacks lucidity of expression. Unlike Wilde, he is never the showman, but
always the poet. Whatever may be his personal eccentricities, he sublimates them
in art. In spite of private quarrels and public scandals, in spite of political feuds and
literary vendettas, malice cannot gainsay the vigor of his diction and the loftiness
of his lyric vision."

To Villon, the old poet's poet, he paid a memorable tribute: "His Muse is both timely and timeless. A child of his own age, his song, abounding in local allusion, possessed what we now call timeliness. But because he penetrates to the core of life, trembling with elemental and primal instincts, he is endowed with the timelessness of the immortals. The voice of Shakespeare whom he preceded by a century, is no fresher than his own. He is as modern as Verlaine, Ernest Dowson or Edgar Lee Masters. . . . Tenderness, irony, ruthless realism and simple faith, pity and pathos, the simile of the scholar and the argot of the Apache, march to an unforgettable tune in the poems of Francois Villon. The note he sounded first of all, reappears in every European literature. Heine especially revels in a similar measure in the peculiar combination of raillery and sentiment so conspicious in Villon."

For the little known poet, John Davidson, he had words betraying a surprising sympathy. He saw Davidson's entire literary life as a struggle against filial piety and religion which "imposed a double harness upon his soul." He said that Davidson's spirit lived in John Masefield and Vachel Lindsay, and he selected as Davidson's most representative work those incomparable ballads "of a Nun," "of the Making of a Poet," "of the Exodus from Houndsditch," "of Heaven," "of Hell," "of Tannhauser," "London," and "Thirty Bob a Week." The selection was a brilliant one, though it had the necessary limitations of Davidson's own poetry.

Of Swinburne, however, Viereck wrote with real enthusiasm, if not quite with the passion of his boyhood. He still felt that Swinburne's verse was "the most melodious and most insolent lyric challenge ever flung into the face of Puritanism." He felt that Swinburne's passion was almost impersonal and surely esoteric with variations from the normal, particularly the love of woman for woman, being of especial interest to him. Swinburne was, by accident of sex, a male Sappho, he said; the passion of his verse was, therefore, not masculine; even in its cruelty, it was feminine. Viereck concluded that Swinburne was the greatest poet of the Victorian era and also the greatest bore of the times because of the defects of his virtues.

In 1923, before his alliance with Haldeman-Julius was complete, Viereck published, through Thomas Seltzer, a book of one hundred short pages, previously serialized in the Hearst papers, entitled *Rejuvenation: How Steinach Makes People Young*. The book appeared under the *non de plume* of George F. Corners, which is a free rendering of the German of Viereck's name. It was the first of his potboilers, but its journalistic qualities were so good that the great Freud himself suggested to Viereck that he ought to write a similar book on the subject of psychoanalysis. Instead, Viereck poured the strange metaphors of Freud over every book he wrote after the war. The *Rejuvenation* was lucid in its exposition and sound in its judgments, but the author made no secret of his sympathies for Steinach and his hopeful attitude toward the new science created by the man. He said: "If we halt the insidious advance of Age, may we not, in time, challenge Death?" There was the little boy running down the stairs to escape Death! No wonder Steinach's research appealed to him. His little book was the first popular interpretation of Steinach and a preliminary study to *My First Two Thousand Years*.

There were several reasons for the anonymity adopted by Viereck. The effect was that the book did no harm to Viereck's reputation and did not advance it, either. The two Little Blue Books of his poetry, blazing forth his name and selling in the thousands, did him much good and sent him once more on his way to fame. Viereck was careful that they should have that result. He sent copies of the booklets to every member of the Poetry Society of America, as if to remind them that, without a license, he could practice the art of poetry. He sent copies to libraries and public institutions. He wrote to men of letters throughout the country, expressing the hope that the modest garb of the booklets would not obscure any faint loveliness of the poems themselves. James Branch Cabell, Robinson Jeffers, Hudson Maxim, Edwin Markham, Richard Le Gallienne, Frank Harris, and others assured him that the loveliness of his poetry was very much in evidence, and he felt deeply content. As a Christmas gift, his wife, delighting in symbols, bound the set of Little Blue Books. They symbolized that he was once more interested in literature.

There were over sixty of his poems in the two small volumes, enough to give the full measure of his poetic gift. They included virtually all of his best poems and perhaps a few that might well have been omitted. There were the chief poems of his early volumes and a few fugitive pieces which had never appeared in book form. Each Little Blue Book commenced with a word of introduction, the one on the theme of being discovered and the other on a poet psychoanalyzing himself. In the one introduction, Viereck said that his rediscovery as a poet occurred sooner than he had anticipated. He gave Haldeman-Julius full praise and told him that if he regretted that he was not the first to proclaim the merits of Viereck's verse, he should remember that America, too, was discovered before Columbus. He paid his respect to the poets who had excommunicated him and to "the new lyric suck-lings": "without rhythm, without sense of beauty or any sense whatever," their work "illustrates the acme of futility." In the introduction to the second Little Blue Book, Viereck hearkened back to the spirit of the marginalia with which he ended *The Candle and the Flame*. He foreshadowed an autobiographical volume which would make a psychological grouping of his poems. Some few years later that book was actually published. The Little Blue Books gave the initial impetus which made possible some of Viereck's later achievements.

Through Haldeman-Julius, he got to know Dr. Isaac Goldberg, a critic then first achieving a small measure of fame by virtue of a civilized outlook which stemmed from Havelock Ellis. Through Goldberg he met Henry T. Schnittkind, associated with Goldberg in various literary labors, and through Schnittkind, he became acquainted with Paul Eldridge, perhaps the most important literary contact of his life since those early days when he was a comrade of William Ellery Leonard and Ludwig Lewisohn. The alliance with Eldridge meant the doing of work which had long plagued Viereck, work which did almost as much for his name and fame as had *Nineveh* in those very distant days of long ago. Several matters intervened:

politics, the ticker, journalism and the basic habit of restlessness, but gradually all of the intervening forces were removed. Not long after Eldridge and Viereck met, Eldridge inscribed one of his books "To George Sylvester Viereck whom I met in the Great Desert, by an accident or fatality too beautiful to be divine. . . . Yahweh, fearing us, severed our paths for too long a time—but Lucifer—may his name be blessed!—united them."

It is a story of permanent interest that thus grew indirectly out of the Little Blue Books. It is the thematic motive of the next ten years of Viereck's life.

29   THE PROGRESSIVE POLITICIAN

Viereck began to lose just a little of his interest and perhaps a wee bit of his faith in the German cause. His disassociation from the Steuben Society represented one phase of this change. The composition of his magazine, *The American Monthly,* represented a more important phase. He tried to make it less parochial, less narrowly German, and more of a truly American magazine. It was his hope to convert it into a general circulation journal. He gathered such shrewd newspapermen as his friends Emile Gauvreau and William J. Rapp, who had had experience with Macfadden and Hearst. He began to publish purely literary contributions. He started a drama section, with himself as its editor, and as an interest arouser he began a controversy over whether drama critics should be hanged after five years' service. The magazine became more and more one of a general appeal, but, alas, the appeal was not represented in circulation figures. The magazine seemed to be losing German readers without gaining new ones. Viereck hoped to start a new magazine for Macfadden into which he might pour his thoughts and energies. He also thought of starting a literary vehicle of his own. The magazine's contents can be gauged from its proposed title, *Aphrodite.* But the idea, like so many others, was still-born. Viereck became advisory editor of the Macfadden publications, largely through Fulton Oursler, almost causing an internal revolution in the Macfadden organization.

The history of the *American Monthly* took a new turn, a most curious one, in the fall of 1927. A leader of the Steuben Society, a man of the most incongruous personal traits and career, purchased it. The man was David Maier, who had played so active a role in La Follette's 1924 presidential campaign in association with Viereck. Although a Tammany man, united by friendship with "Jimmy" Walker and the other Democratic chieftans, Maier had strong progressive sympathies which stemmed from his personal experiences and his racial inheritance. He was a cousin of the banker Otto Kahn and deeply interested in German affairs. And he was a Jew. Early in his career he had made the sort of mistakes which might ordinarily have disqualified him for life. He had gone to jail for particularly nasty offenses connected with his running of bawdy houses. He had been a sort of collector for Tammany, but instead of breaking down as the result of the disgrace, he entered into a phase of much usefulness, vitiated too often by the ghosts of his past. He rose to the eminence, American style, of a banquet in his honor, and men of consequence, including Viereck, Senator Borah, Senator Copeland, and Victor Ridder were proud to sit at the table with him. Maier aspired to own an organ of opinion and ultimately succeeded in purchasing the *American Monthly* from Viereck. When news of the change in ownership reached Doorn in Holland, contributions from the imperial personage in exile who signed himself "O.W.K." ceased.

In the issue of October 1927 appeared Viereck's touching, if possibly grandiloquent, valedictory. Viereck called the reader's attention to the truly remarkable fact that he had been at the helm of the magazine from its start in August 1914. The magazine had appeared without interruption, first as a weekly and then as a monthly, for thirteen long years, despite threats, boycotts, and intimidation. It had unflinchingly demanded fair play for the Germanic race, both here and abroad. It had done its best to keep the country from war and had made Viereck the least popular person in the United States, with the exception of Eugene Debs. Viereck said he was at that time too busy to worry about his personal fortunes, particularly his literary fame:

When the fate of the world is at stake, a handful of verses does not weigh heavily in the balance.

I fought back as hard as I could. I make no apologies. I regret nothing. I recite these facts without bitterness, for I never stifled the voice of my conscience. I never ceased to oppose wrong. And I was rewarded by the unflinching loyalty of my readers. Many brave souls went through worse hells than I, because they could not speak.

I did not quit under the roar of the guns nor did I quit, when after peace was declared, sniping continued.

Today the battle in which I enlisted is won.

War Psychosis is dead.

The myth of Germany's guilt is dissipated. The fable of German atrocities is exploded. The loyalty of Americans of German descent, both to their racial ideals and to the United States is triumphantly vindicated.

I sacrificed more than one decade of my literary life upon the altar of truth and fair play. I am justified in returning to my own gods, to devote myself to my true vocation. I am a poet, not a politician. Only a world cataclysm could hurl me from my Parnassus into the arena of political strife.

He emphasized that much work remained to be done and that constant vigilance was necessary but that there were others competent to do the work, David Maier for one. "Where I, owing perhaps to temperamental limitation, played a lone hand, he will find cooperation." Viereck promised advice and contributions regularly. "I am not deserting the ship," he said. "I am merely stepping back into the ranks."

Thus ended Viereck's last experience as an editor up to that time, and the end came without real regret on his part. Unfortunately it did not carry with it a severence from all journalistic activities. That was one of the principal mistakes he made in the years which followed.

30 "AMBASSADOR" OF THE KAISER

There were those who found Viereck's mention of his relationship to the Hohenzollern family offensive. Viereck protested often enough that he was not seeking, and never had sought, to presume upon any such relationship. At the very beginning of his career he had said that he did not think the matter of much consequence: "it is far more important that I am the spiritual descendent of Edgar Allen Poe." That was his overt opinion in those distant days, but to a greater extent than he was willing to believe, the fact that he could regard the German royal family as related to him colored his words and actions. He began to feel inwardly that the Kaiser mattered more and Poe less than he had thought. This was sensed first of all by his foes and then by his friends and they felt that he was predisposed in favor of the Hohenzollerns; that his dynastic instincts, so to speak, conditioned his conduct and beliefs.

The frequency and warmth of Viereck's references to Kaiser Wilhelm II were noticeable. In the columns of his various magazines the Kaiser was mentioned often and with fervent praise, long before the world went to war. His first serious discussion of his royal relative was, of course, in *Confessions of a Barbarian*. In that book there was rhapsody, unconfined, almost uncritical, without the benefit of a personal encounter with the emperor. The meeting that was to have taken place was cancelled because the Kaiser was in difficulty due to the criticism aroused by a published interview with him that had just appeared in a London newspaper. Viereck's poetic tribute, *William II, Prince of Peace,* was also written without benefit of firsthand knowledge, and throughout the war Viereck acted as the Kaiser's apologist without once meeting him. Nor did any letters pass between them until the world war began. Such worship from afar was bound to take on a new and personal form. No doubt Viereck's aim from the first was to meet and truly know the man who had meant so much to him. His eager pursuit of the great men of his day could not stop short of the German emperor. The Kaiser's own words best tell the story of Viereck's conquest of the exile of Doorn.

On December 19, 1926, the emperor sent Dr. Harry Elmer Barnes, then engaged in writing on the genesis of the war, a letter of considerable importance. After expressing "great satisfaction" over the fact that Viereck had placed the *American Monthly* at the disposal of Senator Owens and Dr. Barnes, the emperor said that the three were a "fine combine" in the battle against German war guilt, and he wished, in his quaint way, "success to this Triplice." He continued:

> My relations with Mr. Viereck, date from 1921 when he visited me here [at Doorn] and placed his pen and paper at my disposal for the clearing up of the War Guilt Lie and personal defense and other topics. Since then I have regularly sent him material partly in form of private letters, partly in form of articles, which he edited or used or prepared for the press and got published. In his valiant and strenuous fight for my person he slowly converted many Americans of the press, and others from their idiotical standpoint relative to me as the Devil who let loose the War. I am personally indebted to him for much help and advice in this matter. No other American Press or Syndicate or single person has been allowed to publish anything about me except through Mr. Viereck. He having established relations with all the influential or leading papers, syndicates or editors who were at last persuaded to take another view of me and even articles from me or inspired by me. Thus he has become the *centre* of all material relating to my work, the sole *exponent* of my ideas, with my full confidence in the way he best thinks fit for their dissemination.

And as it was in 1926, it remained, although the initial reason for the intimacy of the two men ceased. Until World War II began, nobody any more believed in Germany's sole guilt for World War I, thanks largely to Viereck; nobody any longer wanted to "hang the Kaiser." But the friendship of the two men remained strong. There was a time when their relationship appeared to be strained. That was after the appearance of *My First Two Thousand Years,* Viereck's chronicle of the Wandering Jew. The Kaiser then wrote to Viereck in a manner that displayed more sorrow than anger. He wondered how Viereck, a Christian gentleman, could write as he did. It troubled him that Viereck wrote apparently so irreverently of the religious ideas and symbols that were so dear to him. It was long before the partial estrangement vanished; perhaps it never wholly disappeared. In general it can be said that "the little Viereck" was the one person who could talk back to Wilhelm.

Viereck was not consistently sycophantic in his relations with William. He was respectful, loyal, kindly, friendly, sympathetic, and affectionate—like a son, in short, with an independent mind. But he was not blind, although more than once he defended the Kaiser's actions when silence would have been best. When the Kaiser had hateful things to say of the immortal Heine, Viereck sought to excuse him on the ground that Heine had sneered at some of the Kaiser's female ancestors. To be sure, Viereck did not alter his own high opinion of Heine, but was it proper for him to defend the Kaiser's purely personal outburst? The Kaiser's personal anti-Semitism did not influence Viereck's views of the Jews.

Strangely enough, Viereck and the Kaiser never discussed their kinship—never as much as mentioned it to each other. Viereck speculated about the matter in print more than once, and he talked about it in private often enough, but there was only one bit of evidence that the Kaiser himself was aware of the relationship. On one occasion the Kaiser, half-smilingly, referred to Viereck as "mon cousin"—the traditional royal mode of addressing a royal kinsman. He made no point of it; the address may have been unconscious and unintended, but there it was.

The first milestone in the personal friendship of the two men created an international sensation. After the Kaiser's abdication of the crown and his departure from Germany, curiosity about him was general and became feverish when Lloyd George raised the hue and cry of "Hang the Kaiser" in the course of a political campaign in England. Every newspaperman in the world aspired to publish a genuine interview with the deposed monarch, and in their absence the columns of the press had article after article of gossip and surmise, some of it malicious and some merely ill-informed. The royal guest of the Dutch government persistently refused to permit a journalist within his household, for he felt that he had always been wronged by the press. He had the feeling that a reporter was some form of low creature with whom an emperor and king could not talk familiarly; one lost face when one took a journalist into one's confidence. Then along came the little Viereck and the rule was broken for the first time: and only Viereck broke the rule thereafter. After 1921 it became his annual custom to see the Kaiser, he and Mrs. Viereck generally spending a week with the household at Doorn. As the result of the first such week, Viereck's initial important article on the Kaiser was written. It appeared originally in the Hearst papers in America and was recognized at once as the first important word from Doorn. Great headlines greeted it, and it was copied in one form or another throughout the world. In Germany it added fuel to the flames of an interminable controversy.

In Germany since the war the population had been divided in two camps: the friends and the foes of the Kaiser. Maximilian Harden was the leader of the foes, and he was joined by Theodore Wolff, of the *Berliner Tageblatt* and others, many but not all of them Jews. Ultimately, the biographer and literary journalist, Emil Ludwig, became the chief opponent of the Kaiser, his book on William being the literary testament of the opposition. It was difficult to say who led the Hohenzollern forces in Germany. In a sense Hindenburg was the leader. Some felt that Hitler was the great Aryan hope for the recall of the Kaiser, but he soon made mincemeat of the royalists' wishes. He stole some of the Kaiser's thunder, opposition to Versailles and all. Hitler was only the Kaiser vulgarized beyond recognition, with a gory streak of sadism, of which the Kaiser was hardly guilty, and a vile coat of ignorance alien to William. The Kaiser was essentially a Christian and a gentleman, in the best meaning of those misused words; Hitler was neither. Who then was really the ex-emperor's chief representative? Many felt that Viereck played the role, though he resided in America. Certainly in Germany, attacks on the Kaiser often enough were attacks on Viereck, but those who defended the Kaiser too often refrained from mentioning Viereck, lest they give offense by coupling their names.

The Kaiser told Viereck to feel free to call upon him whenever he required any information through personal visits, letters and cables, and frequently Viereck found it necessary to accept the offer. Rumors involving the imperial family were constantly circulated, and it was necessary to counteract these stories with authentic information. When the Crown Prince suddenly reentered Germany, it was wise to ask if it was with the advice and consent of his imperial father. When Hindenburg ran for the presidency, it was necessary to inquire if it was with the advice and consent of the emperor. When the Kaiser remarried, the newspapers found it to be their pressing concern, for readers undoubtedly were eager to learn the details of the royal romance. Soon enough rumors of discord in the household at Doorn were rife and of conflict between the emperor and his children. Viereck would cable for confirmation or denial of the various stories that crowded the front pages of newspapers throughout the world, and the answers received from the Kaiser would make the headlines, sometimes in a double spread. Viereck was the one to whom men inevitably turned for enlightenment on subjects relating to the imperial fortunes.

He knew the emperor intimately. He knew the new mistress of Doorn, the Empress Hermine. He was perhaps close enough to the Crown Prince to be called a friend; they were approximately of the same age and had collaborated in the writing of the Crown Prince's book, *The Truth About My Life*. Other members of the family and the household were not unknown to him, and they all knew Viereck's family as well. The Kaiser, like every one else, found Gretchen Viereck delightful; with a friendly insistence he once made her sit and knit while he conversed and read to her. Invariably he asked to be remembered to Gretchen and to all the little Vierecks and even to the Vierecks' dog, Ajax, whom he regarded as particularly intelligent and faithful. With the *gemutlichkeit* of a good German he sent "greetings from house to house," and they were returned with fervor. In the day of sorrow the Kaiser and the Kaiserin did not fail to remember their friend across the sea; they were among the first to console Viereck when his father and mother passed away.

Perhaps the chief token of the regard in which Viereck was held was his being chosen to assist Hermine in the preparation of her memoirs, published in 1928. Viereck was a collaborator and more and a special note in *Days in Doorn*, the empress's book, acknowledges that fact. Hermine furnished the material, and Viereck did most of the writing, subject to her veto. The book had a tender charm about it that was wholly feminine. It was well calculated, in brief, to make friends for the royal household. Its chief motivation was the refutation of the tales told against the Kaiser. Germany loved the old empress, Augusta Victoria, too much not to resent the Kaiser's remarriage. It was essential to counteract the mischief done by the scandal-mongers and ill-wishers, and Hermine's book was the answer to the royal prayer.

The book begins with a lengthy prologue written by Viereck and appearing under his name: a shrewd, informal and seemingly ingenuous account of the wedded life of William and Hermine. Can a man love more than once, Viereck asks, almost in a tone of a human interest writer on a tabloid newspaper, and he answers his question in a plausible manner. One gets, by design, the image of a loving couple at home. Sad things are told, and enemies are castigated, but the general feeling of love and charity remains. The book silenced those who would have it that the imperial pair were at war. Viereck's desire, patently, was to paint the picture of a cultured, loving woman ministering to the wants of a sorrowful old Christian gentleman who stands in need of affection and understanding. In this he succeeded admirably.

Viereck's effect upon the household is perhaps best seen in that section of the book in which Hermine tells of her favorite authors, particularly those Americans for whom she cares most. Of American writers of the older generations, she cares most for Poe and Mark Twain, among Viereck's favorites, too. Of living American writers she has high praise for Fulton Oursler, Paul Eldridge, and Alexander Harvey, all close friends of Viereck's. Two of her favorite German writers are Herman Sudermann and Ludwig Fulda, not unknown to Viereck, and she admires Heine, despite her husband, and Bernard Shaw. Of course, there are others, too, and these are not always according to Viereck's tasts, for Hermine had read deeply in the world of literature. Viereck constantly exchanged views on literary and political subjects with the emperor and his wife, and it is no cause for wonder that the more impressionable and modern of the two was more amenable to his views.

Viereck's familiarity is also shown in the conversational tone of the prologue to the book. When interviews with crowned heads are often so stuffy in their formality, it is refreshing to find conversations as intimate in their manner as those which Viereck reports. He addresses the old Kaiser on every theme, seemingly without inhibitions, and the Kaiser appears to reply as one human being to another. Considering the etiquette which hems in a king even in exile, the tone of the conversation is memorable. There is an appealing verbal picture of the Kaiser in a book, by Viereck, called *Glimpses of the Great,* which appeared after *Days in Doorn.* In it Viereck reports a conversation which took place while both men were trudging toward the House Doorn in the rain. The Kaiser answered the salutation of all who greeted him on the way, each time with an unfeigned friendliness that did him credit. He talked to Viereck of the divine appointment of kings, but he emphasized that all tasks, from the lowest to the highest, are divinely appointed. He talked like a man who had never been accused of arrogance.

There emerges from a study of the truly intimate documents relating to the Kaiser—his letters, for example, insofar as they were published—the feeling that he was an intriguing combination of contradictory impulses; in that respect he was certainly a blood relation to Viereck. His communications to Viereck superbly displayed the blend of the modern and the medieval that Viereck often pointed out. The letters, incidentally, were written in English by the Kaiser himself. His correspondence was not ghost-written. Idiomatic speech, mixed with the quaint, was there, the Kaiser using such expressions as "that is the Nigger in the woodpile" with a remarkable naturalness yet also using such archaic language as that already quoted. His ideas were of a similar turn, eminently sane and remarkably unreasonable by turns. In discussing world events he was generally plausible and sometimes brilliant. In discussing religion he was often dull and generally pedantic.

It is not too much, then, to say that no one seeking to depict the era dominated by the World War I can afford to ignore the interdependence of these two strange men, William Hohenzollern and Sylvester Viereck. It is not generally known, for example, that for a number of years the Kaiser annotated much that Viereck wrote, his books no less than the editorials that appeared in the *American Monthly*. Those who read that magazine may have wondered at times about the identity of a knowing person who signed his articles, bearing a London dateline, with the mysterious letters O.W.K. Nonetheless, there is reason to believe, they were written or inspired by the Kaiser, the cryptic letters meaning merely "One Who Knows." Often Alexander Harvey edited these O.W.K. articles; a particularly congenial task to Harvey, owing to his admiration for the Germans in general and their former ruler in particular.

It was natural for Viereck to write of his relations with the Kaiser—not merely a series of articles but a full length book. Who was better qualfied than Viereck? The professional writer must make copy of his experiences and contacts; all is grist for his mill. But still one could not help inquiring if Viereck had the necessary objectivity and courage to write a thoroughly honest and forthright book about a then living man of importance for whom he had such personal affection as the Kaiser. Viereck realized this himself. He remarked that he found his task a difficult one and, as if thinking of himself, that it is difficult, perhaps impossible, to perform a painless autopsy upon a living person. He seemed to be steeling himself to the task.

As if to protect himself, Viereck adopted various literary devices. Those arch-conspirators responsible for the Treaty of Versailles were unwittingly responsible for the chief Viereck strategem. They wrote solemn phrases into the treaty of peace about trying the Kaiser. That trial, of course, never took place; they perhaps never intended to have it take place. Viereck, however, put the Kaiser on trial in his book. He let the accused have his say and the friends of the accused were called as his witnesses. The events of his life passed in review as on the witness stand. There was a corps of prosecuting attorneys and a staff of advocates for the defense. This permitted Viereck to say all that had to be said, if he so desired. Viereck called psychoanalysts to the stand. They probed the subconscious motivations for the actions of the Kaiser and those close to him, the same method, with a different twist, as that used in the Roosevelt volume and in a later volume about Colonel House.

Viereck's book, *The Kaiser on Trial,* then, was one of the tests of Viereck's integrity. One can almost anticipate his handling of the theme and its degree of success when examining the methods he employed and the results he obtained in earlier books. In his various studies of personality, the best of which have been assembled in the volumes called *Glimpses of the Great* and *The Strangest Friendship in History*, one sees Viereck at work and at his best. These volumes appeared in actual time later than *My First Two Thousand Years.*

31 COLONEL HOUSE
FORGIVES HIS ENEMY

In 1915 the portfolio of Dr. Albert, which had been purloined under tragi-comic circumstances, was placed in the lap of Colonel Edward M. House and William G. McAdoo, alter ego and the son-in-law, respectively, of President Wilson. At that moment the fate of the German cause in America was in their hands, and the fate, more than incidentally, of George Sylvester Viereck as well. Acting with astonishing acumen, if possibly questionable taste, the two men turned over the contents of the purloined portfolio to the *New York World*—and cooked the German goose to a crisp. That was perhaps the first time that the mysterious and ubiquitous Colonel House influenced the destiny of Viereck.

Too soon, America was at war with the Central Powers. Viereck had to pull in the bold sweep of his sails, while maintaining what he professed to believe an intellectually honest course. Only his youth and the romantic qualities which made him a poet prevented the war years from becoming a complete hell on earth. There was a certain quaint malice in outwitting foes who were intent upon destroying one, and Viereck displayed verve and resourcefulness at the game. He survived with only a temporary eclipse of his sense of humor, but during the humorless period which followed the termination of the war, Viereck was savage in his denunciation of President Wilson, Colonel House, and the others whom he blamed for dragging the country into the war and, above all, for "the crime of Versailles." August Heckscher, the genial financier, was not the only one who told Viereck, in a kindly spirit and in a private letter, that he was too bitter. But Viereck thought otherwise, and in issue after issue of the *American Monthly* he hit at his wartime foes. He supported Harding and Debs—one never could be sure as to which one Viereck actually voted for! Harding's attitude showed that he regarded Viereck as one of those responsible for the defeat of the Wilsonian forces, and the former German propagandist took an energetic part in the 1924 campaign of the indefatigable Bob La Follette. That campaign seemed to wash away the wartime impurity from the soul of Sylvester Viereck. When the five million votes cast for La Follette were counted, Viereck, consciously or unconsciously, took count of his own losses and gains and steered his ship in another direction—away from the bitterness and the strife.

He might have made the turn earlier if his foes had sooner shown a willingness to forgive, but the many rebukes he received only confirmed the rancorous hatred he felt for those who, he believed, had misled first themselves and then the country. He had, for example, in 1921 sent to Woodrow Wilson, then in retirement, two articles by Dr. von Mach, making grave charges against the former president. "Inasmuch as we have no desire to be unfair, especially to political opponents," Viereck had written to Wilson, "I shall be glad if you care to avail yourself of my offer, to place at your disposal the columns of my magazine for any rejoinder which you may wish to make." Almost immediately the reply of America's wartime president arrived—written by his secretary: "Mr. Wilson requests me to return herewith the enclosures sent in your letter of September twenty-ninth and say that he does not care to read anything by Dr. Edmund von Mach or to receive any communication from you"! In anger Viereck wrote to the ex-president's secretary that the feeling expressed in his reply "is entirely mutual." Still angrier, he said that "nothing short of public duty could induce me to communicate with Mr. Wilson;" but inasmuch as Mr. Wilson's actions affected "the honor of the United States no less than his own," he had hoped for a reply.

During the war there had been times when Viereck was minded to praise the president and his man, House. There had been an issue of *The American Weekly* having a photograph of Colonel House in the place of honor on the cover of the magazine. The same issue of the magazine lauded the colonel in a leading editorial and contrasted him favorably with those crying out for a crushing defeat and punishment of Germany. At first Viereck's praise was little more than a ruse of war, but as the inspired rhetoric of Wilson poured forth, he began to hope that there might be a peace of justice. It was only a vague hope, but he dared not abandon it. Then came the tempting of Wilson by the devils of Old World diplomacy and his consequent fall. Viereck's hatred knew few bounds.

By 1929 Viereck was able to write of the world war and his share in its manifold ramifications with some genuine objectivity—as if from Olympus. He could write of himself and others with good humor and complete freedom from personal rancor. The Viereck who had taken so active a part in the war now seemed another person that the Viereck of 1929 could treat as an outsider. At that time he began writing a series of articles for the *Saturday Evening Post* on the propaganda activities of the various belligerents. The articles appeared anonymously, and this device enabled him to be more restrained and impersonal in his viewpoint, with the result that the articles attracted wide and favorable attention.

Among those who read the articles was Colonel House, then in retirement but evincing eager curiosity about public affairs. He naturally made inquiry about the anonymous author and was delighted as well as surprised to learn that Viereck was the man. The colonel wrote to Viereck at once, on August 18, 1929, thanking him for the pleasure his articles gave him. "I seldom read articles or books relating to the war," wrote Colonel House, "for I got a full measure of that greatest of human tragedies while it was in progress, but I am glad my attention was called to your brilliant, informing and valuable contribution to one of its most sinister features.''

"You have presented both sides in a spirit of fairness that one seldom finds,'' the generous-hearted former foeman continued, with that gesture fully forgiving the wartime lapses of Viereck. "I hope you may publish the articles in book form and that they may have wide circulation, for you have cast a wholesome light on the evils of propaganda upon which our people may well ponder.''

That was all the colonel said in that first letter, but it was sufficient to excite the Viereck entourage. Viereck was in Europe at the time, expected back the following week, but his representative, Dr. Maerker Branden, wisely assumed that "he would wish me to lose no time in acknowledging your very gracious letter to him and express, in his behalf, sincere and deep appreciation of your kindness.'' The man knew his employer! "I shall let him have the letter just as soon as he arrives and I know he will read it with much pleasure and wish to write to you himself of his keen gratification.'' And immediately upon Viereck's arrival in New York, he wrote to Colonel House, suggesting a chat "sometime.''

That was the beginning of an extraordinary friendship, one of the most fruitful contacts Viereck ever made. Viereck's desire to meet the distinguished men and women of his day was not merely the journalistic climber's yen for celebrities. It sprang, rather, from a genuine yearning to absorb each man's knowledge, viewpoint and personal qualities. It is the vampire instinct so crudely set forth in his early novel on the subject, a sophisticated and subtle absorption of the gifts of others. Before long Mr. E. S. Martin, who, like House, had been one of Viereck's wartime foes, could truthfully write to Viereck of Colonel House's pleasure in Viereck's company, a pleasure which Mr. Martin now shared.

The first important result of the alliance was an introduction by House to a book by Viereck that must have astonished students of history and confounded many of Viereck's detractors. The book was *Spreading Germs of Hate,* the propaganda articles in augmented and improved form. The year of publication was 1930, less than a year after the receipt of Colonel House's surprising letter of forgiveness.

The Foreword, by House, began:

When the World War was raging, and charges false and true were made by one belligerent nation against another, few would have been willing to prophecy that eleven years after peace had been made there would be found anyone who had been in the thick of the contest who would write of it so calmly and so fairly as George Sylvester Viereck has done in this book.

[The book] will remind us how foolish and partisan we can be in times of high emotional tension. . . . Now that the world has become calm and reason once more rules, we can read with pleasure and interest such a book as Mr. Viereck has written, and wonder how and why we so nearly lost our balance during the trying days of the Great War.

To be sure, the colonel did not assume responsibility for Viereck's facts, but the reservation was that of a man trained in the school of restraint. The foreword implied more than it said, for the bond of affection between the two men was beginning to be closer.

Viereck gave voice to the new insight he began to gain from his association with House. In his own introductory chapter, which he styled *After the Battle*, he said, "Some of my friends, whose hearts are still in the trenches, cannot forgive me for being forgiving. They expect me to harbor forever the rancors and raptures of war. To them I reply with this little poem, written after sitting metaphorically at the feet of Colonel House and listening to his astonishing disclosures." The poem reached the pinnacle of Viereck's gift for epigrammatic lyricism. It gave final expression to a world mood:

> I fought for what I deemed the right,
> I saw the Truth. I was her knight.
> My foemen, too, were thus aflame,
> Blind chessmen in the obscure game
> Of some malign divinity.
> Now, with unfolding eyes, we see
> The paradox of every fight,
> That both are wrong and both are right,
> That friend is foe and foe is friend,
> And nothing matters in the end.

"And nothing matters in the end"—that was a refrain that ran somewhat through Viereck's past life and whenever a sense of defeat and disappointment gripped him. The friendship with Colonel House mattered; it mattered emphatically, and Viereck cultivated it to the full. This implies some importunity on his part, but such was not the case. The gentle man of mystery became as avid for Viereck's friendship as Viereck became for his. Viereck's inborn deference for older men, the result, as he knew, of his "father complex," necessarily charmed House, just as it had won Shaw and Freud and Einstein and the Kaiser and other men who had said farewell to the stress and sorrows of youth in the fashion of the immortal Rabbi Ben Ezra.

Spreading Germs of Hate told the "secrets of German propaganda," of "British Paper Bullets," of Uncle Sam's propagandistic fervor, of "Irish Wit and Gallic Candor" in the field of propaganda, of the alliance of politicians and propagandists; it told, in brief, of all phases of the dread disease that infects public opinion. It told such things in a style rich with drama and yet calm in its essential tone and method. The book was replete with incidents—undoubtedly the finest collection of such stories in print—for Sir William Wiseman, Colonel Norman G. Thwaites, and other propagandists had supplied Viereck with their best tales. There had been many intimate gatherings of these men. Over the teacups and between cocktails, the former foes had exchanged views. They were friends now, proud of their exploits and yet repentent, too. They did penance by confessing their sins, and thus *Spreading Germs of Hate* became a book of confessions. The moral of the book was that the forms of propaganda are too mutable, too cunning, too insidious and deadly for anyone to be entirely immune from their ravages, but good sense and humor make a fairly adequate innoculatory serum.

Authorities even in academic circles hailed the book as an important one, a source book of inestimable value. Some felt that Professor Harold D. Lasswell's study, *Propaganda Techniques in the World War* was a more sober and more adequate analysis of the subject, but Professor Lasswell felt otherwise. He said that Viereck made one of the truly basic contributions to the study of propaganda, a volume that could not be ignored by those who would understand why we fought in 1917 and why we fought again. Lasswell believed that propaganda was a newer and subtler form of tribal war dance in which the populace joins until all are hypnotized by the spell of the tom-tom. That is an explanation certainly of the black spell that held America in its grasp in 1917 and sought to destroy such men as Viereck who did not yield to it.

Throughout the book Viereck pays homage to Colonel House, but it was in a later volume that he paid his friend the full measure of his devotion. That volume bore the melodramatic title of *Strangest Friendship in History* and did not appear until 1932, after serial publication in the magazine *Liberty,* to which periodical Viereck was now contributing with some frequency. The book, it must be confessed at once, is marred by theatricality, yet it will take its place in the select library of indispensable historical books despite the fact that it reads like a novel.

There are, however, more serious questions about the merits of the volume. The questions concern Viereck's assessment of Woodrow Wilson, for he not only praises his new-found friend, the colonel, he also speaks highly of the ex-president, whose policies he had railled against bitterly and seemingly without respite. How sincere were Viereck's beliefs and, above all, his success in driving home the points he made about Wilson? The book itself does not give a complete answer.

In July of 1932 Viereck had written to the widow of President Wilson. His letter was so persuasive in tone that one marvels at the fortitude of Mrs. Wilson in ignoring it. Viereck in his letter confessed that he had been a foe of Wilson's policies, but he added that a study of various documents and numerous conversations with Colonel House convinced him of Wilson's "sincerity and the nobility of his purpose. I see him now," Viereck said, "as a warrior battling for an ideal that was perhaps too sublime for his age. I believe that when he promulgated the Fourteen Points and laid down certain fundamental principles of international cooperation he gave expression to hopes which will reverberate in the heart of mankind forever." He asked for the privilege of talking with Mrs. Wilson "for a few minutes—in Washington or wherever it may suit your convenience."

He did not receive Mrs. Wilson's cooperation. She did not remove the interdiction placed by her on the letters of her immortal husband, and she did nothing to ease his task, for certainly much in the book offended her and she could anticipate those things. Viereck had written of Wilson's ill-fated trip to Europe: "Messiahs should travel alone. Woodrow Wilson set forth to save Europe with Edith Bolling Wilson. Caparisoned from head to foot in purple, a purple dress, a purple hat and a purple plume, she cast a purple shadow athwart the friendship of the two" (Wilson and House). Certainly Mrs. Wilson could not delight in such forthright language.

But others did aid Viereck, some with enthusiasm. There were Dr. Dumba; Count Johann von Bernstoff, the German ambassador; members of Wilson's cabinet, including Bainbridge Colby, T. W. Gregory, David F. Houston, and Newton D. Baker; and Frank L. Polk, Joseph P. Tumulty, Sidney E. Mezes, Justice Charles Evans Hughes, Louis Seibold, Prof. Charles Seymour, Shaemas O'Sheel and Miss Frances Denton, "the Colonel's able secretary who knew and kept more secrets than the State Department." Mrs. Viereck, the lovable Gretchen who could be as serious as a schoolmarm, A. Paul Maerker Branden, and Fulton Oursler did more than their share in inspiring Viereck and lashing him into completing the book.

Of course, Viereck drew freely upon his own experience, as he said in the introductory note to the book, for he had known the chief actors of the drama he unfolded: Wilson himself and House, Clemenceau, McAdoo, Bryan, Page, Burleson, Morgenthau, Ludenforff, Foch, Briand, the Kaiser, and many others. Viereck realized that he was thus equipped with a more intimate viewpoint than that of the ordinary historian. And the intimacy of his viewpoint accounted for many of the successes and failures of his book. When he confessed that he was more often guided by psychology than chronology, he admitted, in effect, that he was governed too often by surmise. Viereck said at the end of his course-charting introductory chapter that House's good intentions, like Wilson's, helped to pave mankind's way to hell. Such intentions caused Viereck's feet to slip often enough, but such slips enlivened the work, their very brilliance compensating for the factual inexactitudes and glib generalities.

The heart of the book is revealed in its concluding paragraph. "For all his might," said Viereck, "Wilson could not stand alone. In every fruitful enterprise he borrowed the Colonel's brain. I shall not impute feet of clay to the idol. I concede that they are living flesh. But they are not his own. Woodrow Wilson stalks through history on the feet of Edward Mandell House."

Viereck had originally planned to conclude the book with a fantasy styled "A Rendezvous in Heaven," depicting, in dialogue form, the reunion of Colonel House and President Wilson, but he was persuaded to discard it. Wilson, "not yet an angel, still a man," stretches out to grasp the hand of House as House picks his way through the clouds to the anteroom of heaven. Wilson tells House that there are some things to discuss before he can gain "the serenity compatible with Elysium." The subjects they discuss and the conclusions they arrive at amount to a benediction on the matters and things with which Viereck's book deals. In the playlet form, the clash of personality in the case of "psychic messmates" is particularly well realized. Wilson says, as a last word, "When I was chained to my bed I was surrounded by the four walls of my dream. Sitting in the anteroom of heaven I was forced to look reality in the face. That was my purgatory.'' House counters: ''Mine was to talk to you here, saying the things I should have said on earth.'' The little drama has a marked resemblance to one of those included in the volume that Viereck had published many years earlier. Instead of the aesthetic mood, there is here the note of high sincerity befitting a tragedy that could be told by ancient poets.

The basic chapter of the book is the one called ''Symbiosis,'' wherein Viereck attempts to prove that ''the relationship between Wilson and House was not that of host and parasite.'' ''It was,'' Viereck says, ''a psychic messmate-ship,'' in which both conferred favors, the one making up for the deficiencies of the other. Through their symbiotic union, Wilson and House jointly consummated the program of liberal legislation that distinguished the first three years of the Wilson administration. They were co-partners in conceiving the Fourteen Points. They helped make peace before America entered the war, and once America was in, they helped fight the war and went to Paris in the same spirit of unity. Then a break occurred: House never saw Wilson after the return from the Peace Confer-ence. Viereck helps to solve the mystery of the break. He points in the direction of Mrs. Wilson and one other unnamed person. That interpretation, true or false, is totally unnecessary to the success of Viereck's general thesis, just as the general thesis, true or false, does not diminish the success of the book. It is an extremely interesting and valuable commentary on a period that will intimately influence all people for generations to come.

Colonel House felt that Viereck had treated him with generosity. Their union became stronger, and the two men found themselves in surprising agreement on many aspects of international and domestic affairs. They compared notes, so to speak, at all times. Each storm cloud that appeared over Europe was observed by them together. Each contributed much of value to the other. Inevitably in the mind of each arose a query as to what would have been the result if they had met earlier—before America's entry into the war. Might they have been able to prevent that tragedy?

One example of their common vision lurked on the horizon. Twenty-one years afer Sarajevo, the European scene was again smoldering ominously. The world stood at the crossroads. Was it to be the end of western civilization, as Spengler and Norman Douglas and others had so vociferously predicted? Fearing the worst, Colonel House wrote an article for *Liberty* magazine. It appeared in the September 14, 1935, issue and was called, appropriately enough, ''Wanted—A New Deal Among Nations.'' The article began with a direct reference to Viereck: '' 'Italy must expand or explode.' This statement was made by Il Duce to George Sylvester Viereck some years ago.'' It ended in a message that had to be heeded if our civilization was to endure:

> Just as social peace cannot prevail without some adjustment of the capitalistic system, so international peace cannot be preserved without

drastic territorial readjustments. Great Britain, France, Russia, and the United States must receive Italy, Germany, and Japan on terms adjusted to present world conditions and recognize their insistence upon being given their proper part of the colonial resources of the world. Chaos and catastrophe will be upon us unless those that have among the Powers are willing to share in some way with those that have not.

Bernard Shaw immediately answered the article in his typical way: "Explode and be damned." But soon enough Shaw changed his opinion and began to approximate the Viereck-House viewpoint. House's article had repercussions in Germany, in Italy, in Japan, and at the counsel table of the League of Nations in Geneva. It was destined to have more emphatic results in the future, for it was perhaps the best expression of a principle that commanded the war guns of a large part of the globe.

I have styled it the Viereck-House viewpoint because to me it appeared the wedding of the views of both men. It was interesting and instructive and painful to watch as the years unfolded.

More and more Viereck took House into his confidence on both the little and big troubles of his life. When Viereck's pro-Nazi activities brought much abuse upon his head, he protested to House, particularly against a long and libelous article in a Philadelphia newspaper which referred to Viereck's almost forgotten World War I activities. Viereck labeled the article a tissue of lies and feared that it was part of a conspiracy to crush him. He particularly resented the effort to prove that he was legally guilty of certain high crimes during the war, and he poured forth his grief in a long letter to his friend. House replied in a manner sufficient to soothe Viereck's troubled nerves. "Miss Denton and I were laughing about your being called a spy. . . . I never knew a man with more mental, physical and moral courage, and you say, at all times, just what you think." And the good old man had begun his letter to Viereck: "My dear Friend." Viereck needed no further consolation. He abandoned the idea of suing the paper for libel. "Publish and be damned!" he thought, knowing that little vindication could come from a court of law.

It was in 1936, I believe, that I met Colonel House. He wrote briefly to me of his "friendship and admiration" for Viereck, and he agreed to meet me shortly thereafter.

The strength of the Colonel's voice, its assured tone, its occasional brusqueness intrigued me. I was struck immediately by his appearance, the impeccable taste of his clothes—not a line misplaced, all, indeed, in mathematical order! Each hair of his pale mustache was in place. The slight stoop of his shoulders was scarcely noticeable. None of this suggested the almost eighty years through which he had passed. His talk was clear and unhesitant, his enunciation good, with just the least suggestion of a Southern drawl. Colonel House shook my hand, beckoned me to a chair, carefully shut the two doors to the room—one he had to shut twice—and then he sat down opposite me. The methodical manner of the man impressed itself further upon me. I momentarily glanced around the room. Not one of the many books was out of place; not one picture hung awry; not one piece of furniture was deflected. The room suggested the man himself, as orderly as a star in its course. I could not help asking myself how Viereck contrived to charm a man whose life was so well ordered. I left with my impression of the intimacy of the two strengthened but not really explained.

He questioned me first as to what I had in mind in connection with my book and how well I knew Viereck. I told him that I had corresponded with Viereck for eight years at that time, that I had won generous cooperation from him and was spending much time with him.

He listened carefully, inserting a question here and there. My attitude seemed to satisfy him. At any rate he thereafter spoke in what appeared to me to be a decidedly friendly manner.

"What I know of Viereck and what I could tell you could perhaps be summarized briefly," he said. "Perhaps you had better question me. That, at least, will save time?"

And question him I did. None of any questions seemed to offend him and some he seemed to relish; all he answered fully. His desire to be helpful was obvious. There was no brusqueness; in fact, he was almost leisurely in his narrative, giving me various asides on his early life and his European experiences and his views on preparedness and pacifism. "I am a paper colonel," he said. "I tried to get rid of the title, but I couldn't. It persisted, and I soon found a certain usefulness in it."

I am a pacifist . . . But I believe in a large army and navy to assure peace. Some peace organization, the name of which escapes me, asked me to speak at one of their gatherings and to join with them. I told them that I do not go out at all; but I invited them to send a committee to me to ascertain my views. I told them just what I am telling you, that only if the other nations respect our strength will we have peace—unless all of the nations disarm. We alone cannot do that.

It was after the election of Wilson but before his inauguration that I spoke with Wilson on the subject of war and preparedness. I told him that war in Europe was inevitable within a short while unless we had the military force to compel peace. I told him that an army of 1,000,000 was a necessity, not an active army but something in the nature of a reserve army. He agreed and sent for Leonard Wood to draft plans. Wood, as a military man, was delighted and went to work on the plans with spirit. I suppose it was a good plan; I do not know. But we learnt to our dismay that it would cost one billion dollars. Wilson said, 'Congress will never authorize that much!' and, of course, I was forced to agree with him. [One billion then was the equivalent of many billions in our inflated economy.]

He added as an after thought, "The World War cost us sixteen billion dollars." (With today's inflation, the figure is much higher, of course.)

"We are the only nation that can buck England in a naval race. If I were President, I would advocate the most powerful navy for this country.

"But Germany and, for that matter, the other nations, are another story, as far as England is concerned. England will not permit Germany to approach it in naval strength. France and Russia have been ready to attack Germany, given the word from England. If Germany would attempt to equal British naval strength, England would give the word. Hitler's speech yesterday was meant to reassure England. Possibly some of my advice was heeded by Hitler. I had told my views to Viereck and other friends of Germany. Perhaps they relayed it to Hitler. That is all right as far as I am concerned."

"I was born two years before the Civil War and I remember the period of violence that followed the War. In Texas, a fearless fellow—you see a drawing of him on my table—*Liberty* just sent it over to me the other day—helped to put down violence by force of character. Virtue plus strength will overcome the forces of ill. Parallels can be drawn for today."

His assessment of Viereck reflected the healing effect that time had had:

When I first met him I was astonished to find him much less prejudiced than I had imagined. He has prejudices even now; he instinctively favors the German viewpoint. But now his prejudices do not destroy his sense of fairness. I think that he is anxious to do justice to everyone and all causes. I think that he has no selfish motives and that he is essentially selfless in the expression of his views.

He knows American opinion and psychology. He is close to the center of things. He has the ear of important people and their confidence. And, of course, he understands the German psychology. In my opinion, he is of more value to Germany than any one outside of that country, although I do not think that the German government is fully aware of it or fully appreciates it. He means more to Germany than any Ambassador or Minister or Envoy. He is, of course, the foremost German-American.

I asked the colonel if he thought of Viereck as a poet or a practical man of affairs, and he replied, his face lighting up, "To me Viereck is always a romantic figure, always the poet, although he has a full grasp of the practical. He has a charm that is almost impossible to resist, once one knows him. He is one of the most charming, likeable men I know."

"How close are you to him?"

"That I cannot say. He is one of my most valued friends—and our friendship is in the process of daily development. . . ."

"I think Viereck is one of the most *unusual* men of our day," he continued, giving the word *unusual* more meaning than I have ever heard it given.

"If I may say so, Viereck's life has the same *unusual* quality that my life has had. You know, I have never held public office and yet I have played a part in the scheme of things. Viereck's life has been unique, too. . . ."

"Is Viereck accurate in his reports of conversations, meetings and the like?" I asked, welcoming the opportunity to bring up the subject.

"Yes, but he is always eager to be corrected. When he sends anything to me, he tells me to tear it apart—the more corrections, the better."

In spite of Colonel House's congeniality and his frankness about his relationship with Viereck, I departed with the vague feeling that, like everything else associated with Viereck, I still lacked the complete picture. Somewhat later I questioned Viereck over a period of several days, attempting to penetrate his many personas and glimpse the real man. Of course I failed, but this encounter is interesting in several ways: for how it counterpoints my interview with Colonel House, for how it shows how far Viereck had come since the rancorous days of World War I and afterward, and for what it pointed to in the future.

"I suppose your first long trip made a particular impression on you?"

"No," he replied. The subject did not seem to interest him.

"But surely your first ocean trip impressed you."

"Yes, I made up my mind never to cross the ocean again. That was in October, 1897. Since then I have crossed so often that I have lost count. I have traveled for pleasure and in search of material; but the ocean as such means nothing to me. In fact, you hardly see it while traveling!"

Did art, music, reading, recreation mean as little to this poet?

"I have no extensive knowledge of painting, sculpture, the graphic arts, architecture, the theatre, the drama, the novel, the fine arts and literature in general," Viereck said, almost in a tone of vaunting.

"My favorite novel is *My First Two Thousand Years,*" he said. "It is probably the most extraordinary book published in English in the first third of the twentieth century. The importance, the depth and the philosophy of this brain child of mine and Eldridge's was overlooked because of the glamor of the story and diction. This book of ours is a charming thing."

"I like none of the classics," he emphasized. "I am not interested in the fine arts or in general literature except for the poets. I never visit museums and galleries; they bore me; they make me ill. I used to go to the theatre when I was dramatic editor of *Current Opinion,* but now I attend only two or three times a month. I read all the time—but only the books of my own choice and wayward fancies."

Knowing Viereck's dislike of mere knowledge, it took something in the nature of courage to ask him to what extent he was interested in economic, political and social problems, the so-called serious things of life.

"I have been involved in such things, chiefly through personalities in whom I was interested," he said. "When I battled for the Lord it was under Roosevelt. I was interested in La Follette and in Debs, and of course I am interested in Germany and German-American relations, but I am interested in all these things only if they are dramatized in some personality.''

"But what form of government and society do you favor?'' I asked. "I favor an oligarchy,'' he said, "if I am one of the oligarchs.''

"And for which form of society have you the greatest antipathy?''

His answer was unhesitant: "The dictatorship of the proletariat. Why? Because I am I. I do not like the beehive or the ant hill. I suppose people can somehow live under any form of government; but while a choice remains, mine is *not* communism.''

"Will a choice long remain?''

"Perhaps not,'' he was quick to admit. "Communism, like other evils, may be inevitable. Fascism may be a necessary evil in emergencies. But they are not for me. I sometimes describe myself as a conservative anarchist, which, being translated, means that I want to be left alone, to work out my own destiny and to escape boredom in my own way.''

"Are there any politicians, economists, sociologists that interest you?'' I asked, forlornly.

"Only the picturesque ones, like Hitler and Mussolini,'' he replied. "I simply don't like economists and sociologists. Why? Because I don't.''

"What does money mean to you?'' I asked suddenly, anxious to trace a tangential course that might somehow pierce the heart of the bored aesthete.

Viereck thought for a moment. "Money,'' he said, playing with the word, "is a thing to be spent. And it is a symbol of power. I do not hold it in disrespect, as you know. I once had half a million dollars!'' (This, I point out again, was in the pre-inflation days when such sum was a considerable one.)

"But what do possessions mean to you?''

"Nothing! I could live in one room with one hundred books, a few pictures and a comfortable couch. . . . I have always earned a good deal and spent much more. I do not need to hold fast to symbols of affluence. . . .''

"Does fine living appeal to you?'' I asked.

He answered at once, "It is my natural state,'' forgetful of the "one room with one hundred books, a few pictures and a comfortable couch.'' In other words, he played with poetic dreams of the simple life, but aspired to all the luxuries that adhere to the financial barons of our day.

"Do fees and royalties affect your writing?'' I asked, hardly expecting a frank response. I reminded him of Art Young's penetrating analysis of him as one too much in love with luxuries and those who can afford them. He thought Young right, but he added that it was only natural for him to favor the true aristocrats, rather than the herd. "I belong in their company,'' he said.

"How do you differentiate between your journalism and your literature?'' I asked.

"Journalism,'' he replied, "may be literary, but it contains the element of decay. The very thing that makes it timely robs it of immortality.''

"Why, then, do you indulge in so much journalism?''

"Because it amuses me. . . . It is my game of golf."

And so, by easy steps, the conversation progressed to the consideration of the more than thirty men who are included in Viereck's book *Glimpses of the Great,* the memorial to his talents as an interviewer. Viereck said that he once replied to a customs official who inquired as to his profession, "Lion-hunting!" But the various interviews have certain elements of distinction that lift them above ordinary celebrity-seeking.

"Don't you dwell too much on politicians and royalty and such?" I demanded.

"This is a political age," Viereck insisted, forgetting his professed indifference to politics. "Royalty always interests democracies. . . . Bear in mind, too, that at least one half of the book is journalism, and emphatically not literature. . . . "

"I wrote out my interviews, making notes as I talked, he said. "Being unable to read my notes, I consulted my imagination. To that my interviews are indebted for whatever poor merit they may possess. For accuracy they were submitted to my sitters and carefully revised. I made each man say what he wanted to say and should have said, and what he authorized, reporting not the accidental or the casual, but the important."

Still there was an expression of doubt on my part.

"My function was sometimes purely decorative. I kept my tongue in my cheek at times, but ordinarily I was extraordinarily honest. I selected generally only those of my contemporaries who interested me. I tried to meet men who were, in Wilde's phrase, symbolic of their age. I selected men who stood for some great world current or because they were convenient mouthpieces for me. I cared most for those who said the things I would like to say. Most of the men, especially those older than myself, liked me. My feeling is that you portray others to portray some phase of yourself. You write history and biography and fiction for the same reason."

"Does *Glimpses of the Great,* then, contain all of the men and women you deem the greatest of this age?"

"This book is, in a sense, a kaleidoscope of human intelligence," Viereck had said, in a foreword to the volume, "a mirror of mankind, in the first quarter of the twentieth century. It records the pulse beat of the age." "Is there a tune to which the World Spirit dances?" Viereck asked, and answered at once: "I think there is." He said that "in every age the tide of thought, despite mutinous eddies and backwash, flows in certain specific directions." Every age, in short, has its tune. His book, he believed, gave "an echo of the complicated rhythm which dominates the postwar world."

His contacts with Bernard Shaw call for special consideration, as Shaw was one of the few men deeply respected by Viereck, intellectually and as a human being. It was not too much to say that he revered G. B. S. for certain qualities in Shaw that he found in himself. Shaw asked him if he made his living in any way other than by writing, Shaw's implication being that writing was not quite honest as a means of earning a livelihood. "Like you, Mr. Shaw," said Viereck, "I live by my wits."

When I sent Shaw a questionnaire about Viereck, Shaw forwarded an amusing and revealing response. He said that he has known Viereck "ever since he was an adult. But my personal contacts with him hardly total up to three whole days." I could almost see Shaw fingering a pencil and a pad and adding up the length of each interview and multiplying the result by the number of interviews; he had an inherent love of mathematical tricks!

"We have always spoken our minds to one another on the subjects we discussed; but those were public subjects," he said. "I have never been in his house."

He had been asked for details and incidents of the acquaintance, and replied that there was: "Talk, talk, talk. No incidents."

When asked for his Viereck letters, he said that he kept no correspondence. "It is a mischievous habit."

"What aspects of his career and work most interest you? Why?"

"I am too old to be interested in anybody—even in myself," he replied. "I never know what he is up to."

As for his opinion of Viereck's position in American, German and world literature, he could only say: "Ask me 300 years hence. He is echt Deutsch." As to his preference among Viereck's writings: "I never read them." His place in international politics and affairs and in history: "Don't know. Neither does he." The reasons for Viereck's success or failure?—"His brains." What in Viereck's personality or character most interests or irritates him? "He doesn't irritate me. I like the German touch in him." Shaw's general reaction?—"On the whole, pleasant."

Shaw had, as much as any man, contributed nuggets to Viereck's fund of self-amusement, but neither man had deeply influenced the character or the career of the other. Shaw's personality touched all the bright young minds of the day—Viereck's no less than the others—but he did not lead any man to probe more deeply into the darkness of his own soul. Freud had done that and, perhaps, Einstein, and both men had been basic in the later career of Viereck. In the Viereck guestbook there is a heart with two squares in it, drawn by Einstein. The heart is Einstein's own, the two squares stand for Gretchen and Sylvester, the whole thing symbolizing that the Vierecks were then close to the heart of the great physicist.

The most obvious sign of Viereck's return to respectability was his social life. Viereck had acquired from his father and from Plato the symposium habit. Louis Viereck as president of the *Deutsche Schiftsteller Verband,* initiated symposia for Ludwig Fulda, Prof. John W. Burgess and many other distinguished men. Following his lead, his son subordinated music and dancing to talk and discussion at the parties held in the Viereck home. One such memorable gathering was the farewell party held on a May evening in 1936 at his home of many years, at 627 W. 113th Street, off Riverside Drive, in New York City. In a short while, the Vierecks were to say good-bye to their old home and face their friends in an apartment. To them, that denoted the passing of an epoch in their lives. All save one person came very early; none departed until the next morning had almost arrived.

The guests present were as varied as the conflicting desires of Viereck's own soul, and they were indicative of the forces that were at play that evening.

There sat to one side a man who had broken bread with Swinburne and Wilde and Whistler; one who had observed them with trained yet sympathetic eyes and who could report them with understanding. W. Orton Tewson was a man in his middle years, perhaps older, who glowed with a quiet excitement that became more intense as the evening wore on. "Whistler was a beast in many respects," he said. "Wilde was ever kindly, ever likeable." There was a sharpness in his tone that made each syllable of his talk stand out.

Then there appeared the vision of a man from a strange, new world. A tall, thin man, whose eyes blazed with an unearthly light, entered the room so quietly that one was hardly aware of his presence. He bowed himself to his seat, to his right Gretchen, to his left Sylvester. He beamed upon them paternally. He greeted the guests with a kindly nod. Before he could be introduced, Tewson blurted out, "Nikola Tesla!" Tewson's eyes appeared dim with emotion. More than thirty years before, the *Times* had sent him to interview Tesla, then in the midst of a controversy with Edison. Now he was seated once again near Tesla, ready to learn the intimate secrets of the man's soul.

The atmosphere warmed the heart of the poet-scientist who was chiefly responsible for our modern technological world. Tesla, who, in the opinion of many, had almost single-handedly established the science of applied electrical mechanics, with his inventions of the rotating magnetic field and systems of arc lighting and alternating power transmission, was in a communicative mood. He told his life story unostentatiously, simply, with quiet eloquence. He told of his platonic affairs of the heart. He explained the inventions that have made the world his debtor. He told of his plans, of his credo, of his foibles. It was a tale of wonders, told with guileless simplicity.

That same house had seen Einstein, Hauptmann, Hirschfeld, Sinclair Lewis and countless others. It had been a gathering place for many notable spirits. Its walls told the story of these men and women, and many were there that night, a virtual register of important intellectual, social, and political figures of the time. Its host carried their personalities within his own personality, like a chameleon reflecting their many lights and shadows. Viereck was comparatively silent much of the night, but he was subtly responsible for the intellectual thrills of the evening. His personality, insidiously, charmed all who were present. There could be no doubt that these human touches meant more to Viereck than the stern visage of duty. Like a sponge, he avidly soaked in the riches of those around him.

32 THE CHRONICLER OF
THE WANDERING JEW

Anyone reading the body of Viereck's verse, even the titles, would have suspected that all history was to him a continuous pageant or panorama. To him the first king, the last monarch, and all the intervening princes are brothers. Their costumes might vary; the boundaries of their kingdoms might change; time might wither the grasses growing on the hillsides of their fields; and commerce might expand like a bubble about to burst. But they are all kindred, all part of the procession of a common humanity. "Aiander" envisions man, "Aiogyne" woman, in their course through the centuries. "Nineveh" "The Parrot," "The Plaint of Eve," "Children of Lilith"—to name varied examples—have the same grand sweep of a poet who delighted in seeing life richly and whole.

When the Balkan wars were raging in Europe as the sinister prelude to a worse conflagration, the idea for a book took possession of Viereck's mind. It would be a novel of a new genre, a thoroughly modern variation on the theme of the Wandering Jew. It was to deal not so much with the indestructible Jew as with eternal man. It was to trace the course of mankind through the centuries since Christ. All that was common to the generations of man would be portrayed: the constant human characteristics, the recurrent types, the wonder and the squalor of existence. It would be a connected narrative of an epic sweep, the prose poem of humanity, an erotic interpretation of history, the gospel according to Freud. The more Viereck thought about the theme, the more it excited him. He felt that there were illimitable possibilities in the book that could enrich the literature of the world. However he realized that, in spite of a great idea, *The House of the Vampire* had been an almost complete failure. Now he had a far greater idea, and he wanted to make certain that it would not collapse. He began to write his book of books, the idea firm in his mind, the devices of the tale secure. But, somehow, the spirit of life was lacking. He had a story in tatters, and he wanted a cloth of fine velvet.

At that time—1914—he went to visit his parents. On his return to America, he brought with him a sheaf of poems, the passional leaves of *Songs of Armaged-*

don, and he had with him certain additional ideas for his book of the ages. He decided to see his faithful friend, Hugo Munsterberg, before proceeding to New York and the work that lay ahead of him. He had already discussed the work with the Harvard savant and had won his eager interest, Munsterberg applied hypnotic treatment in an effort to fit Viereck's brain into a groove of concentration, so that the work might be completed. Viereck now hoped to win further encouragement and aid from the great psychologist, but, alas, gory clouds darkened the European skies like beasts about to leap upon helpless men. Europe was at war; apocalyptic rumblings of disaster were heard everywhere. Munsterberg was oppressed. All culture seemed to him at that moment futile; the writing of a novel seemed insolence to the high gods. The epic of the Eternal Man could abide the issue of the war. He persuaded Viereck that, for the time being, he ought to forget everything except a vigorous defense of the Fatherland. He put aside his story. *The Fatherland* was founded, and a period of public life dawned for him as he doffed his literary mantle.

There were moments when the idea of the book plagued Viereck. When he was most convinced that the Central Powers were fighting a righteous war that merited his constant support, he felt occasionally that his calling was literature, not propaganda, poetry, not politics, enduring works, not journalism. He had those moments particularly when he talked with that strange literary cavalier, Dr. Hanns Heins Ewers, who was in America at the time. Ewers, too, was battling for the Fatherland, and like Viereck he had adventured into many types of literature. He wrote stories that suggested Poe. He was a poet of distinction and an essayist whose lines had a beauty that could be both blatant and intensely subdued. He knew the little world of creeping things as did Fabre. He was the sort of scholar and man of letters who could grasp instantly the strength of symbols like the Wandering Jew. To him Viereck confided the basic ideas of his book, which by then he had begun to call *Mr. Isaac Laquedem,* one of the many names for the man supposed to have been doomed by Christ to wander for all time in all places.

In January 1918, while America was at war with Germany, Viereck sent to Ewers, who was still here, the rough draft of the prologue and the first fourteen chapters of his book, expressing the hope that Ewers would complete it. He asked Ewers not to say that it is inartistic to finish the work of another man. Did he not remember the great dictum of Goethe about seizing ideas that served an artistic purpose? If you refuse, said Viereck to him, the book may remain unfinished forever.

Nothing of a definite nature came of Viereck's overtures, except a crystallization of Viereck's views on the Wandering Jew theme. And so more long years went by. It was now the year 1924. Viereck had just completed his services on behalf of La Follette, and he was near the end of his association with Haldeman-Julius. The long-ignored manuscript of the chronicle of the Wandering Jew tormented him, but still he felt unable to resume work on the book. At that time he received an inspiring letter from Henry T. Schnittkind of the Stratford Company, a Boston publishing house that was then making the effort to establish itself in an influential position in the literary world. Schnittkind asked Viereck if he would care to prepare his autobiography, or perhaps a novel, for publication by the Stratford Company. It was obvious that what the company wanted, above all else, was Viereck's autobiography, which Schnittkind felt would be a fascinating book. Viereck informed him that the novel he had in mind would be a more truthful biography than anything published as autobiography. "What in my character or career pleases you?" he asked Schnittkind, playing as fondly with the idea as he had in the past. At the same time he wrote to Horace Liveright to tell that lively publisher that there seemed to be a revival of interest in his work. He mentioned that, while he had refused to write his autobiography, he could put a good deal of his secret life into his novel dealing psychoanalytically with the Wandering Jew. Perhaps with urging he could finish that story, but certainly not without it.

The kettles began to boil. Liveright expressed much interest in the book; his inquiries kept pace with Schnittkind's. Viereck seemed to pit one against the other, as if to arouse his sleeping instincts to complete the book by creating an atmosphere of seduction. The book would be teased out of him. Narcissus would answer the obliging mirror. He wrote Liveright a long, tempting letter, substantially like the one he had written to Ewers six years before and Liveright became more interested; so did Schnittkind. Which would win? It was a game worth watching. Liveright had three of his men go over the rough draft of Viereck's manuscript, and he himself read it. One reader briefly dismissed the book as bad. It is, he said, "a Viereckian version of the '10,000 best known epigrams' and badly done at that. There is no chance in the world of its escaping the censor." Another reader wrote with tremendous gusto of the manuscript. "In this book," he said, "is seen in all its power the terrible megalomania of Viereck. Any book of his, anything he has ever written, deserves more than cavalierish treatment if only because of its interest as a psychopathic study. There is an interest in the man, so conceited, so tremendously egotistical and so futile that makes anything he has ever written a fascinating study." He then went on to pick out, with considerable shrewdness, the flaws of the manuscript, and he concluded in a spirit of prophecy: "His story is fascinating, there are excellent and penetrating pieces of writing, it is unflaggingly interesting, but he has threaded it on an unimportant and unworthy and a too-consciously perverse thread. The book will undoubtedly be published by someone. It will be talked about and will get someone a lot of notoriety. Its sale will not be large. And its pretensions are unworthy of its accomplishments. I am, I think, against it. Someone else should read it." Liveright himself felt that the staccato style was against the book, but he was interested in it and wanted to see it again. Viereck felt stirred by the penetrating criticism.

Meanwhile, Schnittkind continued on the trail. He suggested that James Branch Cabell might be an ideal collaborator, for, he said, it is just the sort of thing in which Cabell reveled. A little later he suggested that Paul Eldridge, hardly known to fame, might yet prove to be a good associate. To arouse Viereck's interest, he sent him two little books that Eldridge had written, the one of them called *Our Dead Selves*. It was, as Eldridge subtitled it, an *Anthology of the Lowly*, a tender record of what the rooster, the hen, the giraffe, and the rest of the animal kingdom might say in self-apology after leaving their earthly habitations. It was of the genre of Masters' *Spoon River Anthology* but not a whit less original or adequate in diction and philosophy. The words of the rooster give a sufficient indication of the merits of the volume:

> The Sun was a red balloon
> Which I blew high—high—
> Beyond the mountain peaks,
> And balanced on the sharp point
> Of my crowing.
> As my head was chopped,
> I heard a loud and sudden clap—
> I knew the Sun had burst.

There were others of equal and surpassing merit. Viereck was delighted and sensed a kindred spirit. He told Schnittkind he would like to meet Eldridge, but he expressed himself as not quite sure that the man had the constructive ability to write fiction, an ability which Viereck confessed, he himself possessed "only in a limited degree." "What I need," he said, "is not so much a man with many ideas, but a man who has the storytelling faculty and patience." When Schnittkind expressed regret that Eldridge was not the man, Viereck hastened to reassure him: "I merely expressed some doubt," he said; "it is quite possible that he may be the man."

The two men met. Eldridge was not yet forty; Viereck had just reached the forty mark. Eldridge had lived for long in several European countries. He had studied at several great centers of learning and had won his doctor's degree at the University of Paris. He had delivered a series of lectures at the Sorbonne on American literature and at present was teaching romance languages in a New York high school. He had written poetry and short stories and plays. He had been called, and he was, a master of irony. Havelock Ellis, Isaac Goldberg, Van Wyck Brooks, John McClure, Vincent Starett, Benjamin De Casseres, and others had praised his work, but he was unkown and hardly rising to fame. He was withal dreamy and hopeful. He and Viereck took to each other at once, their friendship by all indications reaching a perfect lyrical intensity. Whenever Eldridge mentioned Viereck, his love for the man was obvious.

Max Beerbohm, that most whimsical of modern essayists, should have written of the uses and meanings of inscriptions in books. Even sloppy, mawkish, maudlin words, written on the flyleaf of a printed book are meaningful, as full of revelation as any passage in the Bible. All such words are the intimate communication of a soul, particularly when the person has a soul. When Paul Eldridge, in an inscription said that he had met Viereck "by an accident or fatality too beautiful to be divine," his very soul spoke, in spite of the disingenuous sounding language he employed. Earlier that very year he had given Viereck the second copy of the deluxe edition of his book, *Irony and Pity,* and had inscribed it "To Sylvester, whose mind is entangled with mine like the roots of a tree." The language he penned later in the year showed how far their intimacy had progressed in very few months, and five years later their souls spoke in unison. Not a speck of doubt could be seen on the horizon when, on the first day of the year 1931, Eldridge gave Viereck yet another book. "O mighty Growler," he wrote on the inviting first leaf, "Hearken to thy High Priest, Kotikokura, and bless George Sylvester Viereck, thy Son, flesh and rib, upon this day! Wind thy thousand tails about him, and protect him from all evil! Make him powerful like unto Thee, that all may exclaim: Another Great Ape." There was a playfulness and a tenderness that betokened an almost ecstatic regard, a harmony that could not be broken because it was in tune with some inner need of both men. Only two years passed now and Eldridge gave Viereck another book—a final gift. He wrote on one of its pages words, which, in another man, might mean much but which, coming from Eldridge, mark the disintegration of a great friendship. The greeting ran with an unusual snap, from "Paul" to "my constant friends, Sylvester and Gretchen." The cycle of friend-ship was completed; there could be no more to it, but for the moment neither man realized it. That was the tale that inscriptions told. That is the subject for an essay by some Max Beerbohm or Christopher Morley of our day.

It is, also, the story of the Viereck-Eldridge collaboration, surely one of the most unusual associations in literary history. Books have been written in collab-oration before, particularly in the field of drama, from the earliest times to today. Works of scholarship are often produced in that fashion, novels less often, and one can scarcely imagine a poem that is truly a joint product. The elder Dumas, perhaps the originator of mass production in literature, had a whole school of collaborators; Erckmann and Chatrian, the de Goncourt brothers, Mencken and Nathan, these are a few of the varied individuals who have joined their literary fortunes. Gilbert and Sullivan present another sort of collaboration. Fascinating queries as to the reasons for such associations inevitably come to mind. What inner compulsions or external caprices motivated them? What induced their success or failure? Can a unified work of permanent value result from the cooperative effort of artists?

The case of Viereck was of particular interest. Here was a man who had achieved prodigious fame in his own right, a fame perhaps out of proportion to the merits of his work, but real in every respect. At the height of his acclaim no enemy could deny that he had reached some sort of height from which he could look down on other men of letters. And he had no little respect for his own merits. He felt that he was gifted to a superlative degree, that he was a man of genius—perhaps America's foremost poet and certainly in the company of Poe and Whitman. He was talented in a dozen fields of literary endeavor, fluent and bristling with ideas. The world, to him, was brim full of material. Freud, in particular, had explored intellectual continents for him. He felt that he had vision and a novel outlook. Yet he sought a collaborator and found him in Paul Eldridge.

Years later, after the two men had parted company, an explanation was besought from Viereck. He was reticent at first, and then he said that he had always refused to analyze his and Eldridge's method of collaboration and to consider the reasons for the alliance:

"When you have a child before you, how can you tell whether the share of the father or the mother is greater? In our intellectual relationship I have been the father—the generative principle. I had most of the pleasure and Eldridge had most of the labor. But, of course, this is not entirely true. His mind reacting upon mine was independently creative. It is almost impossible to tell the origin of the various genes from which has sprung the personality of our brain child.

"The fundamental concept is mine, the execution largely—but not entirely—his," Viereck said on another occasion. "Mine is most of the ideation, his are most of the images.

"The book had to be written, because it is in a sense, the record of my own emotional and intellectual experiences. But somehow it needed a double parentage."

The abrupt, too logical, and sometimes too brutal style of the original manuscript needed a soft focus, a blurring of the edges, and these Paul Eldridge supplied. Eldridge was a poet of refinement, his literary gentility a necessary complement to Viereck's rougher manner. The two men realized that each had much to offer the other, and they regarded themselves as intellectually wed and often referred to the union of their minds. They never quarreled. "We invariably agreed in important matters," Viereck has said, "and did not consider it necessary to quarrel over details."

Eldridge proceeded to rewrite all that Viereck had written, supplying a softer tone to the work, as Viereck outlined the general plan of each chapter and of the book. The two men discussed the outline, and the incidents and characters grew out of their talk. Viereck introduced here and there flashing phrases, such as "unendurable pleasure indefinitely prolonged," which he thought essential to the ideation of the book. At home, Eldridge would write the chapter and then read it to his literary partner. Sometimes Viereck would accept what Eldridge had written. Often enough they would wrestle over it until its form was changed. Again Eldridge would rewrite it, and once more the two men would reexamine it critically. In a sense it was a struggle to blend two distinct literary rhythms, and sometimes it could not be done. Now and then they came to a chapter which Eldridge refused to do. In such cases Viereck wrote the first draft. But certain chapters were Eldridge's favorites, one on Spinoza belonging almost entirely to him; and there were others, too. On the other hand, the interview with the Borgia pope, Alexander VI, the episode centering around Bluebeard, the eery narrative of the Florentine twins, the meeting between Appolonius of Tyana and Cartaphilus are almost entirely Viereck's, but, in general, one cannot disentangle the contribution of the one from the other. They were the parents, and the book was their child.

While the two men were working on the book, they were filled with excitement and often discussed their plans with their friends, winning the wholehearted belief that they were writing a masterpiece. Dr. Isaac Goldberg made a solemn announcement to that effect in the *Haldeman-Julius Weekly,* and Fulton Oursler told William H. Briggs, of the distinguished publishing house of Harper and Brothers, about the book. Mr. Brigg's interest much stirred, he wrote to Viereck so that he might be permitted to read the manuscript. The collaborators sent the first half of their book to Mr. Briggs and several men at Harpers read it. "I think all of us who have read your extraordinary story feel that you are on your way to a masterpiece," Mr. Briggs wrote. "I think I can say for all of us here at Harpers that if the second half is maintained at the level of the portion which we have seen, we should then feel like undertaking the publication of the book with vigor and enthusiasm. In many ways we can see that it may be an epoch-making book."

The manuscript was again sent to Liveright, and his reader felt that the collaboration with Eldridge had helped the book in some ways and harmed it in others but that, all in all, he could not recommend its publication. This was an unexpected blow to the two men, who felt they were doing memorable work. They were destined to receive more such blows. Simon and Schuster, an enterprising new firm, kept the manuscript ten weeks and then rejected it after writing: "No manuscript that we have had in our whole publishing experience has been harder to decide on than yours. It interested us enormously and loomed up as one of the biggest editorial projects we had ever encountered." They rejected it because they had commissioned Dr. Will Durant to write a biographical story of civilization, which they felt covered somewhat the same ground.

The two men began to regard the book as a White Elephant and consoled each other. "Mon Cher," wrote Paul to his partner, "to hell with the rest! We know that we are remarkable fellows, don't we?" Their experience with the publishing world was generic, a sort of allegory for all serious artists.

Tiring of the effort to find a publisher in America, the two men went abroad, Eldridge to his favorite haven, Majorca, and Viereck to the Fatherland. Eldridge remained and Viereck returned. In August of 1927 Viereck was able to write to Eldridge that he had placed the novel in Germany! Benvenuto Hauptmann, son of the great Gerhart, was to translate it (he did not), and Paul List of Leipzig to publish it. "I shall use the fact that the book is being published in Germany in order to put more life in our efforts to place it here," Viereck said, while venturing the fearful thought that American authors would increasingly be compelled to publish their books abroad "because the police in Boston and obscure postmasters elsewhere arrogate to themselves the right to censor literature." The very next month Viereck was able to write to Eldridge that he had found a publisher in America— Macaulay. The long quest was over, but Macaulay insisted upon various changes, for such is the way of publishers.

To Viereck's letters announcing the good news, Eldridge replied, with mounting enthusiasm. "Querido Amigo," said he. "It would be Germany, naturally, where an intelligent book could be published. You know that any arrangement you make is always welcome to me. Cartaphilus never goes wrong!" And in his excitement he closed the letter with the best of wishes to everyone, including Ajax, Viereck's dog!

The two men worked at the job of condensing the long script, but eventually it was on the press. Viereck busied himself with the task of obtaining the necessary publicity, sending Macaulay's man, Davin, letters filled with material that he thought would make good press releases. He told Davin of James Branch Cabell's hearty welcome to the reentry of the Wandering Jew into literature. He emphasized that the fall of 1928 was to see the publication of three books by him: *My First Two Thousand Years, Days in Doorn* (the memoirs of Empress Hermine, written by Viereck in collaboration with her) and *As They Saw Us* (the story of the American armies in Europe as told by Foch, Ludendorff, and others, procured and edited by Viereck). He caught Eldridge's excitement in exceeding measure. After all, it was to be his first truly literary work since the publication of *Songs of Armaggedon* in 1916—a monumental one at that. All the adventures with publishers only intensified his eagerness.

The story of *My First Two Thousand Years* is worth narrating. It is told by Mr. Isaac Lacquedem, alias Cartaphilus, the Wandering Jew, while he is under a hypnotic spell wrought by a psychoanalyst.

Cartaphilus is handsome, intelligent, amorous, and worldly. One of his chief aims in life is to run from his Jewish origin and to become a Roman. In a measure he succeeds. He is a favored captain in the service of Pontius Pilate at the time of the trial and crucifixion of Jesus. The mildness of the Nazarene enrages him because it seems so typical of the submission of the Jews. He hates Jesus also because the man has won the fanatical devotion of Mary Magdalene and John, the two human beings for whom he cares most. Cartaphilus taunts Jesus while He is on the way to Golgatha: "Go faster!" he mutters. The meekness vanishes from the face of Jesus; in anger He says to His tormentor:"I will go, but thou shalt tarry until I return." The words work a miraculous change in the bodily composition of Cartaphilus. Thirty at the time of the crucifixion, he remains forever of that age. (Viereck's dictum: "After thirty nothing matters.") He is slow to realize that he is destined to life everlasting. He sees his contemporaries grow old and pass away. He remains, a living torment to them and to himself. Apparently he is sterile, despite his astonishing physical and mental vigor. Eternal life seems a curse, without mitigating features. He hates Jesus with increasing force, for having doomed him to go companionless and without progeny through the centuries. In anger, he persuades Nero to persecute the early Christians. He swears to everlasting war against the Savior who had perished in shame at the place of skulls. He wanders from place to place, not the hunted animal of the official legends, but unhappy despite his culture, his wealth, his health, his longevity. It seems that the difficulty is that there is no meaning to his life, no quest to hold his attention through the ages. He meets the saintly and infinitely wise Apollonius of Tyana, and the burden of existence is lifted from him. He sits at the feet of the sage and absorbs enough real wisdom to fill the void. Thenceforth, life is a boon rather than a curse; eternity is scarcely long enough to find that for which Apollonius counsels him to seek.

"I see before me a dreary desert of years, a desert without end," Cartaphilus says to Apollonius. "Can life offer me nothing except repetition?"

"What purpose can last centuries?" Cartaphilus asks, still puzzled by the scheme of things. Knowledge, love, hate do not seem enough. Apollonius meditates.

"Have you not spoken of John and Mary, Cartaphilus?" he asks. "The ideal you seek is neither Mary nor John, but a synthesis of both, a double blossom of passion, combining male and female, without being a monster. . . . If you could find John and Mary in one, Cartaphilus, so that touching Mary, you might feel the thrill of John . . . and speaking to John, you might hear the voice of Mary . . . would it not rejoice you, Cartaphilus. . . . All things are possible, Cartaphilus. The World Spirit, in his ceaseless experiments, may evolve your dream. . . . Seek . . . and perhaps . . . you shall find."

In his quest Cartaphilus finds one almost inseparable companion, Kotikokura, and one inconstant, teasing, irresistible lure, the immortal Salome. Cartaphilus had met Salome in the days of Pilate, when she was a princess in Judea. He had sought to win her favors, but she had treated him with apparent disdain, seemingly preferring a pitch-black Nubian to him. This rankles Cartaphilus for many a year, and Salome continues to heap coals of fire upon him. She will not let him possess her, though she gives herself to those, like the Nubian, who are obviously his inferiors. Kotikokura, warm, primitive, faithful to the one he reveres, ruthless to those he dislikes, atones in a measure for Salome's galling coldness. Cartaphilus finds in Kotikokura a salve to his ego and an object whose growth through the centuries is marvelous to behold.

These three, Cartaphilus, Salome, and Kotikokura, sport through the five hundred pages of *My First Two Thousand Years* and through the many pages of the two sequels that followed. In a brief foreword to *The Invincible Adam*, the authors summarize, with considerable aptness, the purpose of their trilogy. *My First Two Thousand Years* was the parent of other books:

> Cartaphilus, alias Isaac Lacquedem, the Wandering Jew, the hero of *My First Two Thousand Years,* is the highly sophisticated, highly civilized modern man, conscious of the feminine component which he inherits from Mother Eve. Doffing the kaftan of the Wandering Jew like his shoemaker's apron, he becomes Wandering Man. Brother to Faust and Don Juan, he seeks unendurable pleasure indefinitely prolonged, and a new synthesis of woman. Every man passes, at least vicariously, through the experiences of Cartaphilus. Salome, his feminine counterpart, is the highly sophisticated, highly civilized modern woman, conscious of her masculine roots. In the course of the centuries the seven veils which enveloped her when she danced for Herod fall from her lovely shoulders. The princess of Judea incarnates the restlessness of her sex. Salome's battle against her biological handicap is the battle of all women. Kotikokura, the companion of Cartaphilus and Salome on their journey through time, is the super-masculine young male, seeking to find himself in the maze of friendship and passion. Together the three books constitute a trilogy of love.

Our Saga of Passion aims to bridge the gulf between the sexes, to establish a truce in their ageless struggle. The essential bisexuality of all life is part and parcel of our doctrine. The latest discoveries of endocrinology and psychology confirm the poetic intuitions of Plato. No understanding of love is possible until we realize that each sex bears within itself the replica of the other.

In all these books we delve into anthropological mysteries. No one can assail the pernicious inhibitions and complexes which envenom the love life of our species without attacking the taboos which dominate civilized man no less than his progenitor in the jungle. In attacking convention one should not confine oneself to the bludgeon; at times it is preferrable to use the stilletto. Science is our ally, satire and irony our weapons. We go to war with a smile. We have a philosophy and we have convictions. But don't expect us to weigh down Pegasus, when his wings itch to fly, with pedantic consistencies. In the last analysis, we are poets, story-tellers, romancers, more eager to spin a yarn than to prove a thesis!

Yet a vast fund of knowledge, not only insight and intuition, went into the books. Viereck had never succeeded in reading through the *Wandering Jew* of Sue, nor had he studied Croly's book or the fragments of Shelley, Goethe, and Heine. He had read, however, the pseudo-source material about the Armenian bishop and the folk legends in general as summarized in various reference works. Old Professor Hubermann, of City College, who had been one of the editors of the *Catholic Encyclopedia,* aided him considerably. His boyhood reading of bizarre histories and romances, the poetic allusions he had gathered in his desultory and eclectic readings of youth and manhood, and above all his familiarity with sexual adventures and with love-lore gave him a proper foundation. Freud, in a sense, was the father of the books, and a volume like Nemilov's *The Biological Tragedy of Woman* (the publication of which in English was due to Viereck) helped much to block in the ideological outlines of Salome, and certain references in William Ellery Leonard's *Two Lives* to woman's slavery to the moon were in back of Viereck's mind. Despite the vast amount of reading done by both men, Viereck and Eldridge, there was no systematic research, no elaborate and painstaking delving into all of the sources. The books were the result, in the last analysis, of Viereck's temperamental eclecticism and his impulse to the expression of contradictory moods. They were the books of a man who refused to hold fast to principles and dogmas. They were, by implication, Viereck's spiritual and emotional autobiography. ''Here are the frailest leaves of me,'' he might have inscribed on the title pages, as he said with frequency during the ensuing years. They were not, in the same sense, Eldridge's autobiography.

At last the first of the books appeared. Some of the initial reviews in the better journals were disappointing. As expressed by one reviewer, several felt that the book was ''fustian,'' rather than ''Faustian,'' pseudo-smart, rather than profound.

They refused to see any serious effort or purpose behind the book. They sneered at what they deemed the pretensions of the co-authors. Others damned with very faint praise. Upton Sinclair took his characteristic attitude, but in an unusually kindly spirit. He wrote to Viereck, not in the least hiding the fact that a copy of the book was wasted on him. Sinclair expressed surprise that Viereck should write on such overlong inanities and abnormalities, "because you really have brains" and "are bored by the very things you glorify."

When the first disparaging reviews were in, Eldridge began to feel that his first hope, that the the book would be caviar to the general and a feast to men of good sense, was all wrong. He wrote to Viereck at that time: "The intelligentsia will dislike us, but the average reader will be delighted." And the average reader was. At least the book sold surprisingly well. Published in August of 1928, the book went into a second printing in November, a third in January of 1929, two more in March, and yet two more in April. By the end of 1930 it had seen twelve American printings and was a best seller and an invitation to more books by the collaborators. It was published in England and in parts of the British Commonwealth. It was translated into German, Dutch, Spanish, Hungarian, and other languages, achieving an international fame.

It should not be supposed that the volume was only a popular success and not a critical one. If there were some critics who disparaged the book, there were many others who praised it loudly. Formidable articles in the newspapers of the leading cities made much of the book. "It is worth waiting two thousand years to greet a book like *My First Two Thousand Years*," said Ryan Walker. Hermann Sudermann, writing from Germany, thought it "great"; Thomas Mann deemed it "audacious and magnificient"; Havelock Ellis rated it "an achievement"; psychoanalysts and students of sex, like Wilhelm Stekel, Magnus Hirschfeld, Eugen Steinach, and A.A. Brill, lauded it. Such diverse personalities as Gertrude Atherton, Isaac Goldberg, and Edwin Markham praised the book. And Liveright was so mournful over his failure to publish it that he agreed to issue any other volume that Viereck might write.

Writing from Paris, Viereck's old friend, Ludwig Lewisohn, picked his words with great care. Their very finicky quality suggested that Lewisohn was sincere in his praise and not acting the part merely of a generous friend. In the measured mood of *Expression in America,* he said that he had taken his time because he "wanted to get a total impression," and now he had it. "The book is in both substance and method of the highest originality," he said; "it is both fascinating and brilliant; the historic pageant is unrolled with a colorfulness and clearness that astonish me. And I am delighted too by the play of implicit wit, the quaint malice of the innuendos, the symbolical pattern sustained throughout. I do hope it will do well and start you toward a second blossoming out in literature." Viereck was delighted, but he wanted a more personal letter. He wanted to know to what extent he was Cartaphilus, Kotikokura, and Salome; the three protagonists of the book. And he wanted to know if Lewisohn saw himself in Cartaphilus or in any other character of the novel.

There were stormy incidents in the course of the book's triumph. Some journalists professed to find latent and even overt anti-Semitism in the book. Several Jewish papers took Viereck to task for his treatment of the subject, their attitude seemingly that, as the great friend and "unofficial ambassador" of the Kaiser, Viereck naturally would follow the lead of his anti-Semitic emperor and intellectual liege-lord. Viereck explained publicly that he "may have been guilty of many follies, but that anti-Semitism is not one of them." The feeling persisted, however, ready to blaze forth, as it did, very few years later. It may be that in sensitive minds certain misgivings lurked, and future events only intensified these doubts. Viereck seemed to have been afraid of them, too, for he was careful to write to Emil Ludwig, whom he was then cultivating, to correct any rumors that may have reached him.

"I understand that they want to suppress your novel in England," said a reporter who called on Viereck at that time.

"They're tantalizingly slow about it," Viereck murmured, the Wildean mood upon him once more.

But soon enough the public guardians of morality in such far-flung places as South Africa, Australia, and the Irish Free State were busy. Africa and Australia were too far away to bother about, but Ireland was another story. Viereck worked strenuously to arouse public interest in his fight against the Irish censorship. He carried his protest to President William T. Cosgrave, in vain. The president replied in a courteous manner, but his courtesy did not make him less firm. George Russell (A E), William Butler Yeats, and Lady Gregory promised to aid Viereck in his fight. Louis Bromfield, Will Durant, H.L. Mencken, Padraic Colum, Shaemes O'Sheel, Louis Golding, Samuel Hopkins Adams, Heywood Broun, and, of course, William Ellery Leonard, and others wrote to Viereck, authorizing him to cite their names in support of his campaign against the literary interdiction in Ireland. It was futile but great fun and, as always, Upton Sinclair made a contribution in character. Sinclair told Viereck that he was embarrassed because he hated "to refuse to do any favor for persons of whom I am fond as I am of you and your wife." Sinclair reminded him that, as a reformer, he defended a book only when there is "some reason" in it. "I cannot see any such reason in your book," he said, "and so I am powerless in the matter. I think you are a lot better than what you write; and I take the reason to be that you are a victim of outmoded ideas of aristocracy which inhibit your human impulses."

But Sinclair was only unconsciously humorous. Bernard Shaw, with malice aforethought, suggested to Viereck that he should kill the Wandering Jew by letting him meet "that intellectual vacuum, William Jennings Bryan." Viereck could afford to be joyous, now that *My First Two Thousand Years* was so great a success. Eldridge could be joyous too. They both cavorted like children at play. When Viereck's forty-fifth birthday arrived, Eldridge sent him a telegram that stuttered with excitement. He announced in a "special to the entire world" that the "latest historical research work confirms assumption that Julian calender was not dated from events which transpired at Bethlehem but rather in anticipation" of

Viereck's birth. He congratulated Viereck "upon the beginning of a bigger and better chapter of your life than you have ever experienced before. Now in the fifth year of our alliance I am anticipating for you steadily increasing literary prestige and all that goes with it. May your literary labors never be interrupted by telephone calls, margin calls or any other calls except those of publishers flourishing advance checks."

They were happy and rightly so. *My First Two Thousand Years* was written and still arousing attention. They were about to complete *Salome,* and *The Invincible Adam* was on its way. Other books were emerging from their minds. There seemed to be no limit to the possibilities of collaboration. Literary history could be made; perhaps it had been made. *Salome* appeared. It, too, was a popular success, but again certain critics were unimpressed, while students of psycho-anaylsis and sex were delighted. The authors felt that age-old taboos mitigated against them, that the subject of the book, woman's periodic subjugation to the moon, was a repulsive theme in many minds. They hastened with *The Invincible Adam,* which Viereck had hoped to call *Kotikokura* or *The Son of the Great Ape.* This time there was almost complete silence so far as the American press was concerned and a decline, also, in public interest here. There were, however, several unforeseen circumstances that made the authors feel that the reception of the book should not sadden them. They went ahead with their plans. After all, the British newspapers were kinder than the American ones. The two men drew parallels between the two presses. The *New York Times* said, "There could be no point in discussing this concocted myth seriously," while the *London Times* thought the book "staggering in the immensity of its scope and in the courageous sweep of its imaginative plan . . . nothing less than the saga of man . . . an astonishing and profound achievement." *The Saturday Review of Literature* of New York had no review of the book, while the *London Saturday Review* said it was a "staggering book" and reviewed it sympathetically. The *New York Evening Post* and *Daily News* had no reviews, either, but the *London Morning Post* and the *Sussex Daily News* made up for the lapses of the American press by describing the Viereck-Eldridge volume as "virile, vivid, original . . . remarkable for a blending of allegory, irony and human . . . in many respects the most outstanding book of the year." While the *New York Herald-Tribune, Daily Mirror, American, Sun,* and *World-Telegram* were silent, British newspapers referred to "brilliant passages of great descriptive power" in the volume and said that the book was "manifestly the work of writers who are poets, story tellers and excellent wits." The general conclusion of the British press was that the entire trilogy was "remarkable . . .vigorous and stimulating."

33   THE SEXUAL RELATIVIST

"The meaning of relativity has been widely misunderstood," Einstein once said to Viereck. The interview was reported in *Glimpses of the Great*. "Philosophers play with the word, like a child with a doll. Relativity, as I see it, merely denotes that certain physical and mechanical facts, which have been regarded as positive and permanent, are relative with regard to certain other facts in the sphere of physics and mechanics. It does not mean that everything in life is relative and that we have the right to turn the whole world mischievously topsy-turvey."

Earlier Einstein said to Viereck that he was "solely a physicist," not a philosopher, but in spite of his own desires, Einstein gave a new twist to philosophy, morality, and sociology. His mathematical concepts have been generalized by some intellectual trick to include all life and all human institutions, and there is the truth of the highest poetry in the popular attitude. When Viereck, like others, described himself as an Einsteinian in morals, he was not playing with words. His tag carried definite meanings of considerable consequence, and as is so often the case, Viereck, the economic standpatter, was the sexual revolutionist, just as the political and economic revolutionist (Upton Sinclair, for example) was often utterly conventional in his sexual beliefs, revolt in one field resulting in compensatory submission in another. Viereck, to atone for his acceptance of the leisure-class theory of economics, toppled over the accepted beliefs in the field of sex. His and Eldridge's saga of passion was his contribution to revolutionary thinking, and it was distinctly Einsteinian. That is, it permitted of no immutable laws, fitting every circumstance.

"What," Viereck was asked, "do you include within the term *sex?*"

"Everything!" he replied. "I am a Freudian."

Add, then, the name of Sigmund Freud to that of Einstein in considering Viereck's ideology of sex, and add the name of Magnus Hirschfeld. To a lesser extent Havelock Ellis, Krafft-Ebbing, Stekel and a few others also conditioned

225

Viereck's beliefs, but not in any commanding degree. The sum total of his acceptance of the ideas of these men was a form of sexual relativity. For hard and fast dogmas, he substituted pliable, ever-changing ideas.

"There is no such thing as promiscuousness," Viereck said. "The element of selection always enters. I have no objection to it, provided the dictates of hygiene and common sense are observed."

One recalled his earlier statement: "Monogamy is absurd, but it is better than polygamy. One wife is enough. But it is a matter of individual taste."

His beliefs were purely pragmatic in this respect. "Marriage is an absurd convention, at best a necessary evil. . . . However, it seems to be the best solution of the sex problem of the largest possible number in our present phase of capitalism. The request for divorce should be sufficient; I agree with Shaw that no reason should be necessary. One should settle the property, to be sure, in a gentlemanly fashion."

He continued: "Courtship is merely the play of one personality upon another. It is intriguing only so long as the personalities involved are intriguing."

"Is there such a thing as perversion?" he was asked, the questioner recalling his brilliant poem, *The Pilgrim*.

"There is no such thing as perversion," he replied, instantly. "I am glad that you have pointed out what I have already indicated about my poem, "The Pilgrim": it does not mention any specific act as 'monstrous,' the meaning being that perversity is purely subjective. Perversion is what the other fellow does and what we don't like in the technique of sex acts. It is not important to anyone except the person himself and his partner or partners. The sole question is of the effect on the respective nervous and glandular system."

Translated into general terms, it means that man as lover should be an anarchist, a law unto himself, within certain broad limits. His consideration as a gentleman should be the sole deterrent to the man seeking to live up to his inmost instincts as a lover. As a gentleman he will know that society has certain rights, but these are narrower than is generally supposed. In matters of taste the lover will ignore, if he sees fit, the customs of the country. He will not harm society or any particular individuals, but he will not act according to majority vote. Though he be one against the world, his desires will prevail so long as they cause no serious harm to others.

By and large, there was a strong resemblance between Viereck's view and those of his life-long friend, Dr. Magnus Hirschfeld, head of the once-famous Sex Science Institute in Berlin. Viereck called Hirschfeld the Einstein of sex because he espoused the theory of sexual relativity. He was not the first to enunciate the doctrine, as Viereck said, but he carried it to its logical conclusion. To him homosexuality, bisexuality, and other practices contrary to the prevailing *mores,* were not pathological but simply variations to be accepted without misgivings.

"Happy marriages," he said to Viereck, "are not made in Heaven, but in the laboratory." This was his epigrammatic way of stating that the modern lover acts by science rather than blind whim. To assist in the scientific process, Hirshfeld established his Institute in Berlin "to study, to teach, to cure, and to afford an asylum" in connection with sexual problems. The conclusion Hirschfeld came to is similar to the one propounded in Viereck's poem, "Slaves": the sexual habits of men and women are determined largely by their internal secretions. It is the solution at which endocrinology arrived, with the important qualification that, while diseases can be healed, ordinarily we cannot change the sexual constitution of men and women. It is, then, not a matter of directing the sexual impulse but of choosing the proper mates, of bridging the psychological gaps, of balancing biochemical structures.

Hirschfeld believed that the traditional division of mankind into two sexes was obsolete. He believed that there were an infinite number of sexes: three principal ones, rather than two, the third being the intermediate sex. One is "male" when certain hormones or chemical agents of the blood predominate, "female" when certain other hormones or chemical agents predominate, and "intermediate," of which there are many varieties. Nobody, he believed, was wholly of one sex, just as no one was wholly good or bad. Since that was unquestionably true, it was only natural that there should be intermediate types, the permutations and combinations being innumerable and adding to the kaleidoscopic zest of life. "Every human being is 'normal,'" said Hirschfield to Viereck, "for no one can escape from his own nature. He is 'abnormal' only if illness, accident or social pressure compels him to act in a manner at variance with the law of his being."

This one of the chief thoughts that went into the making of the trilogy of which *My First Two Thousand Years* is the initial and most interesting volume. One important difference, however, separated Viereck's thought from Hirshfeld's. The great head of the Sex Institute of Berlin believed that only three percent of humanity belonged to the intermediate sex, that small number including, however, many noble human types: Plato, Socrates, Whitman, Chopin, Wilde, Michelangelo, and Caesar, among others. To Viereck the problem was expressed otherwise. He felt that not a mere three percent but all cultured humanity was in search of some synthesis of the sexual types. He called it the quest of the double blossom of passion, yet he implied that it was not a double blossom but a garden of many flowers. He said that humans seek the one person who is all things to them; the answer to our prayers for sexual perfection. The *Two Thousand Year* series is a narrative centering around this impossible dream—hence its chief value as a contribution to the study of sex. It gave flesh and blood to the skeleton to be found in the sex tomes. Scientists necessarily deal with abstractions, and poets with symbols. *My First Two Thousand Years, Salome,* and *The Invincible Adam* were the dynamic unfolding of the newest ideas in the newest of sciences. They were a testing ground for such ideas. Einstein took just a few pages to expound his theories in a coldly scientific fashion. It took many pages and all of the devices of the novelist to humanize his theories and give them a sexual twist.

The chapter called "Antonio and Antonia" is perhaps the most significant in the entire saga of passion as of its time. Despite a certain poetic haziness, it is the most daring chapter, in its way, in the entire field of fiction up to that time, not forgetting certain episodes in D.H. Lawrence's masterpiece, *Lady Chatterly's Lover*. Viereck thought Lawrence's book had to be written for all repressed Anglo-Saxons, but he did not think it a great work of literature. Nor did he overvalue Frank Harris' *My Life and Loves*. He imposed no limits in the literary treatment of sex, for he believed with Whitman that "all were lacking, if sex were lacking." But he did not believe that bluntness of speech is in itself a measure of daring. Certainly the chapter, "Antonio and Antonia," is more daring in its implication than anything in Harris or Lawrence, if subdued in language.

"Who are you?" Cartaphilus asks. The two children, Antonia and Antonio, remain silent and smiling. "Who are you?" Cartaphilus repeats.

"We are Toni," the girl answers.

"Both Toni?" Cartaphilus asks. They nod. "Are you one or two?" the Eternal Man inquires. "We are one and two," the two children reply. Cartaphilus talks with them. He is intrigued as never before by their ageless charm. He calls them his "little sister and brother," but they do not want to be thought of as "little." He cuts his ring in two and gives the parts to them, one little ring to each. He finds himself in love with both children, though he fears the buds are "too tender, too beautiful, to be plucked."

It is time for the children to retire. Antonia throws Cartaphilus a kiss:

Antonio raised his hand half-way, checked himself, and blushed.

I was about to draw the curtains of my bed, when I heard footsteps, hardly heavier than those of a cat, approach. I strained my eyes, but I could see nothing. The hall was very long, and I had time to conjecture.

A soft-tipped finger pressed against my lips. "Sh . . ." I moved slowly toward the wall. The bed hardly felt the weight of her. She pressed her lips to mine. My hands were many mouths, drinking nectar. A long kiss. A pressure of breast against breast, a mingling of lips, a moan. . . .

Like some white weightless feather which a zephyr wafts about a garden, she rose and disappeared in the blackness of the room . . .

Thoughts like many-colored confetti fell softly upon my brain, making beautiful patterns which bore no names.—

Suddenly, I heard the soft footsteps again. Was she returning? Did her lips ache for another kiss . . .? Again the pressure of a finger against my lips. "Sh . . ." Again a kiss, tender and impetuous. Did my hands deceive me? Was not beauty a flame? Was not joy a slow swooning?

I awoke. I rubbed my eyes and forehead trying to remember something—something incredibly beautiful and delicious. What was it? When did I . . .? Was it a dream? I felt a pressure against my thigh. The ruby—a frozen drop of flame—on the head of the serpent.

"Antonia," I whispered.

I placed the ring upon my small finger. It fitted perfectly. I rose. Something fell to the floor.

"The other ring! Antonio?" I placed the ring on top of the other.
They melted into one.

"Who are you?"

"We are Toni."

"Both Toni?"

"Yes."

"Are you one or two?"

"We are one and two."

"Both one?"

"Yes."

How incredibly beautiful!

The Double Blossom of Passion—the almost impossible loveliness
of John and Mary in one!

Phrased otherwise, it is the search for that point at which the two parallel lines
meet. Again Einstein! Salome promises to give herself to Cartaphilus when the
parallel lines meet. That seems both near and far away, both possible and
impossible. Each of the books of the *Two Thousand Year* series ends with the
promise of fulfillment, yet one knows that the search must go on forever. "That
which may be found, is it worth the seeking?" Cartaphilus asks at the end of a
memorable chapter. "All is vanity save love," he says. As the smoke of his
cigarette vanishes, he learns a new truth: "Love, too, is vanity." And as the Son of
the Great Ape falls asleep in the midst of Cartaphilus' ruminations, Cartaphilus
comes to ultimate wisdom: "And the truth of all things is—irony."

The judgment that Viereck pronounced on his own masterpiece may not be as
vain a misjudgment as some suppose. It is easy to dismiss a work of the scope of
the saga of passion, much easier than to consider it with the care it merits. The
work may well be a monument in the long and thwarted history of human
tolerance. Its inevitable tendency is to make intelligent men receptive to sexual
notions that may have been abhorrent to them. It insinuates a belief in the
reasonableness of the concept of sexual relativity. In young minds, particularly, it
is a seed that blossoms into understanding. Its influence would have grown had not
Viereck caused his name to become a brand of unspeakable infamy.

My First Two Thousand Years and its sequels ought to be seen as philosophical novels comparable to Norman Douglas's *South Wind*. One should not presume
to make fatuous comparisons, it is true, but both are novels of ideas, both cerebral
and yet rich with character and incident. The Viereck-Eldridge novel is more
passional but not less philosophical in tone. It impresses one as a profounder book
than the *Jurgen* of James Branch Cabell, for Cabell's book, although bearing a
superficial resemblance to the Viereck-Eldridge novel, is built upon a slim foundation—its manner conceals the paucity of its ideological content. Jurgen's formula,
"I will drink anything once," is superficial as compared with the quest of
Cartaphilus. That is why one can try Cabell's book only once, while *My First Two
Thousand Years* rewards more than one reading. (Still, Nathan Leopold managed
to read Cabell 26 times in prison.) The older novels of the Wandering Jew have

scarcely a superficial resemblance to Viereck's, because Croly and Sue and the others lived in an anomalous world in which sex did not exist. Viereck, like his hero, Cartaphilus, wallowed in sex: always thirty, always potent.

How can one translate *My First Two Thousand Years's* ideas and incidents into the changes and chances of Viereck's own life? In spite of his seeming candor and his exhibitionism, Viereck placed definite limits on what one may say. He felt that the truth can be told only when the man is dead and buried and all his friends and relatives and loves are in their graves. Living people are not mummies, he insisted, and they must not be troubled by the skeletons in their closets. One may scandalize continents by one's seeming candor and yet contrive to hold one's own intimacies sacrosanct, save to the extent one chooses to open the gates. Ideally, that is not real candor.

Some years ago, one of the great American autobiographies was published. The author sought to tell a plain and unvarnished tale, as the folk expression runs. "All that I have written is true," he said, "It is true of America. It is true, in other degrees, of mankind." And most of American believed him. The book, although a serious one, went into many printings, but the truthful author said to his dearest friend, "I wish I could have told the truth in this book of mine! The most important things are not there." This candid man had an all-important paragraph in his book that was simple in language; every word was unambiguous; every thought was crystalline, with the result that men and women read the paragraph and assumed, without thinking about it, that they knew what the paragraph was about. Strange to say, none of them really knew, for the author had done a brilliant job of conceal-ment: he had used apparent candor as an instrument of secrecy. The paragraph was the door to the man's life, but the key had been thrown away! This passage is enough to prove that psychoanalysis is, in many respects, merely a new vocabu-lary, having as its unconcious motivation the concealment of the obvious.

The same candid autobiographer once pranced up and down the stoop of the house of the husband of his lady love of later days and shouted, in challenge, "I am shameless!" Perhaps he was, just as it was Viereck's boast that he had said and done more daring things than any one then writing literature. This belief is compounded of many particles. One of them is the element of exhibitionism, the same instinct that has led some people to follow the cult of the naked. The substitute for a naked boy is a naked word or thought. Another element of the belief is wish-fulfillment, unconscious to be sure, for Viereck had an instinct toward the truth, even if he was guilty of concealments. The desire to shock and bait the bourgeoise, the instinct for a rigorous literary expression, some understanding of the sacred law of individuality embodied in the theory of relativity—these were among the other particles of Viereck's belief in his own frankness.

Once Viereck discussed certain of his greatest friends. He talked of them with the affection and understanding that one bestows only upon old friends who have not been found wanting. There was, notwithstanding, a wholesome frankness in his speech that matched the frankness with which one of these friends had discussed Viereck! In both cases it was "love's fine wit," not malice, that spoke.

"I believe that I am more normal than they are, because I have not suffered from repression," Viereck said. "I have responded to the demands of my nature."

It is quite possible that this was true, but it nonetheless was an anomalous situation to find Viereck vaunting not his sins, but his normal nature. The explanation of what might otherwise be considered a cryptic remark was found in Viereck's theory of relativity. It is lawful for any man to answer the song of his own soul by an echo of its divine tune. That is what Viereck strived to do. Einstein never suspected that certain of his mathematical concepts would become scripture for a poet of passion!

34   THE POET TURNS
PSYCHOANALYST

Just as prattle about Einstein's theory was at one time on all lips, so to an even greater degree, perhaps, has the Freudian nomenclature become common property. Psychoanalysis is one of the key sciences of our day; the ignorant, no less than the learned, have borrowed the theories and, above all, the language made familiar by Freud. This country particularly has been avid in its acceptance of the great Austrian psychologist.

"I appreciate the compliment, but I am afraid of my own popularity in the United States," Freud once said to Viereck, as reported in *Glimpses of the Great*. "American interest in psychoanalysis does not go very deep. Extensive popularization leads to superficial acceptance without serious research. People merely repeat the phrases they learn in the theater, or in the press. They imagine they understand psychoanalysis, because they can parrot its patter."

Yet Freud himself was largely responsible for the vulgarization about which he complained. His defense of lay analysis, his insistence that a medical eduation is often a handicap to the psychoanalyst, and the polemical character of much of his writing encouraged the glib patter about which he complained. That Freud did not include Viereck in the group of vulgarizers is evinced by many things, not least of all by the fact that he expressed the desire that Viereck write a popular interpretation of psychoanalysis similar to Viereck's book on rejuvenation. Viereck did not write the one book on the subject that Freud desired for the very good reason that all he had written in the last several decades of his life stemmed from Freud. Viereck's writings, his correspondence, his conversation, his thoughts and dreams were drenched with psychoanalysis. It was an all-absorbing interest, an obsession, that determined Viereck's course of conduct for many years. Every serious error the man made, especially the worst error of his life, can be traced to the astonishing influence Freud had upon him.

"It may be that those who live by psychoanalysis shall perish by psychoanalysis," said Viereck in one of his best passages. "Psychoanalysis robs hate of its sting. Perhaps it also deprives love of its halo. By penetrating into the innermost tunnels, the deepest galleries of the mind, until it reaches the very root of Self, it may destroy those emotions and processes which cannot exist save in the haze of illusion. Under the scalpel of analysis, maybe art withers and affection dies. It cannot give us the love that passes all understanding but it can give the understanding that passes all love."

When questioned about this statement, Viereck said that psychoanalysis had taught him one thing that it had not taught Freud: to understand and to forgive all. Long before, he had said to Freud that psychoanalysis enforced the lesson of Christian charity, but Freud, Jehovah-like, had thundered an emphatic denial. He insisted that tolerance of evil is by no means the necessary result of knowledge and that psychoanalysis points out what should be exterminated. In that same conversation the great man had said to Viereck that when he noticed the growth of anti-Semitic prejudice in Germany, and in German Austria, he ceased to consider himself a German, but preferred to call himself a Jew. This disappointed Viereck, because it seemed to him that the father of psychoanalysis should dwell on heights, beyond racial prejudice and personal rancor. The conversation served to point out the essential difference between the two men and made abundantly clear the various failures of Viereck's life.

Viereck's interest in psychoanalysis dated from the years before World War I, almost, indeed, from the beginning of the new science. He used to have long discussions about the subject with his learned friend Professor Munsterberg. A great psychologist of the old school, Munsterberg was not greatly impressed by what Freud had to say, though he gave respectful attention to what the young poet had to say of the subject. He no doubt realized that it was inevitable for Viereck to be interested in a science that gave sex the preeminent position. Was not sex the very essence of the life of the poet of passion? Why, then, should he not seize upon the ideas of Freud and make them his own? He had been prepared for Freud by Hirschfeld, Havelock Ellis, Krafft-Ebing, and the others whose writing he had devoured as a young man. These men, he discovered, were just foundation stones in the vast pyramid that bore the name of Freud. Almost as soon as he grasped the man's idea, his epic of the Wandering Jew began to shape itself in his mind. Just as Freud had taken the old Oedipus legend and other symbols of the past, he would take the imperishable figure of the Wandering Jew and remold it, so that it might be a fit symbol for a psychoanalytical history of mankind.

At the same time Viereck began to think of his poetry in the terms of the Freudian science. He began to ask himself what inner meaning was hidden in the core of his verse. "Inhibition," his early poem about his parents, particularly betrayed his new-found interest, and *The Candle and the Flame,* the volume in which it appeared, showed the same mounting excitement about psychoanalysis. Marginalia in the book were in the very spirit of Freud and his name was mentioned once, though his inspiration would have been obvious to the knowing, but it was in

the book about Theodore Roosevelt that Viereck paid his first great tribute to the
Austrian psychologist. That book was, in every sense, a Freudian analysis of the
Rough Rider. Through it, Viereck cut his eyeteeth, so to speak, and was ready for
more thorough work in the new field. First this was done by way of fiction—in *My
First Two Thousand Years*—and then by way of the greater fiction that is styled
autobiography. The great sacrifice Viereck placed on the altar of Freud was a book
called *My Flesh and Blood,* described on the title page as "A Lyric Autobiography
with Indiscreet Annotations." The book appeared in 1931 and was, by and large,
the most important book Viereck ever wrote, with the partial exception of *My First
Two Thousand Years,* important to some degree as literature and more important as
a mirror of his age.

Some rhymster summarized the contents of *My Flesh and Blood* in a poem
called "Absit Reticence":

> He writes, "Reader Beware!"
> And flits on to confess,
> His great loves and small
> (All kinds, more or less)
> In verse and in prose,
> Both begging for censure,
> He tells each affair,
> Each tender adventure . . .
> Casanova is here
> And a cambric-tea Wilde.
> Emotions are probed,
> And reactions are filed . . .
> And when you are done
> The thing that impresses
> Is what a stout ego
> This rhymer possesses.

In short, the book is the one that Viereck foretold in the introduction to one of
the Little Blue Books he prepared for Haldeman-Julius: psychological groupings
of his various poems and explanatory remarks on the verse and the various
episodes of his career and aspects of his character that were foreshadowed by
them. A good proportion of Viereck's best verse appears here, most of it included
in his previous books and some of it new. *My Flesh and Blood* thus called for
double analysis, first as poetry and then as autobiography, for it was much easier to
place the verse in relation to the poetry of its age than to evaluate the psychoanalytical trappings.

"Caveat Lector!" Viereck exclaims in a passage that unites good writing
with bad. "I ensnare my emotions, pierce the gaudy things through with a pin, and
mount them in a glass case like a collector of butterflies." The sense of melodrama
becomes too artificial for comfort, as Viereck continues, "I admonish the reader to

peruse my poems before, guided by my annotations, he ventures with me into the labyrinth of my soul,'' and becomes shrill as he warns, ''He who enters here does so at his peril.'' But some measure of verbal restraint leads him to admit that perhaps ''the flame of psychoanalysis flickers deceptively. Maybe it is only a magic lantern throwing upon the screen some image inserted by the manipulator.''

In a confessional that acts as an introduction to the book, Viereck opines that all art is a form of exhibitionism and every poet an exhibitionist, that his own books are a succession of intimate personal revelations, generally on a sexual plane, that despite his preoccupation with the war and public affairs, his real course is the zigzag one of attempting to reconcile the sexual types. He reviews briefly his thirty-year harvest of verse and marvels at its freshness, though he concedes that America had at length begun to catch up, thanks to him. He feels that he cleared away the rubbish of old taboos and emancipated the American Parnassus from the baneful New England conscience. Sensing his inordinately high self-valuation, he suggests that he needed the armor of conceit more than others because of the war psychosis that took him as a victim. Art, he says, does not float in a vacuum; it requires some frame of reference to the physical world, hence the autobiographical and psychological annotations. These soundings of the unconscious deal with the various complexes of his poems: Eros, Lilith, Eve, Jesus and Oedipus, the struggle between libido and extinction. Naturally, Viereck eschews too pedantic a classification, nor does he vouch for the absolute authenticity of his annotations. Again, ''caveat lector!'' ''In spite of boyish boasts and youthful reminiscences of other men's music,'' he concludes, ''my heart blood flows through these poems. My best verse vibrates with my own pulsating rhythm. In my constructive moods I impart to my work something of the Faust that slumbers in every German. Simultaneously my verse reflects the destructive self-analytical attitude which, in spite of my Nordic blood and Nordic forebears, makes me a brother to the Wandering Jew.'' He invites the reader to:

> Behold the naked ghosts that haunt my soul,
>   Spawn of strange nights, a scarlet brotherhood.
>   Partake of me. This is my flesh and blood.
> Caress my body when you touch this scroll.
>
> This is my life. Thus have I made my bed.
>   The roses of Priapus, passion-born,
>   Shall be my pillow, mindful that the thorn
> Still pricks and rankles when the rose is dead.

In short, some of the most striking language and thought to be found in the entire body of Viereck's work is contained in *My Flesh and Blood*—and also some of the worst. The strength of the volume and its weakness are found in the quintessential language employed. Where a paragraph might properly be employed to convey the thought in a smooth and effective manner, Viereck uses a sentence or a phrase, with the result that the writing too often is top-heavy, epigrammatic to a degree, so freighted with cogitation as to be too rich for ordinary diets. Nothing is deadlier than spiced diction, for the average palate runs from intellectual condiments. The defect is not simply stylistic; it springs also from Viereck's rabid determination to make points out of the pointless. It is a matter that must not be dismissed lightly.

Sigmund Freud was the bearded angel that troubled the waters of Viereck's soul and transformed him from a poet to a psychoanalyst. Viereck's penetrating friend, Fulton Oursler, told him that psychoanalysis had taken everything from him and given him nothing in return, but Viereck denied the assessment, saying over and over again, that psychoanalysis had given him understanding though it had ruined him as a poet and lover. He said that he committed suicide as a poet by learning too much about the mechanism of the unconscious; that, as a result, he ceased being spontaneous as a poet and as a lover.

To be sure there are great lines and stanzas in some of his later poems—all of "Slaves," for example, and "After the Battle" and "The Hero"—but these are short poems, and Viereck's total poetic harvest after World War I was small, though he later experienced a poetic rebirth during World War II. His tendency in his verse, even more than in his prose, was to condense, to distill, to quintessenial-ize. He wrote verses big with thought, epigrammatic outbursts, lines illustrating the verities of psychoanalysis and endocrinology. Of course, thought has its place in poetry; truly great poets, like Shakespeare and Goethe, are great thinkers as well, but the intellectual content of their lines is concealed, implicit rather than direct; it is incidental, unpremeditated, unobtrusive. Even Swinburne mixed thought with his music.

Viereck's early poems, the passional studies of his youth, were luxuriant with thought but more luxuriant in language. There were wild, exotic flowers of the jungle, and a few hothouse plants, bred in the library. Lines like those of the poem, "Respite," showed that Viereck might have recaptured the early mood, but they were only momentary echoes of what could not again be captured:

> I shall not, dead, miss Love's sublimities,
>   The pageantry, the passion, and the smart,
> But only this: the sweet proximities
>   Of flesh to flesh, of heart-beat to the heart.
>
> I shall not, dead, remember anything,
>   The sun, the moon, the waters and the lands,
> The wild adventure of my journeying:
>   Only the weary flutter of white hands.
>
> Let earth the maggot feed upon my brain,'
>   Let me forget the rime, the rune, the rose,
> If but this vision to the end remain:
>   A little body, birdlike, nestling close.

Viereck said that all poets are instinctively psychoanalysts. So long as it is a matter of instinct, little harm, much good flows from it. The important thing, as Viereck said, is for the creative artist to understand it and then to forget it; it must be an ignored part of his unconscious equipment. It is better for the poet to *feel* than to *know;* when he has forgotten psychoanalysis, he may begin to feel. Viereck's difficulty was that he was not able to submerge the Freudian theories in his unconscious. His verse was ruined as a result. He insisted that new meaning was given to his prose, but he admitted that it had not increased his happiness. It had, indeed, increased the distance between himself and the rest of the world. The mock gift of understanding was his sole reward.

The reviews of *My Flesh and Blood* fell easily into various categories. There were critiques of the poetry, critiques of the author written by laymen, and, finally, analysis by men of science. Louis Untermeyer had his usual uncomplimentary say, but his unfriendliness and the resentment of some others were forgotten in the face of the tender appreciations written by Charles Hanson Towne, John Neihardt, and others. Most gratifying of all to the poet turned psychoanalyst were the appreciations written by those who were leaders in the field he sought to make his own. *The Medical Journal and Record* of New York City was generous enough in its praise, written from the viewpoint of the medical profession, and even more pleasing were the words of such men as Stekel, Brill, Wittels, Jeliffe Smith, Lehrman, Payne, and Benjamin. Stekel hastened to write Viereck: "I have not read in a long time a book like *My Flesh and Blood,* an analytical book, a confession, a sermon, a spring of beauty and truth." Brill, Freud's first interpreter and translator, said that he was so fascinated by the book that he read it all in one session. "To me," he said, "this book is a profound human document by a very versatile and deep thinker." Wittels, author of *Freud and His Time,* was even more enthusiastic than Brill or Stekel. He was, he said, "strangely impressed with the exquisite beauty and magnetic power" of the writing. He said that Viereck had set for himself a courageous task in writing *My Flesh and Blood* but that the book "is an even greater accomplishment"; it is one of the world's great confessions: "a significant event and a bold departure from the traditions of the autobiography." Wittels said that he would not be surprised to find the book taking the world by storm, as did Rousseau's *Confessions.* "I was amazed to observe how deeply you probed into your inner man," he wrote to Viereck. "Your candid, self-analysis laid upon the altar of Freud is a brilliant achievement, and second only to your own superb poetry. That a Viereck should recognize the contribution of psychoanalysis to our cultural development is indeed a noble tribute and—prophesy."

That was Viereck's reward for his long and feverish journeying in the perilous seas of psychoanalysis. "I always find what my hunger needs," he had said. He needed knowledge of the secret of human conduct, and so he found Freud and his disciples. He read the Freudian literature and met the leading practitioners, Freud himself, and all who buzzed around him. Out of a sense of loyalty to Freud, he deliberately refrained from meeting the one whom Freud regarded as a renegade, the celebrated Carl Jung, who might have taught him a few things and who indeed did do so, indirectly. Only reluctantly he met that other great psychologist who had won Freud's resentment, Alfred Adler. The latter he got to know well, and, indeed, collaborated with him in the writing of some articles, but he could not, for Freud's sake, rid himself of an inner antagonism. In other words, despite his vaunted understanding and forgiveness for all, Viereck's loyalty to friends enforced a barrier against even the quest for knowledge. His search was essentially a personal one and had, as has been pointed out, an element of seduction. He also was driven by the impulse to seek out the leader rather than the satellites, however bright. Viereck was not unlike the diner who must see the head waiter, if only to order a cup of coffee. Freud was the fountain head of the new science, so it was Freud before whom Viereck bowed.

The remarkable fact is that he managed to be a deep student, not merely a taster, of psychoanalysis. The subject bcame a profound part of him: it enabled him to write penetratingly of the poets who had interested him, particularly Swinburne, and enabled him, also, to write what was perhaps the one profound analysis of the murder that was called "the crime of the century": the Loeb-Leopold case. Clarence Darrow called Viereck's study of the bizarre murder the best written. The case appealed to Viereck no doubt because it was universally regarded as a characteristic crime of the postwar era. Any misdeed might have served as well for the ordinary student, but Viereck had to analyze that case which attracted most attention.

Freud was his friend and, also, the fly in the ointment of his contentment. The two men met a few times and corresponded with some frequency. To some degree Viereck succeeded in influencing Freud: he inspired Freud's little book on religion and, perhaps, was one of the inspirers of the book on Wilson that Freud projected and, in fact, wrote with William C. Bullitt. Viereck interested Freud in Steinach and the subject of rejuvenation, in which field Freud's townsman was the leader. Freud was apparently fond of Viereck, but he always dealt with him like a severe father with a wayward son. He chided Viereck, took him to task when he sinned against the strict teachings of Freudian psychology, as in *My First Two Thousand Years,* and called him down for making public privately expressed views. Freud and his disciples, including Viereck, were like Jehovah and the children of Israel in the Old Testament: there could be no doubt of Jehovah's love for his sheep, but he would assert his authority even if it hurt.

It was said earlier that psychoanalysis was the root cause of Viereck's worst errors. It should be said, maybe more fairly and accurately, that it was the peculiar effect of psychoanalysis upon Viereck that caused him to err and to stumble and to degrade himself. There is an oversimplification of things that necessarily ensues from Freudian theories, despite the multiplication of complexes and names and viewpoints. It will be remembered that Freud himself was forced to revise the initial concept of the aloneness of the libido as an explanation for human activity and thought. In time he promulgated the "beyond the pleasure principle" concept and began to think that the desire for extinction is almost as basic as the libidinous strivings of mankind. Still, the two principles, whatever their ramifications, are too simple for the comfort of laymen like Viereck. Too often they serve as substitutes for deep thought, which is bad enough, but even worse is the excuse they afford for lax conduct. They serve to hide from oneself disintegration of character; they excuse, in one's own mind, the errors of one's ways.

Understanding and forgiveness of others may very well be a supreme virtue, but forgiveness of self is the reverse of virtue. One way to hold a fallible human being in leash is to keep before his eyes the consequences of his lapses. Once the process of rationalization sets in, be it called psychoanalysis or anything else, the individual is befogged. He is able to transform his vices and make them, merely by verbal magic, virtues in his own sight. This great sin was Viereck's and was the chief reason for his persistence in ways that were at best dubious and at worst morally reprehensible.

One important life experience is illuminating in the way it shows how Viereck's moral decay arose from the capacity for self-excuse.

In 1923 Adolph Hitler was scarcely known outside of Germany; certainly his fame was pygmy in size, as compared to what it ultimately became. His putsch in Bavaria was a comic-opera failure. Adolf had fallen to the ground with such force that he broke his arm and apparently the strength of the Nazi movement. He was vociferous enough and in Germany there were many who took him seriously, but the world at large was indifferent. Viereck met him, was deeply impressed, and wrote a strangely prophetic account of the man. It was offered to the world press and rejected and found publication only in the columns of Viereck's own magazine, *The American Monthly,* where it appeared in October 1923. The article revealed certain important things about Viereck and begs for extensive quotation. "Hitler the German Explosive," the article is called:

Adolf Hitler must be handled with care. He is a human explosive. The very mention of his name induces percussions. Some look to him as a German Mussolini, the savior of his country; others regard him as a violent agitator, thriving on religious prejudices and race contention.

Idolized by his followers, execrated by his foes, he is welcomed by Big Business as the only man in Germany who can take votes away from the Socialists. To some, however, the encouragement given to Hitler by conservative circles seems like an attempt to drive out Satan with Beelzebub.

Viereck then recounted at great length the things Hitler said to him at their meeting. "We must regain our colonies and we must expand eastward," he quoted Hitler. "There was a time when we could have shared the world with England. Now we can stretch our cramped limbs only towards the East. The Baltic is necessarily a German lake. The Treaty of Versailles, and the Treaty of St. Germain, are kept alive by Bolshevism in Germany. The Peace Treaty and Bolshevism are two heads of one monster. We must decapitate both. Our German workers have two souls. One is German, the other is Marxian. We must arouse the

German soul. We must root out the taint of Marxism. Marxism and Germanism, like German and Jew, are antipodes. We wish to purge ourselves from the Jews, not because they are Jews, but because they are a disturbing influence. Foreigners, whether Jews or not, will be permitted to live in Germany only by sufferance.''

There was much more to the article, all of the same foreboding tenor. Viereck's conclusion was threatening in tone:

> Hitler can probably summon more men to arms than the commander in chief of the German Army. His organization compels respect.
>
> Hitler is honest. He is an idealist, however mistaken, who freely risks his life and his health for his cause. He lives simply in a little furnished room. He demands neither wages nor honors.
>
> If he lives, Hitler, for better or for worse, is sure to make history.

Viereck knew, in other words, that Hitler was a tool of Big Business; that he favored the subjugation and even the enslavement of the Jews; that his advent to power meant war in the East; that, in short, the rise of the Nazis meant a period of storm and stress for the world and intense sacrifice for Germany. Yet inevitably Viereck supported the monster. It was purely a process of rationalization in which psychoanalysis afforded the tools. The man reasoned and argued in terms of complexes, neuroses, psychoses, and what not until the human considerations were analyzed out of existence. Black became white and madness a form of reason.

The article on Hitler and its tragic aftermath afford one series of glimpses of the deadly process of rationalization. The collaboration with Paul Eldridge afforded another series, as revealing. Viereck began to notice, or thought he noticed, that while he worked with Eldridge their accord was perfect but that once they were separated, petty differences arose which threatened, in a mild way, to disunite the two men who were so beautifully wedded in an artistic collaboration. At that time Viereck thought of the idea for a novel dealing, once again, with a sort of superman who would bring peace to a world that babbled of love and did battle. The idea was probably inspired by the increase of interest in the subject of international order, which resulted from the growing fear of war. Excited by the idea, Viereck wrote the first draft of a novel called *Prince Pax*. He felt that it was horrible in execution, though he was still enamored of the idea, and turned the manuscript over to Eldridge, who rewrote it. Viereck now felt that Eldridge worsened an already bad book, but his interest in it had vanished. The manuscript was taken to the English publisher of the two men by Eldridge and was released in Great Britain, but Viereck refused to sanction the American publication of the book, with the result that it never appeared here. When events took the course that ultimately they did with regard to Hitler, Viereck, as part of the process of rationalization, began to feel that the sudden onslaught against him by Eldridge was motivated inwardly by resentment over the fate of *Prince Pax*. He began to feel that if it were not for the fiasco of the book, his union with Eldridge would not have fallen on bad times.

Similarly, he began to feel that the differences with the others who began to attack him had some unconscious motivations, really unconnected with the advocacy by him of a regime regarded as barbarous by the civilized world. To be sure, the process was not as simple in Viereck's mind as here so bluntly expressed, and, of course, human beings do too often act in response to petty motives. But, again, it must be emphasized that these rationalizations by Viereck were part of the process of self-exculpation. Freud had been able to guard himself against such self-deception, but Viereck, like so many of the master's disciples, fell easy victim to the tricks of the blind and savage misleaders of mankind. This conclusion can be underscored by a close examination of the facts as they appeared in the first years of the Third Reich.

35 THE BROWN PIT

The July 9, 1932, issue of a none-too-subdued magazine of national circulation contained as sensational an article as had ever appeared in its pages. The article dealt with the head of the National Socialist Party of Germany, the flaming orator Adolf Hitler whose doom had been pronounced by political seers not long before but who had confounded his enemies, the best elements in Germany, by rising to a position of dominance. The article by Viereck was called, with prophetic certainty, "When I Take Charge of Germany—Hitler Shows His Hand." It was in the form of an interview, a dynamic monologue, rather, by Hitler, with Viereck acting merely as the echo.

"When I take charge of Germany," said Hitler to Viereck, "I shall end tribute abroad and Bolshevism at home." Hitler swallowed his tea as if it were the life blood of Bolshevism, Viereck said, while voicing the conclusion that Hitler's triumph was inevitable: "Time and the recalcitrance of the French fight for Hitler." Viereck's article summarized, in Hitler's own words, the beliefs and plans of the Nazi leader, ominous plans with dire threats directed against "aliens." The word *Jews* was not used because the editor of the magazine thought it offensive and could scarcely believe the reports of Hitler's intentions, but there could be no doubt as to Hitler's meaning, except in the mind of a too cautious editor. Certainly Viereck knew exactly what to expect in the event of a Nazi triumph; he had known as far back as 1923, and now, in the summer of 1932, his prophecies were about to be fulfilled.

Only a few months later, the brown shirts were in power. Their leader was in the saddle, and woe to him who dared oppose the Nazi program. Hitler acted speedily, unhesitantly, ruthlessly. Imprisonment, torture, and death were visited upon his enemies. The world learned, to its horror, that Hitler intended to keep some of his pledges. Anti-Semitism was no mere campaign promise; it was an intrinsic part of the Nazi creed, just as certainly as hatred of Communists and

242

pacifists was part of that creed. The world looked on, seemingly unable to do anything, as the crucifixion of a whole people began under official auspices. Hitler was playing the game of the big industrialists, just as Viereck had foretold years ago, and of course it was a bloody game. It meant the freeing of Germany from the shackles of Versailles, but it meant also tumbling into the shambles and ultimately worse shackles. It meant the unification of Germany, but it was the unification and the silence of the graveyard, of unspeakable fear, of despair. It meant the crushing of Bolshevisim and the subventioning of a system that made hope a mockery, for the hope was based on the law of Ishmael.

In the midst of the terror, I wrote to Viereck, urging him, as the leading German-American, to raise his voice against the tyrannous regime that was destroying his Fatherland. He answered: ''I am opposed to anti-Semitism and race discrimination. But I nevertheless welcome Hitler's success in unifying the German people for the first time in two thousand years. I have not seen the new Germany myself as yet. Much that reaches us is propaganda pro and con. And the truth—what is the truth?'' The letter was dated June 19, 1933. No doubt others wrote to Viereck and received similar answers.

Viereck saw the new Germany and returned to America to tell of it. I plagued him with letters, accusing in tone, but appealing to his instincts as a libertarian and a gentleman to speak out against Hitler. So did others write to him. He deplored the ''excesses'' on both sides. He made excuses. He asked for calm. He cited Freud. His friends, many of whom were Jewish, began to be saddened and embittered. Soon accusations were in the air. Rumors of corruption began to circulate. It was whispered that there were strange goings-on. These whisperings finally reached the printed media. They followed one principal course, and that was not a straight one. It was felt that Viereck was leaving much unsaid, on the one hand, and was saying too much, on the other hand. What was the truth, not simply about Germany, but about him? Why did he defend the Nazi regime?

In *The Nation* of November 29, 1933, there was featured an article entitled *Nazi Politics in America* by Ludwig Lore. Spread over the cover of the magazine was the compelling interrogation: ''Are Nazi agents spreading propaganda here? If so, who and where are they?'' The article dealt with Colonel Emerson, Ludecke, Spanknobel, other such characters, and their questionable activities. It told of the formation of the Friends of the New Germany and the malodorous efforts of that group. Then it got to such friends of Viereck's as Frederick Franklin Schrader, who had assisted him with the *Fatherland,* and Ferdinand Hansen, but still there was no direct reference as yet to Viereck. ''The brains and purse of all the propaganda activities of the American Nazis,'' Lore went on to say, ''are in the General Consulate in New York, while the Embassy is kept informed. Up to June 21 of this year, and probably since that time as well, these offices subsidized a number of German and American writers of repute and paid the cost of other propaganda activity''; but gradually German-American businessmen assumed control over the propaganda. The German Propaganda Ministry, however, watched carefully and its effort became more elaborate and extensive. Approximately three months earlier, said Lore, it arranged with Carl Byoir and Associates, for the distribution of informative material on the "New Germany." Under the terms of this contract George Sylvester Viereck went to Germany with Carl B. Dickey, to look around and to interview Hitler, Göring, Goebbels, Frick, Schacht, and most of the other Nazi dignitaries; "these absolutely unbiased and objective impressions [this was the Byoir characterization of the material] will be served up to Americans in a series of widely syndicated articles in the near future. . . ."

Lore's article was perhaps the first important one on the subject of the activities of American Nazis that mentioned Viereck. The article implied much more about him than it said, and Viereck was constrained to reply. His answer appeared in *The Nation* of December 20, and later disclosures were to prove it a model of concealment and distortion. The letter did not make one misstatement, but it left unexpressed most of the material facts. Its inevitable tendency was to mislead; it suggested exactly the things it did not say. The letter did not say that Lore misstated the situation; it said that the article "does more credit to the author's imagination than his accuracy." It did not say that Viereck was not under contract with Byoir; it did say that he did not visit Germany "under the terms of any contract with Carl Byoir and Associates." It did not say that Byoir had no contract with a German agency; it did say that there was no contract with the German government, "to the best of my knowledge." It ventured the thought that there is nothing wrong with distributing "informative material" on Germany, but it said nothing about paid propaganda. "I never befouled my father's nest," said Viereck. "But I always preserve my intellectual integrity. If I write about the New Germany," he added, saying nothing of his intentions, "I shall do so sympathetically. But I shall retain a sense of detachment." His parting shaft was that rumor of disturbances and difficulties should not be exaggerated and that his "colleagues" should not "ignore Hitler's stupendous achievement in fashioning a new economic and social world out of the wreck of the old." In other words, the letter was a good specimen of unhealthy shrewdness. It deceived only Viereck.

Lore, in his reply, reiterated and expanded what he had said in his article, but he admitted that, knowing Viereck's favorable view of Hitler's Germany, he was puzzled that Goebbels, the Nazi Propaganda Minister, had to go out of his way to persuade Viereck to "new expressions of enthusiasm." He quoted Hellmuth von Gerlach's statement about Viereck, that "his old love for the Hohenzollerns does not rust, although he has been able to combine it profitably with his new love for Hitler. . . ."

Under date of October 1933 there had appeared the first issue of Isaac Goldberg's "monthly survey of people and ideas," called *Panorama*, initially the sort of magazine of interest to Viereck. Indeed, he was listed as one of the editors, as was Henry T. Schmittkind, through whom he had met his dear friend and collaborator, Paul Eldridge, who was one of the editors. But soon Viereck's name was removed from the masthead, and an implied explanation in the form of an open letter from Goldberg to Viereck, who was addressed as "Herr German Apologist" appeared shortly afterward. The letter charged that Viereck, who should have been the last one in the world to do so, because of the debt he owed to Jews, was casting gratuitous aspersions upon the Jews. Goldberg did not question Viereck's right to approve the Hitler regime, but he said that Viereck could not justify the official persecution of a people. Goldberg challenged Viereck to state publicly that he approved the Nazi regime with the exception of its anti-Semitism. The letter was a masterpiece of impassioned writing and deserves to be remembered as one of the best appeals from an embittered heart. "Your writings, ex-poet, rather than any words of ours, condemn you," said Goldberg, in concluding. "You, more than we, are in exile. We honored you too long with our friendship. Now with your enmity we ourselves are honored."

When Viereck's attention was called to this magnificent letter, before he had actually seen it, he said that he would reply to it if it was sufficiently well-written! The result was a double spread in the February issue of *Panorama*, entitled "Documents Towards the History of Nazi-ism in the United States" and subtitled "Goldberg-Eldridge-Viereck Correspondence Upon Hitlerism and Viereckism." In short, Paul Eldridge, his friend of friends, had turned decisively against Viereck. As Goldberg observed, the letters were far more important than they appeared to be at first glance. "They represent," said Goldberg, "a moment of that eternal vigilance which is the price of liberty." Viereck's letter he characterized as a series of evasions. In it Viereck accepted Goldberg's initial challenge and publicly declared that, with the exception of his anti-Semitic program, he approved wholeheartedly of Hitler's dictatorship. He said that he would certainly not desert the 99 percent of the German people merely because he sympathized with the suffering of the 1 percent; that no money could buy his silence when Germany is traduced; that despite his admiration for the Jews, he would not renounce his German heritage. He charged some Jews with seeking to embroil this country in a war with Germany, and he said that such Jews were only incidentally Americans. He charged that the Nazis had discriminatory laws because of the actions of some Jews, but he said that he would do all he could to alleviate conditions.

In a mood of self-pity, Viereck might have said of Eldridge's assault on him, *"Et tu Brute!"* But it was Eldridge who felt outraged; he felt as if the wife of his heart and hearth had turned into a woman of the streets. Eldridge's sincerity could not be doubted for one moment. He said that he had bided his time, when mutual friends condemned Viereck, hoping that sooner or later Viereck would disprove the accusations that were being made but that his hopes had been in vain. Now there was no other alternative, he felt, than to say, "I accuse!" And accuse he did. He called Viereck's letter "a mass of half-truths, subterfuges and saccharine sentimentalism." "As usual," said Eldridge to his discarded friend and collaborator, "you will discover loopholes, do mental pirouettings, be facetious, invoke Freud and all his complexes, and like a Knight Errant, secure in his golden armor, you will ride forth. But the rest of the world—the world that should matter to you—will as in Anderson's fairy tales see you naked!" The letter, like Goldberg's, was a masterpiece of invective, because it was not consciously fine writing. It was torn from Eldridge, like a tortured limb, and his suffering rose to a shriek. But as yet the case against Viereck was largely inferential. There were rumors pointing accusingly in Viereck's direction, but no public proof, no incontestable evidence that he was bought and paid for. One could not be blamed for prejudging him, for surely a man upholding a barbarous regime ought to be under suspicion, whatever his professed motives. The town rang with the excitement of what many regarded as an affront to New York's million or more Jews when a monster mass meeting of pro-Germans was held in Madison Square Garden. Viereck did himself incalculable harm because of his association with those who were unquestionably anti-Semitic. His speech before 25,000 Nazi sympathizers was a foolhardy act. One little incident shows this sufficiently.

I had made a dinner appointment with Viereck without knowing of the mass meeting. The appointment was for the evening following his speech. Meanwhile, someone telephoned me, asking me to dinner. I told of my prior appointment. "That bastard!" the other exclaimed, "break the appointment! You should not be seen with such a man!" The incident was typical of the reactions in many quarters. This friend of mine was one who ordinarily was disinterested in social issues; like Viereck, he felt that self-amusement was the end and aim of life. But in the face of a tragic situation he reverted to an attitude of social awareness and adopted the prevailing belief with regard to Viereck. A Jew who associated himself with Viereck had to search his soul to assure himself that he was acting properly. I, for one, often found myself probing deeply, in the effort to reassure my heart and brain that nothing within me was befouled. Here is an extraordinary human being, I said to myself of Viereck, who is acting exactly as he should not. Is it not worthwhile attempting to learn the reasons for such perverse conduct and perhaps to change the man's course? Perhaps I was foolish, but I persisted, nonetheless.

When I called on Viereck after his speech, I was determined to say nothing of it. Viereck, however, brought up the subject. Almost at once he said, "Tell me frankly what you think of the speech I delivered last night." Later that evening we were at a restaurant frequented by literary men and journalists. The editor and the business manager of a leading New York newspaper that energetically espoused the cause of the Jews against the Nazis were present, both men gorgeously drunk and one of them in a mood for speech-making. Ignoring the Semitic sweep of the nose of Viereck's friend, he discoursed foully on the Jews. They were leeches, he concluded, blood-sucking parasites who ought to be exterminated. Viereck turned to me and said, "And I am supposed to be an anti-Semite!" The newspaper proceeded in its pro-Jewish course with drunken interludes of secret anti-Semitism, one supposes, by the business manager.

Viereck's speech had begun provocatively: "I am not a member of the League of the Friends of the New Germany. But I am a friend of the New Germany. I was the friend of Germany under the Empire. I was the friend of Germany under the Republic and I am, today, a friend of Hitler's Germany. I am not, and never will be an anti-Semite." Every word of the speech was challenging and it ended in a mood of defiance: "We Americans of German descent want peace, not war. But we shall not remain silent in the face of these sinister machinations. We shall no longer submit to intolerable insult. The insolent demagogues who mislead some of our Jewish fellow citizens must realize that Germans and Americans of German descent have rights which even professional German-baiters are bound to respect.

> "We don't want to fight—
> But, by Jingo! If we do,
> We've got the brains, we've got the votes,
> We've got the courage, too!"

There was a minimum of good sense in the speech, and its general tone was necessarily an offense to all Jews and Gentiles who resented the attitude of those defending a reactionary regime. Wherever it was quoted—and very damaging passages were extracted—it aroused anger. Paul Eldridge felt impelled once again to enter the fray. He dubbed the speech "a mass of lies, sprinkled with particles of truth, like strong condiments to hide the foulness of the meat. If history ever records your name," he declared with prophetic tenseness, "it will say: George Sylvester Viereck preferred darkness to light, falsehood to truth, hate to love, prejudice to reason, a world of slaves to a world of freemen and will brand your memory with one word: 'Shame!' "

Soon the whole controversy was lifted somewhat from the realm of conjecture. Public demand and the instincts of politicians led to an official investigation by an arm of the federal government: an enlightening spectacle within its limits, important not only in connection with Viereck, but in itself.

On March 20, 1934, the House of Representatives passed a resolution empowering the speaker to appoint a special committee for the purpose of conducting an investigation of "(1) the extent, character, and objects of Nazi propaganda activities in the United States, (2) the diffusion within the United States of subversive propaganda that is instigated from foreign countries and attacks the principle of the form of government as guaranteed by our Constitution, and (3) all other questions in relation thereto that would aid Congress in any necessary remedial legislation." Thereupon the Speaker appointed the committee, which was popularly known as the Dickstein Committee, even if Representative Mc-Cormack of Massachussetts was the chairman, while Dickstein was only the vice-chairman. Senator Thomas W. Hardwick of Georgia was named as the committee counsel.

The committee employed special investigators to make preliminary examinations and conducted executive hearings prior to the open and public hearings, for the ostensible reasons of procuring proper evidence and protecting the reputations of persons from unwarranted reflections. It conducted twenty-four executive hearings and seven public ones at Washington, New York, Chicago, Los Angeles, Asheville, and Newark, and took 4,320 pages of testimony and examined several hundred witnesses—an imposing record. But, unfortunately, congressmen have to think of their constituencies, and there are various personal factors that come to the fore in an investigation conducted, after all, by politicians. The Dickstein Committee was far from an exception in this respect, with the result that there was something indecisive and unsatisfactory in its proceedings. It is, however, worth examining the record so far as it relates to Viereck. The atmosphere in which the investigation was conducted, the acrimonious encounters, and the bearing of Viereck, as much as what was actually said, are of much interest.

The name of Viereck first got into the public hearings when Carl C. Dickey, an associate of Byoir, was called to the stand. He stated that Carl Byoir and Associates was a partnership consisting of himself, Carl Byoir and Vincent Lancaster; that they had been in business for about three years, their main business being travel promotion; that they had formerly done business with the National Committee of Jews and Christians, an organization to combat intolerance; that all of them were definitely opposed to anti-Semitism, strongly advised against it, and at no time carried on such activities; that they knew Viereck for some while and he was instrumental in getting a contract with the German Tourist Information Office; that for this Viereck received a monthly salary of $1,000, commission of $750 per month, an office and a secretary; that for this money Viereck advised the Byoir firm about Germany ("He was supposed to know everybody and everything in Germany, a sort of encyclopedia to be consulted"); that an office was established by the Byoir firm in Germany; that they did not report to the German government, although presumably the government knew of their services and did not disapprove; that the Byoir firm issued regularly an economic bulletin to a select list; that there was nothing improper in this bulletin or in any other publications issued by them; that they had consulted with the various German consuls but only on the general theme of the work called for by their contract and on the possibility of getting more business and the like; that they sought similar business but had little of it. Dickey was an unflustered, matter-of-fact witness who carried himself well.

On July 9 the committee renewed its public hearings in New York City. Raymond Moley, the first of President Roosevelt's "brain trusters," was called as the first witness. Senator Hardwick was careful to bring out, through his initial question, that Moley had no present offical or direct connection with the government of the United States. Losing no time, the senator had the series of articles on Hitlerism in America, which had appeared in Moley's magazine, *Today*, introduced in evidence. Moley brought out that the articles were thoroughly checked, under his general supervision, by competent people, and that all of the documents were in his possession. "These statements," he said of the articles, "are understatements rather than overstatements." The articles, incidentally, did not mention Viereck. Moley expressed the opinion that any organization in this country possessing precisely the same purposes as the Nazi organization in Germany was a menace to the institutions of this country and that it was thoroughly improper for a German citizen, occupying an official position, to subsidize propaganda in this country against people here. So ended his testimony. Accompanied by the thanks of the chairman and the deference of the entire committee, Moley departed.

The next morning Viereck was called to the stand, his counsel, Mr. Langley, an associate of Judge Cohalan, close at hand. The attorney requested leave to make a statement, but the chairman refused to entertain any such offer. He advised Mr. Langley that he could counsel his client as to his constitutional rights but could do no more. "Mr. Chairman," Mr. Langley persisted, "this has to do with information that has come to my notice which affects a member of the committee and persons attached to the committee. I think you may want to. . . ." "The gentleman will please desist," demanded the chairman. Viereck now spoke up: "Mr. Chairman, may I make a statement before. . . ." "You may make no statement," the chairman informed him. "Even if it affects the integrity of a member of your staff?" Viereck asked. He was told to answer the questions simply and without argument. "I do not think there is any court in the world that would be so unfair as not to permit one to make a statement," Viereck declared. "If you are here to try to create a scene," the chairman put in. "No," Viereck interrupted. The questioning proceeded, with other such exchanges of compliments.

Mr. Langley suggested to the chairman that a copy of Viereck's speech at Madison Square Garden ought to be read into the record, but Senator Hardwick observed that he did not see the need of it. "It is only Professor Moley's statements, I believe, that are read into the record," said Viereck with heat. The senator changed his tone somewhat and asked Viereck if he wanted the speech introduced in evidence. Viereck replied that he certainly did, that he stood behind every word of it. The chairman said that it would be received as an exhibit but not printed in the record. "Well," said Viereck, "Will Professor Moley's articles be put in the record?" No answer.

Senator Hardwick wanted to know the attitude that Viereck had taken at the time of World War I and was informed that Viereck regarded the war as a great mistake and largely responsible for the world economic collapse. Viereck tried to tell of his war record after America entered the conflict. "If you persist in going beyond the proper limits of an answer to a question, I shall have to be stern with you," the chairman warned him. "You want to find the facts, do you not?" Viereck retorted.

Senator Hardwick wanted to know about Viereck's acquaintance with "Mr. Hitler."

"Before meeting him, I conveyed to him certain ideas suggested to me by the American Ambassador at Berlin," said Viereck.

"Did you not tell Mr. Hitler that in your opinion it would be a hundred times easier for any friends of Germany if Germans would make a distinction between the good Jews, what Germans call the good Jews, and the internationalists who are opposed to any country?" the senator asked. "Yes, sir," replied Viereck, may explain, I told Mr. Hitler, for instance, that it was a great mistake to have posters displayed at some watering place, that Jews are not permitted to bathe here. He agreed with me. He said that the instance which I cited was unauthorized and then he asked me whether there were not quite a number of beaches in America where Jews were not welcomed. And I, much to my humiliation, had to admit that he was right. Chancellor Hitler said that he had not declared war on the Jews, but that the Jews had declared war on him; that he had done the Jews no harm; that he had merely curtailed some of their special privileges and prerogatives."

And so, by very gradual steps, each punctuated by a battle, they arrived at the Byoir contract. Viereck said that he thought he was largely instrumental in securing that contract and that he received an adequate fee for it, the compensation mentioned by Mr. Dickey. "You also advised men like your friend Kiep, the German consul here in New York, did you not?" Senator Hardwick asked. The answer was in the affirmative: "On the general aspects of public relations. I was considered as an expert in these matters, not only by the Germans but by others." Dr. Kiep, he said, had paid him $500 a month for four months or so. "It was purely a provisional agreement," Viereck added.

"Is Dr. Kiep a man of large personal means?" the committee wanted to know.

"I think so," said Viereck.

"Do you know where he got the $500 a month with which he paid you?"

"He told me that he secured it from friends in Germany, but I suspect it may have come out of his own pocket."

The committee wanted to know if Viereck entered the Kiep payments to his account books. "No," said Viereck. "I made a memorandum of them and they appear in my income-tax statement." The committee wanted to know if he had any regular books, and he replied that he had such; "but these cash payments, much to my surprise, were not entered in those books, but they are entered and appear in the working papers of my accountant." The $1,750 per month from Byoir was, however, received in checks and entered in his books. Viereck observed at this point that he is not very good at bookkeeping; that he writes books, and does not keep them; that his books do, however, show the sources of his income.

While admitting that such advice naturally affected German-American relations in general, Viereck said the contract had no other function than "mere advice." Senator Hardwick wondered if Viereck understood that the advice might be relayed to the German government, and Viereck said that he would not be surprised in the least. The senator wanted to know if he got anything out of the $4,000 that had been paid in cash to Byoir by Dr. Kiep. Viereck said he was not sure, but that he should have.

"I guess you would have claimed it if they had not paid it to you," the senator remarked.

"I may do so after these proceedings are over," countered Viereck.

"In other words," continued the senator, "you did not know about that $4,000 until that evidence was brought out in Washington?"

"I would not say that," commented Viereck, "but the matter was rather trifling."

"What kind of service did you give Byoir and Associates in connection with this work?" Viereck was asked.

He replied: "I should say the sort of service that an important lawyer gives to his clients—advice."

The chairman wanted more information. "I interpreted events and personalities for them. I gave them a number of articles which I had prepared myself, including an interview with Dr. Schmidt, the Minister of Economics, and another interview with Dr. Schacht, the president of the Reichsbank," Viereck continued.

The committee's examiner inquired if Viereck was in close and constant contact with the German Foreign Office when he visited Germany.

"I would hardly say that," he parried. "I have many friends in the foreign office and I visited them—not only in connection with German-American relations but for material for interviews and articles and books. But naturally they sought my advice." For the publication *Speaking About Hitler,* Viereck had contributed, he said, advice and excerpts from the press, derived from his very careful study of the newspapers. He added that neither Hitler nor any German official had ever advised him about the impression his articles had created, nor did he think that Byoir received any such advice.

Senator Hardwick now read Viereck's statement to the press, released after the Washington hearings and denying any impropriety in the Byoir contract. In the statement Viereck again repudiated anti-Semitism but reasserted his faith in the New Germany. "When the full truth is known, it will appear that no one labored harder than I to discover the way out of the German-Jewish dilemma," Viereck had said. "Events justified my attitude in 1914. They will also justify my stand in 1934. Whatever the gods may hold in their lap, here I stand; I can do no other."

Viereck tried to get the reasons why Dr. Kiep paid in cash into the record, but he had extreme difficulty. Viereck did not know if he had ever before or afterward been paid by a German consul in cash, but, he said, he did not think so. He said he made no inquiry to learn the sources of Kiep's money and did not know for what personal matters he spent the money. Finally, he was able to get in the explanation as to why the Kiep payment was made in cash: "Dr. Kiep was under the impression that there had been a system (of espionage) extending to the banks, and that any such transaction would come to the attention of Germany's enemies, and it would be misrepresented."

The chairman wanted to know why Dr. Kiep had to conceal the matter if he had no concern about it. Viereck answered, "I am not Dr. Kiep, but I suppose because of the complaints on everything German and the conduct by Germnay from the conspirators."

"You accepted the $500 cash under those circumstances?" asked the chairman, more by way of exclamation than question.

"With pleasure," Viereck answered. "If you handed me $500 I would take it, too. In fact, I have to present a bill to the committee for my trip from the country."

Congressman Dickstein wanted to know why the German railroads had to pay approximately $108,000 for a mailing list that could easily be obtained for less; that was his interpretation of the Byoir contract. "You can get law from the law books," replied Viereck, with mild irony, "and yet you used Mr. Wickersham, Mr. Untermeyer, and Mr. Dickstein. You go to experts." Dickstein, not silenced by the ironic compliment, wanted to know if the German railways were under the control of the German government, and he was assured by Viereck that everything in Germany is under such control.

The real explosion occurred during the testimony of Ernst Schmitz, representing the German Tourist Information Bureau. He was the man with whom the American negotiations for the Byoir contract were carried on, principally by Dickey, Viereck, and the Byoir associates. Schmitz said that he had entered into the contract with Byoir without instructions from Germany and then had submitted it to the home office for consideration. He knew that Viereck had discussed the contract with people in Germany because Viereck had told him. He had had contracts similar to the Byoir one throughout the existence of his organization. Publicity firms had been employed for certain jobs, such as the distribution of literature, but none of them, other than Byoir, had had an eighteen-month, or yearly contract. He thought the amount paid to Byoir was not high for the type of travel promotion work they had done. They sent a man to Berlin to open up an office there and constantly advised the office here as to the questions that came up from time to time: the sending out of booklets about the Oberammagau Passion Play and the like. Schmitz said that he had not known the amount of Viereck's compensation, but he had assumed that Viereck was in the employ of Byoir and would be paid. He looked upon Viereck as a sort of "lobbyist" for Byoir and did not know that Byoir was also doing work for Dr. Kiep and had been paid $4,000 in cash by him. Schmitz was a calm witness. His answers appeared to be spontaneous and proper. Suddenly the tone of the inquiry changed, and the best row of the session ensued.

Congressman Dickstein had taken over the questioning. "What was the occasion of your giving free passage to Burton Holmes and other writers in this country?" he asked. Schmitz said that it was the usual thing and that some of the men given passage were friends of his. No, there was nothing connected with propaganda, nor were there any orders from the embassy or from Berlin.

The chairman was a bit dubious. "Did you get any orders from Berlin about giving free transporation?" he demanded, backing up Dickstein.

"We get every year——" Mr. Schmitz began.

"Did you? Yes or no," the chairman broke in.

Schmitz tried to explain. "As a matter of fact——" he resumed.

At length the chairman told Schmitz he might make a statement. "I understand," said Schmitz, "that the chairman of the House Committee on Immigration asked the North German Lloyd for the same courtesies that we extended to various newspaper men."

"To what?" Dickstein wanted to know.

"For a free trip to Germany," he was told by Schmitz.

"But he never got a free trip. He paid for it," Dickstein put in.

"But he got minimum rates for superior accommodations," Schmitz persisted.

"But it was paid for," Dickstein repeated. "There is no use beating around the bush," Dickstein added. "I am the chairman of the Immigration Committee." The furies were unloosed. Epithets came fast and ferocious.

"No further questions," announced Dickstein.

"Just one question," insisted the chairman. That was the prelude to another speech by him. "As chairman of this committee," he said, "I cannot permit and will not permit you, Viereck, and Langley and this is your combination; Langley is your attorney; Langley is Viereck's attorney. Langley undertook to impugn the integrity of this committee yesterday. . . . But Mr. Langley has corrected that fact."

"I have not done anything of the sort," Langley interjected, "and I still stand by it, that my information reflects on a member of this committee. You did not bring it out in public."

"This gentleman here is looking for a scene," the chairman stated.

"Now, just a minute," said Langley. "Have you ordered that I be removed from the room?"

"No, no. . . ." The chairman repeated that the action was ungentlemanly. A word or two more and the questioning was over.

As of February 15, 1935, the committee submitted its report, the first section of it dealing with Nazism. It complimented the twenty-odd million Americans of German birth or descent who had refused to participate in Nazi activities despite the strenuous efforts made to win them over. "Several American firms and American citizens as individuals sold their services for express propaganda purposes," said the report, "making their contracts with and accepting compensation from foreign business firms. The firms in question were Carl Byoir & Associates and Ivy Lee—T. J. Ross. Carl Dickey, junior partner of Carl Byoir & Associates, testified that his firm handled the contract with the German Tourist Bureau with the fee for services set at $6,000 per month. He testified that the contract was secured with the help of George Sylvester Viereck who received $1,750 per month with free office space and secretary as his share of the $6,000. The committee finds that the services rendered by Carl Byoir & Associates were largely of a propaganda nature. . . ." The report went on to say: "Viereck admitted that he discussed the Byoir contract with a German Cabinet office before it was entered into. He further testified that he had also been paid the sum of $500 monthly for 4 or 5 months by Dr. Kiep, former consul-general in New York City, which was paid in cash for advice of a propaganda nature. . . ." Finally: "The first payment in the contract amounting to $4,000 was made by Dr. Kiep . . . in cash." Most people were constrained to accept these findings as true and went even beyond the committee in condemnation of Viereck and his cohorts.

In concluding its report the committee recommended that Congress should enact a statute "requiring all publicity, propaganda or public-relations agents or other agents or agencies, who represent in this country any foreign government or a foreign political party or foreign industrial or commercial organization, to register with the secretary of state of the United States, and to state name and location of such foreign employer, the character of the service to be rendered, and the amount of compensation paid or to be paid therefore." The other recommendations were directed largely against the communist movement, for the Nazi investigation ended up as the prelude to an onslaught on the reds! This was the committee that evolved into the House Committee on Un-American Activites.

As might have been expected, the chief difficulty in connection with the Dickstein Committee resulted from the failure to specify what was meant by propaganda. The word was used with abandon, without being defined. The only documents introduced in evidence relating to Viereck were the Byoir contract, his Madison Square Garden speech, and the publications called *Speaking About Hitler* and the *Economic Bulletins*. The Hitler publications were excerpts largely from the American press, none of them supporting the persecution of the Jews and most of them condemning it strongly. The *Economic Bulletins* condemned the boycott here but said nothing against the Jews. The themes were trade and travel and economics, and there certainly was nothing of an extreme nature. To be sure, the committee had unearthed material against some persons operating here, but no connection was shown between them and Viereck. There was nothing even of a circumstantial nature connecting Viereck with them. His activities, sad as they were, were not sufficiently defined to justify all of the charges against him, but the inevitable inferences could do him no good.

Much more shrewd and decisive were the results of an investigation conducted by a radical journalist named John L. Spivak. He had been connected in his preradical days with Macfadden on one of the tabloid papers of New York and had precisely the sort of experience that fitted him for merciless interrogation of those who had skeletons in their closets. His series of articles, called "Plotting America's Pogroms," appeared in *The New Masses*, the left-wing magazine, from October 2 to December 4, 1934. Subsequently the articles were reprinted in pamphlet form and then they were incorporated in Spivak's book, *America Faces the Barricades*. The series received unusual prominence and was quoted in journals opposed to the left wing. In the first article of the series, Spivak promised to prove, *inter alia,* that Ralph M. Easley, head of the National Civic Federation, distributed anti-Semitic propaganda imported into this country by George Sylvester Viereck, "paid Nazi agent," and that Easley secretly tried to stop the German boycott and reported on these efforts to Viereck.

In the sixth article of the series, published first in the *New Masses* of November 6, 1934, Spivak reached the subject of Viereck. The article was called "Anti-Semitic Duet: Easley and Viereck," and the cover of the magazine showed the two men singing notes that looked strikingly like swastikas. Here is a sample of the contents of the article. Spivak reports himself as having phoned Easley, whose secretary asked him to wait a moment. "The minute stretched out to four by the watch—just long enough, I judged, to trace the call and get several people listening in on extension wires. Then

> "Hello," said a sharp voice.
> "Mr. Easley?"
> "No, this is Mr. Stevenson——"
> "Not Arch Stevenson of the old 'red-baiting' fame?"
> "This is Mr. Archibald Stevenson!" the voice said with dignity.
> "What is it you wish to see Mr. Easley about?"

"I should like to see him about his anti-Semitic activities. I know, of course, that he does not like Communists, but what I want to know is why he is carrying on anti-Semitic work—what that has to do with his hatred of Communism." . . .

Let us now, since they worked so closely together, see what sort of person George Sylvester Viereck is. Mr. Viereck is an author, journalist and editor. I will not go into his literary history. I will merely say that he is one of the shrewdest propagandists I know. He himself does not commit himself to writing. However, Mr. Easley did enough writing, for both of them.

In his article Spivak said that it was not necessary to devote space proving Viereck a Nazi propagandist, but that it was important to know his financial condition before and after Hitler got into power. Viereck, he said, lost almost his entire fortune in the crash of 1929 as a result of large and unwise speculations. "In March and April, 1933, after Hitler got into power, his bank accounts show that he suddenly had large sums of money. Early in October he returned from another trip to Germany and he had still larger sums available." Then in March 1933 Dr. Kiep gave Viereck a retainer of $500 a month—in cash. "This retainer," said Spivak, "was supposed to have been deposited openly to his accounts and recorded in his cash book as money earned for legitimate advice. I saw his cash book—there is no entry for these sums except one $500 entry on page 114 which *does not disclose the source.*"

At this period of financial prosperity for Viereck, Easley suddenly got interested in stopping the Jewish boycott of German goods, wrote Spivak. "On March 27, 1933, Viereck and Easley got together, with Viereck guiding the professional patriot in moves—to stop the boycott. Three days later . . . Viereck cabled the ex-Crown Prince of Germany, Vice Chancellor von Papen and Dr. Hjalmer Schacht." Then Easley got busy and arranged secret conferences, said Spivak. Those who attended were Justice Joseph M. Proskauer, Max J. Kohler, Louis Wiley, all three Jews, and members of the national Civic Federation. "The plea was shrewdly made to the Jews that a boycott would result in a counter-boycott with the inevitable development of race hatred. . . . All that the Jews were told about Viereck was that he was 'willing to cooperate' with them."

A special committee was appointed at Viereck's suggestion to arrange for a good will Commission to Germany and, on May 13, 1933, the group cabled Schacht, who immediately sent them a cable of welcome. "Easley was constantly meeting with and writing reports to Viereck and introducing him to prominent Jews," wrote Spivak, telling of some of these meetings. One report, marked confidential, was dated June 6, 1933. In it Easley suggested a plan of procedure: a booklet by the American Jewish Committee, containing the Jewish case against the Hitler Government; then the committee of the National Civic Federation would make a statement of its offer of mediation (Easley vaunting his organization as the only nonpropagandistic body); "of course, the answer to the American Jewish

Committee's pamphlet will open the way for the National Socialist Party of Germany to give its whole case; then the Federation will stress its efforts for peace." Spivak declared this to be a tricky scheme to stop the boycott here and open the door to Nazi publicity against the Jews. Fortunately, said Spivak, the Jews got suspicious of Easley's "sudden interest," and that terminated his efforts.

"At this period," continued Spivak, going on a tangential course, "the patriotic Mr. Easley became intensely interested in disseminating Adolf Ehrt's book, *Communism in Germany*, which though purporting to be an attack on Communists, is actually filled with cunning anti-Semitic propaganda, the best kind to get across. Easley, with Viereck maneuvering and advising in the shadowy background of international intrigue, worked desperately to get Jews to endorse the book." Waldman and Proskauer read the book and denounced it as anti-Semitic. Said Proskauer: "Any book, which directly and by innuendo, identifies Jews and Communists, is an anti-Semitic book. That is the essence of the situation. The rest of it is embroidery." The former justice advised Easley to abandon the project, but Easley, assisted by his wife, proceeded to distribute copies free of charge from the federation offices. The book, Spivak added in capital letters, had been "IMPORTED FROM GERMANY BY GEORGE SYLVESTER VIERECK TO BE USED FOR PROPAGANDA PURPOSES." The copies, 20,000 of them, had been consigned to Viereck.

That, Spivak knew, was the climax of his article. It closed with some questions to Easley, centering around the Ehrt book: "How much money did you get from George Sylvester Viereck to help defray the cost of distributing this anti-Semitic book? How much did your wife . . . get . . .? Did Viereck suggest giving him (Pelley of the obnoxious Silver Shirts) these copies? What other propaganda material did Viereck ever give you to distribute which he imported from Germany?" Spivak offered no proof of the insinuations and innuendo contained in his questions. Did he have any proof?

It is time now that we attempt to arrive at the truth of the various accusations made or insinuated at the Dickstein Committee hearings, in Spivak's articles, and elsewhere. This much cannot be gainsaid: Viereck received cash from the German consul Kiep, suspicious circumstances surrounded his relations with Kiep and the first payment of cash to Byoir, and the secrecy justified queries and more on the part of thoughtful men. There was no direct proof that Viereck disseminated anti-Semitic propaganda other than his involvement with the Ehrt book and other decidedly suspicious circumstances. There was no proof that Viereck was connected with offensive organizations, but he was guilty of defending a government which, in the eyes of most civilized human beings, was a degradation, and this was bad enough. But he was accused of going beyond mere expression of opinion. He was accused of selling himself to the propagation of an inhuman cause, that of anti-Semitism.

To what extent was this true? Take, first, the Ehrt book. The cover of it shows the Reichstag fire, and under the picture is the name: *Communism in Germany! The*

Truth About the Communist Conspiracy on the Eve of the National Revolution.
There are 179 pages in the book. The text of the book is Hitler's statement made on
September 1, 1933: ''At the beginning of this year there were weeks when we were
within a hair's breadth of Bolshevist chaos.'' The book ends with the statement:
''The destruction of the Communist Internationale is a task for the nations of the
whole of the Christian and civilized world.'' The space in between is a docu-
mented exposition of the system and history of communism in Germany, surprising in its detail. The authenticity of these documents is questionable despite the
offer of the General League of German Anti-Communist Associations to make the
proof ''available for seriously interested students of public affairs.'' But there can
be no doubt that the book is, by and large, a study of the subject it purports to
discuss, namely, communism in Germany. This is emphatically not to say that it is
not contaminated by the most hateful and blatant tone of anti-Semitism. Whenever
a Communist is also a Jew, that fact is stated, and such statements occur quite
frequently, and in a few brief passages the author identifies communism with
Jewishness, as if they were mutually associated. On page 28 the author says, ''It
must not be forgotten that the Social-Democrats of republican authority, formed
part of the same front of Marxism, Judaism and Pacifism as its hostile brother, the
German Communist Party.'' On page 31 he says, ''The teachers and leaders of
Communism in Germany also came direct from the school of the old Russian
Jewish Revolution.'' On page 155 he states, ''The fight in which they [the brown
shirts] fell was no less honourable and vital than the German defensive war of
1914–8, with the difference that the other sides of the barricades were not manned
by honourable soldiers of a foreign nation, but by criminal cliques of the lower
orders and misled members of our own people in the service of a rootless,
international group of Jewish and Marxist intellectuals.'' And on page 178: ''The
total contrast to Jewish-Marxist Bolshevism is exclusively represented by German
National Socialism.'' Clearly this is rampant anti-Semitism.

What did Viereck say in defense or in mitigation of his connection with so
vicious a book? He explained that the book was shown to him by the author, who
asked him to help reach the American public. Viereck thereupon read the book,
''though perhaps not very carefully. Everything,'' he said, ''was done in a hurry.
There are undoubtedly some sentences in the book which can be interpreted as
anti-Semitic. If the Jews insist on affiliating themselves with extremely radical
movements, they can blame no one but themselves if an attack on radicalism seems
like an attack on the Jews.'' Viereck did not think that he ever discussed the book
with any Jews, and he said that he had nothing to do with copies of the book having
been given to Pelley of the Silver Shirts; indeed, he never knew that they were
given to Pelley. He had nothing at all to do with the circulation of the book, he said.
It was consigned to him because while he believed that Easley would distribute it,
he was not sure. If Easley had failed to distribute it, Viereck said that he would
have tried to interest some other organization. The duty, he said, was paid from the
German side. He had no expense in connection with it and no financial interest of

any kind. He did not pay anything to Easley or Easley's wife, despite Spivak's innuendo: "these matters were arranged between the German publisher or the organization which sponsored the book and Mr. Easley."

Viereck said that he first met Easley when preparing a series of articles on communism entitled "The Web of the Red Spider," published in *Liberty*. Since that time he met him a few times, perhaps a dozen in all. Easley, he said, took an interest in the German-Jewish question and wanted to prevent the controversy from spreading to the United States, for one thing, because American business was being affected. The only writing of Viereck's that Easley knew were his articles on political subjects. "During the War he wanted to shoot me," declared Viereck. "Now he thinks that would probably have been a mistake."

Viereck claimed that he was not a member of the National Civic Federation, that he simply met Easley, Woll, and various trustees at the offices of the federation. Easley sent to him and to numerous others reports marked "confidential" about various matters relating to the German-Jewish question and to the campaign against communism. Viereck did not know which of his letters were in the possession of Spivak, but he knew that Spivak got those letters from the file of some member of the federation or some member of the German-Jewish Committee to whom Easley sent duplicates. He said that he had nothing of importance in the way of letters from Easley that were not in Spivak's possession or quoted in the *New Masses* articles, that the letters that he had received related to routine matters, and that he believed that Spivak quoted the letters accurately, though he had not checked them carefully.

Viereck said that he and Easley tried to persuade the German government to change its rulings against the Jews and at the same time to bring pressure on the Jews to stop their anti-German activities. Viereck showed Easley his cables to the Crown Prince and others so that Easley might see that he was doing his best to exert pressure on the German government. Viereck had sent the cables, he said, because of the solicitations of his Jewish friends. Rabbi Elias, the same man who had once induced him to join the Christian Committee for Palestine, called on him and urged him to do his best. He was assured by various persons claiming to speak for the Jews that if Germany relented in its boycott, the Jews would relent in theirs. Then Easley arranged for meetings of representative Jews and Christians to discuss the serious problems of reconciliation between Germans and Jews. Those to be invited were determined by Viereck and Easley. They included John Ross Delafield, James W. Gerard, Herman A. Metz, Joseph M. Proskauer, Victor and Bernard Ridder, Frederick B. Robinson, Louis Wiley, and other Jews and Gentiles. The sessions were executive, that is, secret; but a stenographic transcript was kept of the proceedings. Among those who spoke were Viereck and Victor Ridder. The discussion was "thrilling and dramatic," Easley said in his confidential report on the subject which is here blended with Viereck's statement (the two accounts do not differ from each other): their differences were with Spivak.

Easley's report carried this revelatory heading: *"Anti-Semitism and Nazi-ism Abhorrent to Americans—Movement for Unity Among all Racial Groups—Pro-*

*posal on German and Jewish Citizens to join with the National Civic Federation in
its Warfare against Communism.''*

Easley's statement said that the genesis of his endeavor "to be helpful in the
German-Jewish controversy dates back to the morning after the Madison Square
Garden mass-meeting held on March 28, 1933, under the auspices of the Ameri-
can-Jewish Congress which then launched its boycott of German goods.'' Mediation seemed the proper procedure to Easley, and he was assured by the State
Department at Washington that it would be "not only approved but appreciated."
At the time the association with Viereck was formed and the various meetings
culminated in one held on May 4, 1933, at which a resolution was passed
unanimously, authorizing the sending of a good will commission to Germany. The
first paragraph of this resolution stated that "the anti-Semitic program of the
German Government announces a violation of fundamental human rights and such
violations are provocative of international discord in fields of political and economic action.'' The resolution had as its declared purpose the neutralizing of racial
antagonism and the maintenance of "good will and normal economic relations"
between America and Germany.

"The Jewish members having magnanimously suggested that, lest it antago-
nize the Germans, none of their group should be on the special committee
authorized under the resolution,'' the committee was made up of Woll, Delafield,
George MacDonald, Herbert S. Houston, Easley, and Viereck. They secured the
cooperation of Dr. Schacht, but circumstances forced them to hold the project in
abeyance. Viereck said that the Spivak articles were *not* responsible for the delay
of the project.

Viereck said, returning to the Byoir contract, that he met Carl Byoir some
years previously through Sam Woolf, the artist, when he tried to arrange an
interview with Machado, the Cuban dictator who was employing Byoir as his
publicity man. Viereck said that he took a liking to Byoir, which was not lessened
by Byoir's admiration for his poetry. (Byoir had poetic and literary aspirations
himself.) Viereck felt that Byoir's work for the oil man Doherty and for the Cuban
government showed that his organization was equipped to handle the German
contract, and so the connection was made. As to the details, Viereck stood behind
every word of his testimony before the Dickstein Committee. He said that other
than the Byoir contract and the Kiep association and some letters to the press,
spontaneously written both before the contract and after its expiration, he had not
been associated with the Nazi government, the Nazi party, or any agency thereof in
any capacity, or with any German business or agency or individual. He denied
Spivak's charge that in March and April 1933 his bank accounts suddenly showed
the receipt of large sums of money and he denied that after his trips to Germany
there were further and still larger sums in his possession. The only money he had,
he said, flowed from his contract. Viereck denied association with the unsavory
individuals discussed in Spivak's articles, but he admitted knowing Col. Emerson—"we are friendly but distant"—and Rumely—"we like each other but rarely
meet"—and the members of the embassy staff, of course, and some others. Since

Spivak alleged no reprehensible connection between Viereck and the underworld of American Nazidom, that seemed to put the matter to rest, except to mention that Viereck said he advised the Friends of the New Germany not to publish violent diatribes against the Jews and other matter likely to harm rather than help Germany. "It proved impossible to keep them in line," Viereck commented.

Viereck's attitude toward the Spivak articles was curious. He said that he read them only casually; that they contained little that was new and much that was not so; that they were filled from the garbage pail of the Dickstein Committee—that is, they contained the material discarded by the Committee; that the articles had no appreciable effect. Of Spivak he said that the man was a bright young journalist, probably sincere in his radicalism; that he knew and rather liked him; that the man had no sources that were not accessible to any capable journalist; that he did not know how accurate Spivak was, but that he was probably more accurate than the average sensational reporter writing for radical publications. In connection with the articles, Spivak called up once, Viereck said, but he never spoke to him personally and he placed no material at Spivak's disposal.

Viereck wrote out a reply to the series, but he never sent it in to the *New Masses* because his friends advised him "to let sleeping Communists lie or lying Communists sleep." They said that there was no object in engaging in a controversy with the Reds (later Viereck felt that he should have replied "because I never shrink from a fight").

Fortunately for Viereck's reputation at the time, there appeared more to be said for him. Still more fortunately, his views of the *Schone Adolf* seemed to change radically in the ensuing months. However, it should be abundantly clear by now that Viereck was determined to be pro-German against any odds. His mind was prepared to defend any blackness, so long as it was a Teutonic blackness. Had he accepted no compensation, had he entered into no formal affiliations with German agencies, he might have avoided the worst pitfalls, for his activities would not have cried so desperately for explanation and he might have retained a greater sense of detachment. He might even have played the role to which he aspired, that of the reconciler; at least, he might have learned more readily that the Nazi regime did not desire a reconciliation and so he might have reached the higher patriotism, rather than the abominally low nationalism to which he clung. He might have seen that the brown shirts were an abomination, both to true lovers of Germany and to the world.

Many months later Viereck readily admitted that the Byoir contract and the activities centering around it were tactical mistakes, but he still refused to concede that there might be any moral turpitude or mental weakness in what he had done. It is sometimes difficult to overcome the inertia of rationalization! Viereck soon enough was prompted to forego his mad defense of the Nazi regime, though he would not publicly chastise Germany. The Byoir contract was terminated by mutual assent, and Viereck refrained from making public defenses of the Third Reich save for isolated acts here and there, as when Germany violated the Locarno Treaty. At length he was able to make it known that his belief in Hitler simmered down to his feeling that National Socialism was a medicine that Germany needed at the time. As for the persecution of the Jews in Germany, he said "that it is legally a monstrosity, economically a catastrophe, ethically an error, politically a blunder, intellectually an imbecility, humanly a barbarism, esthetically bad taste."

To be sure, it should be counted on the credit side of Viereck's ledger that he had definitely repudiated the Jew-baiting activities of the Nazis, but one should not overpraise him for this. Despite some muddled persons, the Jews were far from being alone in having just cause for complaint against the brown shirts. The Catholics, a section of the Protestants, the trade unionists, the Social-Democrats, the liberals, the pacifists, all of humanitarian Germany, could decry the brown blight. But Viereck did not rise to defend them. He preferred to believe that all of Germany, except for a very small minority, supported Hitler. He preferred to forget what he once knew, that Hitler represented big business; that he was the ironfisted spokesman of a minority group, successful for the time being in hoodwinking the majority by playing on their sense of inferiority. Because some Germans applauded the "triumphs" wrought in their name by Hitler, Viereck continued to whisper hoarsely that Hitler had rejuvenated his people. Viereck, to be sure, was pro-German, but his pro-Germanism was that of the ruling clique. The son of the Hohenzollern socialist had become the apologist for those very things that were obnoxious to all men of good will. The cycle of reaction was complete.

And, alas, as would be demonstrated later, Viereck had not truly terminated his activities for the Nazis. They had simply been transformed and concealed. In the end, he was to pay bitterly for his lapses.

36   IS IT THE END?

A boy whittles on a sizable block with or without a definite goal in mind. He decides, almost without thinking, that first this portion of the block and then that ought to be removed. Sometimes the immediate result is beautiful; more often it is without meaning. But in the end the block is a pile of shavings and less than a memory. Has something similar been done to Viereck in this book? Has every part of him been whittled away until he has lost all substance? His writings apparently have been denigrated; his philosophy has been trampled upon; his character undermined; his career treated cavalierly. What, then, is left? He himself, in a mood of despondency, implied that nothing was left. In a letter to this writer, which will shock those who think of Viereck only as an unrestrained egotist, he said:

> I wonder whether you are not engaged, after all, in a wild goose chase. I have made several scattered reputations, but not one great reputation. The people who like my German do not like my English. The people who like my verse do not like my prose. The people who like my politics do not like my literature. The people who care for my journalistic efforts are interested in nothing else. There are not enough people who hate me enough or love me enough to assure the success of the book.
>
> Even in the field of literature I have dissipated my efforts. If I had written only fiction, or only verse, or only psychological studies, I would probably have achieved some eminence in any one of these spheres. As it is, I am afraid that I have added nothing to the world's treasure, that will interest anyone one week after I am dead, or entitle me to more than a cross reference in the annals of mankind.
>
> Drop the book. The game is not worth the candle.

And if that is the case, we are again, as in the beginning, confronted with the recurrent, Why. Has this book justified itself? In a spirit of utter seriousness, befitting this age of catastrophe, unrest, and transition, men demand of a biography that it give some valid excuse, some compelling reason, for imposing itself upon a troubled world. The feeling, made especially vocal by some of the warring proponents of revolt and of reaction, is that the individual means little, perhaps nothing, and that tendencies, forces, impulses count for much, perhaps all. Hence a man should be the subject of a biography only if he echoes some typical sound, not merely a scarcely audible gurgle of the stream of life; or, expressed in the now historical phrase, a man must stand in some symbolical relation to his age or to humanity itself, if we are to make him the subject of serious study.

Let us accept the belief, even if it robs life of some of its unpremeditated glamor. We may easily fit Viereck into the frame of things and show, as we have, that he played a special role in the life of our times. But important reservations are to be made in the general theory of the unimportance of personalities. We may begin with the thought that the arithmetic of life is only a primitive form of mathematics, less logical than some of the economic determinists would have it, two and two becoming less or more than four in the fallible human brain. In spite of all the theorists, men do not always function with machinelike precision; the human equation imposes itself, or, if you will, the machine breaks down despite the two-and-two logic of its construction. Hence we cannot always build upon a rule of symmetric cause and effect. We must reaffirm some measure of belief in personalities and qualify a purely mechanistic and rationalistic philosophy.

Personalities like Viereck are the sometimes dangerous and sometimes beneficient curves and bends in the course of the stream of social tendency. The intellectual mariner will be concerned with the twists and turns of the river of life—with its peculiarities of personality—as much as he will be concerned with the normal direction. Each Tom, Dick, and Harry of us, made confident because we do not carry a burden of knowledge, thinks himself a social engineer, and as such we cannot afford to ignore the one man, in this case Viereck, who helps shape the stream. The solicitous thought is that we cannot always recognize a great man; but who is so deaf that a loud sound does not impose itself on him?

Therefore, write a biography of Viereck, so that, interred in a book, he may be catalogued in the universal library and forgotten like a million needless notables before him. This may delight the crowd of his detractors, but there is no more than cynical satisfaction in it.

Each age has set before itself the task of preparing a record of its foibles, sins, and virtues, its men of note and of ill-fame, its deeds and misdeeds. The age calls upon all who have some special knowledge of any one man or tendency or event to set forth their testimony. Maybe the record is applauded in its day, for it is generally of the day only. But soon the archives of the time gather dust and are consulted less and less, except by pedants. In time the world rids itself of all that was transitory, all that looked genuine in its day but which was really tinsel and veneer. What remains becomes ever so much more precious, becomes human scripture, indeed, as its relation to the commonplace becomes obscured.

Many then begin to feel that all the acquisition of facts, all the laborious accumulation, is a foolish process. They urge that time itself, which they personify with religious naivete, be permitted to choose the fit and to discard the chaff, unassisted by the scribes. Here again we have the mental confusion which mistakes itself for wisdom. The process of creating scripture is not an automatic one. It is the result of the unconscious exaggeration of scholars and the enthusiasm of hero worshipers. Through these different men, different tendencies, different events are successively given the center of the stage, which may or may not belong to them, and judgment is then passed by the best critical minds. This successive spotlighting results in the necessary elimination of men, tendencies, and events. Left to chance, however, there would be no real judgment, merely fortuitous elimination and the falsification of history.

The bare process of choosing a man as the subject of a book is an unwitting admission of partisanship. We may struggle for so-called objectivity. We may don judicial robes. But we remain the advocate and special pleader. For thus we serve the race and assist in the process of selection. It is enough ultimately that we know that our success depends not on the blindness of our advocacy but upon its wisdom. If this book has preserved all that was memorable in the life and writings of George Sylvester Viereck, one should be content that one may have added a permanent page to the records of our day.

Throughout his life, as we have seen, Viereck was a public figure and attracted enormous attention. There were periods when scarcely a day passed without the mention of his name in the press and at public gatherings—in our age a test of importance, at least for the day and hour. The circumstances were not merely sensational in the ephemeral sense. They were, in more ways than one, unique; and so they merited attention. A full knowledge and understanding of early twentieth-century American literature is hardly possible without a knowledge and understanding of Viereck's early poetic career, the period during which he was the wonder child of American letters. Complete knowledge and understanding of America's part in World War I is hardly possible unless Viereck's role in it is known and understood, nor can we know truly and identify surely the erotic impulse in modern literature without knowing and identifying Viereck's contribution. Finally, the most characteristic phase of our latter day tower of confusion is the propagandistic fervor, and surely it will be conceded that Viereck's role as a propagandist was a preeminent one. In that field he may be considered generic.

His career should, therefore, be studied, despite his self-denigration, for all that is significant in it. It is sheer stupidity or hysteria to say, as do many of Viereck's former friends, that because of his sins a great, shroudlike silence should cover him. The cry, "Never again Viereck," is as senseless today as it was during the years of World War I. Granting the worst that may be said of Viereck, his career compels attention and should be recorded. The saints and sages and soldiers are not the only fit subjects for biography. The devil is entitled to his advocate, and generally gets it, not for the devil's sake but so that the rest of us may be enlightened and the times served. Elementary truths all of these, but in the tumult of today the obvious wears a heavy veil.

Such thoughts necessarily flow from the letter, already quoted, that Viereck sent to me one day in a mood of extreme despondency. But that was not quite his feeling, nor an approximation of what he inwardly thought. A letter to William Ellery Leonard is much more representative, for it is only natural that his deepest truths should spring from a contemplation of his lifelong association with Leonard and Ludwig Lewisohn. Within a comparatively short while a little book about Lewisohn was published and volumes about Leonard and Viereck were projected, the various biographers consulting each of the three men and, in two instances, each other. Viereck was asked by Clara Leiser, Leonard's would be biographer, for the letters that Leonard had written to Viereck in the past. Out of a sense of delicacy, Viereck asked his old friend if it was agreeable to oblige Miss Leiser. He first said that he was not sure where the letters might be found but then confessed that he might know where they were but was afraid of the emotional disturbance that might result from examining old and dusty files; afraid, too, of the indecision created by the struggle to retain many things which perhaps should have been destroyed.

"I realize that some of our correspondence has been superficial," he wrote to Leonard.

> I have always felt that I did not need to correspond with you; that whenever we met we would completely understand each other; that we could always begin where we left off. Also at various times my bosom contained much perilous stuff, with which I did not want to burden you, since you had already too many burdens of your own. I have often sent you clippings, etc., not because they were intrinsically important, but merely to tell you that I am still there, that I still love you, and I am still deeply interested, also perhaps still deeply interesting.
>
> The reason why you are still a poet and I have ceased to be one is that you take the things that happen to you more seriously than I take the things that happen to me. May be my shell is harder; may be I am more shallow, or may be I am so complex, that the various forces in me balance each other, and so create the illusion that there is no emotional ferment.
>
> I wish I could love anyone as deeply as you do, but I am incapable of such love, perhaps because I have fallen out of love with myself. I am Narcissus, who at the age of 50 discovers the bald spot on the back of his head and the increased curvature of his stomach. May be the world would still enchant me, if I were not completely disenchanted with myself.
>
> There was a time when I seemed to be Antinuous, Hadrian, Narcissus, Don Juan, Casanova, Catullus, a young God, slim, passionate,

golden-haired, desired by all and desiring all; forever young, forever in love with himself, until the mirror told me that I was mistaken. I did not cease to be desired, but I ceased to desire.

The fear of such a thing pursued me long ago when I was still in the twenties (see "Iron Passion"). I realized that what matters was not any love given to me, but my own inability to love others, or to love deeply even myself.

There was also the fear of approaching age, which I expressed when I was nearly thirty, in my sonnet "Antinuous at Forty," and in the phrase which appears somewhere in "The Candle and the Flame"—"After Thirty Nothing Matters."

In the last stanza of "The Three Sphinxes" I have told my fate:

> And lo, the spring's breath faded from Love's charm,
>   The sunshine from his hair,
> And in his arm
>   The arrows turned to rods.
>   He heeded not the silent years that crawl
>   Like uncouth spiders. Weary, cynical,
>   Self-conscious, disenchanted stood he there,
>   The oldest and the saddest of the gods.

It was George Sylvester Viereck who spoke, not Eros, but when I wrote that poem I was still a God, albeit the oldest and the saddest. Today I am no longer God, but a rather tired mortal, to whom life offers nothing, except at best mild amusement.

I had many great other shocks. The first when I discovered that I was not the greatest genius that ever lived. The second shock: that I was not even the greatest American poet; perhaps not even a great poet at all.

I became the spokesman of fair play for Germany. I fought and lost the World War. Then I became an interpreter of great men and a philosopher of tolerance and understanding. Subsequently I discovered that I probably knew nothing at all about great men, or about great philosophers, and my world clashed between my instinctive affection for Germany and my affection for philosophy and tolerance.

The final shock was financial. I thought I was independently rich, or at least well-to-do. Then came the depression and swept away all my reserves. I am today poorer than I ever was in my life. When I was born, it is true, I had nothing, but at least I had no debts. Today I am weighed down by obligations and have debts; hence I may say that I have less than nothing. Die schone Welt ist zerstort!

But at least I have the fragments of dead dreams and dead loves, and here and there an understanding soul like you.

It is quite possible, though not likely, that Viereck was play-acting, without realizing it, when he wrote to his old friend in such terms of disillusionment. The letter is added proof that there is no sorrier game than that of self-amusement. It is an insult really to the spirit of an age which is largely tragic and certainly deeply serious. The hedonist in a day like ours is an obscene anachronism from the social viewpoint and becomes fit for the deepest circle of hell. One hopes, therefore, that Viereck assumed his customary hedonistic attitude through the utter weariness or disgust that often result from a tense and serious contemplation of life. One looks at a mad world, hears the gibber of idiots, and seeks refuge in the sanctuaries of the mind. Hedonism, so-called, is often only another name for a brave front. Was it so in Viereck's case?

Once in conversation Viereck insinuated part of the answer in the form of a useful figure of speech. He is, he said, the strangest tree in the arboreal kingdom. One season his branches bear scarlet flowers, phallic lilies, all of the blossoms of passion. The next season the gorgeous flowers of love are gone and in their place is Dead Sea fruit. Another season rolls by, and this time swastikas peep ominously from all of the branches. Thus throughout the years the tree brings forth each season something different. The chief difficulty with this is the unpredictability of the yield. It is often enough to cause the observer to give up in bewildered disgust. Instead of saying, "Perhaps the tree will yet bring forth fruit pleasing to my senses," the one who contemplates the exhibition is likely to turn away petulantly. This accounts for some of the disillusionment on Viereck's own part and for the extreme variations on the theme of the man played by his friends and foes.

It is profitable to summarize the diverse views and perhaps build a harmonic picture out of them. The reflections from a thousand twisted mirrors may converge and become one clear impression.

The very shrewd father of individual psychology, Alfred Adler, had much to say of Viereck. To him Viereck was a good species of the pampered child. The only son in the household of very kind and well-educated parents, his half-brother having left home, Viereck did not miss the experience of being singled out, Adler said. Because of his mental progress in childhood, he was burdened by himself and by others with too great expectations. "His admiration of outstanding men of very different qualities is surely the outcome of his worshiping his own singularity as he has seen it," Adler suggested. His philosophical outlook toward life was necessarily that the world should be a playground for a few selected persons to whom should be granted the obedience and the submission of the others. In short, Viereck suffered from a high-brow, aristocratic attitude, and only the kindness he received in childhood gave him the patience to listen to views in opposition to his own. His real aim was to evade the problems of life. "He finds it hard to be bothered with competition or with disadvantages common to us all." He preferred the companionship of older men of accomplishment, who gave him the impression that they were hailing him as an equal. The danger he automatically faced was that he was too prone to accept views merely because they had strongly aroused the interest of a part of his generation. He resented growing old and coming nearer to death. The thought that life might go on without him, that he might no longer be with those who are in the limelight, scared him. He was rich in concrete examples and comparisons. He had an imagination that contrasted the old with the new; that was, indeed, more ready to look backward than forward. And he was essentially Teutonic in culture.

The renowned European physician, Professor Johann Plesch, who attended several of the crowned heads of Europe and, incidentally, once saved Viereck's life, came to conclusions that were in some respects similar to Adler's.

Of the dead and of journalists one should speak well or else remain silent, Professor Plesch said. Plesch thought of Viereck as essentially artistic in nature and, as such, capable of vicarious experience. Sparkling in all colors, he might become in a trice the very one on whom he had concentrated his thoughts. Such a spirit cannot be logical; for logic is the privilege of profoundly boring philosophers. A philosopher may wait a hundred years to attain his just rank, but a journalist must be heard at once, even at the cost of truth and personal convictions. From the journalist's buzz saw fall chips on friends and foes, but they are not to be taken seriously, for they turn lightly with the wind. So Viereck's successes and failures were not to be measured quantitatively. As the breeze rose, so would his worshippers and his opponents; now one group would be louder, then the other.

In the finely split personality of Viereck, Plesch was most sympathetic with his struggle against old age, his playing at hide and seek with the eternal laws of nature. Viereck simply did not acknowledge the rights of nature, Plesch said. He felt that he had to resist the inevitable pull from the cradle to the grave; he disregarded all that reminded him of disintegration and death. Against such naivete, Plesch stood powerless; he did not want Viereck to open his eyes and see his aging figure in the mirror. He preferred that Viereck not live his real life but reside in his phantasies.

Dr. Wilhelm Stekel regarded Viereck chiefly as a lyric poet who could have become preeminent had it not been for his too many interests. In Stekel's phrase, Viereck split himself. He should never have written books in collaboration with others. His was an extraordinary talent and a fascinating personality who did not reach his potential genius perhaps because he was a neurotic with inner restraints.

Another great psychoanalyst, Dr. A. A. Brill, said that he always thought Viereck a man of broad vision, but the stand Viereck took on Hitlerism convinced Brill that Viereck was "a very neurotic personality, too tied to the past to see beyond very small horizons." Brill, too, was impressed chiefly by Viereck's personality, the psychological insight of his writings, his versatile interests.

Viereck's "staying power" as an object of controversy might be best illustrated by the response I received from a former friend of mine and Viereck's, a writer of distinction and a man apparently of the broadest tolerance, who excommunicated me with awful oaths when he learned of my preoccupation with Viereck. His farewell letter, telling me to scratch his name off my list of friends, landed upon me with the vicious impact of a triphammer, numbing my power of thought at the time.

> Your letter about the proposed life of Viereck filled me with loathing. Some Christians turn the other cheek. And you—a Jew, a liberal!—*lick* the other cheek, and not of the face.
>
> What is there in this turncoat's life to write about? His betrayal, not only of the Jews, but of every liberal impulse? His sale of self to the highest bidder? His lying? His treachery to his friends? Couldn't you have left that job to some Nazi pederast? . . .
>
> There are laboratories where dung is examined and reported upon. Take your proposed life to one of these laboratories, and at the same time, visit some friendly psychiatrist.
>
> You have my sincerest condolences for something that must have died in you, and still remains without burial. The putrefaction rises to your brain and suggests such biographies as the one you plan. . . .
>
> Your purpose in life should be higher than to go around cleaning toilets.

And across the questionnaire I had sent him, he wrote, in large letters of scarlet, a single word: "SHAME!"

This friend said, in a second letter, that even to write an attack upon Viereck was to elevate him to undue prominence and to solicit information from him was to sink to the lowest level of self-degradation. This righteous man was not alone in hoisting me on the spear of his contempt, but there were some who went to the other extreme in their attitude towards Viereck, placing him in a beau role that was almost too pretty for comfort. If there were some ready to roast Viereck, there were others more ready to toast him.

I recall a carefully sealed letter I once received from an intimate friend of Viereck's. The letter was marked "private and confidential," and I was sworn to secrecy about its contents. Do not draw a picture of Viereck as a Don Juan or as any sort of unconventional person, the letter warned me. Hush! He is a faithful husband who loves his family and vaunts the scholarly prowess of his sons! The writer begged me not to tell Viereck his traitorous opinion of his good qualities, for he seemed to feel that Viereck joyed in a self-drawn picture of a swashbuckler of many carefully cultivated vices.

Is it not possible that Viereck's self-drawn picture of himself as a man of many sins was accepted too readily, much to the man's hurt, just as he too often created mystery where none existed? The same friend who threw moldy vegetables at me cited, in support of his low opinion of Viereck, an alleged statement by Viereck that he aspired to be the greatest poet and at the same time the greatest scoundrel of his age. Viereck was neither the greatest poet nor the greatest scoundrel. His sins were generally not individual misdeeds but socially reprehensible acts, which were, of course, far worse. Some thought that a purely Marxian summing up might produce the nearest thing to a definitive statement.

To that end, an active Communist read the first draft of the book and offered suggestions. The man's devotion to the communist cause was vouchsafed by the many times he had sojourned in prisons throughout the country during his struggle against "the ruling class." In the quiet of his cell he read the manuscript dealing with a life so different from his own, and passed judgment. What follows is a free rendering of a left-wing interpretation.

Unlike my former friend who excommunicated me with awful oaths when he learned of my preoccupation with Viereck, my friend of the left found nothing wrong with the choice of subject. A writer has the privilege, he said, nay, the right, to choose whichever subject appeals to him, and in considering a human being like Viereck, or any other writer, one must fit him into his times. In what section of society did he move? What social conditions prevailed? Whose viewpoint did he assimilate by virtue of his mode of life? It will be seen that Viereck's extreme individualism was the logical effect of a society where individualism for the few on top is made into a categorical imperative, a divine right based on a denial of individualism and freedom to the many. Viereck's life, the evolution of his views, will be seen, if examined carefully, as quite similar, by and large, to those of other writers in his circle. Their outlook was essentially a counterfeit of those rugged individualists, Morgan, Ford, Hoover, Hearst, and Raskob. As social conditions change, as capitalism goes into its world crisis, as the revolt of the masses becomes more widespread, as fascism becomes an attractive way of preserving the rule of the privileged few, then the hangers-on of the wealthy class become more outspoken in their hatred of communism. Viereck was only typical in this respect.

Viereck should be portrayed in such a way, said my radical friend, so that the reader will grasp clearly his antisocial nature. To portray him merely as an interesting figure is not only not enough—it is harmful. Let us phrase the matter otherwise. A medical man is absorbed in the study of a cancerous growth. He notices, with mounting enthusiasm, the intimate details of the malignancy. What if he should, in his excitement, attempt to yank the cancerous limb from the living person while exclaiming, "What a specimen! I'm going to preserve it in alcohol." One would deem him mad as a March hare, despite his learning and zeal. One should not, then, view Viereck simply as a fascinating specimen, though he is that. Each chapter of a book about Viereck, my friend concluded, should be a subtle condemnation of him and his ideas as well as of the system which fosters men like him.

Does this book satisfy the left-wing ideal? Should it? One looks at the thousand twisted mirrors which strive to reflect Viereck. A glaring light confronts each, so dazzling in intensity as to become audible. One seems to hear a shriek of dismay at the very thought of converging the mirrors. One must conclude that Viereck, being an extraordinary human being, was no one personality to be summed up in one of the glib phrases, but a figure split into a thousand fragments. This book attempts to assemble the fragments. The moral tags are only incidental.

Even so, one is constrained to end on a moral note. One is inclined to nod one's head, oracularly, and say that Viereck's story was that of a man who would have everything and give little in repayment. He would have fame and fortune and all of the fine fruits of genius. He would spin a web of luxury about himself, though it prove to be a trap for himself and for others. True, he wanted to live in an atmosphere of beauty and inspiration and song, and was willing that choice spirits share his couch in paradise. But he was unwilling to pay the price. He was unwilling to believe that heaven asks much, especially of a nympholept of beauty. Much as he loved the spirit, he would not sacrifice anything of the flesh. To him the fleshpots of Babylon meant more than any insubstantial vessel of divine moonbeams. A dreamer like Vachel Lindsay might go about in imperial America as a mendicant, exchanging wisps of beauty for bread. Viereck could never do that; his Odyssey was that of a regal barbarian. When the world was a generation or two younger, Lindsay traveled afoot in the East, visiting only the lowly and preaching to them his gospel of beauty; he told the story humbly in *A Handy Guide For Beggars*. At the same time Viereck went abroad splendidly. He saw the great ones of the earth and had much milk and honey in the banquet halls of the mighty; he wrote of his rich experiences exultantly in his *Confessions of Barbarian*. One need not measure the respective artistic heights of the two men in order to conclude that Viereck's failure in life as well as in letters was that he had none of the self-denying, world-abetting spirit of the Franciscan monk; he would not pay for the beauty and the grandeur given to him so prodigally by the Lords of Earth and of Heaven.

> All I have wrought and praying wrought so well,
> Disturbs the iron chorus of the spheres
> No more than beating of a sounding brass,
> Or the thin tinkle of a leper's bell.

POSTSCRIPT

As with so much else about his life, what befell George Sylvester Viereck in the years following the events recorded earlier in this volume may be told on three discrete levels: the official reports of his criminal cases in the United States courts; a simple autobiographical narrative called, somewhat melodramatically, *Men Into Beasts;* and some poetry of a quality not attained by Viereck since his golden youth. These might be described as the objective, or factual; the subjective, or personally predisposed; and the creative, which transcends all that one might justly criticize.

Following his first conviction in the United States District Court in the city of Washington for violation of the federal Propaganda Agency Act, Viereck appealed, unsuccessfully, to the United States Court of Appeals for the District of Columbia. Fred Vinson, who later became the Chief Justice of the United States, wrote the unanimous opinion, a rather lengthy one of almost twenty printed pages, for the reviewing court on September 21, 1942. According to this opinion, Congress had passed a law in 1938, during the height of the furor here over Nazi propaganda, requiring "political" agents of foreign principals to register with the State Department and to keep such registration up to date with supplemental statements semiannually. Viereck had registered and filed supplemental statements. It was charged that in three of the supplemental registrations he had willfully omitted material facts, a crime under the law. A jury had convicted him, which presumably meant that he was guilty beyond a reasonable doubt of all material elements of the offense. Viereck claimed that many prejudicial errors had been committed at the trial, but as Justice Vinson observed, there was no contention of the general insufficiency of the evidence, and, according to the judge, no such contention could be made. So if the conviction were reversed, it would have to be on purely legal grounds rather than on factual considerations.

Viereck contended that he had properly filled in one inquiry as to the nature of his business by declaring himself simply an author and journalist. Viereck objected, too, to the forced exclusion of one of his attorneys from the trial and to misconduct on the part of the prosecution. The defense brief claimed other errors of law and procedure, several of them quite technical and not impressive to the reviewing court. That tribunal felt that the law required the revelation of the details of agreements and activities, not merely the sort of generalized conclusion set forth by Viereck. The trial court had instructed the jury that the law required the registrant to reveal all of his political activities, whether or not he was acting as an agent for a foreign principal in connection with those activities.

At great length and in astonishing detail Justice Vinson analyzed each jot and tittle of the Propaganda Agency Act, as amended, and concluded that the government prosecutors and the trial court were right in their interpretation of the statute's requirements and that Viereck was wrong. Viereck should have revealed that he was more than simply "author and journalist." He should have revealed the full extent of his work as "a very active propagandist." Viereck had registered as an agent for two foreign principals, the Munich Newspapers and The German Library of Information. He did not disclose his direction and control of Flanders Hall, a publishing company interested in political subjects. He did not disclose that he had organized and been active in three similar political groups: Make Europe Pay War Debts, Islands for War Debts, and, possibly, War Debts Defense. Nor did he disclose his help in the preparation of a deceased United States senator's views on political topics. Finally, he did not disclose his assistance in disseminating the political views of various congressmen. These views, the court said, coincided with his own views and "those of his foreign principals from whom he was receiving a large income."

As to each of these omissions from the required registrations, Justice Vinson entered into great detail as to the entangling facts revealed by the evidence adduced at the trial and concluded that they showed willful violation of the law. The court made much of Viereck's book *Spreading Germs of Hate,* introduced into evidence by the prosecution over Viereck's objection. The court gave a somewhat unflattering assessment of the book as proof that Viereck knew his way in the tangled web of propaganda. Even where there might have been doubt about evidence or the examination of witnesses, the court resolved the doubt against the defendant, despite the usual presumption of innocence. The court concluded: "The asserted errors concerning the procedures at the trial either are nonexistent or appear small and nonprejudicial in their proper perspective. It is clear that we should affirm."

Less than two months later, on November 16, 1942, an unusually short time, the Supreme Court of the United States granted a petition for the review of the case on most of the issues. On February 1 and 2, 1943, the case was argued before the highest court. The court reversed the conviction and ordered a new trial. Chief Justice Stone, a man distinguished for his punctilious regard for constitutional rights, wrote the opinion of the highest court. Justices Jackson and Rutledge took no part in the consideration or decision of the case. The great liberals, Justices Black and Douglas, dissented from the opinion, feeling that the conviction should be sustained.

The Court held that the Foreign Agents Registration Act, before amendment in 1942, required and authorized the Secretary of State to require of registrants a statement of only those activities which were carried out in behalf of foreign principals. Because the jury had been instructed that the political activities of the defendant had to be reported in statements to the Secretary of State even if they did not pertain to his foreign principals, the conviction had to be reversed. The Court did not imply, in any way, that Viereck had not engaged in unreported political activities. So far as the majority of the Court was concerned, it was a question of exactly what the statute required. The Court added, by way of further warning: "As the case must be remanded to the district court for further proceedings, we direct attention to conduct of the prosecuting attorney which we think prejudiced petitioner's [Viereck's] right to a fair trial, and which independently of the error for which we reverse might well have placed the judgment of conviction in jeopardy."

Justices Black and Douglas believed that the statute under which Viereck was charged, tried, and convicted was reasonably susceptible to the interpretation given in the jury instruction which the majority of the Court found to be in error. They analyzed the statute carefully and came to a different conclusion; but while they shared the Chief Justice's concern for prosecutorial fairness, they indicated or at least implied that they did not regard Viereck's prosecution as unfair." . . . Earnestness or even a stirring eloquence cannot convict him of hitting foul blows." They stressed: "The jury found, and it is not questioned here, that the petitioner [Viereck] was a paid German propagandist engaged in various business activities, in all of which he made use of the same kinds of propaganda calculated to further the interests of Germany in the United States."

So Viereck had to go to trial once again; and once more he was convicted on six counts for violations of the penal provisions of the Foreign Agent's Registration Act; and once more he appealed to the United States Court of Appeals for the District of Columbia. On January 10, 1944, that court affirmed the conviction in an opinion that made quick work, this time, of all of Viereck's contentions. The court professed to find support for its ruling in the very opinion, written by Chief Justice Stone, reversing the former conviction, and it referred approvingly to what Justice Vinson had written sustaining Viereck's conviction in the earlier Court of Appeals case. "If, perchance, there was error in one or more of the trial court's rulings on evidence which we have just discussed (which we emphatically deny), we still feel, under the record in this case, that any such error was nonprejudicial and so inconsequential that in no event would it justify a reversal at our hands of the judgment below."

Again Viereck petitioned the Supreme Court of the United States for a writ to review the case. This time, his funds having been completely used up in the course of the protracted litigation, he asked for leave to proceed as a pauper, in which case he would not have to pay the costs. This motion the Court granted. At the same time, on March 27, 1944, the Court denied the petition for leave to appeal. The case was at an end, and Viereck once again had the prison doors shut upon him, a wretched end, it would seem, to a career that had begun with a measure of glory if not grandeur.

In this case just discussed Viereck alone was tried twice, and there were four appeals to the higher courts before the matter was resolved by his serving time in prison. But this case, complicated and costly as it was, represented only the beginning of his legal woes. On July 24, 1942, he was indicted by a District of Columbia grand jury which had been reviewing the matter and hearing evidence for a year under the tutelage of the same United States attorney who was declared to have struck "foul blows" when Viereck was first tried alone. Indicted with Viereck were twenty-eight assorted defendants, including isolationists, anti-Communists, anti-Semites, Nazis, Bundists, Fascists, rabble rousers, and others, all charged with violations of the sedition and conspiracy sections of both the Espionage Act of 1917 and the Smith Act of 1940. A second indictment was voted approximately six months later, on January 4, 1943, by a second grand jury. Then, on February 7, 1943, William Power Maloney was removed as special assistant in charge of this sedition case, and O. John Rogge was appointed in his stead. This was followed by a third indictment which removed twelve defendants named in the original indictments and added eight new defendants. Viereck was included in all three indictments. In the third indictment his co-defendants included Joseph E. McWilliams, Lawrence Dennis, Gerhard Wilhelm Kunze, Gerald Winrod, Herman Max Schwinn, William Dudley Pelley, Elizabeth Dilling, Elmer J. Garner, Ellis O. Jones, Robert Noble, and several others, all known, in varying degrees, for their opposition in various forms to America's participation in the war. Some were creatures crawling out of the woodwork, others like Lawrence Dennis and Viereck were considerable persons.

It is doubtful that there was any defendant, certainly not Viereck, who knew or worked with all of the other defendants. In a conspiracy case it is not necessary that the parties know each other. It is enough to prove beyond a reasonable doubt that they were each involved, in some material way, in a common criminal undertaking and that overt acts were committed.

Regardless of the merits of a gigantic conspiracy case, the government courts trouble for itself when it proceeds with such a case if the defendants and their attorneys are resourceful and determined. Confusion, if not chaos, is a certainty. In this case there was confusion compounded. In the end, after months of what passed for a trial, most of those who had favored the indictments were appalled by how the case was working out. Months were consumed in presenting evidence; there were motions of all kinds, good and bad; there was every kind of tactic intended to make it difficult, if not impossible, to convict or to sustain a conviction. Only in an American political trial can there be such bedlam. Finally, the presiding judge died. His health had not been improved by the case. After his death, the government made a special effort to bolster its case by sending Mr. Rogge to Germany for an investigation of records of the Third Reich. Nothing helped. The case was ultimately dropped.

Viereck and the others were free at last to pick up the pieces of their broken lives and to see if they could put them together. Viereck certainly tried to do so and more nearly succeeded than the others. In a very real sense, the meaning of his existence was lost because of his various legal travails and their causes. He spent the balance of his life trying to justify himself. True, he also tried to carry on the profession of letters and, at times, succeeded rather well; but, in the end, he was thwarted, defeated, and cast down beyond repair. Most people felt that this result was preordained and deserved.

Thus far I have tried to avoid the jargon of the courts in my presentation of Viereck's legal difficulties, but my account necessarily has a technical cast that does not stir the emotions. Viereck was able to write in his own behalf with a clarity and seeming sincerity that could be persuasive if one forgot the basic truth of the situation. I will digress for a moment to tell that truth as I saw it contemporaneously with these events.

For a considerable period of time, Viereck and I had corresponded. Sometimes, we were in almost daily communication. We exchanged hundreds of letters, and we saw each other on many occasions. I knew him, his wife, his children, and some of his friends with a degree of intimacy. I read everything available by and about him. I did all of the many things that I have recited in the early pages of this book. I wrote the bulk of my book relying upon what I had learned. Then a process of disillusionment set in, slowly at first, then swiftly.

For some years we did not write or visit each other, partly because for much of this period Viereck was in prison. My natural compassion would have caused me to correspond with him and even to show sympathy. I do not believe in trampling upon the downtrodden. I wrote bitterly about him for what I thought would be the last time in an article for the winter 1944-45 issue of *The Chicago Jewish Forum*, a very fine literary and political journal published by my unique friend, Benjamin Weintroub. I decided to drive home my meaning by considering Viereck in the light of his long-time relationship with the Yankee born poet, scholar, linguist, and phobic William Ellery Leonard, who had just died, and the Berlin-born Jewish author and critic par excellance, Ludwig Lewisohn. Appropriately, I called the article "A Bizarre Fellowship." After telling of the origins and development of the friendship between three highly diverse creatures, I concluded:

> Lewisohn, in the thrall of work, can forget anybody; and Viereck, a prisoner to his overwhelming ego, has cast a dark shadow over the old association. Yet it affords a clue to the disgrace into which the Wonder Child has fallen. Viereck, the Nazi propagandist, is the same clamorous exhibitionist who first greeted Leonard in 1902. Having failed to receive continuously the desired notice and compensation through literature,

Viereck turned to other fields of endeavor. Their baseness did not deter a spoiled brat who felt contempt for the petty strivings of others. It is a tragic story that will some day be told in its proper perspective when Viereck and his precious Nazi paymasters are ground into dust.

But part of the story should be sketched now in order to invite the later full chronicle. Not long after the appearance of his little volume of German verse, Viereck's first work in English was published by Brentano: a slender book of sensuous exotic plays. Then appeared a book of lush rolling verse called *Nineveh*. No poet since Byron created so great a sensation over night. Today it is difficult to believe that all over America the young poet was talked about and praised by such diverse characters as the President of the United States, the bellowing Teddy Roosevelt, and the discerning critic, James Huneker. Viereck was looked upon as the leader of a poetic renascence. He was lionized, and he strutted about as if the acclaim would last forever. But almost as soon as he reached the heights, his descent began. By 1914 it was clear that other literary voices were gaining ascendancy over his: Sandburg, Lindsay, Masters, Millay, half a dozen others. It was then, for the first time, that he became the sinister spokesman for warring Germany. He was a founder and editor of *The Fatherland*, the uncompromising defender of the Teutonic cause. Again there was notoriety, excitement, money, the deceptive indicia of success. After the Armistice, Viereck remained for a time a literary outcast. It was bitter gall for a man of his immodest temperament. Then in collaboration with Paul Eldridge he wrote a series of novels about the Wandering Jew. There were elements of greatness in the series; but it was obvious by the time the third volume appeared that Viereck had written himself out. The creative impulse was becoming feebler. Hitler came to the rescue of the jaded artist who forever sought superexcitation. Once more he became the agent of a marauding German government. By now it could mean only moral collapse, an end to any semblance of righteousness. The bizarre fellowship of Viereck, Leonard, and Lewisohn was at an end.

Later, Viereck's son Peter said that this essay of mine had given him greater insight into his father than anything he had ever read; and peevishly, Viereck inquired why this should be so. Eventually Viereck, too, found much to admire in my essay while not agreeing, of course, with its bitter conclusion.

It is only fair that we return now to Viereck's defense of himself as expressed in his little book *Men Into Beasts,* first published in 1952 by Fawcett, a leading paperback book publisher, and sold by the thousands in several printings as such books are wont to do. If Viereck thought the book would restore him to popular esteem, he was doomed to disappointment, as he probably surmised in his more perceptive moments. Viereck had risen to renewed fame and prosperity after the First World War despite the toll taken by his propaganda activities. He had had a

rebirth as a journalist and serious writer. Leading publishers like Hearst, Macfadden, and Oursler sought him out. But he had not yet gone to prison, and he was
young and of a resillient nature. Now he had the bar sinister of prison and the
handicaps of age, ill health, and lack of funds. He had other handicaps, too, of a
more subtle nature. After all, Imperial Germany was not Nazi Germany. Defending the Kaiser was more forgivable than praising Hitler. Still, *Men Into Beasts* left
the impression that Viereck was confident, courageous, and able once more to
overcome.

The book was republished in hard cover in 1955 by another famous prison
inmate, Samuel Roth, who professed great admiration for Viereck and gave him
the opportunity to express himself in verse and prose. Roth went to prison again on
federal obscenity charges because of his magazine, *American Aphrodite,* in which
Viereck had a place of refuge and publication. The latter Roth case resulted in the
landmark decision on obscenity in which the Supreme Court affirmed the right of
the states and the federal government to punish for that offense, which it tried
unsuccessfully, it should be said, to define. Viereck's association with Roth was a
natural one. Both had an affinity for writing about scarlet sins, as well as normal
human sexual appetites. Roth wrote an eloquent publisher's introduction to *Men
Into Beasts,* declaring that he was presenting the book ''as the humble and sincere
testament of an authentic artist, living under intolerable duress.''

I have the very first copy of the book that came off the press—so, at least, a
note by Viereck, dated February 18, 1955, proclaims. It is from this edition that I
quote Viereck's introduction as the best summary of the book as well as Viereck's
own judgment on his legal travails:

> FOR ALMOST FIVE YEARS I was Uncle Sam's involuntary
> boarder in the District Jail, Washington, D.C.; in Atlanta, Georgia; and
> in Lewisburg, Pennsylvania. Atlanta is a preserve for hardened crimi-
> nals and repeaters—''recidivists.'' Lewisburg, on the other hand, is
> sometimes jestingly dubbed a ''gentleman's country club.''
>
> The District Jail is a cross between an ordinary jail for minor
> offenders and a full-fledged penitentiary. Its turnover is enormous. Some
> of its guests stay only a few days; others, like myself, spend years behind
> its walls. Still others are whisked away to eternity on its electric chair.
>
> In the present volume I have described life in prison from the
> inside. I have written the truth as I experienced it. I wish to hurt no one,
> least of all the men whom society regards as its debtors. To protect them,
> I have altered appearances, changed names, and juggled dates. Aside
> from such devices and inevitable occasional lapses of memory, my tale
> is authentic. The incredible things I describe are true. They really
> happened.
>
> It may seem surprising that many inmates revealed their most
> guarded secrets to me. Reticences are apt to fall by the wayside in the
> enforced intimacy of jail. Boredom makes prison life one long bull

session. Men talked to me frankly because they were sure that I would listen to them without prejudice. I could not have won the esteem of men like Havelock Ellis, the foremost pioneer of sex knowledge in England, Magnus Hirschfeld, head of the Institute fuer Sexual Wissenschaft in Berlin, Sigmund Freud, explorer of the dynamics of sex in the unconscious, and Alfred Kinsey, who stripped away the hypocritical pretenses with which we Americans attempt to conceal the facts of life from ourselves, if I could not look truth in the face without blush or snicker.

In the pages that follow I shall say little about my own trial. I was accused of violating an obscure subsection of the booby trap called the Foreign Agents Registration Act. I was compelled to register because I worked for a foreign principal, the German Library of Information. It is perfectly normal for great powers like England, France, Italy, to maintain information centers abroad. There was nothing sinister in my connection. In accordance with the law, I registered not only once but three times. My contract specifically exempted me from any involvement with the Nazi Party and its doctrines. It clearly stated that I would engage in no activity incompatible with my duties as an American citizen. When the cold war of the Administration threatened to embroil us in actual warfare, I severed all my German contacts, including my lucrative employment by the Library. That was months before Pearl Harbor.

My sworn statement was carefully prepared by two competent attorneys. The statute in question was so badly drawn that it had to be rewritten three times by Congress to make it intelligible. According to some quirk in the law I was not permitted to prove that four hundred of five hundred registrants had made the same mistake as I did (if mistake it was).

My case had been assigned to Federal Judge T. Alan Goldsborough. The Government forced him to withdraw by threatening to charge him with "bias" against the Department of Justice. They preferred their own handpicked judge. Fulton Lewis, Jr., points out that this was probably the only precedent within a decade or so except for the Government's demand on Judge Luther Youngdahl to disqualify himself in the case of Owen Lattimore.

My constitutional rights were trodden underfoot. At the climax of my trial, the Judge arbitrarily deprived me of the attorney of my choice who was to sum up my case. The Supreme Court reversed the verdict of "guilty" on the ground that the Judge had made legal errors and that the Government had used "foul blows" against me. This is the language of the Court, not mine.

The ruthless treatment to which I was subjected elicited vigorous protest in the press and in the United States Senate. Taft, Wheeler, Langer, Nye and others excoriating the Department of Justice, hailed the decision of the Supreme Court. This infuriated sinister pressure groups within and without the administration. They determined to "get" me. Deprived of the counsel of my choice, impoverished by the expense of my first trial, I was "convicted" when war psychosis was at its height. I would not have been convicted if I had been able to engage the services of the brilliant attorney who won my case in the highest court in the land.

It may be of interest to note in this connection that the Supreme Court of Ohio, reinstating an attorney who had pleaded "guilty," declared that a violation of the act involved no "moral turpitude." It was merely an "administrative measure." Nevertheless I was incarcerated under harsh regulations with maladjusted individuals whom society regards as "common criminals." The conditions under which they serve their sentences tend to turn men into beasts. I was unable to secure parole because the same sinister elements who were responsible for my first indictment dragged me into the farcical Mass Sedition Trial, conducted on the model of Moscow. After three years and three inept indictments, the Sedition Trial was thrown ignominiously out of court.

Shortly after my release from prison, a letter came from George Bernard Shaw. "I say, G.S.V.," he wrote, "though you don't explicitly say so, I gather from your address that they let you out after five years. You seem to have stood it with extraordinary spirit. Most martyrs are duds."

I make no claims to martyrdom. I do not regret my years in prison. How else could I have met so many murderers, thugs, forgers, thieves, rapists, pimps, male prostitutes, drug addicts, and dipsomaniacs on terms of complete social equality? My incarceration has taught me much. It has widened the circle of my experience. I can well say with Terence, the great Roman playwright, "I am a man; nothing human is alien to me."

Viereck had a rebirth of his poetic skill during the years that he was in prison and afterwards. Poetry is said to be a young man's art. Certainly, Viereck was young enough, a mere child and then a youth, when he produced the verse that, for a time, made his name familiar to the general public as well as literary circles. Much of this early verse was deeply felt, much of it was a form of posturing, and sometimes it was a combination of both. Often there were elaborate displays of technical skill, and more than occasionally it was sincere, even spiritual and substantial. The experience of having his life catch up with him was unique to the extreme for Viereck. While on trial and in prison, he had to think through all that was happening to him and to those he loved. It was not enough to write prose pleas in self-defense. Something more was needed. He had to make something meaningful, lyrical, and enduring out of what he was going through. More often than might be supposed, he succeeded and proved that there was still some essence in him that was creative, cogent, and beautiful. The good and the bad were compartmentalized.

What he wrote was basically for himself. In a sense, he had to prove that he still felt deeply and could evoke images worthy of a considerable poet. He wrote sonnets, odes, and lyrics in various forms, simple and complex. Sometimes one could not be sure whether what he created was poetry or an elevated kind of doggeral. In any event it was highly readable, appealing, and forceful even to those who might be unsympathetic to the man who had created the verse.

There was the problem of publishing what he had written. At best, poetry is seldom a salable item. We generally give stones rather than solace and sustinance to poets. In Viereck's case it was doubly difficult. Who would dare to publish the poetic offerings of one who had sinned more than once, in ways that most Americans found unforgivable? Viereck was fortunate to find a sometime outcast and jailbird like himself, Samuel Roth, who republished *Men Into Beasts* after it had run its paperback life and devoted substantial parts of at least three issues of *American Aphrodite* to Viereck's prison poems. And later, in July 1958, a little magazine called the *Wisconsin Poetry Magazine* devoted its entire issue to some of these poems.

There were moving lines dedicated to his wife Gretchen. When the verses were composed, she was close to him. She was his window to the world, his shield against his tormentors. They clung to each other desperately. She was then in St. Luke's Hospital in New York. He wrote with simple conviction:

IF YOU HAD DIED
If you had died, beloved, there would be
No hope, no dream, no solace left for me.
The wells of song within me would have dried
    If you had died.

If you had died, I were indeed accurst,
No sop of hysop to assuage my thirst
Or stay my soul but newly crucified
    If you had died.

If you had died, my foeman would prevail,
Piercing at last my spirit coat-of-mail,
Me, stripped of valor and bereft of pride,
    If you had died.

In another poem he told of his prison companions and particularly one pal, combining the common speech of "cons" with the high exultant lyricism of true poets. It begins:

When the long night begins to taper
My cell is thronged with memories.
Where's Goldilocks? Where Joe the Raper,
Jakie the Goniff, where are these?

Dopey the Swineherd, Three Gun Harry
Who hides in prison from a shrew?
God knows in what far stir they tarry,
I miss them all but none like you.

Into my mental vision's brackets
Crowd pale-faced jailhouse cherubim,
Six Minute Maxie, Lord of rackets,
Curley the Redhead, Hepcat Jim,
And Jitterbug, joyrider merry,
Boss of the colored kitchen crew,
Who was more kind than mercenary,
Where are they gone? And where are you?

It ends:

When I paid you a stolen visit,
With what inimitable grace
You warmed for me the brew illicit
In an unhallowed fireplace.
The paltry tin cup was your chalice,
The coffee dregs your honeydew,
The filthy jug became a palace
Since for the nonce, it harbored you.

"Genius," said some, while others called you
"The master con-man of the can."
I knew: whatever had installed you
Behind these bars, you are a *man*.
And, erring knight or gay knight-errant,
You were my pal, my comrade true,
Steel walls and rods were no deterrent,
Straightway my hand reached out to you.

The longest of the prison poems is called Bastille, D.C. It is the hardest to
judge. It begins:

In Uncle Sam's D.C. Bastille
Black bean soup is a sumptuous meal,
A putrid apple is a prize;
We watch each bite with greedy eyes.
Bugs in the breakfast food are meat,
Stark hunger makes each mouthful sweet:
Mouldy potatoes, stews that stink,

The liquid offal that we drink—
They call it coffee in the clink.

The surly turnkey gives the sign,
The tincups rest. We fall in line.
With twisted smile, with grin that mocks,
We drop our tin-spoons in the box,
They clatter as we scurry by
Under the keeper's watchful eye.

It ends not quite convincingly:

Sam is the knight that bears the light,
His valiant armies' conquering might
Across six continents is hurled
To bring Four Freedoms to the world.
For distant cousins, brown of skin,
For Chinamen and Bedouin,
Sam's gallant Yankee legion fights,
But we, his children, have no rights
For though you prate men should be free,
In Uncle Sam's Bastille, D.C.
Your phony Freedoms will not jell.
And laughter splits the sides of Hell.

And there is the "Portrait of an Alley Cat," which tells us a good deal about
Viereck as well as his subject:

In some dim doorway, chance-begot,
Half cherub and half alley cat . . .
Phosphorous eyes that find their mark,
Like a young tiger's in the dark.
From mouth, like Cupid's curled to kiss,
Pour raucous curses, obscene hiss.
"F— you and f— the universe!"
You mutter as you snatch a purse.

A black cascade of boyish curls
Falls on your forehead like a girl's
With fag atilt and lips asneer,
You lay a broad or roll a queer.
The saucy dimple on your chin
Bespeaks no consciousness of sin,
And cross your face flits everywhile
Shyly a wayward angel-smile.

You never quail when blood is spilt,
In your quaint decalogue of guilt
There's one offense that spells disgrace,
"Rat on a pal"—and so lose face.
No cop, no court, no stir can quell
Your charming insolence. In Hell
You'd give the Devil tit for tat,
Tough cherub, winsome alley cat!

What I have here set forth is only a sampling of the prison verse that ought to be published one day as Viereck's only justification for his misspent years.

During his postprison years Viereck wrote two novels, one pseudonymously, the other under his proper name, neither a deathless masterpiece but both showing some of his old skills as a storyteller.

All Things Human was published in 1949 by Sheridan House in New York under the name Stuart Brent. It is almost 400 pages in length and deals with a protagonist named John Stuart Kent, described as a millionaire banker and aesthete. Kent experiences "all things human" in marital love, unsanctified love in various forms with girls, boys, men, and women, bouts between children and parents, business success and failure, a trial for murder, an imprisonment—everything good and bad that might befall a human being. In a sense it is much like Viereck's own speckled life. His hero, Kent, like himself, has known all forms of lubricity, success, and degradation. Viereck hoped the book would launch him into a new career crowned with success, even if he had to hide behind a name not his own.

The Nude in the Mirror, a shorter work than *All Things Human,* was published in 1953 by the nondescript Woodford Press. It was also published in a British edition. It was issued under his own name, and it made no appreciable impression. But he proved to himself that he could write once more if given the opportunity. What the book lacked most was the evocative and narrative skill of his one-time collaborator, Paul Eldridge. The ideas were all there, the luxurious setting, a parade of ancient and modern lovers, something of what had made the Wandering Jew series so successful. Viereck could not spell out the details. He created essentially a skeleton rather than a whole man, certainly not the richly human tapestry that distinguished *My First Two Thousand Years*.

In *The Nude in the Mirror* Viereck was eager to make it known that he was the one who conceived, in 1910 or 1911, and carried through with Eldridge, much later, the spirited saga. In an introduction he was almost as provocative as in the past. In the very first sentence he declared: "Critics will ridicule or ignore this book because it explodes the ramparts of masculine conceit." He said all that he could, almost shrilly, to arouse readership, but he failed, not necessarily because his book was lacking in quality. He failed largely because of the public anger that had brought him to trial and imprisonment.

Viereck will be remembered for neither of these novels. He deserves to be recalled for the prison poetry of which I have presented only an insufficient sampling here.

After a lapse in our correspondence for several years, Viereck sent me a letter dated August 15, 1947. Except for a failure to address me by my first name, a mere "Gertz" substituting for the more familiar greeting of earlier days, the letter was almost as cordial as if there had been no break in our relations. "In looking over my files I found some of your letters," he wrote by way of excuse for resuming the correspondence. "I am back, having lost everything except my sense of humor. I am not living with Gretchen who has become a Catholic, and serves the Church as Margaret the maid."

He was to say more on the departure of his wife as the correspondence progressed.

The effect of the time spent in prison? "I have not grown much older in jail, in fact, I recommend jail as a health resort to my friends." Apparently, I was still a friend in his mind, however tentatively. He offered to send me some of his poems, "if you are interested." He would welcome my reaction. And he wanted to learn about my children. He said nothing about my wife, Ceretta, although she had always been very kind to him, despite her distrust of him. He clearly held no brief for wives at the time. In spite of myself, I did not find the resumption of correspondence unwelcome.

In the next letter, dated August 26, he remonstrated that it was not necessary for me to tell him in every letter how much I despised him. "Incidentally, I am not yet a carcass." Much of the letter was written with the style and substance that had distinguished him in those years when he was at his best:

> I am greatly impressed by your Bizarre Fellowship. You have grown greatly in comprehension. Your psychological insight is more profound than when you first attempted to write my life. This does not mean that I necessarily agree with your interpretation. However it is perfectly true that craving for what you call super-excitement, rather than the profit motive, influenced my decisions.
>
> Gretchen, after giving away whatever money I left with her to Jewish refugee committees and the Catholic Church, deserted me completely more than three years ago. This left me without funds and without access to my papers and closed many avenues of communications. She was, at one time, while I was Mr. Roosevelt's prisoner, my window to the world. Before I was the God, now I am the Devil in her cosmos. My place has been taken by the Rev. John Oestreicher, himself a convert to Catholicism.
>
> Gretchen, I understand, puts on working clothes in the morning and goes to the rectory where she washes clothes, scrubs floors, and prepares food bought at her expense. She is known only as Margaret the Maid. At night, about ten o'clock, she slips home, puts on, I presume, her silk undies and her mink coat. The priest ruthlessly exploited her. He and her

psychiatrist, a Dr. Jacoby, completely dominate her life. She has not read a newspaper in three years, and does not listen to the radio, but goes to Mass every day. I would not be surprised if she were canonized by some Pope.

I bear her no ill-will, but would like to help her. If I had lived with her for the last five years, I would indeed be what you so gently called me—a carcass.

I have had some interesting talks with my son Peter and his wife. I have forgiven him the fact that he made me a grandfather before my time. Gretchen has broken with him too. The shock of [their son] George's death, my own misfortune, and the jealousy of the Moon has undoubtedly shattered her mind. She is now like a person possessed, no longer her own charming and considerate self.

He then suggested:

If you wish to finish your book about me, don't wait until I'm ground to dust. I am pretty well grounded now.

He said he would no longer impose any restrictions upon me. It was clear that he was almost excessively eager that I continue.

He concluded with both malice and insight:

I assume that the Anti-Defamation League and other terrorist bodies have already sharpened their knives to intimidate editors who might be interested in my work. I am surprised that the Jewish Forum printed your article, which strikes me as a little masterpiece, in its own fashion.

Give my love to young Tarzan [my son Ted] and to Marjorie [Margery]. All girls are potentially vixens. Did you ever read Lady Into Fox? It is about a man who thought he was married to a woman, and found he was married to a vixen. I never expect to go through that experience myself. Poor Gretchen, in her battered mental and emotional state, has told some malicious lies and half-truths about me. However, as I say in one of my poems, which I may send you after you recover from the initial shock:

Is this the scourge the Moon with malice sends
To hapless woman, when her summer ends?

On October 3, I got new insight into a somewhat changed man; once unsympathetic to blacks he now had the beginnings of understanding:

. . . I am entirely with you in your effort to bring about racial understanding. In former years I had no contacts whatsoever with our colored population. I met them only as elevator boys, hewers of wood, and drawers of water. Now and then I came across a Negro poet, but that was something else again. I shared the general American attitude of ignoring the problem—the policy of the ostrich. In the Chateau Roosevelt in Washington, known as the District Jail, I met a charming cultured colored lady. She was the secretary of Mr. Gill. It was she who encouraged me to write my novel and helped me in many ways. She opened my eyes to the fact that there is really no difference between us and them except the complexion.

I now have a colored secretary—a West Indian boy, who is not only efficient and loyal, but highly intelligent. He is a World War veteran and a Senior at City College. He is devoted to me and I am fond of him. The color question does not enter at all.

I hope you will succeed in your fight for civic rights, but that does not mean that the battle is won. Jews were Prime Ministers in England, and had an important share in the intellectual life in all Europe, but Anti-Semitism still persists. In fact it is now stronger than before Hitler—not only in Germany. Consequently I am afraid it will take hundreds of years, and maybe bloody revolution, or certainly a complete change of heart before the race questions are finally settled. Maybe that day will not come until the atom bomb throws our whole civilizaton into the discarded.

He declared that he was not an anti-Semite, that his Jewish and half-Jewish friends were once more friendly to him—all except Paul Eldridge, his collaborator in the Wandering Jew novels.

He recommended a book by Upton Close critical of the Anti-Defamation League. When I attacked the book, he wrote on October 30: "You have changed, but not for the better. Once you were a dispassionate critic of life. Now you are a partisan and a zealot."

I had said that the truth about him would kill him, and he responded: "Why should the truth kill me? Why do you want to kill me anyway?"

He told me of a "delightful letter" he had received from Bernard Shaw, then in his ninety-first year and almost as sharp as in his heyday. In his old impish spirit, Shaw wrote: "And so your lady threw you over! Take care—she may come back." Shaw had never deserted him. The old cynic was essentially generous hearted.

On February 17, 1948, he complained again: "Editors are still too terrified of the Anti-Defamation League to print anything of mine." It was a complaint that he was to repeat from time to time without offering proof of his charge.

On July 9, 1948, I received news of a volume of verse:

I am now completing a book of poems to be entitled "Laughter in Hell." I have written a preface of thirty pages, which explains my attitude and tribulations. I have also added an Appendix with legal documents etc. I would like to send it to you after it is completed if you have the time and goodwill to go over it carefully, and if you promise you will use nothing you may find in it against me directly or indirectly until the book is published. What you do afterwards is your affair. Now that I am completely separated from Gretchen, I care less about such things. I presume your portrait of me will change somewhat like the picture of Dorian Gray. "The marvelous boy who perished in his conceit" will become a brown shirted villain in your imagination.

He expressed a willingness, on July 28, to look at the poems of my son Ted, then twelve years old:

I shall see no stars of David dancing in his verse. There are no swastikas in mine. Of course we are doing everything in our power by our blundering policy to revive National Socialism. I suppose you heard the story of the man who appeared in a DeNazification court and announced that he was a Nazi. "You should have confessed this fact three years ago." "Ah," he answered, "three years ago, I wasn't a Nazi."

On August 10, he finally sent me the promised manuscript of his new volume of poetry, saying:

. . . Be as ruthless in your criticism of my literature as you are in your criticism of what you consider my politics. If any poems are weak or unworthy of me, they must go out. If the entire thing is not worth while, say so. I am too close to it to be able to judge.

As I delayed commenting on the poems, he grew increasingly impatient and wrote reminder after reminder. On September 21, he added an interesting bit of news: "Until a few days ago, I was still in what is called 'constructive custody,' now I am free." He seemed to be little inhibited earlier. He could hardly be less so now.

On September 28, he opined:

I know you are very busy and probably immersed in the Wallace campaign. I am with Wallace against war, but I am not with him in the appeasement of Soviet Russia and the slaughter of Germany. If I vote I will probably vote for Norman Thomas.

He was completely mistaken as to my political attitude but could hardly be pleased that I was for President Truman in that year of political miracles, 1948. Learning my views, he wrote on October 5:

I wouldn't vote for Truman or anyone else remotely connected with the New Deal. In fact I have not even registered even though I could do so. If

I voted at all it would be for Norman Thomas, although I have not got much enthusiasm even for him.

Around this time, October 29, he sent me his first photograph "since my release from the shackles of the New Deal," commenting that I did not "deserve it." All of this time, he was still calling me "Gertz" rather than anything more intimate.

Finally my long critique of his poems reached him, and he took my criticism seriously enough to comment upon it at great length in his letter of Armistice Day, 1948. He dismissed my loathing of some of his activities as simply a salve to my conscience. ". . . . You don't hate me in your heart," he said. Item by item, he took up my criticism of the individual poems, agreeing in part, disagreeing sometimes, striking a sort of poetic balance. One coment was of special interest to me:

> . . . In the Nuremberg poem, I admit the blood guilt of the various persons who were murdered by a travesty of justice—a lynching which we attempt in vain to legalize. I think that our action and the fortitude shown in the end by the men who were hanged, redeems them to a large extent—even the unspeakable Streicher. However you will note that I carefully restrained from making them saints in a Christian heaven, but opened for them only the Nordic Valhalla. There is only one line which partakes of a finality which I call great: "The rope is hallowed by a brave man's death."

On April 26, 1949, he informed me that he expected to be in Chicago in May for a few days. "You can then renew your admiration or detestation, or both." The trip did not take place at that time. Later I was to see him both in Chicago and in New York.

At last, on June 15, 1949, Viereck resumed the habit of calling me "Elmer" rather than "Gertz." Perhaps he had recalled the remark of his old literary idol, Oscar Wilde, that he was Oscar to his friends and Mr. Wilde to all others. Wilde was still on his mind as he wrote about the tragic and gay poet, both under his own name and pseudonymously, for Samuel Roth's haven, *American Aphrodite.*

At this time, too, Ludwig Lewisohn, his oldest friend, resumed writing to him, initially to comment on some of his poems, shown to Lewisohn by Peter Viereck. Viereck commented in his letter of July 19: "He was always my friend, even if he disagreed with me as violently as you did."

A considerable period of time elapsed—the balance of the year 1949, all of 1950, and much of 1951—before I heard from Viereck again. He had been quite ill, suffering from a cerebral vascular thrombosis. He thought it was, perhaps, a punishment for his many sins, which "do not include any prejudice against the Chosen People." In a letter, written on August 13, 1951, he said: "I sometimes describe myself as half blind in the right eye, half paralyzed on the left side and almost dead in center but that is an exaggeration." In fact, he never really improved in health. There seemed to be a steady decline in health, finances, and literary fame. As in the past, he distilled a sonnet out of his difficulties, calling it "In Contemplation of Dissolution":

> Death's messengers, as in the fairy tale,
> Knock at my body's ramparts day and night,
> My heart with ceaseless hammer-blows they smite,
> My pulses rush like racing steeds, then fail.
> Laboriously advancing to its goal
> My blood-stream grapples with obstreperous veins,
> My breathing falters, stabbed by obscure pains,
> And in my ears mad sextons tug and toll.
>
> I walked upon life's highway with the great.
> Fame gave me sprigs of her unwithering crown.
> Love kissed my mouth. Adventure was my mate.
> I spurned disaster and defied man's frown:
> Now half amused, half curious I await
> The final knell that rings the curtain down.

On September 5, 1951, he told of a visit to his son Peter, adding the unexpected sidelight: "I see Gretchen occasionally. In fact, we both visited Peter together, but we live apart and are apart except for memories of the past. She is still a Catholic and goes to mass every morning." And he sent a poem, not simply on bodily dissolution, but on finality, "Ode to Swift Death." After a rather lame start, the ode concluded with something of Viereck's old affrontery:

> Chase me not as a hunter to its lair
> Pursues the hare,
> But take me as a bridegroom takes his bride,
> Ere my loins shrivel and the years deride
> My pride's eclipse.
> While I am I, I welcome your embrace,
>
> But do not tarry, tarry overlong!
> Smite, while a smile still blazes on my face
> And on my lips
> A song!

Meanwhile, his old friend Bernard Shaw had died, and I commented in glowing terms on Shaw, whom I vastly admired. The admiration has grown with the years. Viereck commented on October 29, 1951:

Of course I agree with you about Shaw. He was, in spite of his monkeyshines and little poses, the greatest literary man of our generation and probably a greater playwright than Shakespeare. Of course Shakespeare is hallowed by tradition. Shaw deals with certain social problems of our own time. As a result some of his stuff seems dated. But not his great plays like Caesar and Cleopatra (his wife's favorite and mine), St. Joan and many others.

In the same letter he dwelt upon the possible publication of his poems, about which he was not cheerful:

> I could probably find a few people among my friends who would be willing to guarantee the publication of a book of poems or subscribe to a substantial number of copies in advance. But even that is difficult, largely because the people who like my lyric and erotic verse abhor my politics. On the other hand, those who are interested in my politics are not interested in my verse. Moreover both would be embarrassed by the audacity of some of the themes. If the poems should not be published before my demise, maybe you will find a way to have them appear in print. I cannot rely on Peter in this respect.

The last sentence was added in handwriting as a kind of sad afterthought.
Around this time he was expecting to see us. When we failed to appear, he sent a one sentence letter: "Elmer, where art thou and where is your Eve?"
His poems were still troubling him when he wrote to me on January 17, 1952:

> I presume you have given up the idea of coming here. There is something I would like to discuss with you. I have made a will dividing my very small estate between Peter's children, my wife and a nephew. I have left my manuscripts to Peter. This will include Jail Portraits or whatever title I choose to call them. There is a chance that they may be published within a year or two. But if they are not brought out by Peter within a year of my demise I would like you to have the right to publish them.

I was startled that, despite our vast differences, Viereck still thought of me in such trusting terms. As I valued his poetry more than his personality, I was pleased. Viereck returned again and again to the theme.
During this period of time he had been disposing of his letters, books, and other literary effects through a rather strange character whose views were much more slanted to Nazism than Viereck's views had been. My letters had been included, inadvertantly, Viereck claimed. He needed to get the financial means to live, he commented in a letter dated January 24, 1952, as significant for that reason as for his sorrow over his rather ambivalent relations with his surviving son:

> Another reason for disposing of pictures and letters was this. When my father died I casually looked over his stuff and overlooked important

letters from such people as Marx, Engels and Bebel. I am afraid the same fate would await my own correspondence. Peter is very busy and, like myself, rather impatient. He admires my poems, knows many of them by heart, remembers even passages that I have forgotten, but does not have the moral courage ever to refer to me or to them. It seems to me that historically, irrespective of the merit of my verse, I have a certain place in American literature. At any rate my son should not join the boycott against me. I know your position, but I also know your literary integrity, and that in spite of the paragraphs holding you secure against "defamation," you will not be brutal in your portrait of me. Incidentally if the case were reversed and if I were making a speech at the Poetry Society, as Peter will this month, I certainly would not ignore him.

In a postscript to the letter, he added: "Heine spoke of someone as being a young man with a great future—behind him. You can say that of me. Most of my work was done before the cataclysm."

Viereck, having much time to contemplate the wreckage of his life, often made shrewd and sometimes cynical comments about himself. Of special interest was a passage in his long letter of February 15, 1952:

I really have no political leaning whatsoever. I am interested in men, not in causes. My last political enthusiasm was [Theodore] Roosevelt and after that, in a minor key, LaFollette. I presume ancestral roots and my descent from the family that once ruled Germany, as well as my love for my father, was primarily responsible for my entanglement with the Germans and Germany. It was not a matter of money. I could have made just as much or more if I had changed side. Moreover there is the imp of perverseness in me which compels me to choose the unpopular side. I once described myself as an inverted chameleon that always adopts a color at variance with its environment.

Still self-conscious about the sale of his effects, he commented in the same letter:

Van Nosdall claims to admire me greatly as a poet. But I detest his anti-Semitic attitude. He is far more pro-German, pro-Kaiser and pro-Hitler than I ever was. Though not German, he was a member of the Bund. He represents a peculiar psychological problem—the over-compensation of some inferiority complex. But he has been decent with me and made a few thousand dollars for me when I needed them.

And his son Peter was on his mind as always:

You are right. My relations with Peter are somewhat ambivalent. We love (and distrust) each other to some extent. But he always comes to see me when he is in New York. I usually have dinner with him and his mother. People tell me that he looks exactly as I did, although he is taller and handsomer. My poems have influenced him considerably, even if he has not the courage to acknowledge that indebtedness. But I guess he has suffered a great deal on my account. To some extent his reaction involves some form of the Oedipus complex. I admire his brilliance, even if I do not understand many of his poems. But as I always said, genius is hereditary in our family. I trust it is also hereditary in yours.

One cannot understand Viereck without insight into his relations with his highly gifted son. Having known both for many years, I have realized this more than most. Peter, too, has been concerned. He has striven to make me understand the sad situation. He has been of much help to me in the course of the revival of this book. As he said recently, he was a child when we met, and he is now a grandfather, an observation made more than once by his father. It would be well to gather up now some of the strands in this tangled relationship.

While his father, years previously, was trying to walk a tight rope, with less and less success, between his loyalty to America and his commitment to the Nazis, Peter Viereck was deeply absorbed in the study of what had led his ancestral land once again to establish a gigantic war and propaganda machine that threatened to engulf the world. Peter and his younger brother George had always been interested in public affairs, not often echoing their father's viewpoints. I recall that on at least one occasion, while in the Viereck home in Manhattan, I had observed Sylvester Viereck brush aside some penetrating question by one of the boys, who then, disconcerted, turned to me for an answer. I had not often seen such curt conduct on Sylvester's part, at least not so far as his very bright boys were concerned. Later when one of them, I think it was Peter, was graduated from Harvard, I asked Sylvester what I could give the young man as a gift. I was told that he would like the two volume work on Soviet Communism by the Webbs, the famous Fabians and companions of Bernard Shaw who had gone to Bolshevik Russia, briefly, and had then composed a monumental tome telling the world the virtues of the Soviet system in contrast with our own capitalist anarchy. Peter and George continued to probe, each in his own independent way, and they developed strong antipathies for all authoritarian governments, all ant societies, whether of the right or of the left. Their father, too, professed a dislike for nonindividualistic societies, but it had not stopped him from entering into arrangements of various kinds with German agencies, his ancestral pull being stronger than his dislike of much for which the Nazi government stood.

So Peter Viereck labored on with his studies, so inimical to much that his father was thinking and doing. It culminated in a book of striking originality and profundity called *Metapolitics—From the Romantics to Hitler*. It was published in 1941 by the prestigious Knopf firm and immediately won a success of esteem, caused, at least in part, I am sure, by the contrast between the views of the son and the father. Peter's theme was that Nazism had its roots in the German past, long before the Treaty of Versailles, so glibly blamed by many Germans, including George Sylvester Viereck, for the rise of the Third Reich and its infamous institutions.

"I have tried to show that Wagnerian romanticism is the most important single fountainhead of Nazi ideas and ideals," Peter says at the very end of his book. "How appropriate, then, how peculiarly fitting, that nazism's nineteenth-century prophet, in his best and sanest moments, damned the Nazis in advance. In those inspired moments, Wagner warned that Germany would some day sacrifice all her best qualities of wisdom, art, science, and peace for the sake of ruling the world by military power. . . ."

There was much in the book that the elder Viereck could not have liked despite any admiration he may have had for the intellectual capacity and scholarship of his son. There was always a strong current of ambivalence, as we have seen, and it encompassed not only differences in ideology but in poetic styles and content as well. Both were, indubitably, poets. Peter received the Pulitzer Prize for an early volume of his verse, just as George Sylvester had been hailed as a poet in his youth. But they were basically worlds apart, and George Sylvester did not hesitate to voice their differences in letters to me and others, including Bernard Shaw.

In a copy of *Metapolitics* that Peter presented to his father on September 30, 1941, soon after publication, Peter wrote:

On your 27th wedding anniversary, voila my first direct descendant.

To my direct paternal ancestor

this so-called "war mongering" book on the direct and indirect ancestors of the Nazi plague is inscribed with———
well, definitely mixed sentiments!

but with
AFFECTION ALWAYS
from
Peter

Before the end of the year, the United States was at war with the Nazis, and both sons of Viereck were in the uniforms of American soldiers. Peter fought with our forces in Africa. His less fortunate younger brother, no less brilliant and brave, fought and died at bloody Anzio beachhead on the shores of Italy.

Fourteen years after his presentation of his first book to his father, after the war was long over and Viereck had spent years on trial and in prison, after both men had written many books, both in verse and in prose, Peter inscribed a copy of his latest work, *The Unadjusted Man,* with these significant words:

TO G.S.V.
unadjustedly
often admiringly,
and ever affectionately,
Peter

In a letter to me dated October 16, 1956, not too many years before he began living in Peter's home, Sylvester wrote with curt finality: "As far as Peter is concerned, I agree with Bernard Berenson, who said he was 'the least bad of the new poets.' "

Earlier, on March 23, 1953, he wrote what may have at least some elements of truth:

> Peter receives a great deal of publicity, but he lacks his father's gift of turning laurels into dough. Both as a polemicist and as a poet he owes more than he realizes to me. As a matter of fact he probably realizes it deep in his heart.

And to Peter, he wrote a long, undated critique after the publication of Peter's new book of poems, *The First Morning*. It is a brutal form of integrity for one poet to write to another, his first-born son, in this fashion:

> I do not know what to tell you about the book. I read two-thirds on the day I received it and found very little I could understand. I read most of it over again the next day and was still equally puzzled. In your first and second book of poems I found a few that appealed to me including The Dawn Horse and Kilroy etc. But in this book I find only a few individual lines which contain what I would call magic, or if you will lyric sex appeal.

Then Viereck continued no less destructively while trying to show understanding:

> . . .Probably all this is my fault. I belong to the first decade of the 20th century and maybe the 19th whereas you belong to the mid-20th century. I had hoped that you would advance or lead back poetry as you did in some poems to the great stream of tradition, but in this book, at least, your evolution has been entirely the other way. I resent its pedantries, its mixture of criticism and verse. It smacks of Pope, except that Pope would have expressed himself intelligibly. Maybe I got up on the wrong toot. Maybe I am only a relic of the past. I am not yet ready to render a final judgment. I must go over the book again in another mood. I would be interested in getting the reaction of others. Maybe they will help me.

It was perhaps the Strauss family all over again, the elder not being able to tolerate the younger. This may be the age-old story of the war of the generations, but it does not wear well on a sensitive person.

Viereck tried to soften his blows later in the letter when he wrote:

> I had a very pleasant dinner with your mother. We ate at the Brass Rail on Park Avenue which has excellent food but bites deep into the pocketbook. However, we had to celebrate the birth of your lyric baby, even if in my opinion, it may be a curious deviation from human norms.

Early in 1952, I believe, I met with Viereck again. It was while I was attending the sale of a famous collection of Lincoln memorabilia at a well-known New York gallery. The meeting was not as long or as relaxed as we had hoped. The years have obscured my recollection of what either of us said, but there must have been considerable strain in the meeting, as there was in a later one that year. By that time Viereck was again aware of my wife Ceretta's existence and referred to her, as well as to the children, in his letters. We could not help recalling that many years earlier he and Gretchen had greeted the birth of our first child almost with hosannahs. Now Sylvester and Gretchen were irreparably estranged, and our own relations with him, although feebly cordial on the surface, had a kind of distrust that was never overcome. Perhaps it should not have been. There was so much to regret and resent and explain. I could not be as critical of the wreckage of the man as I had been when he was in his prime, almost exultant in his unpopularity. The letters were generally as revealing as they had been long ago. Many of them almost demand quotation, but the tone has already been set, and there is no point in redundancy.

It was intriguing to learn through his letter of March 17, 1952, that his somewhat impoverished son Peter was debating at the Rand School with Corliss Lemont, son of the Morgan banker, on Communism and Russia. "I shall be there," Viereck wrote, "but I shall be still as a mouse." It was ironical that the man of rich parentage was espousing the Communist cause, while the poor poet was hostile to the Soviet pretensions. I could not help recalling again that I had given one of the Viereck boys, probably Peter, a copy of the tome on Soviet Communism by the Webbs as a graduation gift. Since then Peter had become as anticommunist as his father but in a different fashion. Peter intellectualized his opposition; his father popularized it. Viereck expressed it well in his letter of March 30, 1952:

> Martin Dies and others have harmed me personally, but I think that they, as well as McCarthy, were necessary callers in the night to alarm the people. McCarthy, I am sure, would disapprove of me on more counts than one. I am, as you know, a conservative on everything except sex. I am, however, an individualist and believe in free speech. I once suggested that I might run on a ticket for free lunch, free speech and free love. I have, at times, been compelled to support certain extremists near

what Theodore Roosevelt called the "lunatic fringe." But it was usually a defensive measure because I, myself, was under attack from the lunatic fringe on the other side.

Viereck was often surprised to learn facts already known to others, as when he wrote to me on May 22, 1952:

I have met an interesting German refugee who has given me five fascinating books on the history of the German Jews. I think he would like me to write a book on the subject. I did not know that the Jews had been living in Germany for nearly two thousand years, although I do dispatch Cartaphilus [hero of his Wandering Jew saga] to the Rhine in *My First 2000 Years*. It seems that these Jews became Roman citizens and emigrated to the Teuton lands, where they were completely assimilated. Some, who were not, argued at the time of official pogroms, centuries ago, that they were not "Christ Killers" since they had become Roman citizens and lived in the Roman Empire before that most distinguished member of their race—Jesus Christ.

On June 30, 1952, Viereck wrote an almost pleading letter about the possibility of coming to Chicago for a visit:

A friend of mine, a young lawyer is going to Chicago by car to attend the convention. He and his friends are Taft men. They will take me along. I am not particularly eager to go because it would be more comfortable to watch the proceedings of the convention on television. But I would like to see you and one or two other people. I also want to show you the family album and family history which I expect to deliver to my nephew, Louis. On the way back I shall stop in Columbus.

My going depends on my consultation with my doctor who is looking me over this afternoon. If he has no objection I shall go. If not, I shall inform you by air-mail or telegram. I expect to leave here Saturday morning and arrive sometime Sunday. We will drive day and night. Can you find a place where I can put up for two, possibly three nights? It can be modest, but I must have a chance to take a bath or at least a shower. If so, please let me know by wire or air-mail.

In my condition both financial and physical, I don't want to race from place to place and pay an exhorbitant price for a night's lodging.

You may have been a poor correspondent of late owing to your many activities, but I suppose you can reserve one evening for me or one afternoon. I would like to see your wife and the kids.

Of course, I wrote to him that he would be welcome to stay in our home. We put him up in the room and in the very bed later occupied by Nathan Leopold,

Henry Miller, Carl Sandburg's daughter Margaret, and others who had become parts of our eventful lives. We saw a good deal of Viereck. It was the most extended visit we were destined to have with him during the remainder of his life. There was, as I have noted, a kind of strain in our relations. I was too uncomfortable. Some of the past history which had appeared to recede in our new correspondence came to the fore again. We invited no guests to share Viereck with us until the always generous Ceretta scolded me for my keeping Viereck hidden away as if he were a dirty secret. Thereupon, when we were invited by old friends to visit them, we asked if we could bring our guest along with us. They assented, but later we learned that, with relatives who had suffered and in some instances died in Nazi Germany, they were not very happy about extending hospitality to one whom they still regarded as an apologist for the Nazis. Thus I learned again that it is easier to forgive than to forget. If Viereck sensed this disquietude he did not say so then or later. His discomfort was only with his companions on the highway, those who had driven him to Chicago, whose neo-Nazism he professed to dislike. Viereck sent affectionate greetings and thanks from New York to all of us including our German Shepherd dog, dubbed by him "the noble Knight." Thereafter he would refer to our dog in affectionate terms, almost as if grateful that the animal had no knowledge of the history of our guest.

From Chicago he had gone to Columbus, Ohio, to visit his beloved nephew, the one person who had invariably showed him great generosity. As he wrote:

In Columbus, Ohio, I had the unique experience of stepping on my grave and sitting on my tombstone which my nephew holds in readiness for my demise. All this took place on the anniversary of my first stroke—Bastille day. My Bastille did not fall but it was severely damaged.

He fairly bubbled with a kind of good humored excitement:

Peter's wife says I am the only gentleman in the family. Maybe it is possible to be both a gentleman and a genius if you belong, as I do to the 19th century, although I have seen more than one-half of the 20th.

I hope that Teddy has his new car, and that Knight has not taken another bite out of one of the kids. I believe three is the limit—at least in New York. It would be, indeed, a pity to see so aristocratic a hound get into trouble even if he had the best lawyer in town.

On July 26, 1952, he expressed himself on the Presidential election:

Well, you were right about Stevenson. It was clear from the beginning that Eisenhower and Stevenson were the choice of the Invisible Government composed of politicians, malefactors of Great Wealth and possibly representatives of the ADL. I would rather vote for Stevenson than Eisenhower, except that I think that the rascals ought to be put out to give the rascals that have been starving for 20 years a chance at the crib.

He was more at home in commenting upon a poet, on August 7:

As to Ezra Pound, he is an important literary figure, but he travels along erratic paths. I do not pretend to understand him, especially in his present phase. But I am against caging nightingales, even if the nightingale is naughty. And after all, he is a poet.

This was another way of saying that he too should not have been imprisoned, whatever his views and activities, for he too was a nightingale rather than a crow.

In letter after letter, he told me that he was hoping to write his autobiography, "or rather two. One on my political life and the other to be published (after my death?) on my love-life." He thought that neither would interfere with my book about him. If he wrote either book, I have not seen evidence thereof. His health and his poverty were continuously interfering with his plans.

On September 16, he was filled with intense excitement as he communed with his oldest friend:

I visited Ludwig Lewisohn at Brandeis College. We had a delightful reunion. It seems that neither he nor Eldridge know much about the Jewish Book Club to which they merely lend their names. Ludwig made an interesting remark. He said that I am a poet but that I do not care for literature as such. I wonder if that is true. I really never cared for the classics, in fact I never read them. I care very little for contemporary literature. Few books and few poems have appeal for me. It is an interesting observation from an interesting person. Remember that Ludwig knew me when I was 16.

Ludwig says that I am a philo-Semite (he knows that I am) but he says that the philo-Semite is worse than the anti-Semite from his point of view. I want to assimilate the Jews who can be assimilated whereas he wants them to go to Zion. Personally I don't see why the Jews must keep their special holidays. They should have done what the Catholics did, synchronize their feast-days with those of the Pagans. The calendar is out of joint. It has been changed many times. No one knows which day is Saturday. The Jews could just as easily make Sunday their day of rest. But no, they must always have some difference, always unnecessrily. The younger generation does not believe in most of these things but accept them for the sake of their more orthodox parents.

Lewisohn also urged me to write my autobiography. He said that it should go somewhat like this. "No matter what my political opinions might have been, Fate and my antecedents predestined me to be involved in the affairs of Germany."

As the presidential campaign progressed, Viereck shifted his views, as he told me in his letter of September 18:

. . .I like Stevenson's wit, but now that Eisenhower has seen the light I am somewhat more favorably disposed toward him. As far as the old parties are concerned, I say a plague on both your houses.

I do not like McCarthy personally. I certainly disapprove of his silly attacks on the sexual conduct on the part of various members of the State Department. But I welcome his attack on Communism, even if he exaggerates and is blatant. Every movement must have an extreme right and left wing. It is what T.R. called the lunatic fringe. I put my own friend Keith there. I told him so.

On October 29, he told me that "Gretchen had a major operation followed by various complications including pleurisy and kidney trouble. But she now seems to be on the road to recovery. I see her every day at the Lenox Hill Hospital." By November 20 Gretchen was back home. "I see her almost every day which takes quite a bite out of my life. She is improving slowly and will not be able to resume her work in the Newman Club for several weeks." On February 4, 1953, he wrote that he was not seeing Gretchen at all, except when Peter was in town. "She asked me not to call her up or visit her because my presence 'upsets' her." Thus the reward for the faithful non-resident husband. How much this hurt him he did not say, but the pain was apparent.

In his letter of June 5, 1953, a year after they had driven him to and from my home in Chicago, Viereck told me of his break with Keith Thompson and Edward A. Fleckenstein. "I still like them personally but I find it necessary to disassociate myself from them emphatically politically." They were unreconstructed Nazis and anti-Semites, and Viereck was charged by Barry Gray, a radio commentator, with using them as his fronts. So his past continued to plague him. He could try to forget it, but others could not. Futilely, he wrote Fleckenstein:

> America is an amalgam of many races and creeds. Whoever stirs up the melting pot renders a disservice to his country. I never attended your meetings, except a Christmas celebration, wholly unpolitical, in which I said politely that I have returned to my first love, the Muse and have exchanged the arena of politics for Parnassus. I am with you in all activities serving to build a bridge between Germany and the United States. I am humanly for you, but I cannot follow you into any venture likely to destroy the amalgam of American citizenship.

So, innumerable letters were exchanged between us. Just as in the case of his son Peter, our relations were ambivalent at best, more so on my part than on his. I was increasingly conscious that there would be a sudden termination to the renewed friendship. Under date of April 2, 1956, I was advised by Viereck's secretary that he had suffered "a mild stroke which seems to interfere somewhat with articulation." Still, he was going to take an ocean trip because his doctor thought it would be good for him. Other letters from the secretary, rather than from

Viereck himself, followed. At that time my wife Ceretta was in very somber shape as the result of an automobile accident, which occurred while she was going, in inclement weather, to assist at a child guidance center. Helping children was the great passion of Ceretta's troubled life. Viereck repeatedly inquired about her himself and through his secretary. At this time, too, our dog Knight, who had so beguiled Viereck when he was a guest in our home, died as the result of surgery. Viereck wrote: "Knight's life was worth living if it inspired an immortal ode by your son." Ted, then a college student, had lessened his grief with the poem he composed at the time.

We next heard from Viereck from Florence, Italy, where he was Peter's guest.

On September 6, 1956, Viereck told me that he was back from Europe:

I spent a month in Italy with Peter and five weeks in Germany. I saw Schacht, von Papen, Krupp, and spent a day with Prince Louis Ferdinand and his Russian wife, at the old seat of the Hohenzollerns, Burg Hohenzollern in Hechingen. I had a serious attack of colitis during the last two weeks, which I spent in a spa.

Prince Louis Ferdinand had raised his glass "To *our* ancestors," and this pleased the German-American royalist greatly. He would never cease to take pride in his Hohenzollern blood. As Emil Ludwig had said, he, being illegitimate in descent, was more royalist than royalty itself.

On September 11, he told me:

I expect to write a number of articles about my trip, which I'll send you when and if they appear. Much to my amazement, Hitler left behind three monuments, the Autobahnen, the Volkswagen and—anti-Semitism. The Germans at large, certainly the intellectuals, were not anti-Semitic in Hitler's day. Many are now anti-Semitic owing to various psychological and economic factors which I shall try to explain. Of course, I did not conduct a Gallup poll, and may be mistaken in my impression.

On November 20, he told me he had met Herman Hagedorn, his old German-American foe, "and we buried the hatchet—after forty years." This was not as joyous as the reunion with Ludwig Lewisohn, who died too soon thereafter. Leonard Abbott was gone also. All of his friends of yesteryear seemed to be dropping like autumn leaves. His turn would come very soon, he knew. But he could report that he had rejoined the Poetry Society at their request—after forty years—apparently, a magical period of time for him. On December 2, 1956, he wrote to me from Lenox Hill Hospital that he was suffering from an attack of hepatitis, the same ailment which was complicating Ceretta's increasingly tragic life.

On February 25, 1957, Viereck wrote that he had been in the hospital for nearly seven weeks. On March 11, he reported:

I, too, have not recovered from my ailment. I feel tired and nauseous, and my blood pressure has increased decidedly, in spite of my loss of weight. It seems that Nature eventually makes life so unpleasant for us, that it is no great burden to cast it off.

I am sorry for Ceretta. I am sorry for you. In a less moralistic civilization you would find solace elsewhere, without yielding one iota of your love for your wife.

On May 16, he told me that he had "done practically no work of consequence for nearly a year. . . .I am exceedingly feeble. It is only my spirit that is unbroken. Money, too, is scarce with me."

At this time I was hard at work in the effort, ultimately successful, to get Nathan Leopold, the thrill killer of 1924, out of prison after a generation of confinement. Viereck was unsympathetic in his letter of July 18, 1957:

I am of two minds on the subject. I do not believe in "punishment" because I do not believe except in a very limited way in the doctrine of free will. However Society must protect itself against certain offenses, especially murder. I have no objection to the lethal elimination of unfit human material. It is possible that Leopold may now be entirely different from what he was when he committed the crime. But I am not sure that Society should take any chances in such cases. In fact I would not have objected to his lethal elimination after the crime even if he was demonstrably insane at the time. Remember the Thaw case and the brainstorms that continued long after his release.

If I met Leopold personally and was impressed by his intellect, I would probably change my mind. But if I was Governor of Illinois, I would remember my responsibility to the country.

To me it was a matter of ironic interest that Viereck, so much in need of sympathy himself, could show so little concern for Leopold, whose crime, infamous as it was, scarcely ranked in evil with a defense of the Nazis. Leopold, in turn, was unsympathetic when later I defended Henry Miller. What is there about the maimed that depletes the glands of sympathy?

On September 10, I received another doleful letter:

I too, have my share of trouble. I have been in the hospital for for nearly six weeks, after being sick for nearly ten days at home. I had a combination of pneumonia, an infected urinary tract, acute colitis, and finally a prostate operation.

Regards to you and your wife. Hail, and I would almost prefer to say—farewell.

On November 12, he was still suffering from the aftereffects of the prostate operation, which had confined him in the hospital for two months. "I am still half alive. I look upon my present life as a brief detour from the final goal."

A bit later, in an undated letter, he dwelled again upon Leopold:

> . . .As my secretary, a young college student, reminds me thrill murders have become quite common place today. I am sorry for Leopold, but I would not want to live with him or near him, even now. It seems to me that society had to pay very heavily for his maintenance all these years. I hope you will win your case in any event. I shall try to get Leopold's autobiography when he is ready. I have read most books about the case including Compulsion.

Scarcely had I achieved my great triumph in the Leopold case and the acclaim, it seemed, of much of the world other than Viereck, when I was shattered by the death of my wife of many years, a remarkable woman who had always seemed on the verge of tragedy and yet had been able to mask her sorrows with much verve and gaiety. For a long time I could dwell only upon my unfortunate Ceretta. I told Viereck of my wife's death, and he wrote to me, briefly but movingly on May 18, 1958:

> If you were a poet you would have written your letter of April 28, in verse. It is a poem. I keep very few letters nowadays but I shall preserve yours. I presume it is a consolation that something of Ceretta lives in your children. How old are they now? Think of Ceretta as living in Neverneverland. She must have had several of the qualities of Peter Pan and Tinkerbell.
>
> I sometimes think that life is so short that it is hardly worth living.

I heard again from Viereck on July 18, 1958, when he congratulated me on my son's graduation from college. He added: "I am fairly well but I am in a sterile mood. No poetry, no romance, no sex. And you remember Whitman's 'Yet all were lacking if sex were lacking or if the moisture of the right man were lacking!' "

The last letter I received from Viereck, so far as I can determine, was dated July 31, 1959, more than a year after his previous letter. Its occasion was my marriage to Mamie, my present wife and the source of the new joy that has come into my life. The letter was short and sad: "I hope that your marriage will be the exception to the rule, and that you both will be happy. There is only one thing that is worse than being married, and that is not to be married."

Undoubtedly, what he wrote to me so curtly was a reflection of his relations with his wife. Gretchen and he were never reconciled, and he never really accepted this "desertion" on her part. He must have felt that he could win her back, just as he had charmed her when she was his child bride many years earlier and throughout most of their life together, in woe and weal, until World War II. This was not to be. He domesticated his frustration, his sense of betrayal, his longings, in poem after poem. They may momentarily have eased his pain, but they did not change her, or him, in any way. She was steadfast in her determination not to return to him.

His health constantly worsened. He had repeated strokes from which recovery seemed less and less likely. He had to give up whatever independence he derived from living alone. In the late 1950s, he moved to the home of his son Peter in South Hadley, Massachusetts, where Peter was a professor at Mount Holyoke College. Despite their differences in politics, poetics, and personality, each now found much to cherish in the other. There was a kind of reconciliation, which Peter found a very moving experience.

One day Viereck picked up a new edition of his son's *Metapolitics*, which had been out of print for a time. It was Peter's classic study of the roots of Nazism. Sylvester looked through the book and remarked to his son that he now recognized that Peter was right in what he said in his book, and he confessed that his own viewpoint had been erroneous. He said his error was to assume that because atrocity stories of World War I were false, the same must be true of World War II. Peter still was not sure, he told me, whether or not his father was simply humoring him.

Peter felt that his father was ambivalent about Nazism and Germany, despite the price he had paid for his propaganda activities for the Third Reich. Peter believed that it was he rather than his father who loved German culture; hence, Peter's wrath at the Nazis who barbarized it. He believed that his father privately hated Germany and had wanted in his younger days to be at least 200 percent American. Later Viereck felt guilty about that hate and made up for it by becoming 200 percent pro-German, to the point of ignoring or disbelieving Nazi atrocities that everyone else of good faith could plainly see.

Viereck once told Peter that he resented his own father's dragging him to German cultural meetings when he wanted to steep himself in English culture. He loved English poetry. He loved everything about the land that produced such lyricists. But after his father died, he felt guilty about hurting his father by rejecting the German heritage. He tried to make amends, posthumously. He went overboard. One extreme led to another.

Human nature, as Peter said to me, is much too complex for one to be too certain in one's judgments, particularly when a character such as his father is under contemplation. Perhaps Viereck sought out Freud and others versed in human psychology to discover himself or even to flee from the unwelcome image that he saw.

Peter hinted at these things in the new edition of *Metapolitics* which his father saw in his home. He could not write about the family tragedy in a vulgar exhibitionist way. He had to be more austere and oblique, but he was clear enough to be followed by all who knew him.

At last, on March 18, 1962, Viereck was freed from the torments of the last years of his life. Death must have been a great release for him. I could not help thinking of the agony of Madame Bovary's last hours. When he died, few could have predicted that he would be remembered, despite what must be regarded as a very remarkable career and an extraordinary personality. Most people would have said that his claim to survival was in his generous and gifted son Peter. Before he was gone, Peter had written a poem about his father which he called, appropriately, *Benediction*. It appears in Peter's book of verse *The Persimmon Tree*, published in 1956. The copyright is in Peter's name, and I acknowledge his generous permission in quoting it as his, and perhaps my, farewell to a tragic figure of our century, George Sylvester Viereck, poet, propagandist, personality, self-confessed barbarian, and unconfessed, self-tormented satyr.

BENEDICTION
(To my Father)

When the first vague years, the years of questions and toys
Resolved into years of the boy with his nose in old fable,
    It was good to hear a father's voice
    Across the lull of the breakfast table.
When the second fate, the years of answer and choice,
Diffused into years of the youth on the parapet,
Where maps went rainbowing round such tallness
    In outspread valleys of my whim,
Then earth was good in multicolored allness,
And I loved all of it. But loved not him.

The third fate ambushed. Then the three roads met;
I faced the enemy the Sphinx foretold.
Again, again the ancient rites unfold.
Must all men play out fables to the end?
    Are men themselves not fates?—to bend
Their chains to rungs? I will outbless that curse,
I praise alike the young years and the old:
The enemy the Sphinx foretold, I slew;
That, too, was good—forgive my doubt, my smallness—
It all is good, it all is good, him I loved too.